# TWENTIETH CENTUR'

# TWENTIETH CENTURY BOY
## The Marc Bolan Story

*Mark Paytress*

SIDGWICK & JACKSON
LONDON

First published 1992 by Sidgwick & Jackson Limited

This edition first published 1993 by Sidgwick & Jackson Limited
a division of Pan Macmillan Publishers Limited
Cavaye Place London SW10 9PG
and Basingstoke

Associated companies throughout the world

ISBN 0 283 06171 5

1 3 5 7 9 8 6 4 2

A CIP catalogue record for this book is available from
the British Library

Phototypeset by Intype, London
Printed by Mackays of Chatham PLC, Chatham, Kent

The author would like to thank the following for permission to quote from their work:
Essex Music Group for excerpts from 'Chateau in Virginia Waters' and from the sleeve
of the 'Prophets, Seers And Sages . . .' album; Morrison Leahy Music Ltd for the short
passage from 'The Warlock Of Love'; Wizard (Bahamas) Ltd for excerpts from 'Dandy
In The Underworld', 'Spaceball Ricochet', 'The Slider', 'Left Hand Luke', 'Teenage
Dream' and 'New York City'; William Heinemann Ltd/Jonathon Green for extracts
from 'Days In The Life'; John Peel, Nigel Cross, New Musical Express and Spencer Leigh.

# CONTENTS

# ACKNOWLEDGEMENTS

So many people have contributed in some way to this book, none more so than Cliff McLenehan, whose encyclopaedic knowledge has provided an invaluable safety net. He also raised several pertinent points concerning the analysis, and I'm sure would have made many more had not time, and the slight inconvenience of him being on the other side of the English Channel not been against us. Someone else who had much to say regarding several of the more general points raised in the script was Peter Doggett, my editor at *Record Collector*. Unfortunately, I've still not been able to convince him that Bolan is closer to Lennon and Dylan (in the widest possible sense), than to Noddy Holder, as he suggests. I don't think we quite realised how much our approaches to rock 'n' roll diverge once we peer beneath our shared passions for Elvis, Sonic Youth, the Kinks and others. He argued the case against the inclusion of some passages which he felt entered the realm of the heretical, but having the last word on this occasion, I couldn't resist!

Andy Davis and Fiona Bleach also read the script and made many valid suggestions, and while I was sorry that another long-term colleague, John Reed, couldn't, he did at least have time to cast an eye over the chapter that dealt with his pet subject, the mod era. The finished book would have been far less substantial without the assistance of Martin Barden, Ros Davies and Dave Rimmer, all of whom made scrapbooks and exclusive information available to me, not to mention many interesting ideas and recollections. Many of Marc's closest colleagues, relatives and business associates enlightened my evenings and weekends as I laid the groundwork for this book, and I must single out Marc's brother Harry Feld, his producer Tony Visconti, and his record-spinning friends Jeff Dexter and John Peel for getting behind the project wholeheartedly. Tony and John had every reason not to grant 'just one more' interview about their old friend, but both were kind enough to respond to my persistence with incisive and entertaining assessments of Marc and the cultures he inhabited. Jeff opened several new doors for me to pursue; while Harry unlocked many mysteries regarding Marc's childhood days. I'm only sorry that this lengthy hike into his past came so soon after the death of his parents, Sid and Phyllis Feld.

Almost everyone I spoke to gave me far more time than I expected, and I'd like to extend my thanks to them, in alphabetical order: Keith Altham, Mick Box, Joe Boyd, Pete Brown, Jeff Dexter, Andy Ellison, Harry and Sandy Feld, Jeff Griffin, Bob Harris, Mike Heron, John Hewlett, Vic Keary, Mike Leander, Bill Legend, Donovan Leitch, Gered Mankowitz, Mike McGrath, Colin Miles, Simon Napier-Bell, John Pearse, John Peel, Frances Perrone, David Platz, Mike Pruskin, Pete Sanders, Tony Secunda, Clive Selwood, Captain Sensible, Helen Shapiro, Susan Singer, Danny Thompson, Chris Townson, Tony Visconti, Allan Warren, Mick Wayne, plus two close friends of Steve Peregrine Took who preferred to remain anonymous.

I am also grateful for conversations I had with June Bolan and Richard Jones, but which, for different reasons, never quite formalised into an interview situation. Both Tony Howard and Mickey Finn had their own reasons for not speaking, and I respect and understand the decisions they made. I was disappointed not to locate Theresa Whipman, not least to verify the spelling of her surname. She spent a lot of time with Marc at a crucial period in his life, and has always eluded biographers. So of course, do Riggs O'Hara and The Wizard . . .

I'd also like to thank the following for their assistance: Nina Antonia, Marc Arscott, John and Shan Bramley, Alan Clayson, Steve Cook, Nigel Cross, Jed Dmochowski, Noel Hammond, Pat Hehir, Kevin Howlett, Paul Johnson, the late Malcolm Jones, Uwe Klee, Faebhean Kwest, Spencer Leigh, Lorne Murdoch, John Platt, Danny Secunda, Nikki Sudden, Mike Torry, John Tracy, Dave Williams, Barry Winton and all at the *Record Collector*, not forgetting my editor at Sidgwick and Jackson Helen Gummer, who'd first got wind of my interest in Bolan a couple of years ago.

On a more personal note, I'd like to mention my parents Erika Lewis and Norman Paytress, who were forced to live their lives to the sound of the Rolling Stones and the Move; later, Captain Beefheart and Jefferson Airplane; and later still, the Sex Pistols and Throbbing Gristle. I think they found Marc Bolan and T. Rex a welcome relief.

Sadly, they won the argument over the piles of weekly music papers, which had been kindly passed on by a family friend and the first vinyl junkie I ever knew, Pete McConnell. He didn't know what he'd set in motion when he started to pass on his cast-off singles, like the Beach Boys' 'Good Vibrations', the Beatles' 'Penny Lane'/'Strawberry Fields Forever' and the Move's 'I Can Hear The Grass Grow'.

And then there was 'The Wizard', a guy named Mick who briefly lived next door. He was my Martin Kauffman figure. Together with my similarly music-crazed sister, Julie-Anne, I used to peer out from behind the curtains as he literally floated past, happy and glorious in a full-length woman's fur coat and long, Peter Green-style hair. We laughed at him and admired him at the same time. One day, I was invited into his house to look at his records. He'd built his own record player – a stereo! – and painted it in the swirling psychedelic colours of the day. He laughed at the Dave Dee, Dozy, Beaky, Mick and Tich photo I'd brought in to show him ('the best thing about that is the motorbike they're sitting on,' he said of the *Rave* cover shot). Deeply wounded, maybe, but I was transfixed by the strange world I'd entered. He played me the Who, Pink Floyd, the Jimi Hendrix Experience and Tyrannosaurus Rex. I remember thinking that the sleeve to *My People* was absolutely marvellous, but only recall hearing 'Debora'. Mick, once of 88 Shelbourne Road, Bournemouth, circa 1968/69, make my year: get in touch!

A special thanks must also go to my dear friends Fiona Bleach, who was wholly supportive, and to Trevor King who gave me no help whatsoever throughout the entire project.

# PRELUDE

**'The only philosophy I had as a kid was that a human being is an art form.'**
Marc Bolan to Danny Holloway, *New Musical Express* magazine, 1972

I never saw Marc Bolan and T. Rex. They appeared in Bournemouth on the night of 9 May 1971, where the Winter Gardens played host to the first signs of what was later described as 'T. Rextasy'. I would have loved to have been there. The nearest I had got to any pop stars at that stage was having the members of the Move sign their names in my red autograph book, signatures that shared pride of place with those of the local football team, visiting third-division team players, and, for some strange reason, several junior school friends.

Bolan returned to the Winter Gardens on 20 February 1976, the day before my seventeenth birthday. I didn't see him then either. His circumstances had changed almost as much as mine. He had lost his subcultural edge; I believed I had found mine. Having plunged headlong into the culture on which he had turned his back several years previously, I could see little attraction in watching him going through the motions, even though the thought crossed my mind that he had slipped out of public favour so much that I would probably be able to talk my way in backstage. By that time, I had all the Tyrannosaurus Rex albums, together with the prerequisite early T. Rex recordings, and what I really wanted to know was why he turned his back on the style of those twelve months I was so desperately determined to relive – 1967.

It was a close decision, but I clearly remember making the decision not to go. Instead, a friend, Mike Channing came round, the red light bulb and the joss sticks would have been profoundly turned on, and we probably played Soft Machine's *Third*, Can's *Future Days* and some Dead and Airplane. In those intensely polarised days, that was worlds away from 'Dreamy Lady' and 'London Boys'. In my mind, Bolan had lost everything he once had in abundance. And because I had thrown myself whole-heartedly into what I imagined he once represented – and so perfectly too – the apparent travesty of his present act was made all the more obvious. He had had the face, the hair, the songs, and the added kudos of emerging from the *underground*, a word which carried with it a near-holy sense of mission – and opposition. Marc Bolan was now firmly on the wrong side of the divide: he had clearly become the problem, not the solution.

I never was reconciled to him, at least not until the morning I heard he had been killed. Marc Bolan had become a mystery once more, freed from the terminal decline which had seen him parading on children's television programmes in an ever-more absurd succession of costumes, playing lukewarm versions of his former three-minute glories, and ballooning into the Gary Glitter-type figure from which he had always sought to distance himself. I hadn't even noticed that he had slimmed down or, being firmly committed to the *NME* and not *Record Mirror*, that he had started to champion the new musical cataclysm known as punk rock.

Marc Bolan was never allowed the luxury of fully coming to terms with the new wave. The opportunity of seeing whether he would have climbed out of his dreamy doldrums inhabited by dragons and dandies, and proudly lined up alongside Lou Reed, David Bowie, Syd Barrett, maybe even Gary Glitter, as Old Farts who managed to light up the blank expressions of the punks, was denied. Bolan's final album, *Dandy In The Underworld*, had been less than an earth-shattering achievement, but there were signs that he was up to some of his old tricks, ready to recast his die. He made many changes in his career – reflected in his dress, his music and his world view – and while these were often perceived as marked and dramatic, they were the result of several months' careful thought. Throughout 1977, he had been deliberating. It is not difficult to imagine Marc pursuing a regenerated career in his self-styled role as 'Godfather of Punk', embracing its celebration of noise and its abiding need to *do* something, even if that something was little more than give the music industry a kick up the backside. Bolan, whose drive towards the mainstream had in no way compromised his need to maintain an acute sense of difference, nailed his own sails to punk in much the same way as he had done to the early mod movement, the Dylan-inspired Romantic notion of the pop star as artist, and the belief that music was entwined with a much grander social project, as postulated by the hippies.

It is equally feasible that this next shift in allegiance may have produced nothing worthwhile. Since he made the transition in 1971 from subcultural stylist to mainstream maverick with a cultural category of his own, glam rock (though he preferred to call it cosmic rock), Bolan had tended to coast. The dynamic of his adherence to the various youth cults of the sixties had been to displace the crisis prompted by the realisation that each human being is as much alike as he or she is different. He sought to channel that displacement into a need to accentuate that difference, and then magnify it into something unique and important.

By 1972 – as the biggest-selling musician in the country – he had achieved just that, but the drive which had sent him spinning inexorably from the streets of Stamford Hill to the newly invoked category of Superstar had been rapidly supplanted by the desire to celebrate his success. Whether punk would have fully rekindled that original drive again is doubtful. But Bolan's compulsive habit of redrawing his own musical parameters in accordance with contemporary trends – which had gone horribly wrong on occasion since 1973 – would, I am sure, have resulted in some better records, as he embraced its style and ethos with more conviction.

Punk, perhaps more than any other youth movement, concerned itself with the break-up of the sense of the 'unified self'. It was media literate and had a healthy tendency towards demystification. Its stars were 'anti-stars', iconoclasts who set into reverse pop's – sorry, rock's – quest to follow film into the rarified pantheon of the Arts, with a capital A. Bolan, long regarded as a loud-mouthed, overdressed impediment to rock's sober quest towards establishment recognition, could see aspects of himself in punk's project, and was able to close off any obvious contradictions and anomalies (Bolan demystifying the role of the Star?), just as he had been doing for the past twenty-five years.

As an unknown pre-teen named Mark Feld, when he gazed back at his mirror reflection, he didn't see a young, Hackney-bred kid destined to remain confined by the tight-knit culture from which he sprang. Instead, he found freedom by entering into a fetishistic love affair with idealised versions of himself. By tinkering with the façade, he was able to transcend the reality of the conformist, standardised life patterns of those around him. It was a predicament that was shared by many thousands of the first post-war generation all around the world – but that didn't hamper the overriding sense of the *unique*, individual quest.

Having first designed himself in terms of media icons of the day, from big-screen heroes like Davy Crockett to new pop idols like Elvis Presley and Cliff Richard, as Mark Feld he substituted naked emulation for a more rewarding construction of self, fashioned from an increasingly diversifying set of influences. At first, Mark was concerned only with the obsessively detailed world of sartorial elegance, but as he aspired beyond being the self-styled king of a few streets in Hackney, this visual artistry was gradually complemented by empowering new reference points appropriated from a different culture.

Inhabiting the 'low' esteem cultural space of fashion and the 'high' domain afforded to poets and creative artists, provides the best sense in which Marc Bolan was what he coined a '20th Century Boy'. His commitment to both has generally excluded him from pride of place in existing rock histories, many of which now need rewriting to reflect changes in contemporary thinking. The first generation of rock scholars came from the 'lit. crit.' tradition, and thus the importance of the lyric was privileged far beyond its requirements. Sound, style and music as a social process are at least as important, and I make no apologies for attempting to address that imbalance during the course of this book. That Marc Bolan saw himself as a poet, and why, is at least as important in my view as playing critical football with a line-by-line dissection of that poetry.

It is 1992: fifteen years after his death, time has been rather kind to Marc Bolan. The open sores his defection from the underground once caused have long been forgotten. New generations are able to listen to his music without imagining him as some kind of Judas. To be successful in pop music and shout about it was tantamount to treason at the time Bolan did it. Pop determinedly sought to elevate itself as rock, and so the showmanship and braggadocio that accompanied his move into the mainstream at the start of the seventies was made unwelcome by those intent on hijacking pop music away from its teenage audience. The response to Marc Bolan brings to mind a phrase I once heard applied to another public figure whose name escapes me – that he was resented by the courtiers but loved by the people.

Marc played out his power politics within the sphere of popular music and popular culture. His self-assertion – through his clothes, music and poetry – is the voice of the Twentieth Century Little Man. Denied access to traditional sources of power, he cultivated a seemingly impenetrable self-belief and tapped into a creative muse that found an audience more than willing to share his fantasies, his escape from normality. But Bolan wasn't an eccentric. Apart from several months later on in his career, when he lost control of his life in a drug-inspired retreat from the world that inspired him, he was fully aware of what he was creating. He may have shunned his schooling as irrelevant, but as an observer of popular trends, both musical and cultural, he was a highly tuned, astute student, outwitting many of his art-school contemporaries.

Today, a pleasing image no longer necessarily signifies a 'lack' in the quality of the music. Madonna and Prince are the eighties editions of Marc Bolan, except that they probably have better business advisers and, what's more, are prepared to listen to them. Bolan wanted to do it all himself. While the magnificent persona of the perfect glam idol remains his creation and his alone, so too was his inability to transcend it. Such was the cloying strength of his appeal at the height of T. Rextasy that when it began to pass, he could never quite shake it off. Everything he did inevitably referred back to the months he spent as the biggest pop superstar in Britain and Europe.

Contemporaries like David Bowie managed to stake out new territories and guises. Marc Bolan could only ever be Marc Bolan. The appeal of what he created remains stronger than ever. Everybody likes Marc Bolan records. Advertisers like them so much that one company paid a reported seven-figure fee to use one of his songs to sell pairs of jeans. Subsequent rock stars have attempted to use parts of his image, often with revolting consequences, probably because the sum of Bolan's constituent parts was considerably less than the whole – not that there was anything necessarily *coherent* about his overall persona.

During the course of this book, I have attempted to trace the development of the Marc Bolan everyone remembers – the symbol of those carefree months during the early seventies when the name of the pop game seemed to consist of a strange desire to wear ridiculous costumes while passing off several old rock 'n' roll riffs onto a new teenage audience. But Bolan's appeal was always deeper than that of the one-dimensional glam artist. Poet and teenage idol, obsessively image-conscious yet painfully aware of traditional creative values, he embodied a series of contradictions that ultimately meant that he defied easy categorisation. More than that, he managed to strike a balance between mainstream acclaim and the decidedly offbeat appeal of a cult artist.

It is this juxtaposition of the familiar and the strange that informed much of his life, and which provides the backdrop to this book. The Marc Bolan 'story' is a tale of the struggle between the desire to maintain a strong sense of individual self and the prevailing trend towards homogenisation. Bolan answered with songs that often sounded like other people's, and yet at the same time, remained uniquely his. That's why he remains one of the most successful recording artists in the world.

# CHAPTER ONE

**'Fantasy baby is all I got.'**
Marc Bolan, 'The Third Degree', 1966

**'It was fame I wanted – an illusion – like James Dean. I mean, I never thought it would be real. Marc Bolan is an illusion. I'm Mark Feld.'**
Marc Bolan, *Look-In* magazine, 1974

**'The Greek artists, the tragedians for example, poeticised in order to conquer; their whole art cannot be thought of apart from contest . . . ambition gave their genius its wings.'**
Nietzsche, *Human, All Too Human*, 1878

In the modern age where the human personality has fragmented under an imposing artillery of external influences, Marc Bolan tried on more hats than most. Straight adaptations of movie monsters and cowboys as a child gave way to imitations of early idols like Elvis Presley and Cliff Richard, before he began to cast himself in the mould of the youth styles of his teenage years. Marc became a Modernist, a Face, an Individualist, a beatnik and a flower child, before drawing from each to construct his most perfect identity – the glam rock idol. The need to reinvent ever more exemplary incarnations of self provides the shifting terrain of subcultural style with its basic motivation, and is closely bound up with social standing. So it was with Marc Bolan. Like so many post-war teenagers, Bolan chose to express his subordinate status by dramatising his life via a succession of adopted characters, which were reflected in his dress, his lifestyle and his music. It may have looked like deviant behaviour from the outside, but ultimately it was used to serve his own interests, as he sought to extend his sense of empowerment from being top dog in the streets of Hackney to a star of global proportions.

Bolan was always happy to remind interviewers of his

working-class origins, if only because it reflected well on his achievements, but he rarely discussed his family background. Even during the early months of 1972, at the height of what was quickly dubbed 'T. Rextasy' and when every newspaper and magazine sought a new angle on the Bolan phenomenon, Marc kept his family out of the public eye. His parents rarely gave interviews to the press, while his elder brother Harry was such a well-kept secret that some of Marc's closest friends scarcely knew of his existence.

Despite the professed humble origin, Bolan also liked to claim French ancestry on the back of the deviant spelling of his Christian name, though this, like so many of his autobiographical pronouncements, was nothing more than fantasy. Before choosing to spice up his name with a dash of ersatz Euro-glamour in his late teens, he was born Mark Feld in Hackney Hospital in London's East End, youngest son of a lorry driver and a market-stall seller. You do not need to look back far into the Felds' ancestry to find a *bona fide* European connection though, albeit one quite removed from the connotations of style and sophistication that French blood would have given him. Mark's paternal grandfather Henry Feld was born on 21 March 1894 in White-chapel, and was of known Polish-Russian descent. His parents were probably among the many thousands of Jewish émigrés who fled the pogroms and resettled in East London in the wake of the assassination of Tsar Alexander II in March 1881.

Given Mark's later obsession with self-presentation, and the fact that many of London's poorer Jews sought to earn a living in the clothing business, it's perhaps surprising to discover no family interest in that line at all. Instead, grandfather Henry's hands were put to somewhat less delicate use. By trade he was a porter in Smithfield meat market, and supplemented his income by indulging in the lucrative 'sport' of illegal bare-fist fighting, where you fought till you fell. He wasn't the only meat market worker to do so: transporting large animals all day obviously provided good training for squaring up in the park after work. Sometimes Henry Feld would get his tasks confused. Legend has it that on one occasion, when a horse had the indecency to stand on his foot, he retaliated by punching the animal between the eyes and knocking it out flat. Justice was meted out later when Henry was forced to take early retirement while still in his late forties after getting slapped on the head by a side of beef.

Many years earlier he had met and married a local girl, Betsie Ruffell, on 3 December 1913 at the United Synagogue of London. The couple soon moved out of Whitechapel to nearby Stepney, and by the time Mark's father, Simeon, was born on 22 August 1920, they had settled a mile or so north of Whitechapel, at 9 Reeds Mansions, Gosset Street in Bethnal Green.

Henry and Bessie (as she preferred to be known) gave their six children a Jewish upbringing, so when Simeon later married out of the faith, this became a source of considerable, if under-stated friction. Certainly, in later years, despite the close proximity of his parents whose large family had prompted a move further north to Stamford Hill, Simeon's own family rarely mixed socially with the Felds, and contact was usually restricted to weddings and funerals.

Although considerably slighter than his father in stature, Simeon maintained the family's meat trade tradition for a time by getting a job at Blooms, the kosher butchers, until he was called up for war service. Poor eyesight limited his spell in the British army to just six weeks, but Sid (as he was more commonly known) was intent on playing a part. After his acceptance into the Dutch merchant navy, he spent much of the war working as a steward on a munitions ship travelling between Liverpool, New York and the West Indies.

Back on the home front, Phyllis Winifred Atkins had left school to join the millions of women who manned the factories in support of the war effort, working in the Earls Court Exhibition Centre building, which had been transformed into a munitions factory. Phyllis lived nearby at 32 Kinnoul Road, in north-east Fulham, where her father, Henry Leonard Atkins, had previously owned a small greengrocer's shop. It never generated much income, and after the birth of Phyllis, on 23 August 1927, and three other daughters, Henry's wife Elsie was obliged to take early morning cleaning jobs for the idle ladies of South Kensington in order to make ends meet. By the time Phyllis reached working age, Henry had ceased trading to become a dust destructor, operating the incinerator at the end of the refuse collecting process.

Sid Feld had returned home before the war's end, and joined the Ministry of Supply's payroll as a porter, winning the heart of young Phyllis Atkins in the process. Sid impressed her with tales of his high seas exploits and, regardless of the seven-year

age difference, the pair became sweethearts; so much so that by
the end of 1944, seventeen-year-old Phyllis discovered she was
pregnant. Propelled into action by the standards of the day, the
couple were married on 31 January 1945 at Fulham Register
Office, and took up residence in the top rooms of a three-storey
house in Stoke Newington at the cost of 15 shillings per week
rent, inclusive of rates. Later that spring, Phyllis was evacuated
to Walton Hall, a stately residence just outside Wakefield in
Yorkshire, where on 25 June 1945, the Felds' first child Harry
was born.

Now with a family to support, Sid – who had held a driving
licence before the war – found a job with a local road haulage
firm. Long-distance lorry driving wasn't ideal for a man who
preferred his own bed to the anonymity of a guest-house, but
barring a short interlude selling hairbrushes during 1947, Sid
went on to spend much of his life on the road. During the
immediate post-war years, in the days before tachographs recorded the speed and distance covered by heavy goods vehicles,
the system was open to abuse by firms keen to out-travel and
out-pace their competitors. But this worked to Sid's advantage,
too. Instead of driving directly from one destination to another,
he would go all the way back to London to load up again so that
he could spend the night at home.

Home was 25 Stoke Newington Common, a large late-
Victorian terraced house owned by a Mr Ambrose, who occupied
the middle floor. The Felds' four rooms were on two levels – a
kitchen and bathroom were situated at the top of the long flight
of stairs, with a back bedroom and a large front living room which
looked across the common a few steps higher. The glorified patch
of green opposite was actually no bigger than a small football
pitch, but, like the railway line linking the suburb with Liverpool
Street Station beyond that, it gave a welcome feeling of space to
the occupants of these relatively cramped conditions.

An attractive feature of the row of houses was the stone
columns topped with ornamental Corinthian capitals. Among the
Gothic style moulds on number 25 and its immediate neighbours
were a bird of prey with outstretched wings, an 'Old Father
Time' figure, and a distinctive, cream-coloured long-necked
swan.

There was another Mark Feld, whose fate adds a cautionary note to the moral back-slapping that resounded throughout the Allied territories in the immediate post-war euphoria. Unlike his brother Simeon, this Mark – the youngest of the four Feld boys – was a physical lad who wasn't averse to getting into the odd scrap. He had served in the army during the war and by 1946 was stationed at the Burton Dassett camp in Warwickshire. It was, by some accounts, a poorly disciplined establishment, with cases of shots being fired indiscriminately and soldiers regularly going AWOL.

This indiscipline reached a horrific climax on the night of 19 August 1946 when Feld, asleep in his billet, was struck with a truncheon and suffered a fatal blow to his head. Apparently, following an outburst of trouble, thirty-five-year-old Patrick Francis Lyons of the camp military police, and the acting company sergeant major, Sgt. Henry Storey Crampsie, ended a night of drinking by paying Feld a surprise visit. It was alleged that Lyons told Crampsie beforehand that he intended to 'do Feld up', that Feld was a bad soldier, and that he 'would fit only one place and that was Belsen'. Lyons later claimed that his intention was only to frighten Feld. 'When I was about a yard from the foot of his bed,' he told the court, 'Feld jumped up and came for me. I struck out with my truncheon and aimed what I thought to be a light blow at his shoulder.' That blow, which was indelicate enough to fracture Mark Feld's skull, earned Lyons a conviction for manslaughter, although the judge, sentencing him to ten years' penal servitude, told him that he was as nearly convicted of murder as possible.

Private Mark Feld 14709755 received two posthumous tributes: the Under-Secretary of State for War sent a service medal to his mother, Bessie Feld, and his elder brother Simeon named his second son in his memory.


Nineteen forty-seven was the year the baby boom peaked at 20.5 births per 1000 of the population, which was hardly a surprise considering the return of hundreds of thousands of active servicemen and the lifting of the spectre of war. It was also the year when the Labour government sought to transpose the camaraderie of the wartime spirit into the economy, first nationalising the British coal industry, then laying down plans to do the same to the railways and to electricity. There was even a National

Health Service on its way. Working people, who had made so
many sacrifices since the outbreak of war, began to feel hopeful
about their futures: children could be planned.

As the nation awaited the arrival of the much-promised classless society and a new era of economic prosperity, a second Mark
Feld gave his first yelp to a tiny audience in Hackney Hospital.
It was 30 September 1947; his brother Harry was being looked
after by a Mrs Waterman who had the ground floor flat at number
25. Phyllis and Sid were delighted. They weren't to know that
they would soon be guiding their two small children safely
through one of the coldest winters this century, in a flat that had
no hot water, no proper heating and one or two resident mice.

One of Harry's earliest memories of his younger brother
gives an amusing foretaste of things to come. 'We always played
together when we were young,' he recalls, 'but because I was
that bit older, I had to look after him, which wasn't always easy
because he was always running. He was like a little bullet, and
he had this peculiar way of pushing his feet out sideways as he
ran.

'I particularly remember one winter, around 1951 or 1952,
when there was a heavy snow. It was the only time I can ever
recall six-foot-high mounds of snow in the streets. I took Mark
out into the street and decided to dress him up in my bright red
school blazer and my mum's fur boots. Everyone laughed at
him: he looked a right wreck!' Twenty years later, Mark dressed
himself in costumes that had become considerably more flamboyant, and had transformed the mocking laughter into screams
of unbridled adoration.

Due to the compactness of the Felds' flat, the front living
room soon became a shared bedroom for the boys, containing
twin beds separated by a wooden cabinet. Television was still a
luxury for most families during the fifties, and Harry and Mark
were brought up on the staple diet of American movies, BBC
radio, children's comics and books of fairy stories. The main
point of contact with the world outside of family and school life
was the radio. 'The family always had a radio,' says Harry. 'One
of our highlights of the week was to take it – it was one of the
early portables from Radio Rentals – upstairs to our room at
bedtime, put it on the cabinet, and lie in bed listening to *Saturday
Night Theatre*. The plays were usually quite long, but we always
enjoyed the ghost stories which seemed to be on quite often.

'Mark would love anything that stoked up his imagination. We had the usual comics, of course, and mother used to read us fairy stories like *The Water Babies*. She also used to read excerpts from the Bible to us, not as a religious exercise, but as adventure stories. Because we were too young to understand biblical language, she used to put the text into plain English, so that we could enjoy the adventures of David and Goliath or Daniel and the lion's den. Mark and I also got interested in prehistoric things and dinosaurs. I think he liked the idea that such huge creatures walked the earth, and yet weren't there any more.'

Though dinosaurs no longer stalked the vicinity of what was now London, in post-war Britain there appeared to be a significant new threat. The fifties was a time when leading intellectuals of the day, from both sides of the political spectrum, feared what Richard Hoggart called the 'shiny barbarism' of American mass culture. Cultural critics like Hoggart imagined that a vibrant and 'authentic' working-class culture, as typified by its stoicism, its cycling clubs and its neighbourhood support systems, would be contaminated by a new 'candy-floss world' of fleeting images and instant gratification and what cultural theorist David Harvey later described 'Disneyland aesthetics'. While Hoggart and other well-meaning critics agonised on behalf of the working classes, the establishment were no less concerned to preserve their own interests. If a sea of imported mass culture was to engulf the British way of life, would its own position as custodian of high culture be undermined in this 'triumph of mediocrity' scenario? What Hoggart underestimated, in *The Uses Of Literacy*, his denunciation of bland post-war disposable culture, was the pleasure factor. As part of the new educated 'aristocracy of labour', he had sought to reinvoke the bygone age of his youth, romanticising ugly working men's clubs and 'Don't Dilly-Dally On The Way'-type sing-songs, pastimes that were apparently of the people and not foisted on the people. But in failing to take into account the haste and apparent delight with which the leisure products of the modern media systems were being accepted by the working classes, his anxieties reeked of fogeyism.

Mark Feld revelled in these polished surfaces that lit up post-war British culture. Far from being one of the new breed of passive consumers feared by the nation's moral guardians, Mark, like many of his generation found liberation from the puritan restraint of the traditional working-class lifestyle. The drab mundanity of his Spartan material surroundings contrasted dramatically with the new world of fantastic images, and nowhere was this more marked than in the twentieth century's most seductive dream factory, the cinema.

Harry remembers the impact of Mark's early cinematic heroes well: 'Our mum used to take us to the ABC on Lower Clapton Road or to the Regent [which later became the Odeon] on the crossroads where Amhurst Park meets Stamford Hill. The cinema really fired up his imagination. Through the characters on the screen, he could live another life. If ever he was unsure of a situation, he'd become one of the characters he'd seen or read about as a way of shielding himself. That way he could never get hurt; he could cope with anything. Audie Murphy [the actor who won more decorations than any other US soldier in the war] was a great hero of his. He'd often be Audie Murphy when we played with our local gang. But the very first character that Mark took on was Mighty Joe Young.'

When Bolan later name-dropped Mighty Joe Young, most assumed he was referring to a similarly named blues artist from Chicago. In fact Mark's Mighty Joe Young was a fictional gorilla who, like King Kong, got to star in his own movie, but unlike his predecessor, failed to live on in the public's imagination. The film's plot – a girl befriends a young gorilla in the African jungle and takes it home; the animal is hugely indulged but is shot after alcohol sends it berserk – was tired, but *Mighty Joe Young*, released in 1949, left a great impression on Mark Feld when he saw it a couple of years later. The character provided him with his first protective mask, and the film's blending of the strange and the sentimental was a combination that always stayed with him.


Today, despite encroaching gentrification in the borough of Hackney, Stoke Newington suffers from the urban decay that results from decades of neglect and poor planning. The High Street, once a hive of activity with large department stores and thriving small businesses, is uninspiring and in the stranglehold of a one-way traffic system. Meanwhile, the conversion of the area's large Victorian houses into flats has continued and, coupled with the housing estates which have gradually replaced war-damaged properties, contributes to a general sense of overcrowding. What has remained, though, is a strong nonconformist presence, both in terms of religious faith and political activism. The Angry Brigade, a small group of anarchists best known for blowing up Conservative minister Robert Carr's house in 1971, were based here for a time during the early seventies, and dreams of insurrection are apparent today in the minds of the occasional Class War sloganeer whose political graffiti makes better reading than the countless 'To Let' and 'For Sale' notices.

Stoke Newington's greatest characteristic has been its long-standing tradition as a haven for Dissenters and immigrants. Dissenters, once forbidden to live within the bounds of the city of London, established a thriving community here: among their number in the early part of the eighteenth century was the novelist Daniel Defoe. A century later, a small Jewish community came to the area, a process which accelerated earlier this century when the Jews began to move out of the heart of the East End and into the northern belt that spread from Stoke Newington through Stamford Hill, Golders Green and up to Edgware. More recently, new waves of immigrants from the Caribbean, India and Cyprus have populated Stoke Newington and today the only real sign of the once formidable Jewish presence are the shells of several closed-down synagogues.

Harry and Mark weren't brought up in accordance with the Jewish faith, either at home or at school. The Felds preferred to give their children a secular upbringing, and were happy to send them to Northwold Road Primary School, where the religious content was minimal. Assemblies, conducted by the headmaster Mr Kershaw, himself Jewish, were brief, consisting of one hymn, a reading of the Lord's Prayer, followed by school business. After Mark began his schooling in September 1952, Phyllis walked the short distance up Northwold Road with the boys each morning, returning to pick them up for lunch. Both had no difficulties settling in, and Phyllis soon felt confident enough to take advantage of the school dinner system, leaving her free to accept a weekly job at a friend's fruit stall in Soho's Berwick Street. With the family purse suitably filled, she was at last able to provide her sons with some of the shiny luxuries they increasingly demanded. Among Mark's early possessions was a collection of Dinky cars and a much-treasured Davy Crockett suit and hat, but as the doom merchants had warned, these were soon supplanted by an ever-shifting round of new crazes. Phyllis made the necessary sacrifices.

Mark was a popular and happy pupil at Northwold Primary who got on well with his teachers and enjoyed a large circle of friends. Even at this young age, his chief physical feature was his short stature, although this was more than compensated for by his boldness: he was always ready to play the tough guy – with or without a little help from Mighty Joe Young. Upfront, brash even, gap-toothed Mark rarely showed signs of vulnerability in public. This bravura extended to the apparent delight he began to take in horror films, sparked by an early encounter with the Claude Rains version of *Phantom of the Opera*. But back at home, and with no audience to play to, Mark was barely able to climb the stairs in the dark without quaking with fear. Instead, he'd call upon one of his ever-growing roster of heroes and climb the stairs with a loud roar or a calm swagger, depending on which character he'd chosen to be.

These masks were as much there to satisfy Mark's fantasies as they were for self-protection. By all accounts, he was not a weak or sickly child. On the contrary: he seems to have inherited his strong will from his mother, who was also the source of his dark colouring and, in time, his passion for reading. Although Phyllis would discipline the boys – ensuring they were in bed at a decent hour, giving them a slap now and again – she never babied them. In fact, good communication between parents and sons characterised the Feld household, and problems were usually resolved in an atmosphere free from major upsets or any real fear. One of the few comments Mark later made about his family was that 'there were never any restrictions'.

The Felds weren't great socialisers, but when they did venture out for a drink with Phyllis's market-stall colleagues, they left Harry and Mark with a full stock of lemonade and crisps knowing they'd be able to amuse themselves responsibly. As a cautionary measure, Phyllis always asked the neighbours to listen out in case of any trouble.

The guardian angel was usually Mrs Perrone. She had taken over 25 Stoke Newington Common at the end of the forties, from her brother Fred, who briefly acquired the lease from the former owner Mr Ambrose. The relationship between tenant family and landlord was amicable right up until 1962 when the Felds were rehoused – apart from a short flurry of legal exchanges between March and August 1952 concerning the rent.

Mrs Perrone remembers Mark and the family well. 'I think

Phyllis wore the trousers,' she recalled. 'She was really nice and friendly, a real Cockney. I got on very well with her, though we did have a bit of a duel one day. Little Mark's pushchair was in the long passageway. I told her, "You'll have to shift it, we can't have that in the way!" But we used to get on all right. Their dad was a lorry driver, but he never used to bring his lorry home, thank goodness. They weren't bad tenants at all. Apart from that one instance, they never used to quibble about money. They were a happy family and didn't quarrel a lot.'

Despite the two-year age difference and the inevitable brotherly rivalry, Harry and Mark led a remarkably peaceable co-existence. But it wasn't long before they began to realise how unlike each other they were: and they weren't the only ones to notice. 'Harry? He wasn't like Mark at all,' remembers Mrs Perrone. 'He was quiet like his father. Mark took after his mum. He was much more sociable and jolly as a youngster.' Harry, who inherited his father's fair colouring and his mother's stocky build (quite the reverse of the genetic traits acquired by Mark), agrees. 'We were 100 per cent different,' he admits. 'I realised that from an early age and it became more apparent when he became an avid music follower. My friends were more rough and ready.'

Harry was boisterous, but content. Mark, in contrast, demanded attention. As the younger brother, he felt compelled to keep up with Harry and his friends, a task that was made doubly difficult because he looked young for his age. Instead, he adopted diversionary tactics, like stepping into roles other than Mark Feld and hoping to create an aura around himself. When that proved insufficient, he looked for a new interest to set him apart from everyone else. His immediate peer group had discovered rock 'n' roll. In following them, Mark immediately became several years older: precocious to those who knew the game he was playing, but important, or at least *different* in the eyes of his less-worldly playmates.

# CHAPTER TWO

**'At nine years old I became Elvis Presley.'**
Marc Bolan

**'We used to take the mickey out of him because, quite frankly, he wasn't all that talented. But he was mad about Elvis. He always used to say, "One of these days, I'm really gonna do something with music", and he did.'**
Susan Singer

The close-knit Feld family rarely defied convention. The nearest they ever got to social deviance was spending their Sundays apart. Although there was little contact with his side of the family, Sid joined his father at Petticoat Lane market every Sunday, where they supplied stall-holders with a trellis and cover. Despite his early retirement from the meat market, Henry still retained his old drinking habits which needed paying for, and Sid helped out as a matter of duty, rather than for any financial reward. (When his father died in the early sixties, Sid immediately packed the job in.) While Sid was thrust into the hustle and bustle of London market life, Phyllis often took the boys to visit her family in Fulham. It was a journey that Harry and Mark always looked forward to because the number 73 bus which took them direct to South Kensington, usually passed St George's Hospital at the end of The Mall at 11 a.m., just in time to see the changing of the guard.

On one such Sunday in the summer of 1956, as Phyllis whiled away the journey by leafing through the *Sunday Pictorial* newspaper, Mark spotted something of interest on the back page. It was a typically brash warehouse sale advertisement, but what caught his eye was the illustration that went with it: a spanking new six-string acoustic guitar. He'd coveted one for several months, ever since his father, noting how much his son enjoyed Bill Hayes's 'The Ballad Of Davy Crockett', mistakenly brought home a recording of Bill Haley and the Comets' 'See You Later

Alligator'. 'Just one playing of that and I chucked Bill Hayes out of the window,' Mark later recalled. 'Haley was much more exciting.' Even more impressive, though, was hearing – and seeing photographs of – Elvis Presley, whose singles had just begun to chart in Britain. Mark immediately decided he had to be Elvis, and a guitar was an essential prop if he was going to impress his invisible bedroom audiences with any real conviction. At £9, the instrument didn't come cheaply, but Phyllis dutifully sent off the first of her HP instalments, and on his ninth birthday, in the week that Presley's 'Hound Dog' ripped into the British Top Five, Mark could throw out his home-made contraption made out of orange boxes and elastic bands and lovingly strap his new guitar around him. His snare drum complete with stand, which he'd not had long, stood in a corner untouched.

He couldn't play it, of course. Not for several years. It was more important that he looked right. Standing in front of the radiogram, a monster on four legs guarding the window in the boys' room, Mark perfected the moves of Presley and Bill Haley, the two most visible personifications of American rock 'n' roll music whom he'd recently glimpsed on newsreels at the local cinema. Swinging his new plaything from side to side, stamping his feet in time with the driving 4/4 backbeat and singing along with the barely decipherable words of the latest hits, Mark Feld had become Elvis Presley.

Frances Perrone's living room was directly below. 'Noisy? When you came in that front door and he had that radiogram on, you could hear him down three flights of stairs,' she exclaims. 'He'd be sitting up there in front of his player in that big room with all his records on full blast. Sometimes I used to have to go up there and tell him to pack it in.'

Mark wasn't the only one in his neighbourhood to tune into the vibrant sound of rock 'n' roll, a sound that Frank Sinatra once memorably described as 'a rancid-smelling aphrodisiac'. At the start of the year, while Mark was still drooling over his 'Davy Crockett' record, Lonnie Donegan unwittingly ushered in the skiffle craze with an adaptation of 'Rock Island Line', a song drawn from the repertoire of black American folk-blues artist Leadbelly. During 1956, and for many months afterwards, sales of guitars boomed, alongside a proportionate rise in the filching of tea-chests and the removal of broom heads from their handles. The response to both skiffle and rock 'n' roll was so immediate that many wondered why neither had happened before.

Several others at Northwold Primary shared Mark's passion for the new teenage music. One fellow pop fan was Helen Shapiro from nearby Clapton. 'I was ten years old, a year older than Mark, when I first met him,' she remembers. 'My cousin Susan Singer and I were both very musical, we'd always be singing. We were friendly with two boys in our year at school, Stephen Gould and Melvyn Fields, and when Stephen was given a guitar for his birthday, he suggested we all get together and form a group. In those days, to have a guitar was the height of sophistication and wonderfulness, because Elvis played – well, held – a guitar. Just to walk along the street carrying one was a thrill.'

Despite his age, Mark had already befriended Gould, who lived in nearby Fountayne Road, and his enthusiasm (and his guitar) made him an obvious addition to the fold. To describe the early sessions that took place in Stephen's, and occasionally Mark's, front room, as rehearsals, probably over-dramatises the reality of those enthusiastic get-togethers, although Helen does remember the quintet spending much of the 1957 summer holiday working on songs. 'Stephen and Mark couldn't really play,' she says. 'The guitars were twice as big as them anyway. But they looked good. Mark at that time was this chubby little kid with a quiff. His great claim to fame was that when he combed his hair forward, this quiff covered his whole face. He was very into the look and the whole rock 'n' roll image even then. I've got a very strong memory of him in his brown suedette jacket, with the collar turned up, his quiff and his crêpe-soled chukka boots.

'We obviously grew out of the skiffle movement. I vaguely recall us having a tea-chest bass for a short time, though we never had a washboard. Melvyn kept the beat on the snare drum and brushes while Susan and I sang. There were two distinct camps at the time, skiffle and rock 'n' roll. I was in both because I joined in with my brother's skiffle group from time to time, but Mark was definitely keener on the rock 'n' roll thing.'

Rock 'n' roll brilliantly encapsulated the passions of the emerging teenage culture. Its energy and its volume provided a vibrant antidote to the dullness of school routine, and with most adults tuned into *Worker's Playtime* and the more controlled sound of the big bands, it offered youngsters something that seemed to reflect their own attitude to life. But the appeal of rock 'n' roll was never solely about music. Pictures of Elvis Presley were pinned up on bedroom walls all over the country, and his influence was such that even wised-up pre-teens like Helen Shapiro and Mark Feld idolised him.

It was impossible to erase the effect of that initial contact with a performer whose every move and every vocal nuance was as alien as anything Mark had seen at his local flea-pit. Presley the truck-drivin' boy from Memphis, with an almost unhealthy devotion to his mother, encapsulated a kind of madness. The feverish body twitching, the contorted lip, and above all that blank, emotionless stare combined to suggest that here was someone who was *not quite* at home. That was what Mark Feld could relate to. To prove his devotion, he rushed out and bought 'All Shook Up' long before anyone else in his circle had a copy. The incident was important enough for Helen Shapiro to recall it thirty-five years later.

Mark Feld had a guitar, a borrowed image, and moral support from his fellow dreamers. The next step was to find an audience. Susie and the Hula Hoops (a name mentioned by Mark many years later, though neither Shapiro nor Susan Singer recall it with any certainty) never developed any real instrumental competence, although Shapiro, who had learnt some chords from her skiffle-playing brother, lent a degree of musicality to the proceedings when she brought along her plastic toy guitar. The youngsters' main concern was to perfect their vocal harmonies (although each would take a solo vocal) on a repertoire that included recent Presley hits like 'Teddy Bear' and 'Got A Lot O' Livin' To Do', plus 'Heartbreak Hotel', the song that heralded his arrival in the UK. Two other summer 1957 hits, the Everly Brothers' 'Bye Bye Love' and the Crickets' 'That'll Be The Day', were also rehearsal regulars. Susan Singer recalls endless versions of the latter when the big-thinking quintet played its first public performance at a (now demolished) Stoke Newington café. 'We didn't get paid,' remembers Helen Shapiro, 'we just got endless free cups of tea.'

That summer, Susie and the Hula Hoops also played at a local school, before the arrival of the new autumn term arrested the momentum of the group. Over the months, the would-be pop stars gradually drifted apart, with the final break coming when Helen, Susan, Melvyn and Stephen moved on to secondary schools the following year, leaving Mark stranded at Northwold

Primary. He was not quite alone, though. There was a new young man in his life, one who was far closer to him than Elvis ever could be.

In 1958, Cliff Richard was plucked from obscurity to become the leading home-grown contender to Presley. It's difficult to imagine now, after years of all-round entertaining and ballads offering seasonal comfort and salvation, but Cliff was a serious – and to some, threatening – teen rock idol when 'Move It' charted in September of that year. Mark's well-practised Presley shoulder jerks and lip-curling became all the more convincing when he applied them to the rising British star. He could imitate Elvis's surly demeanour and manic stare, but his baby-face, still buoyed by puppy fat, was better suited to his Cliff Richard. 'He used to do a very good impression of Cliff in those days,' says Helen Shapiro. Harry Feld remembers this latest infatuation as a turning point: 'In his mind, he never ever deviated from the time that he started following Cliff Richard. I think he told himself, "This is what I want", and he single-mindedly pursued that line until he finally made it.'

When Presley was conscripted into the US Army in March 1958, his career was thrown off course, despite his record company's determined efforts to capitalise on the vast reservoir of material he'd pre-recorded before his departure.

Cliff, meanwhile, was the long-overdue British response to the Presley phenomenon. Mark often claimed he met Cliff at the 2i's coffee bar in Soho's Old Compton Street when the singer was still plain Harry Webb and trying desperately to get a gig there. But like the oft-told tale of Mark carrying Eddie Cochran's guitar at the Hackney Empire, this story cannot be verified. Certainly, though, Harry Feld remembers Mark being on and around both scenes at an early age, episodes which have since been immortalised as landmarks in the history of British rock 'n' roll.

In truth, the 2i's – which had opened in April 1956 and gave the world Tommy Steele, Cliff Richard and Adam Faith – was acutely aware of its own importance by the time Mark Feld discovered it, proclaiming itself as 'The World Famous' and 'Home of the Stars' on the sign above its doorway. This proved a magnet to tourists and young hopefuls alike and Mark, who spent most Saturday mornings helping his mother on the market stall nearby, couldn't resist the invitation. When it was cold, Phyllis would slip him a few coppers from her takings and he'd proudly enter the hallowed building and chat to Nora who served the coffees. Mark also scrutinised the jukebox, desperately hoping a customer would put some money in so that he could hear what acts like the Drifters, the Coasters and Ray Charles sounded like. When someone finally obliged, and the Drifters' 'There Goes My Baby' filled the air, Mark was completely knocked out.

Alongside the rise of the 2i's and Cliff Richard was Britain's first indispensable television pop show, Jack Good's *Oh Boy*. Good, who'd originally produced *Six-Five Special* for the BBC, chose to record the shows on Saturday mornings at the Hackney Empire in Mare Street, conveniently a short bus ride on the 106 from Mark Feld's Stoke Newington home. Harry clearly remembers his brother making that journey on several occasions, where he would have caught stars like Marty Wilde, Billy Fury, Lord Rockingham's XI, Adam Faith, and the show's favourite guest Cliff Richard. Occasionally, visiting rock 'n' rollers appeared, and the Eddie Cochran legend – if true – dates from the American guitarist's visit in spring 1960, shortly before his death in a car accident.

By this time, Mark had advanced to the mixed-sex William Wordsworth Secondary Modern School. It was based in the Shacklewell district of the borough, and getting there required a bit more effort than the short walk he took to Northwold Primary. It wasn't long before Mark tired of waiting for the number 73, which dropped him virtually outside the Wordsworth Road site (at fourteen, he moved to the senior building in nearby Albion Road). From his first day there in September 1958, he resented the valuable time school stole from him. Music lessons taught him nothing about the music he liked; art and history occasionally stirred his imagination, but it seemed the teachers did their best to make lessons dull and uninspiring; and sports didn't interest him at all. Confined to his desk with just a pen and paper, he daydreamed his time away, sometimes writing down the scenarios he created in his mind. Some harked back to the fairies and monsters which had enthralled him as a child, a few involved his favourite film characters, others still he'd invent for himself. Nevertheless, inventing stories and imaginative wordplay were merely minor distractions at this stage. It was the near-pathological precision which he'd begun to apply to his outward appearance that now occupied his every waking moment.

# CHAPTER THREE

'I was completely knocked out by my own image, by the idea of Mark Feld.'
Marc Bolan, 1967

'The mod way of life consisted of total devotion to looking and being "cool". Spending practically all your money on clothes and all your after-work hours in clubs and dance halls. To be part-time was to miss the point.'
Richard Barnes, introduction to *Mods!*, 1979

'I've got ten suits, eight sports jackets, fifteen pairs of slacks, thirty to thirty-five good shirts, about twenty jumpers, three leather jackets, two suede jackets, five or six pairs of shoes and thirty exceptionally good ties.'
Mark Feld, interviewed in *Town* magazine, 1962

'Where is the goal towards which he is obviously running as fast as his impeccably shod feet can carry him? It is nowhere. He is running to stay in the same place, and he knows that by the time he has reached his mid-twenties, the exhausting race will be over and he will have lost.'
Peter Barnsley, *Town* magazine, 1962

The Felds weren't in a position to sample every lifestyle product that was offered to the suburban consumer during the fifties. The 'dream houses' that popped up with increasing regularity in Hollywood's post-war output, fitted out with a variety of electrical gadgets in colour co-ordinated rooms, were a million miles from the compact top floor flat at 25 Stoke Newington Common. But the Felds were determined that Harry and Mark shouldn't miss out on what was fast becoming a great British institution – the holiday beside the seaside.

After travelling the length and breadth of Britain by day, the last thing Sid wanted to do in his spare time was get back into a driving seat. There was little compulsion, then, for the Felds to buy a car, even if they were able to muster enough money for a deposit. Mrs Perrone cannot recall the family venturing far, but several photographs and the testimony of Harry Feld prove otherwise. 'We used to borrow a car and we'd go touring,' Mark's brother fondly remembers. 'That meant going as far as we could. It was often a spur-of-the-moment thing. I don't think Mum and Dad ever made their minds up where we were going until the day before we left.

'One of the most common routes was to drive east to Clacton-on-Sea, and then work our way up the coast, stopping off at places like Lowestoft, Great Yarmouth (where we'd visit Dad's brother Arthur) and Mablethorpe. Sometimes we'd get as far as Yorkshire. We'd stay in bed and breakfasts, or else just sleep in the car. Another time we travelled west all the way down to Looe in Cornwall. Mark and I loved the seaside, even though neither of us were very good swimmers. Later on, Mark wouldn't go anywhere near the water in case it spoilt his hair . . . '

By 1960, Cliff Richard, like Presley, had refashioned his style, falling in line with the likes of Fabian, Frankie Avalon and the all-American bobbysoxers. After the success of 'Living Doll' the previous summer, his audience shifted too as parents and 'squares' began to displace his disaffected rebel teenage fans. Mark remained loyal to his idol, even if by this time he was really more interested in the cut of Cliff's jacket than he was in arguments concerning musical purity. He lovingly admired Cliff's ability to notch up a run of six hits that made him the most successful singing star that year, but Mark had seriously begun to worry about his trousers.

The Teddy Boys who cast long, dark shadows in the streets of Elephant & Castle, Clapham, Stamford Hill and Stoke Newington during the mid-fifties had begun to lose their sharpness. The drape jacket, brothel-creeper shoes and bootlace ties which had seemed such a threat back in 1955 were, by the end of the decade, tired and over-familiar. In its borrowing of the Edwardian fashion of 1947, a style originally aimed at well-heeled dandies, the Teddy Boy look was an imaginative – and subversive – refusal of mainstream culture, made all the more powerful when it merged with the arrival of American rock 'n' roll music to create an assertive, and therefore threatening, working-class youth style. But to their kid brothers, it meant little more than a nostalgia for an age that had already seen its moment. In the minds of a new generation of peacocks, wearing anything that resembled Teddy Boy dress in 1959 was marginally less heretical than demanding a return to rationing.

In a memorable interview with *Rolling Stone* magazine, conducted at the peak of his career, Mark told a story which freeze-framed British subculture in transition. Sitting on his doorstep dressed in his black drainpipes, his chukka boots and his Everly Brothers-style blue-striped shirt with its collar characteristically turned up, Mark Feld gazed adoringly as one of those heavy Stoke Newington Teds passed by, radiating perfection from the crease in his duck's arse hairstyle down to the toes of his winkle-picker boots. His envy was scarcely containable. Then the figure of one Martin Kauffman strolled past, dressed in baggy ginger Harris-tweed trousers and a pair of green handmade pointed shoes with side-buckles. He also wore a short dark green blazer and his hair-style had a radical centre parting, with the fringe flopping into his eyes.

Within weeks, Mark had thrown himself headlong into this sartorial battlefield where style was no longer merely an adjunct to the music you listened to. Martin Kauffman may only have been on his way to work when he happened to pass the Felds' home, but to his impassioned observer, the flair he'd shown in perfecting such a meticulously crafted self-image endowed him with a sense of individuality that not even the drudgery of labour could dampen. Kauffman was undoubtedly an early Modernist – one of a group of obsessive stylists who developed out of the modern jazz clubs – and the idea that emancipation came through close attention to the details of dress was the essence of what later came to be called mod culture.

The fading of the Teds and the gradual emergence of the Modernists represented far more than merely a change of tailor. While both subcultures flourished in roughly the same working-class areas, and both screamed out to be recognised, the Teds' uniform was exactly that – a uniform. It consisted of little more than buying the correct outfit and adorning it with the appropriate accessories. The Modernists, meanwhile, were nothing if not eclectic. Instead of sticking to one readily recognisable style, they sought continually to adapt and evolve their dress, combining functional garments designed for the country gentleman with sportswear, ladies' fashions with suits aimed at the city gent. What lay behind this obsessive one-upmanship was the new spirit of competitive individualism that had supplanted the austerity years and, in this respect, Modernist culture in its pure form marked a sharp break with the insular, herd-like outlook of the Teds' world. It should not be confused with what generally became known as the mid-sixties mod 'movement', by which time the ideology – not to mention the styles – had altered considerably.

The self-obsessed almost exclusively male world to which Martin Kauffman and his ilk adhered offered infinite possibilities to Mark Feld. It gave him free rein to turn his role-playing in on himself, allowing him to indulge his manifest narcissism, while also satisfying the compulsion to keep redesigning himself in ever more spectacular guises. It was shameless consumerism – but creative with it. To the young stylists, puritan restraint had gone out with band-leader Victor Sylvester and 'austerity' Chancellor Stafford Cripps.

Frances Perrone noticed the change in her tenants' son. 'He used to leave the house dressed up to the nines,' she recalls. 'He'd become a real little flash boy, that Mark, and he never went anywhere without his rolled-up umbrella. He'd still have his radiogram blaring out, but his room would be dominated by this great big clothes line that stretched from one wall to the other. I used to have a shoe shop in Stoke Newington Church Street and he was forever asking me to make him shoes. I'd got him some made in lizard-skin or snake-skin, but then he got a bit too much. He wanted shoes every other day.'

Mark was too young to have been taken seriously at first by the elder Modernists, as they vied with each other for attention. When he was eleven, in 1958, the 'Italian look' – square-shouldered 'bumfreezer' jackets with narrow lapels and two or three covered buttons; narrow trousers without turn-ups – had already signalled a new peak in teenage sophistication and modernity. Frankie Laine had brought the style to Britain back in 1955, and was roundly savaged by the critics for wearing it at the London Palladium, that near-sacred epicentre of British popular culture. So much for variety. Nevertheless, the pre-pubescent Mark Feld, still without the figure to wear a suit convincingly, pestered his mother for an Italian-style outfit. She took him to a local tailor, but her son's specific instructions regarding the cut left the outfitter flabbergasted.

Frankie Laine had told his adversaries, 'Knock my talent if you must, but not my tailor.' Mark Feld knew he couldn't rely on the goodwill of neighbours or the incompetence of local tradesmen if he really wanted to make it in style. Whereas he'd previously only been familiar with his own Stoke Newington/ Stamford Hill/Clapton/Hackney area and the immediate vicinity of his mother's stall in Soho, having to seek out cheap, efficient tailors widened Mark's territory. A train or bus trip would take him all the way to Alfred Bilgorri of Bishopsgate, near Liverpool Street Station, though if he travelled by bus, he could break the journey to check out Connick's boys' shop in Kingsland Road, Dalston, one of the few places that sold Levi's in his small size. Another regular haunt was a tailor in Leman Street in the heart of the Feld family's old stamping ground in Whitechapel, while further afield was Borowick's of Bow, at the intersection of Mile End Road and Grove Road. For footwear, Mark occasionally used a Greek shoemaker in Robert Street, Euston, until he discovered Stan Bartholomew's in Battersea, and later, the children's department of Ravel in Wardour Street. There were also trips to Anello & Davide, the famous Covent Garden ballet shoe shop, where Mark and his new West End friend, Jeff Dexter (who he first encountered at the Lyceum Ballroom in 1960), bought après-ski boots. A few years later, these reasonably priced and simply made items of footwear with the elasticated sides took off as 'Beatle Boots'.

Mark often summed up his youth by bragging that he had always been a star, 'even if it was only being the star of three streets in Hackney'. To the few close friends in Stoke Newington who shared his hopes, he probably was. Harry remembers his younger brother never being able to pass a mirror, but such extreme vanity was ultimately worthless unless he was able to exhibit what he'd created. Stamford Hill, with the Fairsports amusement arcade (known by the locals as the 'schtip' house; literally, 'to take your money'), cinema, bowling alley and the salt beef bar, became his regular catwalk. Here, he'd meet up with other local *shmatte* fiends, including Eric Hall, Mickey 'Modern' Turner, Gerry Goldstein and two older boys, Peter Sugar and Michael Simmonds.

The ultra-modern world inhabited by Mark and his friends

contrasted sharply with Stamford Hill's formidable population of
Hasidic Jews. Highly visible in their beaver hats, alpaca cloaks,
untrimmed beards and long side ringlets, the religious orthodoxy
of this tight-knit community manifested itself in a desperate
attempt to cling to the eighteenth century lifestyle of their East
European ancestors.

Another vital part of the local 'scene' was the network of
youth clubs which, more often than not, were affiliated to the
many synagogues in the area. Helen Shapiro remembers Mark
making an appearance at her local meeting-place in Clapton. 'He
came in with his crowd from Stamford Hill Jewish youth club,
who were rivals of ours, and I hadn't seen him for a while. The
change was unbelievable. He was very slim, obviously taller,
and was dressed from head to toe in his Modernist clothes –
bumfreezer jacket, button-down shirt, all the gear. He was obviously the leader of this gang and he came in and took the place
over. We all thought, "Who does he think he is?", he was so
sure of himself. But he always had a strong personality, even
when he was nine.' Her cousin Susan Singer also remembers the
transformation. 'Most of us were afraid to go too far,' she says,
'but not Mark. I must say he wasn't aggressive with it. In fact
he was always very friendly and everyone at the dances liked
him. I thought he was lovely.'

Jeff Dexter records a different response. 'He was hated –
precisely because he looked so good. Everyone hated anyone
who they felt had one up on them. People always tried to pick
a fight with you if they felt you were competition. And we were
surrounded by a lot of very rough firms then. A lot of the mods
would dress up in their posh clothes and then go out and punch shit
out of each other. Mark often pretended he was out for a fight.'

Jeff Dexter, like Mark, was absorbed in a scene that revolved
around teenagers who were often much older and much bigger
than him. It wasn't easy if you were young and small for your
age to command respect in places like the Lyceum, where you
had to pass six foot four inch bouncers before you could even
enter. 'You had to be sixteen to get in,' Dexter recalls. 'We were
only thirteen or fourteen, and probably looked no older than
eleven, but we both had as much front as Woolworths. Mark
always came across as a very smart chap with a great sense of
dress. He stood out because he was little and he looked immaculate. But when you were small, you had to pretend that you were

tougher than you were to stave off the aggravation, because you'd often get picked on. Mark always acted like he could fight a giant.

'I remember one incident at the Lyceum where he got into a bit of aggravation and he did get beaten. The other guy got thrown out, but Mark ran off, climbed out of the loo window, smartened himself up, and then strolled back in as if he'd beaten the guy to a pulp. But he hadn't. It wasn't until about a year later that he told me the truth.'

Small stature was also a problem for Mark and Jeff when it came to finding the right clothes in their size, which made tailors like Bilgorri doubly essential. But a trip to Bilgorri, whose reputation was such that many well-known East End gangsters refused to shop anywhere else, didn't come cheaply. 'I know that Mark always had fashion at his fingertips. Whether they were light fingers, I don't know,' says Harry Feld. Mark always recalled this era with fondness, and there is little reason to doubt his own explanation as to how he funded his shopping sprees. 'I was quite a villain,' he told Spencer Leigh in 1976, 'although I never hurt anybody. It came about because I was really into clothes, I mean, obsessionally into clothes. I was about twelve and I'd steal or hustle motorbikes to pay for them. Clothes were all that mattered to me.'[1]

He probably traded hijacked scooters which, by the early sixties, were a fashionable commodity among teenagers. They also provided useful getaway vehicles for impoverished stylists. Mark once recalled a mass raid on a store in Whitechapel where, he claimed, forty Levi's-obsessed youngsters 'liberated' an entire stock of the much-coveted American jeans. His fellow looters scooted off without him and he was left, heart pounding, running for the nearest bus with the booty under his jumper. They'd invariably be a pair of 505s, which were identical to 501s but featured a zip instead of a button fly. Fumbling with buttons was slow, ungainly, and let in an unwelcome draught when you were out on a scooter run.

The other solution to Mark's cash problem was to buy items off the shelf cheaply, then get them customised at home. It was a trick he'd learnt from his mother, who had often transformed an old skirt into pairs of trousers for the boys. Jeff Dexter (who by this time had been plucked from obscurity and was dancing professionally with the Cyril Stapleton Band) often shopped with

Mark at stores as unfashionable as C&A and Woolworths, where they'd invariably find something in the children's department which could then be taken home and tailored to suit.

It was thrift, coupled with the insatiable urge to defy uniformity, which prompted the Modernist scene to take off in new directions, and the relative popularity of the 'Italian look' soon gave way to all manner of sartorial combinations. All Modernists aspired to look sharp, in what was a symbolic refusal of their class position. The cult of the cloth also reflected the drive towards upward mobility, which befitted a nation that had been nudging close to full employment for several years. For young obsessives like Mark and Jeff, looking sharp wasn't the half of it: to their kind, *staying* sharp was the only goal worth achieving. If that meant personally supervising often minuscule alterations to a garment, or changing outfits twice, four, five times a day, then that was what had to be done.

When all-day Sunday sessions at the Lyceum became overcrowded, Mark (who was never much of a regular anyway) would turn disdainfully towards Jeff and say, 'Too many mods here.' There has always been an uncomfortable contradiction between the avowed *personal expression* of subcultural style, and the fact of *belonging* to a subculture, and nowhere is this anomaly better expressed than with the Individualists of 1961–2. The term never really entered into mainstream language, but it was bandied about by the Modernist vanguard in a bid to avoid becoming part of any coherent style. An Individualist – which in effect Mark was – would take the straight mod gear as a starting point, convert it, then throw in something completely at odds with the rest of the outfit. Mark's Stamford Hill gang, some of whom were becoming known as 'Faces' – the ultimate accolade among the Mod fraternity – picked up on this drive towards total originality, and before long, those outside the close-knit network of 'firms' had begun to take notice too.

In September 1962, three of these Faces made it into the pages of *Town*, then *the* lifestyle magazine for men (its only competitor being *Playboy*). Before Michael Heseltine and Clive Labovitch acquired it for Cornmarket Press in 1960, the publication was known as *Man About Town*, and it was only after a radical redesign by Tom Wolsey, and the decision to streamline its title (thus managing to convey a few all-important associated meanings – chic, youth, modernity), that *Town* really began to revel in the deification of affluence. A new breed of photo-graphers, Terry Donovan, Terry Duffy, David Bailey, even future underground guru John 'Hoppy' Hopkins, had their early work featured in its pages; artists like David Hockney were sympatheti-cally profiled; and only very occasionally would an old killjoy like Malcolm Muggeridge be invited to pen an article that threatened to spoil the party.

The theme of the September 1962 issue was 'The Young Take The Wheel'. What are they like? What do they do? What do they want? *Town* enquired, and reporter Peter Barnsley and photo-grapher Donald McCullin (himself a veteran of the Teds scene) were despatched to Stamford Hill to find out. There they found two twenty-year-olds, Michael Simmonds and Peter Sugar, and fourteen-year-old Mark Feld. *Town* called them 'Faces Without Shadows', presumably because the pace of a Face's lifestyle was too intense to cast one. Certainly that was the impression the article sought to create, and the trio were quoted at length to back it up.

In spite of the professed desire to live in a perpetual present, Mark, who was described as 'the most remarkable of the three', showed an early compulsion towards self-mythology. 'Remember three years ago?' he asked his mates. 'It was easy then. We used to go round on scooters in Levi's and leather jackets. It was a lot easier then.' The vision of a twelve-year-old boy dressed to kill on the back of a bike in the streets of Hackney obviously impressed Barnsley. So did Feld's snappy replies to his questioning. He made Mark the star of the article, and McCullin displayed him prominently in six of the ten accompanying photographs.

The well-scrubbed Face from Stoke Newington Common used his moment well, combining arrogance, fantasy and a meticulous knowledge of the scene in equal measure. *Town* reported:

'You got to be different from the other kids,' says Feld. 'I mean, you got to be two steps ahead. The stuff that half the haddocks you see around are wearing I was wearing years ago. A kid in my class came up to me in his new suit, an Italian box it was. He says, "Just look at the length of your jacket," he says. "You're not with it," he says. "I was wearing that style two years ago," I said. Of course they don't like that.'

According to the rules of the day, Mark's conceit was probably justified in that excerpt, but sometimes his embellishments to a story bore no resemblance to reality at all. Take the following passage from *Town*, where a debate on the lack of good London tailors arouses Mark's imagination:

'They aren't good on shoulders either,' says Feld. 'They can't make good shoulders like those French shoulders. I brought a jacket back from Paris – I was in Paris with my parents but I didn't like it much – and this jacket was just rubbish over there but it's great here. Great shoulders.'

Harry emphatically states that the family never went to Paris.

The piece offers a fascinating insight into the minds of the young pleasure seekers, and scratched below the surface just enough to reveal the motor that fuelled the 'exhausting race', the race that the writer was so certain would end in defeat. Had Richard Hoggart, and other radical critics of mass culture read the article, they would have been horrified. Gone were the old values of the working class, where the spirit of community, generosity and modesty prevailed. In their place had stepped rampant individualism, a mean-spirited competitiveness and excessive vanity.

The new gods were the likes of John Stephen, a young salesman at Vince's in Newburgh Street, who'd established his own clothes shop round the corner in Carnaby Street by the turn of the decade and had been doing a roaring trade with the likes of the Stamford Hill Faces. 'All those shops and still only twenty-six or something,' sighed Mark. No matter how or why: success was what mattered. Even Cliff Richard and Adam Faith were still on his mind. 'I suppose they're had-its in a way but they've *done* something. They've made their way at something,' he said.

When it came to issues that extended beyond the much-derided 'baggy seats' and the virtues of women's hatpins, the three young peacocks showed a remarkable nonchalance. Michael Simmonds opined that the 'Ban the Bomb lot' were dead right, but he'd never march with them. Mark supported them too. 'It's all exhibitionist, isn't it? I'm all for that,' he said.

Politics mattered little to mods, but the trio from N16 knew which side they were on:

'I'm a Conservative,' said Peter Sugar. 'I mean Conservatives are for the rich, aren't they, and everybody wants to be rich, really, don't they?'

'They've been in a long time and they done all right,' said Simmonds.

'Yeah, like he says, they're for the rich, really, so I'm for them,'
says Feld.

'Of course I don't know much about it,' says Sugar.

The equation was simple. The Conservative Party looked
after the rich and the sophisticated. No matter that Mark was
sharing a cold bedroom with plaster coming off the walls and his
wet clothes dripping water on to the lino: economic realities
faded into the background as the truth of his own importance
grew ever more apparent. It was politics by association, and
Faces nailed their made-to-measure banner to the glamorous and
wealthy. As Jeff Dexter says, 'Even though you were an oik at
heart, you wanted to be classy. It was the original wannabe
culture. Wannabe boys, wanna create, wannabe rich, wannabe
famous, wannabe loved, wannabe known.'

As the fashions of the Individualists/Faces/Stylists developed, this sense of aspiring towards the rich was more closely
reflected in the dress, and coexisted with the overriding need to
create a look of perfection. The immediate antecedent for this
process was the movement of a few of the original rock 'n'
rollers into the jazz clubs, who sought to replace rebellion with
sophistication. They quickly picked up on the rather ill-fitting,
slightly cramped Ivy League clothes worn by many of the visiting
American jazz musicians. Unbeknown to the clubgoers, Ivy
League dress was originally based on traditional English lines,
being little more than an Americanised version of what an English
undergraduate would wear, with minor modifications such as
the introduction of button-down collars. America's yearning for
the trappings of British culture was then exported back to Britain,
where it fused with the Italian and French looks and formed the
backbone of the Modernist style.

It was probably the features editor, a young Michael Parkin-
son, who decided to play safe when captioning the photographs
in *Town*, which were given a decidedly – and appropriate – grainy
cast. The three youths were portrayed in a variety of outfits, the
details of which were obviously too acute even for the staff of
the country's top men's magazine. But the mix of idiosyncrasy
and tradition was self-evident. One memorable still, depicting
the dark-suited Simmonds and Sugar leaning against a Soho wall,

with a defiant jawed Mark Feld in the foreground, caught this fusion well. Mark is dressed in an immaculate hacking jacket, complete with slanting pockets – a garment usually associated with the horse-riding Hoorays from the shires. However, it has been modified and his customised jacket is unique by virtue of its elongated lapel. The formal trousers, boasting razor-sharp creases, and his collar and tie are less spectacular, but this particular Face's crowning glory is his leather waistcoat. Leather goods were virtually impossible to find in Mark's size (and extremely expensive), but he had managed to persuade Mrs Perrone in the flat downstairs to make him something to his specific requirements. It was a highly prized item, and proved versatile enough to be worn with his best clothes for a stroll around Soho, or as part of a casual combination for roughing it down by the Grand Union Canal.

Years later, Mark described this first taste of public recognition as 'a bummer article'. The reason? '[It] came out about seven months after they'd actually come down to see me and taken the pictures.' During that time, a Face's wardrobe would have been completely transformed – several times over.

Jeff Dexter always thought Mark's crowning glory was his thick, buoyant head of hair, which he wore in a particularly severe style around the time of the *Town* pictures. 'There was an awful lot of what used to be called horizon line around at that time,' he recalls, 'which was a parted college boy haircut raised at the top of the head. Mark's hair naturally raised in the middle so he always looked absolutely immaculate during that period. I envied that little lift in the middle a lot and spent many hours with a hair-dryer in front of a mirror trying to get mine to do the same. After all that effort, it inevitably fell down flat on my forehead after I'd been dancing.' Mark never had that trouble. Besides, he rarely danced.

By the time *Town* appeared in the shops, the Felds had moved to Summerstown, an anonymous district wedged between Wimbledon and Tooting, and dominated by the intimidating presence of Wimbledon Stadium dog-racing track. The house at 25 Stoke Newington Common had been bought by Mrs Perrone's brother during the late fifties, although she continued to occupy the first floor flat. He in turn put the house up for sale in June 1960, but the presence of the long-established tenant families prevented an early sale. The Felds, by then paying 27 shillings per week, still occupied the top rooms at the end of 1961 when the property was purchased by Hackney Council for £2450. Months later, the council finally placed the family in a brand-new building, complete with fitted furniture and their own front door. Unfortunately for Mark, who thrived on the competitiveness of the Stamford Hill scene, this ultra-modern home was several miles away in South London, in an area not renowned for its vibrant, immaculately groomed youth culture.

Despite the addition of mod cons such as a television, Harry remembers the Felds constantly fighting a losing battle with the ageing Stoke Newington building. 'I think Mum and Dad had been on the housing list ever since they'd moved in,' he says. 'Despite having two children, they were told by Hackney Council that we weren't a priority case, because we were both boys. Yet the wallpaper was coming away from the walls because of the damp. You'd never strip the wallpaper off, you'd paper over it. That's what kept the walls up! I can remember tapping on the kitchen wall and hearing the plaster drop down behind the paper. Even when the council rehoused us over to Wimbledon, they still said we couldn't have two bedrooms.'

Summerstown also gave its name to the small back road, adjacent to the stadium, that linked Plough Lane to the busy Garratt Lane thoroughfare. Mark, who had only recently told *Town* magazine that sport was 'not my style at all', was unimpressed by what the new locality had to offer. Summerstown was also flanked by two large cemeteries which, to his mind, were a far more fitting reflection of his new territory. Sid, Phyllis and Harry were happy with colourless suburbia if it brought with it new comforts, but that wasn't Mark's style at all.

The Felds' new dwelling was on a tiny estate of brand-new Scandinavian-designed prefabs. The dozen or so buildings, intended as temporary housing by Wandsworth Council and enticingly retitled 'Sun Cottages', arrived on the site in two halves where they were joined together and erected on stilts. Bolstered by an aluminium skirting and fitted with a small set of steps that led up to the door, each 'cottage' was not dissimilar to a luxury caravan with a pointed roof. There was no garden as such, but each building was surrounded by a paved area, enclosed by a wooden fence. The amount of space inside wasn't that much different from what the Felds had been used to, though Mark's personal space had been further restricted. For the first time in his life, he had access to a genuine front room, but this was at the expense of his shared bedroom with Harry which was barely half the size of the one back at Stoke Newington. The Sun Cottages were cheap and standardised, but at least they were clean, comfortable and warm. To the Felds, and to the hundreds of thousands of families who were relocated during this unique era of investment in public housing, it signified a stake in the much-touted 'affluent society'. Symbolically, they left much of their old furniture behind in Stoke Newington.

Also left behind was Mark's authority over his fellow stylists. Legend has it that he returned to his old patch months later only to be snubbed by a new élite who'd taken over in his absence. By that time, it mattered little anyway. Town – the West End – was where things were really beginning to happen.

When the family uprooted to Summerstown, Mark was only months away from school-leaving age, and his registration at the nearby Hill Croft Secondary School was little more than a formality. He was rarely there. 'School was a waste of time,' he told a reporter in 1972. 'It wasn't a bad place to be when I was five and we spent our time building with bricks. But when the teachers tried to get me to do figure work and writing, I just freaked out. It had no part in my plans for the future.'[2] A Face marooned in the teenage wasteland of south-west London was about as effective as prunes on an empty stomach. Mark needed the oxygen of adulation. He found it in the West End.

In 1962, Soho, with its labyrinth of clubs and rapidly developing network of boutiques, was the mods' Mecca. Phyllis Feld had given up her job at Berwick Street market shortly after moving south, but Mark stalked the seductive square mile with increasing regularity. Sometimes it was to check out the latest stock in John Stephen's His Clothes, where he could buy his trousers off the peg. In part because Stephen catered for the more figure-conscious gay scene at that time, Mark found a good selection of narrow-waisted trousers there to fit his small frame. Invariably, these would be too long in the leg, but before commercialisation set in, alterations in this reputable Carnaby Street boutique were still made on the spot. Mark would also scrutinise the latest fabrics and designs in nearby Domino Male or Vince's in Newburgh Street.

His other reason for frequenting the area was its flourishing club scene. Within easy reach was a boggling choice of R & B (the Marquee, 100 Club); boozy literary conversation (the Establishment); folk (Scot's Hoose, Bunjies and Les Cousins); mixing with the nobs (the Saddle Room); and the opportunity to dance to the latest crop of American black R & B/soul releases at Le Discothèque, the Scene, the Flamingo (which became the All Nighter Club on the stroke of midnight), the Roaring Twenties and the Whiskey A Go Go. Avoiding the Saddle Room, which refused entry to Mark, Peter Sugar and Michael Simmonds on several occasions, the coterie of Stamford Hill Faces would regularly meet their expatriate young friend and pose around the edges of the dance-floors. (Another ex-Stoke Newington contemporary of Mark's, future Sex Pistols manager Malcolm McLaren, belonged to a similar circuit.) Vigorous physical activity wasn't for top Faces. It had a nasty tendency to put unwanted creases in the arms of your jacket.

Wardour Street all-nighters were exhausting affairs. Unless you invested in a few purple hearts or black bombers at 6d a throw, staying up till daylight wasn't always easy, in spite of the volume and the growing tendency to use flashing lights. As numbers increased weekly, clubbing wasn't necessarily the most comfortable way to parade yourself. There was also an element of the 'herd' instinct about the scene which made Mark slightly uneasy. But with the well-heeled desperately seeking to be fashionably working class, and suburban kids like Mark Feld acting out the classless dream, Soho nightlife was a microcosm of the dominant social processes of the sixties – and everyone wanted a piece of the action.

Ever since his infrequent Sunday sojourns down to the Lyceum back in 1960, Mark had been a bit-part player on the club scene. Filled with an abundance of similarly fashion-conscious women, and with pills and alcohol just a knowing nod away, Mark nevertheless remained remarkably self-controlled. In fact, attitudes to drink provided a good test of a mod's 'purity'. Jeff Dexter, whose proximity to elder musicians had weakened his own resolve, says, 'Mark certainly would not drink. It was part of the culture not to drink. You wouldn't be seen dead standing in a pub with a pint in your hand – that was not on! It was oiky.' There was an element of pragmatism here too: top clubs like the Scene didn't have a licence at that time.

If pint glasses resonated with the parochialism of the local boozer, the scooter symbolised the opposite – mobility and cosmopolitanism. On a practical level, they were clean, ensuring those expensive suits remained grease-free. The scooter runs to seaside resorts like Brighton and Southend started as far back in 1959, and grew in popularity along with the rise of the club scene. A common practice was to relocate to a café in Fleet Street – one of the few meeting-places open at six in the morning – after an all-night session in a Soho club. Those able to ward off the effects of the night's high living with a few black coffees would then take off to the coast on their chrome-covered machines; the rest, still buzzing, walked all the way to Waterloo where they'd pick up the milk train. Fights with Rockers weren't on the mods' minds in those days. 'It was a good way of freshening up after sweating all night on the dance floor,' recalls Jeff Dexter, 'and hopefully, you'd find romance as well.'

Mark rarely made the trip, though it wasn't through want of trying. His mate Colin, who worked in Carnaby Street, had a scooter. So did his brother Harry who, while not part of the inner sanctum of the mod scene, still liked to keep himself presentable. He clearly remembers Mark's fear of scooters – which extended to most mechanical things – because he could neither understand nor control them. There may have been a good reason for this. 'There was one occasion,' recalls Harry, 'when Mark set off to Brighton on the back of Colin's Vespa GS 150. It was a lovely machine, immaculately painted, and it sounded like a bomber because the two-inch diameter exhaust pipe had been cut. I'm not sure if they hit a verge or what, but they both went over the top and ended up in hospital. I don't think they ever made it to Brighton.'

Since the end of the fifties, Mark had devoted all of his time to looking good. 'I was', he told the *Observer* in August 1967, 'simply knocked out by my own image.' The soundtrack to this never-ending quest was no longer dominated by Elvis Presley and Cliff Richard. His tastes received little stimulation from state radio, despite the BBC's Light Programme (whose policy of playing only one vocal record in three seemed to last for ever) belatedly aiming Brian Matthew's *Saturday Club* at the teenage market in 1958. Instead, the radiogram back at Stoke Newington (which

was replaced by a more modern 'record player' after the move
to Summerstown) consistently blared Radio Luxembourg, whose
nightly English language programmes, sponsored by the record
companies, maintained a steady diet of pop hits. It was there
that Mark found Cliff's half-hour shows, wedged in between the
next wave of American chart newcomers like Roy Orbison, Duane
Eddy and Ricky Nelson – and Helen Shapiro from Clapton.

Less than four years after her playful entry into rock 'n' roll
with Susie and the Hula Hoops, Helen – with her unusually
mature singing voice – had been spotted by EMI, who placed her
with their Columbia subsidiary label, where she spent 1961 and
1962 notching up hit after hit. The lightweight pop of 'You Don't
Know', 'Walkin' Back To Happiness' and 'Tell Me What He Said'
wasn't really Mark's style, but the transformation from Hackney
living room to national stardom, making guest appearances on
all the major TV and radio shows of the day, had an unreal,
almost magical quality about it. Harry believes that Shapiro's
overnight success had little effect on Mark's drive towards cel-
ebrity, which he felt was already in place by this time. But it
undoubtedly made his goal seem all that more attainable. (Incidentally, Susie and the Hula Hoops was obviously a hot-bed of
latent talent. Susan Singer followed her cousin on to the Columbia label, starting out under her own name, before it was decided
to sever the Shapiro connection which had launched her career
and start all over again as Susan Holliday, with a fashionable
new blonde hairstyle to match. Stephen Gould, the boy whose
guitar had started it all, changed his name to Stephen Jameson,
scored a couple of minor hits with 'Walk Away Renee' and a
version of Lennon/McCartney's 'Girl' as one half of the Truth
duo, and then recorded some solo singles and an album for
Dawn.)

If the songs of Helen Shapiro on the radio didn't whet Mark's
appetite, then the music in the clubs did – at least to a certain
extent. Between 1955 and 1957, rock 'n' roll rebellion was a fusion
of sound and vision which, by the early sixties, had become
somewhat detached. There were no visual icons in the mould of
a Cliff or an Elvis on the early mod music scene. Most of the
artists were black vocal groups, and with little overground
exposure in the media, only a few aficionados ever discovered
what they looked like.

The musical culture Mark stepped into when he entered the

Lyceum Ballroom in 1960 (where Ian 'Sammy' Samwell, composer of Cliff's early rock 'n' roll hits, was resident DJ), or Le Discothèque a year or two later, prioritised sound over visual identification with the musicians who made the records. The 'otherness' of black American culture was celebrated – its language became clubland 'hipspeak', its 'outsider' status romanticised via the (patronising) belief that mods were entering a 'black' domain of street style and an intensely physical pursuit of pleasure (hence the stereotype that blacks were 'body' and not 'mind' people gained further currency) – but there was little close identification with its stars in the dancing clubs. Round the corner at the Marquee or the 100 Club, which played host to a rather different scene, it wasn't quite the same story. There, black US musicians like Memphis Slim and Jimmy Witherspoon would play to hushed, reverential audiences. At mod venues like the Scene, audiences were happy to dance to the likes of the Shirelles and Ray Charles without any compulsion to emulate them. There were no self-styled 'Elmo Lewis's (which is how founder Rolling Stone Brian Jones liked to be known) at the Scene Club.

It is tempting to imagine Mark Feld spending the early years of the sixties desperately seeking out the sound of contemporary black music, on labels like Sue, London and Stateside – music that was an essential part of the burgeoning mod scene. But his affinity with it was not strong enough. While Mark later delighted in name-dropping his early musical heroes – always Presley and Cochran, the Cliff obsession often slipping his memory – he'd usually talk about the black American groups in general terms. The all-important ingredient – identification – was simply not there.

'I don't think we ever really discussed music at that stage,' recalls Jeff Dexter. 'Our main interest was what we wore and where we could get things in our size. That's how we struck up our friendship. Going to the Lyceum and the Soho clubs was just part of the scene. You accepted the music for what it was. We did go to record shops together, but I'm not sure if Mark was totally into the music at that time. I often got the feeling that he didn't see it the same way as I did. I think he spent every penny he could on clothes.'

Jeff's 'feeling' was borne out one afternoon in 1963 when the pair went to the cinema to see *Summer Holiday*, starring Cliff Richard. 'I was slightly upset because I had the opportunity to be one of the kids in the film but turned it down. I went with him to see the film just out of interest, and to see the supposedly good dancing in it, which was actually pretty naff. When we came out, Mark said to me, "That's it! I'm gonna sing just like Cliff Richard. I'm gonna be as big as Cliff Richard. Will you manage me?" I was slightly horrified because Cliff was already part of the old school. While Mark had this absolute integrity about the way he looked and dressed, the fact that he wanted to be like Cliff Richard made me cringe. I actually turned to him and said, "But, Mark, you can't even bloody well sing, so what's the point?" "I'll learn," he replied. "I'm gonna do it. I'm gonna learn to sing, and learn to play. That's what I really want to do."

'I think he felt a bit bitter that I didn't take him seriously, but he wasn't even playing guitar then. He just wanted to get up there and sing and dance around like Cliff Richard. Mark never talked about being a musician. He wanted to be a star. He wanted to be bigger than Cliff.'

Although the release of 'Dynamite' late in 1959 had partially atoned for the heresy of 'Living Doll' that summer, any credibility in the belief that Cliff Richard was an authentic British response to American rock 'n' roll had been buried by the end of the decade. Acts like Johnny Kidd and the Pirates and Screamin' Lord Sutch emerged, but there was little sense of any real British rock 'n' roll movement. The idiosyncratic producer Joe Meek helped plug the gap, but it wasn't really until the Beatles, who based their music on a blend of American soul/R & B and great rock 'n' roll, that the home pop scene was transformed. They introduced a refreshing 'group' sound, a controversial (but nevertheless acceptable) image, and left hysterical scenes in their wake as they assaulted the charts and the concert halls during 1963. More importantly, perhaps, the Beatles altered the rules. It became acceptable for pop stars to write their own songs. To judge singers and musicians on their performance alone was no longer enough. Critics began to look at the composer credits on a record, and songs were evaluated for originality as much as beat or melody. Mark Feld was one of the many thousands who tuned in religiously to BBC Radio's *Pop Goes The Beatles* shows that year, and his enthusiasm for the beat boom – and the criteria upon which it was based – fired his imagination, and his passion for music anew.

# CHAPTER FOUR

'Mark Feld was an early example of what was the downfall of mod, which was the attraction of people who didn't understand what it was about. Mark Feld was only interested in the clothes, he was not involved in thinking.'
Steve Sparks, quoted in *Days In The Life*, 1988

'By the time he was eight or nine he was . . . well, sort of different. He had a head full of ideas – you could see them. He used to make things from Plasticine and did what he called painting with all different coloured paints . . . like all this contemporary lark.'
Simeon Feld, quoted in *Record Mirror* Bolan Special, 1972

'The Romantic is the one who discovers himself as centre.'
G. Poulet, in *The Romantic Movement*, 1966

Bolan's hyperbole reached epidemic proportions during the early seventies, when he outraged critics by claiming to be Elvis Presley, James Dean, Bob Dylan and John Lennon rolled into one, and punctuated his conversation with references to his own 'destiny' and 'genius'. Vulnerability wasn't a word that immediately sprang to mind where the public Marc Bolan was concerned. Or the young Mark Feld, for that matter. But there was a period when the image cracked, which prompted the most turbulent period in his life.

Early defences like Mighty Joe Young and an immaculately constructed outfit were impressive enough when inhabiting the world of appearances, but living in a remote part of south-west London had begun to diminish Mark's self-esteem. Ostracised and with plenty of time on his hands, he exchanged exhibition for introspection and, for the first time, began to look beneath his highly polished exterior. Gaily coloured paving stones and opportunist speculators arrived in Carnaby Street; mods went overground, dressed in parkas and fought rockers on beaches; but all of a sudden, Mark Feld wasn't around any more.

'I went from being a self-styled cult king to a nobody,' he remarked in 1971, adding that 'It was a time of great spiritual crisis.'[1] The move to Wimbledon had been traumatic, but it was probably only the catalyst for this mental anguish. Not every teenager experiences pain alongside growing self-awareness, but few make the transition into adulthood without experiencing some nagging uncertainties – existential, sexual or otherwise. The Romantic ethic, which favours the sanctity of the individual mind over the social domain of materialism and consumption, is inevitably brought to the fore during such a crisis, which is usually resolved when a balance is struck between the competing forces. Some crawl out defeated, crushed by the knowledge that they have to carry the burden of life alone. Others seem to revel in the metaphysical skirmish and emerge, with ego suitably strengthened, adequately equipped to deal with the outside world on their own terms. For a time, Mark appeared to hover, and then it clicked. Whereas Mark Feld's appearance had hitherto done most of his talking for him, he now began to understand that there were other outlets for the power of imagination. He took himself off the street and pursued his new line of thinking.

Having devoted so much of his time to music and clothes, Mark Feld rarely read during his early teens. Changing from one outfit into the next, or replacing an Eddie Cochran record on the turntable with an Elvis hit, brought immediate results; ploughing through books seemed less rewarding, and slightly stuffy. It is hardly surprising, then that one of the first books he ever read was *The Life of Beau Brummell*. He told *Town* magazine's Peter Barnsley about it. 'He was just like us really. You know, came up from nothing. Then he met royalty and got to know all the big blokes and he had a lot of clothes.' But Mark had also taken heed of a cautionary note in the tale of the Regency dandy. 'He came to nothing in the end through gambling,' he said, adding his own moral conclusion – 'I don't gamble.'[2]

There is a direct link between the sixties' passion for all things 'weird' and 'bizarre' and the Individualist's quest to achieve stylistic difference at any cost. While the arrival of the mass-produced mod introduced all manner of contrived combinations (inevitably check-on-check or stripes-on-stripes), the strange juxtapositions once dreamed up by Feld and his fellow Faces had been worn as emblems of non-conformity. Originality. As Mark beat a slow retreat from the mod world, his need to maintain a sense of difference was fulfilled by a new-found fascination for the myths of Ancient Greece and the strange word-games of the world of poetry.

There doesn't appear to have been a critical moment which sparked off this interest in traditional art forms, but it was certainly helped along by several musty-smelling second-hand bookshops in nearby Tooting Broadway. He soon discovered the poets of the English Romantic tradition, such as Wordsworth, Keats, Shelley and Byron, and a twentieth-century writer who drank himself to a premature death, Dylan Thomas. It wasn't long before his natural inquisitiveness took him further afield. He stumbled across the French poet Arthur Rimbaud, whose youthful angst (he stopped writing before he was twenty) was expressed in words that explored the musical properties of verse, and who defied the more emotional flights of imagination associated with the Romantics by employing an obscure mystical style rather than the pretty but well-worn analogies of his forebears. 'When I first read him, I felt like my feet were on fire,'[3] Mark later said.

Mark Feld's discovery of the literary world, coupled with his continued enthusiasm for clothes and pop music, functioned to block off the mundanity of life around him. He'd left Hill Croft Secondary with no qualifications after a brief and uneventful stay, was sharing a room with an elder brother whose interests revolved around pubs and girls, and was living in an indistinct part of London that offered little stimulation of any kind. For the first time in his life, he experienced solitude, having the run of the Sun Cottage during the day while the rest of the family were out at work.

His father continued to drive for a living, making local deliveries for Airfix, and later for Whiteways Cider. Phyllis had changed jobs too. The daily journey from Summerstown to Berwick Street was complicated, and this, combined with the effect of cold weather in aggravating the dermatitis on her hands (which she had contracted while working with chemically impregnated tarpaulins at Earls Court during the war), convinced her to give up the market stall. Instead, she took a clerical post at the National Savings Bank in Parsons Green, a short bus ride across the river. Harry, meanwhile, had landed a job in Wardour Street, the heart of London's film industry, working in the advertising department of Anglo Amalgamated. In contrast, Mark's

entry into the world of work consisted of a visit to the Labour
Exchange, where he was obliged to fill in a form stating his
desired trade or profession, so that he could be notified of any
vacancies in that field. In his characteristic, near-dyslexic hand-
writing, he simply wrote 'Poet'.

If his continued sense of 'apartness' had begun to take on a
new dimension, Mark Feld still maintained an outward sense of
style capable of turning heads. But despite the efforts of his
mother, who did her best to finance her son's dreams throughout
the best part of the next six years, he still needed money to
maintain his sartorial cutting-edge. Harry insists that Mark was
never afraid of work, but it is difficult to imagine his strong will,
coupled with a head full of increasingly fanciful notions about
his own status, enduring the petty rules and routine of a day job
for very long.

Unsurprisingly, Mark's only encounter with mainstream
employment lasted a matter of days. Perhaps out of guilt, he
took two jobs at once: in the daytime he worked at Edgar's
menswear shop in Tooting Broadway, before plunging his delicate hands into the washing-up bowl at the local Wimpy during
the evenings. Inevitably, exhaustion soon got the better of him,
and after what he later called 'one of those Scott Walker numbers'
(an allusion to some kind of breakdown), he retired to the more
measured ambience of the family Sun Cottage. There, his days
were largely spent studying the latest pop charts or a new book
of verse, although the old competitive spirit was never far away,
as the local Jehovah's Witnesses found to their cost. 'He loved
to harass them,' recalls Harry. 'Mark would invite them in for a
coffee, and then he'd harangue them for two or three hours
before they'd get up and make a run for it.'

Mark's future – or apparent lack of it – began to concern his
parents, particularly his father who failed to understand why his
second son couldn't find himself an ordinary job like most school-
leavers. Phyllis was more sympathetic to her son's aspirations.
'I always knew he'd be someone,' she said in 1972. 'It was his
attitude to life. He always got what he wanted.'[4] His latest
demand did not come cheaply. Once again, it was an advert in
a newspaper which caught his eye. Tempted by the chance to
pursue a glamorous career, he persuaded his mother that attending a West End modelling school (which may have been run by
the Lucie Clayton model agency, but no one is quite sure) offering

short instruction courses would solve his problems. The fee of around £100 was astronomical in the days when the average man's weekly wage was nearer £20, but Phyllis raided her own savings in the hope that the sacrifice would be her last. Mark later claimed over-exposure brought his modelling career to a hasty halt, but some have disputed that it ever got off the ground at all. Proof does exist of at least two reasonably prestigious assignments, although whether his mother's investment paid off tenfold, as he once bragged, is doubtful. The fee for a session modelling for Littlewoods' autumn and winter mail-order catalogue, 1964–5, may have helped cover part of Phyllis's initial outlay.

Washable Acrilan viscose trousers were unlikely to have formed part of Mark's extensive wardrobe, and the 'Littlewoods smile' was a far cry from the surly youth pictured in *Town* magazine, but at least the work offered anonymity as well as good money. In a characteristic lapse of memory, Mark never mentioned his assignment for the mail-order catalogue company, finding more credibility in his modelling for the John Temple menswear chain, where he insisted he was the cardboard cut-out in every store. It could be true: he certainly appeared in their 'Styles To Suit You, Suits To Style You' brochure, modelling a variety of outfits, including a high-buttoned continental pin-stripe, a rich golden bronzed worsted cloth overchecked in brown, and a navy serge outfit complete with velvet collar. Years later, a John Temple spokesman recalled Mark Feld as 'just another model selected from an agency in our usual twice-yearly search for new faces. If the figure suited and the face fitted, that was good enough. But he wasn't an exceptional model. And we never used him again.'[5]

'Men of style use the leisureplan,' claimed the brochure. Mark took his earnings elsewhere, far away from the memories of staged photos with a girl and a bottle of wine, and even further from David Jacobs, the grinning, vaguely paternal host of BBC Television's *Juke Box Jury*, who graced the cover – complete with obligatory jukebox – no doubt in a bid to inject a degree of hipness into the company's image.

It was around this time that Mark caught some of the memorable touring acts that played round the country. Barely audible above an audience of hysterical screamers, these were symbolic affirmations of youth rather than events of any great musical value, and the atmosphere of raw excitement generated by the concerts left a lasting impression on the young model. He definitely attended a show featuring the Rolling Stones, the Ronettes, Marty Wilde, the Swinging Blue Jeans and Dave Berry, which rolled into Tooting Granada on 12 January 1964. Yet he maintained a distance from the swelling teen movement, particularly in terms of visual style. Aside from the modelling shots, the only surviving photograph of Mark from these months dates from his brother's wedding, where he turned up immaculately dressed in a white button-down shirt, dark suit, with a hairstyle confirming that the craze for 'Beatle cuts' left his carefully lacquered 'horizon line' relatively untroubled.

Part of the proceeds from Mark Feld's occasional modelling assignments were spent on a new acoustic guitar and, fired by the rising tide of groups springing up in every port and province of the country, he was determined to learn how to play it. Beatles' songs, which were sometimes more complicated than they sounded, weren't the ideal starting point, so he searched back through his pile of rock 'n' roll records discovering that the straightforward twelve-bar changes were much easier to play.

The likes of John Lennon, Paul McCartney and Eric Clapton have all paid homage to Bert Weedon's *Play In A Day* best-selling guide to simple guitar-playing. Almost anyone determined to learn the basic skills of the instrument at the turn of the fifties would have come across Weedon's book, and Mark Feld found it useful too – and probably told Bert so. Bert Weedon, alongside Wally Whyton, Muriel Young, and children's characters like Ollie Beak and Joe Crow, were regulars on *The Five O'clock Club*, one of several new children's television programmes to appear during 1963. Mark's keenness to branch out from his modelling career took him to the studio where the shows were filmed. If he secured any part in *The Five O'clock Club* at all, it was nothing more substantial than as an extra to make up the numbers. But while on the set, he struck up a friendship with one of the programme's regular young entertainers, Allan Warren. Shortly afterwards, Mark had found a way out of Summerstown without suffering any financial hardships: he was sharing Warren's flat at 81 Lexham Gardens, in a well-placed area of London midway between Gloucester Road and Earls Court.

'Mark, like David Bowie, was one of several hopeful pop

people who'd hang around the sets doing bits of extra work,' remembers Warren. 'We struck up a friendship and one day he moved in with his guitar and a carrier bag and stayed for six or eight months. He took over one of the bedrooms, a huge room, and he'd always sit in the same spot by the fireplace with his books and his guitar. Another person who lived with me around this time was Gregory Phillips, who starred with Judy Garland in *If I Could Go On Singing*, and went on to star in *Orlando*.' This last fact provides a link with Mark's claim that he sometimes secured small delinquent roles in that popular children's adventure series, but Warren is unable to substantiate or deny this.

Allan Warren's centrally located flat offered Mark both close proximity to the city nightlife and the solitude of his own room. 'In the daytime,' says Warren, 'Mark would sit in the drawing room with the curtains closed and the light on. For him, the night never ended and the day never started. I think it was because he had this pale porcelain skin which he was very proud of. He didn't like sunbathing: he wasn't interested in the day. But in the evenings, he'd always be out at the clubs. He'd go to the opening of a letter, especially if it gave him a free sandwich.'

Mark stayed at Lexham Gardens from autumn 1964 into early 1965, a period which saw him consolidate his musical ambitions, explore his sexuality and cast himself more convincingly in the mould of the fully fledged Romantic. He'd begun to take a lot of his inspiration from Bob Dylan, a young American singer yet to enjoy any real commercial success in Britain, but whose influence was already striking at the heart of the British pop business. For the time being, the British beat boom, and the newly imported American R & B and Tamla Motown sounds, carried on in the tin-pan alley tradition of the impassioned love song – albeit with different shades of conviction. But Bob Dylan, in mining the rich tradition of American folk-protest music, sat outside pop's boy/girl obsession, and instead chose to follow the example of American folk singer Woody Guthrie by using music as a form of social commentary. At a stroke, Dylan awoke his contemporaries to the potential of the popular song, carved out a space for those unwilling to defer to the group style, and brought a so-called authenticity to popular music by placing his own individual vision above public demands. In so doing, Bob Dylan also provided Mark Feld with his first musical role model since finally giving up on Cliff Richard.

Throughout 1964, almost every male teenager seemed to be in a beat group which, Mark figured, was more than enough reason for him not to. He wasn't interested in sharing the lime-light: he preferred to bask in it alone. Dylan provided a far more suitable role model. He was the 'active man-in-the-mass' – young, cocksure, and on the make. More than that, he shrouded himself in mystery, was self-aware to the point of sophistication, and people described him as a poet. Better still, Dylan's guitar and harmonica skills were rudimentary, and he appeared to answer to no one except his own imagination. In proving that stardom and creative expression were not necessarily mutually exclusive, Bob Dylan represented everything Mark Feld wanted to be. He was a contemporary embodiment of the Romantic values to which he'd begun to aspire.

Other young British singers, like Roy Harper, Ralph McTell, Al Stewart, John Martyn and Donovan Leitch, had also sensed the wind of change, and began to appear on the folk circuit performing a mixture of socially orientated songs drawn not only from Dylan's repertoire, but from the likes of Woody Guthrie, Joan Baez, Pete Seeger and Ramblin' Jack Elliott. While the Dave Clark Five and the Animals sought to emulate the success of the Beatles and the Rolling Stones, and the Beach Boys and the Miracles (closely followed by the several big names from the Motown stable) led the American counter-attack, almost over-night a thousand budding Bob Dylans materialised, strumming an 'authentic' style that particularly attracted singers with a strong social conscience. Mark Feld, who was generally oblivious to social concerns but possessed a strong socially constructed perception of himself, used the example of Dylan to get his own singing and poetic career off the ground.

Back in 1964, in the days before pop received blanket multi-media coverage, record sleeve notes (not to mention cover photo-graphs) played an important role in selling an artist to the public. Writers were enlisted by CBS to 'explain' Bob Dylan, and much of Mark Feld's understanding of the rising star was gleaned from this controlled publicity. He could not have failed to have been intrigued by the comments of *New York Times* journalist Robert Shelton who, on Dylan's first album sleeve, wrote that, 'Mr Dylan is vague about his antecedents and birthplace, but it matters less where he has been than where he is going.'[6] Further on, Feld discovered that, like himself, Dylan 'has been soaking up influ-ences like a sponge', that he 'didn't agree with school', that he read a lot (but not the required readings), and that he admired rockers like Elvis Presley and Carl Perkins as much as acoustic rebels like Woody Guthrie and Jimmie Rodgers. Even more impressive were the sleeves for Dylan's two 1964 albums, *The Times They Are A-Changin'* and *Another Side Of Bob Dylan*, which were crammed full with the singer's poetry, where lucid lines of social comment were beginning to give way to quick-fire flashes of lyrical observation which increasingly teetered towards the absurd.

Inevitably, Mark also acquired a harmonica, which he placed in a holder around his neck, blowing instinctively into the keys in the most obvious imitation of his new guru. However, Allan Warren maintains that the spectre of Mark's old boyhood idol wasn't far away, even after Dylan had alerted him to a superior, creative kind of stardom. 'Bob Dylan was certainly tame-sounding by comparison with the Beatles and all the groups,' he says. 'But Mark looked like Cliff Richard and he knew it, though he wasn't as handsome. Cliff was still the big thing, outside all the heavy groups like the Beatles, and he maintained a nice clean-cut image which Mark still had at that stage. Even his voice was like Cliff's, very toothy, very light.'

After several months spent hibernating in the wilderness of Summerstown preparing for his next move, Mark Feld quickly learnt to wear his new armour – his poetry, his guitar playing and his songwriting – with the same confidence that he once displayed strutting around Stamford Hill with his rolled-up umbrella, leather waistcoat and lightweight camel-hair blazer. But it didn't come easily, and Mark masked any shortcomings with characteristic aplomb, as Allan Warren recalls. 'He'd sit for hours cross-legged and flimsily dressed, playing his guitar, and this would go on and on and on. His dialogue was laughable at the time. He'd always talk about "When I'm a star . . . ", and you'd be thinking, he's never going to go anywhere with that fucking dreadful music, with those cutie bow lips and that broad face. I just couldn't see it. He was like a big fat Tweetie Pie. Yet he'd be absolutely serious and want to talk about it for hours. I certainly wasn't interested in hearing him compare himself with some pop singer whom I'd never heard of. My idea of someone who could sing was Noël Coward. He'd bore us sick on that level. We used to laugh at him, but he wouldn't give up. He was tenacious – couldn't give a toot. It was a full-time obsession.'

Late one night, Allan and Mark (who, despite Warren's

slightly uncharitable remarks, carried the mere remnants of teen-age puppy fat around the face), were sitting in the flat deliberat-ing on their usual topic of conversation. 'We were talking about Mark,' smiles Warren. 'He was one of those people who'd say, "I've had enough of talking about me" (this would be after about three hours!) "now what do you think of me?" I'd think, Oh, God, we've got another three hours' talking about him! I was preparing for my television show, and we hit upon the idea of trying to get Mark on it. He suggested I should manage him, which appealed to me because I thought I might be able to do something with him through my contacts. The following day, I rang the Regent Sound people and asked if we could book a studio in a week's time, then I turned to Mark and said, "Right, rehearse two songs." '

According to Warren, the two-hour session resulted in two separate acetates, one of which contained a version of Bob Dylan's 'Blowin' In The Wind'. This song, which opened 1963's *The Freewheelin' Bob Dylan* album, had quickly become a standard in British folk clubs, but it reached a far wider audience when the popular American folk trio, Peter, Paul and Mary, had a hit with it in October that year. The song's indictment of public apathy to war and wrongdoing in general (which made it immedi-ately popular with the Civil Rights Movement in America) contri-buted to Mark's growing awareness that the world at large wasn't just a bore – it was corrupt. But this had little long-term effect. He wasn't happy with songs of social realism, and never wrote a protest song in his life. Mark's greatest conviction was always that of his own genius.

The song's simple three-chord sequence, punctuated by brief flurries of harmonica notes, made it an ideal choice to launch his recording career, but the memory of it still haunts Mark's first manager. 'He drove me mad with that fucking song!' recalls Warren – and he wasn't the only one. The pair hawked the acetate round the record companies until they secured a meeting with A&R man Barry Green at EMI. He played the songs, pam-pered the pair with endless cups of coffee and kind words – and then rejected them. Nevertheless, records confirm that Mark secured a recording test for EMI subsidiary Columbia at the company's Abbey Road recording complex. This took place on 16 February 1965 between 3.45 and 4.00 p.m. in Studio Three, but he failed the audition. This is probably the occasion when he sang a version of Betty Everett's up-tempo ballad, 'You're No Good', which had been covered in the UK by the Swinging Blue Jeans in 1964. Although a favourite of Mark's, the song was quite inappropriate for his voice, which lacked the necessary warmth and depth to carry it off.

Mark also taped 'Blowin' In The Wind' at a second session around this time, at Vic Keary's Maximum Sound Studios, 47 Dean Street, Soho. The studio originally housed Radio Atlanta, one of the earliest pirate stations, but when the entire operation was transferred to an offshore ship, a lot of the recording equipment was left behind. Keary moved in and, with a basic PA mixer and a couple of ancient tape machines, began making jingles for the pirates using musicians from the adjoining La Gioconda coffee bar in Denmark Street. One day, he got a call from a young singer eager to record some songs. 'Mark was one of the first people to record at the studio,' remembers Keary. 'The studio opened late in 1964, so I guess it must have taken place in January 1965. I'm pretty sure he didn't have a manager with him: Mark was on his own. He recorded "Blowin' In The Wind", "The Road I'm On (Gloria)" and I think he also taped a third song, "The Perfumed Garden Of Gulliver Smith". I thought he was in the Dylan/Donovan mould. Actually, he didn't really make that much impression on me.'

Mark's version of 'Blowin' In The Wind' followed the basic pattern of Dylan's original, but was performed as a tuneful pop song, not as a piece of social comment. The verse containing the crucial line, 'How many deaths will it take till he knows/That too many people have died', was omitted altogether. Mark had mastered the chords, substituted some blue notes on the harmonica in place of Dylan's erratic flurries, yet there was nothing to suggest that he was anything other than an enthusiastic copyist who had no qualms in giving the song a slightly more commercial sheen. 'The Road I'm On (Gloria)' is another non-original, discovered by Mark on the back of an unsuccessful Dion single. Although best known for pre-Beatles hits like 'A Teenager In Love' (recorded with the Belmonts), 'Runaround Sue' and 'The Wanderer', the American singer underwent a dramatic image change in 1963, and for 'The Road I'm On (Gloria)' (the B side of the blues number 'I'm Your Hoochie Coochie Man', issued March 1964), his full-blown pop style had given way to a more intimate backing of an acoustic guitar and harmonica. Once again, the song employed a simple three-chord trick, though the subject matter was far removed from protest. Mark often ruminated on the topic of fate and destiny as his career began to unfold, but even his imagination would have been stretched by the prophetic lines he sang at its outset. 'The road I'm on gal won't run me home,' went the chorus, to the object of his affections, Gloria.

The song carries with it a cruel sense of foreboding but technically the performance was unexceptional. The harmonica playing makes Dylan sound like Larry Adler, and there is considerable stumbling over the picked introduction, which also caused problems as the song fades away. Mark set the tempo at a brisker pace than Dion's original, and while he took the easy option by choosing to strum rather than pick his way through the verses (he dropped the last two), it's obviously the hand of an amateur. Most interesting is the voice, which (with the help of some studio reverb) confidently strives for a maturity beyond its years, but rarely achieves the sense of grief contained in Dion's performance.

Vic Keary's contention that a third song, 'The Perfumed Garden Of Gulliver Smith', was also taped at the Maximum Sound Studios that day is fascinating, but probably incorrect. The original master-tape from the session was made public in spring 1992, and it reveals several takes of 'Blowin' In The Wind' and 'The Road I'm On (Gloria)', but no evidence of what would have been Mark's earliest composition.


The pop business rarely makes decisions on aural evidence alone, and Mark's acetates were accompanied by a series of photographs of the budding bard taken by Allan Warren's friend Mike McGrath, then writing showbiz stories for the top girls' magazine *Boyfriend*. McGrath remembers the session, which took place on the balcony of his Earls Court flat, but has little to say about Mark Feld: 'I find it hard to believe all that stuff about him being a Face,' he says. 'I'm afraid I have to say that he simply said nothing. He was just a pleasant Jewish boy who looked wide-eyed with wonder. He left no impression at all.' Mark wasn't alone in his apparent lack of charisma. McGrath, who had been involved in showbusiness since the age of fifteen, also made the gaffe of describing David Bowie and Reg Dwight (later Elton

John), two other subjects of his around this time, as 'silent and colourless'.

Warren's explanation for the reticence of his client at the 24 guinea photo session was the James Dean influence. 'Mark would often walk around with a moody expression,' he recalls. 'Then he'd start talking transatlantic – "Let's get it on", "OK, cool, man", all that pseudo-American jargon. It really used to make me laugh.' He also remembers the overriding concern during the photo shoot. 'The problem was the face. We had to disguise the fat face. That's why the cap was there, to distract from it and give him a bit of height. And in a way it did, though of course it looks hideous now.' But the image was more contrived than that. In his peaked cap, heavyweight polo-necked jumper, short casual jacket, white jeans and styled suede boots, with the six-string acoustic high around his chest, Mark Feld looked every inch the budding protest singer. His clothes portrayed the casual air of the Bohemian, his gaze, deliberately directed away from the camera, was elusive and thoughtful. The Face that once cast no shadows had forsaken its harshness for the richly toned façade of the Romantic.

Acetates, photographs, even Allan Warren's influence at Rediffusion couldn't do anything for Mark Feld. Neither the producers on *The Five O'clock Club*, nor the record companies wanted to know. After weeks of unsuccessful hustling, Warren's enthusiasm began to wane. Mark remained convinced he was going to succeed, and now, with some recording studio experience behind him, he'd at least achieved something. Only a matter of months earlier, Mark had appeared at noted record producer Joe Meek's flat-cum-studio at 304 Holloway Road begging to be taken under his wing. Meek, who liked to let his sexual fantasies be the best judge of musical talent, seems not to have taken an immediate shine to the young singer. Mark apparently managed to talk his way into the house because he recalled the budgerigar which the 'Telstar' man kept in his bedroom, but 'Sure, kid, record you next week,' was as far as he could get.

Shunned by Meek, and ignored by record and television producers, Mark Feld sought solace in discovering his sexuality. According to Harry, Mark's first sexual encounter took place back in Stoke Newington, with a dark-haired girl with a Mary Quant bob called Terry. But despite his desirability among the local girls, Mark was far too interested in himself and his clothes to get involved in anything more than passing relationships. He maintained this apparent insularity throughout his teenage years, but was increasingly happy to accept the compliments of female and male suitors. Allan Warren maintains that Mark was bisexual at the time. 'He went to bed with anyone, because everyone did in those days. It was nothing new. Rather than go to bed alone, if someone was pretty – irrespective of whether they were a girl or a boy – you'd go to bed with them. You really didn't care either way then, unlike the dull seventies or the mundane eighties when people had different ideas about it.

'Mark loved the girls, but I think, in the beginning, he was very shy with them. He was much more at ease with the boys. Boys took the lead if they fancied him, whereas if he fancied a girl, he'd have to chase her. It really was an ego thing, because he loved himself and he loved to be worshipped. If someone is going to go to bed with him and do funny things to him, he saw that as just another sign of being worshipped.' Much later, Mark spoke about this period of sexual uncertainty. 'When I was fifteen,' he said, 'I wasn't very sure of myself. I wanted to find out so I went with a bloke.'[7] He couched his bisexual tendencies in terms of the need for experimentation. 'It was so that I'd never have to look back and wonder what I'd missed out on. I felt I should try anything once,' he claimed.

Jeff Dexter, who was unaware of Mark's bisexuality, remarks, 'He was definitely more into clothes than girls. Although he was incredibly flash, he still had a certain shyness about him until you got him in a small group, and then he'd come on very strong.' Jeff didn't see much of Mark after 1963, but has heard of his involvement in the Hipster scene. 'The Hipster developed almost immediately afterwards,' he says. This scene revolved around several small French clubs like La Poubelle and St Germaine, where the earliest gays, dressed in John Michael and John Stephen clothes, would go. They had this incredible look where they'd wear these low cut hipster trousers and very tight sailor-type T-shirts, or else very tight Shetland wool jumpers.' According to Albert Goldman's definition, there was little difference between the hipster and the early mods. He wrote: 'The Hipster was [a] typically lower-class dandy, dressed up like a pimp affecting a very cool, cerebral tone – to distinguish him from the gross, impulsive types that surrounded him in the ghetto – and aspiring to the finer things in life.'[8] Of course,

Goldman's hipsters were young, American and black. In London, they were almost exclusively white.

It's possible that the fantasy world created by the urban mod/ hipster existed as a displacement for sexual anxieties. Certainly, there is no doubting a considerable crossover with the gay community, and it wasn't simply the flamboyant clothes and use of make-up by some Faces that hinted at a blurring of sexual orientation. That the emphasis was on consumption/shopping, and the abnormal attention given to self-image, which were both seen as feminine pursuits, closed the gap between the hard man and the peacock. Encounters with characters from the gay scene weren't unusual in Mark's world, and increasingly, as he traversed its boundaries, he continued to add to his string of popular male idols – and win a few admirers of his own.

'People were into beauty in those days,' recalls Warren, 'and Mark was young and he was pretty. And I think that's how he survived. Many people enjoy taking young men out to dinner. There doesn't have to be anything sexual in it. Mark had all that going for him when he was young. He'd bore someone sick going on about his career, but they'd think, "Oh, he's pretty", and order another bottle of champagne. You really didn't need money if you were a pretty boy in the right part of London in the sixties. If you had a modicum of talent and you were persistent, you could get the break very easily, and he had youth, looks, talent and ambition on his side. It worked.'

Unfortunately, it showed little sign of working in spring 1965. By this time, another Dylan enthusiast called Donovan (who had also recorded several songs in a small Central London studio at the end of 1964) had secured a mini-residency on the *Ready, Steady, Go!* television show, been signed up by Pye and finally got to sing his songs for Bob Dylan when the American arrived in London for a UK tour. Despondent but not defeated, Mark returned home to Summerstown. 'I think he went back to mother,' says Allan Warren. 'Basically, we had nothing in common, though we were good friends for a while. Mark was interested in the pop world, whereas I enjoyed the theatre and playing Jack Buchanan records.' Another bone of contention in their relationship had been politics. 'I was right wing,' Warren admits, 'and Mark was left wing, so we often used to argue. I was very into the British Empire and was rather upset that we were losing these colonies. That really used to wind him up.

Mark was very liberal and he'd be furious with some of my attitudes, but in the end he just looked at me and laughed. Being politically poles apart makes good dancing partners in any relationship.'

Mark was made increasingly aware, through Bob Dylan, that politics and music were becoming closely interrelated, and that to be politically unsophisticated in your late teens was almost as shameful as wearing yesterday's fashions. Whether he still believed that the 'Ban the Bomb crowd' were 'all exhibitionist' or not, he joined the big CND rally in May 1965, and a photograph exists of him lined up alongside Donovan, Joan Baez and Tom Paxton at the head of the march. Political agitator was not one of Mark Feld's more recognisable guises, and it is likely the real cause he marched for that afternoon was his own, establishing a symbolic union with some of the most outspoken popular musicians of the day.

Despite his failure to secure a recording contract, and the temporary return to Summerstown, the previous six months had given Mark his first real taste of the workings of the entertainment business. He had mixed with actors and musicians, agents and A&R men, begun to write his own songs and learnt how to approach record companies. He'd also given himself a new name. The main reason Mark's recording session sticks in Vic Keary's mind was the confusion that surrounded the young singer's name. 'He kept changing it,' recalls the engineer. 'When he came back to pick up the acetate, he hung around for an hour or so. I initially typed his real name on the label, although I misspelled it as Selds. Within the space of that hour, he'd crossed that off and put Riggs. Then he changed his mind again and wrote Toby Tyler.'

It may have been no coincidence that Keary typed an extra 's' on the end of Mark's surname. Allan Warren always knew him as Mark Felds, and it's quite possible that this had been the first attempt to jazz up his name. But it still didn't have that all-important two-syllable ring about it – Ha-ley, Pres-ley, Ber-ry, Coch-ran, Hol-ly, Fu-ry, Rich-ard, Dy-lan – and so plucked out of thin air came the name Toby Tyler.

Riggs, the name Mark briefly flirted with before he arrived at Toby Tyler, wasn't conjured up from nothing. One of Mark's friends at this time was the young actor Riggs O'Hara who accompanied him on a trip to Paris. Later, both Riggs and Paris took on near-mythical proportions as a Bolanic mist fell and wrapped both in a cloak of enchantment, but the reality embodies all the mystique of a kick in the face.

Simon Napier-Bell, who became Mark's manager during 1966, was one of the first to hear about Riggs. 'He kept on about him, and in my mind, he was this six foot two Texan oil guy, or a great-looking Hollywood actor type. That's how Mark genuinely saw him. He even put him into a couple of songs. One day, we went out to dinner somewhere, and this unprepossessing figure called out, "Hey, Mark!", and it turned out to be Riggs O'Hara. Mark didn't see things: he just imagined things.'

Riggs may not have lived up to Napier-Bell's expectations, but what is certain is that he was the first of Mark's many 'name' companions – friendships struck up on the basis of the very sound of the person's name. To Mark, whose preoccupation with the peculiar had been given a further boost by the direction Bob Dylan seemed to be taking early in 1965, the thrill of being introduced to someone by the name of Riggs O'Hara for the first time sparked off many associated and imagined meanings, and soon that person took on a whole new identity in his own mind. Riggs eventually drifted out of Mark's life, but their friendship, their shared excursion and the memory of his name were never entirely forgotten.

If Mark could find enchanting things in the mere sound of somebody's name, a trip to Paris – then still the city of romance, sophistication and culture – was destined to set his mind ablaze. It did, and he made reference to this apparently significant adventure for the rest of his life.

He gave the most detailed account of what happened to Dick Tatham in *Diana* magazine. Apparently, it was Riggs who suggested the pair make the trip to Paris. 'We went by boat and train,' said Mark. 'A couple of mornings later I went on my own to see all the art treasures at the Louvre. I was standing there looking at a statue when I heard a voice behind me comment on it. I turned and saw a man of about forty. He looked very distinguished and intellectual and I was particularly struck by his eyes. They were very bright and penetrating.' This gentleman, an American living in Paris with a young girlfriend, invited Mark back to his castle-like residence for a meal. Mark stayed for some

time, digesting his many books on magic and watching in amaze-
ment as his host read people's minds, levitated, conjured up
spirits and performed many other acts of white magic. 'I don't
think anyone has influenced me as much as he did,' said Mark.
Several variations on this theme appeared in print over the years,
although the sinister embellishments from his early telling of the
story were soon dropped. 'They crucified live cats,' said Mark
back in October 1965. 'Sometimes they used to eat human flesh
just like chicken bones. From a cauldron. I don't care whether
you believe it or not. It's a bit scary however false it sounds. But
what can I do? You tell me. It sounds ego; yet it's true.'[9]

No one close to Mark ever believed in the finer details of the
trip to Paris. 'The story I heard,' says his brother Harry, 'was
that they checked into a hotel when they got there. But Mark
found a slug in the bath, said, "That's it!", and they came straight
back home. They were only there for a matter of days, a week
maybe, but certainly not six months and there was certainly no
wizard.'

Jeff Dexter agrees: 'I always thought the Paris trip was total
bullshit. Once he was over the initial shyness of a situation, Mark
could turn on the crap till the cows come home. He was obsessive
about building up his own self-importance, but he was a lot of
fun as well. We all had our own little fantasies that we were a
bit more special than we really were.'

It was this overriding fortification of fantasy which Mark
built around himself that instantly attracted a talent-spotter like
Simon Napier-Bell. 'He told me that he met this magician in a
forest in France and stayed with him for three months,' recalls
the man who later became Mark's manager. 'It turned out that
he'd been to some gay club and this conjuror had picked him up
and taken him back for the night. Mark didn't want to face up
to a situation that was as mundane as trying to find somewhere
to stay for the night in Paris. It was magical, absolutely wonderful. And that's what he managed to do all the time: to take a
mundane situation and see it as some wonderful poetic fantasy.
He was really a poet.'

The culmination of Mark's love affair with all things French
came in the late summer of 1965 when, just prior to signing a
short-term contract with Decca Records, he ditched Toby Tyler
and settled on a more exotic name. Mark, who liked to describe
himself as French cockney, managed to hint at European chic by

altering one letter of his first name, and with a tip of the hat to his latest idol – BO(b dy)LAN – created a new surname. Marc Bolan. It looked right, and it had that two-syllable sound about it. However, one surviving letter predating the Decca contract is signed 'Marc Feld', indicating that the change was gradual.

Another fairly implausible theory concerning the origin of the new name comes from Harry Feld, who says, 'Around that time, he socialised with the actor James Bolam [who found fame himself in the mid-sixties as one of The Likely Lads]. They fell out shortly after, and I have a feeling that this was because Mark used his name as the inspiration for "Bolan".' But this theory is almost certainly wrong, according to Mike Pruskin, who'd recently become Mark's publicist/manager. 'He wasn't even calling himself Toby Tyler at the time we met,' Pruskin recalls. 'He was just plain Mark Feld. But he was desperate to find a name and I think "Marc Bolan" was just plucked out of the air. Originally, it had an umlaut over the 'o' (Bölan), which was even more chic.' It's also quite possible that Marc may have derived the inspiration for his new name from Marc Bohan, the noted French *couturier* then working for the House of Christian Dior.

Eighteen-year-old Pruskin first met Marc while working in Phil Solomon's office as publicist for Van Morrison's Irish R&B group, Them. They immediately recognised that both desperately wanted to pursue a career in the music business and so moved into a basement flat at 22 Manchester Street, a centrally located position behind Baker Street, and began plotting a future for Marc Bolan. With a small black cat called Loog for company, Pruskin hatched schemes to get his friend noticed, leaving Marc free to concentrate on what he now saw as his 'art'. 'He was very picaresque, very dreamy, and would stay up all night playing his acoustic guitar and reading,' recalls Pruskin. 'Tolkien's *The Hobbit* was a favourite of his. He'd read that again and again. Musically, he was very into Dylan. He'd listen to him all the time, pulling out phrases and expanding them for his own purposes. His guitar playing usually consisted of blues songs because they were the simplest. He'd practise his chords, but my most over-riding memory of Marc is him writing reams and reams of poetry. He was constantly writing.'

Having courted several male suitors, Marc now formed his first strong relationship with a member of the opposite camp, Theresa Whipman. Terry (not the same girl with whom he shared an early encounter back in Hackney) would often forsake her dreary flat in a block at Edinburgh House, in Maida Vale, west London, and stay overnight in Manchester Street. In keeping with the androgyny prevalent in sixties culture, Terry and Marc were two of a kind in their thin cords, suede mosquito boots from Millets and navy blue reefer jackets. The blurring of sexual roles was further heightened by Terry's short, boyish hair-style, which contrasted well with Marc's carefully coiffured waves cascading over his soft facial features. Securing favours in the entertainment business hadn't changed overnight, though, and Marc continued to play his hand to the full. 'I think he used his sexuality to get what he wanted,' says Pruskin, 'but that's the sort of game you played to get on.'

Marc's big break finally arrived after the pair managed to arouse the interest of producer Jim Economides, an American best known for producing the college-style harmony group, the Lettermen. Working as an independent producer out of an office in Albert Gate Court next to the barracks in Knightsbridge, it was Economides who first introduced Marc to Decca's A&R man Dick Rowe, who in turn, offered Marc his first record deal.

Decca Records, with a roster of stars which included the Rolling Stones, Them, the Zombies, the Moody Blues and the Small Faces, fast challenged the supremacy of EMI with its stable of successful labels like Columbia, HMV and Parlophone. There had been a couple of hiccups along the way – most notably Dick Rowe's rejection of the Beatles early in 1962 and the Mann-Hugg Blues Brothers (later Manfred Mann) the following year – but the signing of the Rolling Stones helped make amends. The beat and R&B boom was still in full swing, but Rowe, together with his colleague Peter Sullivan, maintained their belief in strong soloists by signing up-and-coming names like Tom Jones, Billie Davis, Marianne Faithfull, Dave Berry, Lulu and P.J. Proby, all of whom had the potential to become all-round entertainers should the pop bubble burst.

No one was quite sure what to do with Marc Bolan, though Dick Rowe felt that the climate was right for singer-songwriters, and sent him along to the label's musical director, Mike Leander. 'He turned up at my central London flat in a lovely denim suit and denim hat, looking every inch like a clean-rinsed Bob Dylan,' recalls Leander, 'and we ran through his songs. The thing that appealed to me most at that stage was his voice, rather than the material. One song called "The Wizard" was quite good, but the others were so-so.

'It was very early days for singer-songwriters and Dylan was a great example for everybody. Marc was very folky but he definitely had new things to say lyrically. He was different, and though he seemed confident in himself, I think he was unsure about the subject matter of his songs, because they were a bit off-the-wall.'

Luckily for Marc, Leander's flat was barely a stone's throw away from Manchester Street, and he regularly descended on the arranger to work on his material. Bolan strummed the basics on his acoustic, while Leander fleshed out the simple chord changes on the piano. But despite the originality of the material, Leander and producer Jim Economides chose the predictable route when it came to recording the songs. 'Back in the mid-sixties, we always recorded solo singers with an orchestra behind them,' says Leander. 'I was a bit stumped to know what to do with Marc, and so I put him in the same light folk category as Marianne Faithfull, who I was also working with at that time. On reflection, that was quite the wrong thing, but at that stage, nobody quite knew what he could do. We just thought, here's a little hot guy who's going to make a lot of noise one day.' When Leander, Economides and Bolan congregated at Decca's West Hampstead studios at Broadhurst Gardens on 14 September 1965, it was Leander's passion for incorporating orchestral sounds into pop records which determined the course of the day. Three songs were recorded: two originals, 'The Wizard' and 'Beyond The Risin' Sun', and a Chicago blues tune that increasingly formed part of a folk-singer's repertoire, 'That's The Bag I'm In'. Containing the distinctly unBolan sounding line, 'I'll never get out of these blues alive', the song was subsequently popularised by Fred Neil on his self-titled mid-sixties album.

Marc's songs were given the Decca in-house hit-factory treatment. Leander's score, performed by an orchestra and a backing vocal group, the Ladybirds, was committed to tape first, while Bolan sang a guide vocal in a booth to ensure that the tempo and key were correct. Once a satisfactory take of the backing track was in the can, Marc put on the headphones and stepped forward – just as Elvis and Cliff had done – to add his vocal. By the time Leander and Economides had finished, there was little of Marc Bolan left on 'The Wizard' and 'Beyond The Risin' Sun', though the mood they created suited the songs perfectly. The arrangements were typical Leander constructions, tight yet sufficiently fragile to complement the strange subject matter. Bursts of oboe, flutes and bells added a touch of exotica, but the single flopped. 'It was a great disappointment when those first tracks made no impression whatsoever,' recalls Mike Leander. And that was despite an active Decca/Pruskin publicity campaign.


During 1965, Bob Dylan returned to the electric rock 'n' roll that had initially inspired him. He also transformed his writing so that his ambiguous but commercially acceptable protest anthems now gave way to lengthy diatribes like 'It's Alright, Ma (I'm Only Bleeding)'. Also on his *Bringing It All Back Home* album, issued in the spring, was 'Gates Of Eden', a song which clearly indicated that Dylan's inspiration now drew from surrealist as much as social/moral sources. Image-drenched phrases such as 'The motorcycle black madonna', 'Two-wheeled gypsy queen' and the 'gray flannel dwarf' only served to fuel Bolan's poetic aspirations. What Charlie Parker did for jazz, what Jackson Pollock did for art, Dylan – by tapping into a highly crafted but seemingly spontaneous creativity – was doing for popular music. Marc, by now steeped in the Romantic ideology of the artist, shared Dylan's perspective – the fusion of art values with three-chord rock 'n' roll, the superior vision of the musician who values self-expression, and the obsessive delight in self-promotion.

Just one glance at the sleeve of *Bringing It All Back Home* revealed to Marc that Dylan's project was unnervingly close to the one he'd mapped out for himself. Encapsulated within its telescopic effect was the carefully constructed world of the latter-day Romantic hero, master of his own tiny universe: a paragon of authenticity measured in artifice. The newly housed Dylan, once champion of the dispossessed, is 'back home', freed from the abstract gestures of solidarity with the hobo (as depicted on his previous album sleeves) and comfortable in his new surroundings of shiny surfaces, with a beautiful woman and a blue-grey Persian cat for company. Now firmly entrenched within the main current of popular music, Dylan had truly become a folk devil to purists like Dave Van Ronk, Phil Ochs and audiences who preferred their singers to perform with a finger plunged into one ear. To say that the subject matter on new songs like 'Desolation

Row' and 'Just Like Tom Thumb's Blues' was uneasy would be an understatement, but in essence the new Bob Dylan celebrated pleasure – through the simple pop rhythms that now ran through his music, through playful mind-games with his audiences, both old and new, and through the careful reconstruction of himself as Pop Poet.

It is that reconstruction which provides the compelling image on *Bringing It All Back Home*. The man who wears his influences symbolically on his album sleeve – Robert Johnson and Lotte Lenya records, a peace movement poster, an oil painting, popular magazines – and throws in a self-portrait and one of his old records for good measure, is in a sense playing the same game as the London mods had done, constructing himself in terms of consumption. Dylan drew on respected Bohemian traditions – protest, poetry, art – whereas the mods dealt in low-esteem culture like dance-halls, clothes and scooters, but both were fuelled by an exaggerated sense of self-importance.

Dylan's playful narcissism however, had strayed into 'Artist' territory, because sections of the literary community had begun to sense that his lyrics were worth a second glance. In bringing pop out of the cellar and into the salon, Dylan's example forged new possibilities which were quickly seized upon by contemporary musicians. But if Dylan balanced precariously on a tightrope that stretched between low and high cultural status, Marc Bolan was still making his way up the ladder to reach that rope. He knew where he wanted to get to, but still wasn't quite sure of the way.

Pop's new-found self-importance coincided nicely with Marc Bolan's birth as a creative force. Not only could its star system satisfy his quest for recognition, it was now ready to bestow 'artist' status upon him as a songwriter and poet. He had the face, the talent, the gift of the gab, and now the record with which to back it up. 'The Wizard' was going to make him a star – or so he thought. Marc, together with his publicist Mike Pruskin and the Decca press office, made the most of the single's subject matter, which was based on the Paris story, and while the *Disc* reviewer wasn't too keen on the Dylan-like phrasing, Derek Johnson at *New Musical Express* was enthusiastic. 'Try and catch Marc Bolan's self-penned "The Wizard",' he advised. 'It has a most intriguing lyric, and his Sonny Bono-like voice is offset by a solid thumping beat, strings and ethereal voices.'[10] The Sonny Bono connection wasn't entirely gratuitous. When Decca signed Bolan on 9 August 1965, it was promptly announced that they were considering material by Bono and Burt Bacharach for his first single.

'The Wizard', which recounted in two verses the tale that appeared as fact in the accompanying Decca press release, was the first of Bolan's many personality songs glorifying imagined or real male characters (a songwriting trait that he shared with fellow Londoners, the Kinks' Ray Davies and the Who's Pete Townshend). The intonation was, at times, very reminiscent of Marc's new idol. Dylan's tendency to drop his voice wearily at the end of each line was reproduced exactly – but the subject matter was obviously more fantastic than anything in Dylan's repertoire. Before the Wizard 'turned and melted in the sky' (which didn't take long: the song was just as much an apparition, lasting just 1 minute 45 seconds), Bolan's description of him conjured up a sense of intrigue rarely heard in pop at that time.

The childlike picture of an enchanting world was maintained on the flip side, where 'Beyond The Risin' Sun' shunned the obsession with men of importance. Instead, it offered a fairyland Utopia inhabited by flying dragons, unicorns and young gods which Bolan, in a style straight out of C.S. Lewis's *Narnia* chronicles (or perhaps *The Wizard of Oz*), placed behind a magic door. This world was as impossible as Bolan's rising star seemed possible, but within a couple of years, when pop had become 'psychedelicised', many groups took on the guise of impossible dreamers. In its naïve purity, the song was almost an 'answer' to the sinful temptation of 'House Of The Risin' Sun', a folk-blues standard which Dylan had covered on his début album, and which the Animals had transformed into a successful piece of mainstream pop music.

Reference to 'the risin' sun' also appeared on 'You're Gonna Need Somebody On Your Bond', a standard popularised by Donovan on his *What's Bin Did And What's Bin Hid* album, issued earlier in the year. While Donovan had quickly been saddled with the British Dylan tag, his music drew from another important source, one generally ignored by the American singer, but closely observed by Marc Bolan. 'I'd begun to take a great interest in the myths and legends of the distant past,' Donovan remembers. 'The folk songs that came from Britain, especially Ireland,

Scotland and Wales, regions with a strong Celtic tradition, had been taken up by American singers like Joan Baez. She sang the Child ballads, songs that had been passed down through the centuries, carrying with them a view of the world that was made up of the remnants of myths and legends.' Donovan was introducing similar material into his repertoire, some of which appeared on his *Fairytale* album issued towards the end of 1965. (There are unconfirmed reports that Marc also demoed three songs from Donovan's début album, 'Donna Donna', 'Car Car' and 'You're Gonna Need Somebody On Your Bond', plus 'Hey Gyp (Dig The Slowness)', a B side from October 1965.)

Sales for 'The Wizard' were poor, but it wasn't through lack of exposure. Bolan promoted the record on *Ready, Steady, Go!* (other guests that week included Johnny Halliday and Sylvie Vartan – interestingly, both French singers), a performance which was marred by the backing band playing out of sync; and he appeared on ITV's *Thank Your Lucky Stars*. Marc also played his first live concerts either side of the single's release. The first took place at the Pontiac Club, based in Zeeta House, 100 Upper Richmond Road, Putney, in west London. The Pontiac catered for a hip mod clientele, where the R&B sounds bounced around the op-art decorated walls. Weeks earlier, the Byrds had appeared there, playing one of the few successful gigs of their entire British tour. But Marc's performance, according to Mike Pruskin, was 'a total disaster. It was like a cartoon, with fights everywhere and people diving all over the place. Marc really wasn't much good on the guitar at that time.' A few months later, he made a brief return to the stage for a university-promoted concert in Wembley, supporting the Nashville Teens, this time apparently accompanying himself with an electric guitar. Rumour has it that he came on during the intermission and played three songs, 'The Road I'm On (Gloria)', 'Blowin' In The Wind' and a new song called 'The Third Degree'. It was a brave move, but like everything Marc Bolan was doing around this time, it met with little success.

Recording three tracks was the norm for the standard one-off Decca contract. In spite of the single's failure, Marc returned to the company's studios on 30 December 1965 to record a further four numbers, all of which – like the version of 'That's The Bag I'm In' taped during the session for 'The Wizard' – have since been lost. It's not certain whether all four, again taped with Mike Leander as musical director, were Bolan originals. 'Rings Of

Fortune' and 'Highways' certainly were, because both were later
recorded and released (the latter as 'Misty Mist'); 'Reality' is likely
to be a Bolan song too. Most intriguing, though, is 'A Soldier
Song', which may have been Marc's own stab at protest in the
mould of 'Universal Soldier' or 'Blowin' In The Wind'. Nothing
came of this end-of-year session, and it appears that Decca
quickly lost interest in Jim Economides' young protégé.

Marc found it easy to create vistas of strangeness and charm,
but he didn't believe in it – at least, not in 1965. In another bit
of prepublicity for the single, he told the *Evening Standard*'s Angus
McGill (who'd first met Marc during the *Town* assignment), 'Personally, the prospect of being immortal doesn't excite me; but
the prospect of being a materialistic idol for four years does
appeal to me.' Old mods, it seems, die hard. McGill later recalled
the visit of the media-hungry Bolan, who arrived at the reporter's
office with his publicist Mike Pruskin in tow. 'I must say I simply
didn't recognise him,' said McGill. 'I had remembered him as a
rather plain little chap, and suddenly, there was the most glamorous young man you'd ever seen, all curls and exotic clothes. He
played the record, which I thought was appalling, and showed
me a sheaf of poetry which struck me as unmitigated rubbish.
But he had determination and such an extraordinary personality
that in the end I think I did write a column about him on the
lines of "working-class lad trying to hit the big time". I never
thought he'd make it, though.'[11]

Helen Shapiro was another to notice the change in her old
childhood friend. 'I hadn't seen him for several years,' she recalls,
'until I ran into him again at Fleetway House, where I was
attending a party – I think it was for *Fab 208* magazine. I said,
"What are you doing here?", and he told me how he'd been
trying to break into showbusiness. I remember he had his Donovan cap on and we discussed old times for a while. Then he told
me he'd been living in Paris for a while with this wizard. He was
very enthusiastic about it, but I didn't really know what he was
going on about. Marc always did have a very strong imagination,
so maybe it was all exaggerated.'

Marc Bolan really believed everything would all fall into
place. Here he was, a recording artist, enjoying several enthusiastic write-ups in magazines, and receiving invites to star-studded music-biz parties. After years of waiting, record company
photographers now sought to capture his beautific image – in the

recording studio, in front of classic oil paintings or in doorways clutching a black cat. Dressed in his smart suede boots, dark mid-length jacket adorned with brass buttons, and with his crown of thick, wavy hair freed from its lacquered imprisonment, Marc was now fashionably Bohemian. His look wasn't quite the 'poverty chic' which swept through the middle-class world of the American beatnik, but it was a lot more subtle than the obviously self-promoting façade of the mod.

With his growing self-awareness came a new subtlety in his demeanour, a cool indifference that again can be traced back directly to Bob Dylan. It was an image – and an attitude – that was very popular with the art school crowd, but as Jeff Dexter recalls, there was always a fundamental gulf between the outlook of the working-class mod and the philosophy of the art school student. 'Once someone like Marc or I had reached the end of our schooling,' insists Dexter, 'we just wanted to be out there. We didn't want to go back to school. We wanted to be grown up and bigger than we were, and the thought of being a student again was abhorrent to us. Art school kids were all spoilt brats who had too much of everything.' Back in the fifties and sixties, the idea of the art schools was fully entwined with the Romantic notion of the artist. Marc had assumed that persona too, but coming from the streets and not the art studio, his priorities weren't necessarily what the art school system had in mind. 'I think he really just wanted to make money,' says Dexter. 'He always had this thing . . . he wanted to make it, rather than create it.'

Keith Altham, then a top *New Musical Express* journalist, remembers Marc at the time of his Decca deal as a familiar hustling figure, hanging round pop establishments like the Brewmaster in Leicester Square hoping to cultivate the right contacts. 'We used to regard him as a bit of an upstart,' he recalls. 'Marc was small and pretty and very full of himself. He would always have a new demo tape or a tale like the one about living with the wizard in France, which we all thought was a bit dubious, even then. Then he'd start coming out with these outrageous statements like one day he was going to be bigger than Elvis Presley, and we'd all say, "Sure, Marc, sit down and have a Coca-Cola." He was very much the young man around town for a while, and then he suddenly disappeared.'

More receptive was Jonathan King, a young singer flushed

with the recent success of his two singles, 'Everyone's Gone To The Moon' and 'It's Good News Week' (the latter as Hedgehoppers Anonymous). At the start of the seventies, he said, 'I knew Marc four years ago and I always knew he would be a monster hit. At that time there were only three people I would allow to sing me their songs. They were Marc Bolan, Scott Walker and Cat Stevens.'[12] Stevens was another hopeful Decca solo artist whose manager, Mike Hurst, shared an office with Jim Economides. Like Marc, he was unhappy with Decca, and Bolan later said that the pair commiserated with each other by playing together and trying to get joint bookings in folk clubs. Their fortunes soon diverged, and while Cat Stevens got shunted on to the label's more adventurous Deram subsidiary (and had great success with 'Matthew And Son' early in 1967), Marc was dropped after Decca gambled on a second single which resulted in another dismal failure.

This time, the session took place at an outside studio, and Decca were presented with the finished masters for the two songs in spring 1966. Mike Leander's deft orchestral touches weren't called upon this time, and instead, producer Jim Economides booked several session musicians (including John Paul Jones, who'd worked with Donovan and the Yardbirds, and later turned up as part of Led Zeppelin) to provide a driving R&B backing on the A side, 'The Third Degree'. The twin-guitar, two-chord assault was a far cry from the 'light folk' treatment of 'The Wizard' (it was closer in spirit to Dylan's 'From A Buick Six', from *Highway 61 Revisited*), but the song was most memorable for revealing the first real sign of Bolan's unique lyric style. The key line, 'Philosophising mad psychiatrist closing off my mind in darkness', added an irreverent delight in wordplay to Bolan's clearly stated interest in the poetry of escapism (and is clearly reiterated in the line 'Fantasy baby is all I got').

'Everywhere I go people laugh at me,' boasted Marc on the A side, and the flip, 'San Francisco Poet', continued the identification of himself with the 'outsider'. 'The days of the beatniks are gone,' he sang, to the uncharacteristic backing of a 3/4 rhythm (scrappily played – by Marc – on acoustic: years later he claimed that this song was nothing more than an unfinished demo; it certainly sounds like it), but if the likes of Ferlinghetti and Ginsberg had had their day, Bolan still found the 'cool' of a poet irresistible.

One of the earliest surviving examples of Marc's energetic sorties into the rarified domain of the poet is 'Sun Songs And Black Masks', five pages of thin pink paper stapled together containing nine short poems, and climaxing with the lyrics for 'The Wizard'. Each piece is carefully typed, as is the author's name, 'Marc Bolan '65'. The subject matter throughout confirms that Bolan's mind continued to flee his urban surroundings, as he evoked Eastern promise, Parisian nights and glorified the state of nature, sometimes in one line: 'Mystic Paris black night, woods, trees, temples and sea . . . ' Fantasy almost always celebrates space, and more often than not – as any reading of Tolkien or C.S. Lewis will confirm – ensures that good triumphs against evil. But not everything radiated beauty in Bolan's world in the mid-sixties, and one of his early nursery-rhymes delighted in chopping off the tongue and wings of a singing blackbird. 'Hee hee', he added as an afterthought.[13]

Two failures out of two on the singles' market, an embarrassing television appearance and a brace of live concert disasters may have been enough for the faint-hearted to call it a day. Marc was undeterred, and now began to broaden his creative juices beyond the bounds of image, music and poetry to embrace art and storytelling. This Hackney-born latter-day Renaissance man began to flirt with a Dada-like banality (one drawing, dated July 1966 and titled 'Inside some chezz', depicts several mice eating away inside a lump of cheese; while 'Electronic Musik Seeped Thru' The Karsy Window' a three-page narrative poem written a month later, is nearer Lennon-style wit than Dylan's work) and the grandiose format of a full-length story. One still in existence is 'Pictures Of Purple People', an eight-scene tale handwritten on twenty-seven pages of an exercise book, and dated May 1966.

The confidence Marc had in his own abilities wasn't reciprocated when it came to those who controlled pop artists at that time. Even something as simple as the deal struck with young Allan Warren, sealed with a primitive contract and resulting in just one ineffective acetate, had prompted Phyllis Feld to make a trip to central London on behalf of her son. This came about after Warren, who had been renting the flat while under-age, finally received a visit from the landlord, David Kirsch (today a well-known property baron), an imposing figure in a long black overcoat who bore a passing resemblance to the actor James Fox. Warren hid his fear and tried to convince Kirsch that, because he always paid his rent on time, he should stay on, Kirsch eventually agreed.

Nights spent sipping champagne at the Café Royal soon took its toll, even on Warren's considerable wage, and he soon found himself owing three months rent at 35 guineas a month. 'I took off to Hyde Park Gate where Kirsch lived,' recalls Warren, 'with Marc's record and photograph under my arm, and I said to him, "Don't you think this is marvellous? This guy could be a star." So I made a suggestion. "Instead of paying you rent, you write off my debt and I'll give you his contract. And you, with all your money, can make him a star." "Oh, what a good idea," he said, "how marvellous".

'Long after Marc and I had parted our ways, David said to me one day, "I've had the most terrible thing happen with that silly contract you sold me. An angry woman called Mrs Feld came into my office while I was in the middle of some business, and complained that I was doing nothing for her son. I told her she was right, I had done nothing. I was so frightened that I gave her the contract and she tore it up there and then. But I've still got the acetate, which is very nice, she's got the contract back, you got off with the rent and Marc will get a proper manager, so everybody's happy." '

If only the cut-throat world of business was always so simple. When Mike Pruskin became Marc's manager in mid-1965, it wasn't long before Les Conn, a Denmark Street publisher who handled Doris Day's Melcher Music publishing company, bought into the deal on a 50–50 basis. Although it's not certain whether Conn or Jim Economides did the negotiating with Decca on Bolan's behalf, the publisher, who was also a scout for the Dick James Organisation, did little to enhance Marc's career. Kenneth Pitt, who managed David Bowie from 1966 to 1970, cited one occasion when Conn took both Bowie and Bolan up to see Dick James, who promptly told him, 'Get those long-haired gits out of here!'[14] Pitt himself toyed with the idea of managing Bolan, and had a preliminary evening meeting on 8 January 1966 with Mike Pruskin to discuss the idea. A month later, Pitt was still weighing up the merits of Bolan and Bowie, but a colleague advised him, in rather unfortunate terms, that 'I think David Bowie will have a longer life.' Pitt went for Bowie.

Mike Pruskin also remembers a meeting with Simon Napier-Bell, then still a young songwriter making his first move into management. Early in 1966, *Ready Steady, Go!* producer Vicki Wickham had approached Napier-Bell with the idea of writing some lyrics for an Italian song spotted by Dusty Springfield while she attended the San Remo Music Festival (that song, 'You Don't Have To Say You Love Me', went on to top the charts in April). In spite of Marc's flawed appearance on Wickham's show, Pruskin and Bolan got on well with the producer, who may well have advised them that her songwriting companion was talent-spotting. The idea, recalls Pruskin, was to ditch Les Conn, but at that stage, nothing came of their meeting with Napier-Bell.

Meanwhile, Jim Economides had been trying to convince Marc that perhaps his greatest talent lay in his looks. The beatniks may had adopted a style akin to poverty chic, but Marc's dressing down was still brought off with the panache of old and at least as much contrivance. Pruskin remembers the continuing obsession with the Look, the talk of his flatmate being reinvented in the James Dean mould, and his own feeling that he'd had enough of struggling to break his charge. 'We weren't making any money and so we parted,' he recalls. 'The crunch came when we became so broke that we had to do a bunk from the flat. At that point I really thought Marc was going to pursue a career in acting.'

Bolan was initially tempted. A few years earlier, he would have jumped at the chance, but that was before he discovered that the world needed his head full of ideas as much it did his face and talent. He later explained that he never felt that close to acting: it seemed altogether too slow for him. Marc's belief in himself as a future musical idol was foremost in his mind. He needed to find a partner who shared that belief, and who possessed the necessary skills and influence to make the fantasy real. That person, Marc decided, was going to be Simon Napier-Bell.

'I'd never heard of Marc Bolan before,' says the well-known pop manager today, forgetting, perhaps, that Pruskin and Bolan had paid him a visit a month or two earlier. Having telephoned Napier-Bell out of the blue, Marc arranged to visit his flat with a tape of his songs. He appeared on the doorstep minutes later clutching his acoustic guitar – but without the promised spool of tape. The manager was immediately struck by the image of his would-be starlet. 'I thought he was a Charles Dickens urchin,' he recalls. 'It's now become very fashionable to wear old clothes – two jackets on top of one another, that sort of thing. Back then it was pretty unique. I certainly hadn't seen any fashion like that around before.' Napier-Bell, understanding that the pop business revolved at least as much around personality as it did musical talent, sensed 'immediate star quality' and did the unthinkable – he invited Marc Bolan in. (Napier-Bell insists that this instant recognition has occurred on no more than three occasions in his entire career: one of the others to make a similar impression was one-time Japan singer David Sylvian.)

Around the time of the success of 'You Don't Have To Say You Love Me', early in 1966, Napier-Bell had been approached by the Yardbirds, then one of Britain's best-selling R&B groups, with a view to becoming their producer. Typically, he ended up negotiating a new deal with EMI and became their manager, but he had the unfortunate task of steering the group through a turbulent period. First came the departure in June of Napier-Bell's original ally, bassist Paul Samwell-Smith, which was successfully resolved when ace session man Jimmy Page was recruited on rhythm guitar and Chris Dreja switched to bass. Before the year was out, lead guitarist Jeff Beck left the group at the start of an American tour, and the group limped on with surprisingly little success, before calling it a day in July 1968 (and metamorphosing into Led Zeppelin).

The Yardbirds were already established by the time Napier-Bell encountered them. By contrast, Marc Bolan was a nobody, raw material that aroused the young manager's thirst for a new challenge. Once inside the flat, Marc sat in a big armchair that accentuated his small frame, strapped a capo on his guitar neck and began to play his songs, without interruption, for just under an hour. Napier-Bell was transfixed, but not by the singer's mysticism. 'There was never an element of mysticism about him,' he says. 'Marc was a wonderful, charming fraud. That was his own fantasy he had about himself. There was nothing mystical in the fact that he was prepared to sit down, quite unabashed, and play all these songs to me; and his guitar playing was appalling. He was absolutely unaware of his own shortcomings. I just loved the voice: unfortunately, no one else did. It was five years before anyone else would even listen. He also happened to be an extremely interesting person, had a great approach and musical attack.'

Between leaving Decca and impressing himself upon Simon Napier-Bell, something strange had happened to Marc's voice.

The youthful, vaguely self-conscious attempt to be a Dylan or an R&B singer on his first two singles had given way to a style of vocalising that was virtually unprecedented in the pop world. It was a remarkable transition which occurred within the space of a few weeks, replacing any professional values concerning diction, intelligibility and holding notes with a voice that went far beyond the bounds of conveying lyrical messages. Its quavering vibrato rendered the lyrics largely insensible, and there was a tendency to punctuate at frequent intervals with sudden bursts of shrill bleating. It was unique, perhaps too much so, hinting at a pure, unrefined haemorrhage from a diseased larynx. Either that or a deranged mind.

Two years later, when Marc was asked about the source of his singing style, he replied, 'I suppose we're trying to imitate the instruments. It's just a development of my mind. I never used to like singing but now it is a great fulfilment, like flying. I think it mirrors what I feel inside.'[15] You don't necessarily need to hunt for the germs of wisdom in his lyrics, or marvel at his economic guitar style to winkle out the secret of Marc Bolan's success. Image and aura were undoubtedly crucial, too, but the hidden appeal of rock music often resides in overlooked ingredients such as the actual texture of a voice. Few singers had a more distinctive texture than Marc Bolan.

Otherworldliness and mental derangement are just two of the meanings that can be teased out from the Bolanic yelp, which was somewhat lucky in view of the aspirations of the emerging youth culture in 1966–7. This newly acquired tool – which some say came from a borrowing of blues singer Bessie Smith's vocal anguish into a white male form, though Marc liked to say it was inspired by playing Billy Eckstine records at 78 rpm – was at least as untroubled by convention as Presley's was back in the mid-fifties, or Bob Dylan's several years later. No style of singing emerges in a vacuum (and if there was an immediate precedent for the warble, it could well have been American singer Buffy Sainte-Marie, whom Marc probably heard during his folk-protest phase) but, like most memorable voices, Bolan's sounded as if it had been blueprinted at conception. It was his most treasured, distinctive and – occasionally – vilified musical tool.

Napier-Bell was sufficiently impressed by Marc's songs, his self-confidence and his attractive image to call up several recording studios, in the hope of booking one that same evening. De

Lane Lea Studios in Kingsway, central London, had some free time and during a two-hour session, several songs were taped. Although never intended as anything more than working demos, these were later scheduled to appear on the *Hard On Love* album in 1972, obviously to capitalise on Bolan's new-found success, but an injunction prevented their release. (Together with songs from later Napier-Bell sessions, these demos eventually appeared in 1974 on *The Beginning Of Doves* album set.) Among the songs recorded that evening were 'The Perfumed Garden Of Gulliver Smith', 'Black & White Incident', 'Observations', 'Pictures Of Purple People', 'Catblack', 'Jasmine '49', 'Charlie', 'I'm Weird' and 'Hippy Gumbo'. None featured particularly intricate arrangements, but the distinctive sound of the voice, the accessible charm of the tunes and the obscure lyrics sufficiently encouraged Napier-Bell to take the young singer under his wing.

'I loved Marc,' he recalls. 'I thought Marc would be the biggest star in the world. Even some of his fantasy about making it rubbed off on me. His voice really sounded magical and I thought people would want to hear it. And the lyrics, in terms of words and feeling, were tremendous. I still think *The Beginning Of Doves* contains some of his best songs, and with very few exceptions – "Cosmic Dancer" for one – they were rarely equalled in his career. When he hit his high point, he wrote some of the best poetic lyrics that I've ever heard in pop. He often talked about being a poet.'

One of the most startling of these De Lane Lea demos was 'Observations', a talking blues based on a simple walking blues riff. It was Bolan's most wordy song yet, if not his most lyrical. He name-drops Brighton, West 1, Maida Vale and Chelsea, encounters guys 'with paintings in their eyes', beggars who turn out to be 'rockin' preachers', rhymes hip slang ('kicks', 'chicks'), and invokes underworld imagery ('zip-gun') and characters ('crazy Sally') in a way that pre-empts much of his later work. There were also the inevitable references to the music he grew up with, most obviously in 'Pictures Of Purple People'. In Marc's hands, this song contrasted good and evil with oblique references to magic, mirrors and maidens, but the inspiration for such delicate subject matter was none other than Sheb Wooley's 1958 top twenty hit, 'The Purple People Eater', an irreverent parody record featuring a speeded-up voice and saxophone. The source didn't matter to Marc: neither did the fact that the finished words may have read as unmitigated nonsense if approached from a conventional standpoint. It was the sound of the words and the imagery they conjured up that were dominant in his mind. The impressionistic, fleeting sense of imagery that Dylan had popularised on his *Highway 61 Revisited* and the just-released *Blonde On Blonde* albums had given Bolan the signal to move even further away from pop's golden rule book.

Securing the interest of one of the new breed of young British pop managers had revived Marc's confidence, enabling him to put the Decca débâcle behind him. Napier-Bell, who thought the Yardbirds were 'a dreary lot', took Bolan on as his new protégé, because he was 'a lot more interesting'. This also offered the manager an opportunity to 'break' an act from scratch. In return, Marc demanded more from Napier-Bell than perfunctory managerial moves. He wanted a patron and a Svengali-figure. 'I remember him complaining once that he couldn't come round and sit in my flat all day when he wanted,' says Napier-Bell. 'He saw a manager almost in terms of someone to live with, a substitute parent. Someone who would help him, guide him, be a partner, talk with him, provide a home, provide him with some pocket money *and* be a manager. Someone who'd do everything for him so that he could go ahead and become a star. There was an element of laziness in Marc.'

The relationship inevitably acquired a closeness which rivalled that of Marc's affair with Terry Whipman. 'I would imagine that his relationship with Terry was rather inventive, like a brother and sister learning together,' Napier-Bell speculates. 'I thought Marc was more gay than straight. He had no great hang-ups about sex. All the figures he admired were men, and I think he admired them to the point of finding them sexually attractive. If his sexuality was more or less evenly balanced, I think he found gay life and gay chat infinitely more amusing. You only have to hear his off-the-cuff interviews and chat between takes. He was always fun.

'Obviously, I was aware of his sexual relationship with me, I was aware that he had Terry, and I was aware that he'd had affairs with various people. He used to come round on the early morning bus from his parents' prefab in Wimbledon and get in bed with me in the morning. How can you manage anybody and not have a relationship with them? The sexual borders had completely collapsed by that time. Straight people thought they shouldn't be straight. In fact, in the sixties, it was pretty difficult to have any sort of relationship with someone without it being sexual. There was a feeling that you were not entering into the spirit of what that decade was about. There was not necessarily any closeness or commitment involved, though. It was of no more consequence than smoking a joint together. I think Marc had a whole series of people with whom he went around having very intimate but very nice, easy relationships.'

Marc's early-morning bedroom discussions with his new manager were, more often than not, plotting sessions for unveiling the new-look Marc Bolan on a record-buying public that was becoming increasingly sophisticated. The wave of American folk-rock, via Dylan, the Byrds and Sonny and Cher, had peaked, while the top British bands like the Beatles and the Rolling Stones had absorbed its influence and begun to look further afield for musical inspiration. Dylan shunned the political, Lennon and McCartney shunned tin-pan alley professionalism. Ironically, as these musical developments gradually prompted a change in relationship between artists and management, Marc Bolan was happy to embrace the old Larry Parnes-style paternalism, at least for as long as it took to make him famous.

Several other demos dating from this time which appeared on *The Beginning Of Doves* include 'You Got The Power', 'Eastern Spell' and 'Horrible Breath', the latter originally written as an advertising jingle for Amplex tablets (and later retitled 'You Scare Me To Death' by Napier-Bell). The song which was chosen to launch him was 'Hippy Gumbo', though Simon Napier-Bell first had to contend with Marc's choice of tactics for promotion. 'He didn't think he even needed to make a record,' recalls the manager. 'Marc said, "Just put some posters up, man, I'll be a star." He didn't really want to play music. He just wanted to be an image. I think he was a bit upset when I said that we had to cut a record. When we left De Lane Lea studio that first night, he said, "Well, that's the album." I had to convince him that the idea was to listen to those and then make *one* into a record.'

Napier-Bell re-recorded Marc's acoustic version of 'Hippy Gumbo', then added a large string section and no less than three double basses, giving the song a claustrophobic effect that would characterise many future Bolan recordings. (Uncannily, the scene-setting drone of the string section would be re-created five years later on Marc's first chart-topping single, 'Hot Love'.) The

Creole-like 'Hippy Gumbo' hinged round a simple five-note blues scale, mirrored by the first public evidence of Bolan's extreme new vocal delivery, and with lyrics disturbingly evocative of Grimm's fairy tales ('Hippy Gumbo he's no good, chop him up for firewood'). The flip-side, 'Misfit', was less extraordinary, with the warbling voice struggling to be heard through a more conventional backing of bass guitar, drums, keyboards and brass.

After negative reactions from every record company in the country, Napier-Bell flexed his muscles within the EMI corporation (the Yardbirds were on its Columbia subsidiary) and found an outlet in Parlophone, the label once looked after by Beatles producer George Martin. Despite another appearance on *Ready, Steady, Go!* on 13 December 1966, the same edition on which the Jimi Hendrix Experience made its British television début, the single fared even less well than its two predecessors, making it one of today's most sought-after Bolan recordings. Meanwhile, Simon Napier-Bell already had another project under way, one which would soon cross paths with Marc Bolan, and finally put his face on magazine covers, his song in the charts and his life at the mercy of rioting audiences. These new protégés of Napier-Bell's were a ramshackle bunch of musicians from Leatherhead known as John's Children.

# CHAPTER FIVE

'All I've done is re-create John's Children, or at least what I wanted John's Children to be like when I was with them. I'm writing exactly the same stuff as I was five years ago. It's no different really except that hopefully it's a bit better and has a bit more insight. And I can play it now; I couldn't then. I could only play "Desdemona" before.'
Marc Bolan, *Zig Zag* magazine, 1971

'It was like ducking Marc in the deep end and then pulling him out again and saying, "See, you can do that. That's what you can get away with without being any good. Imagine what you could do with a good band and some good songs." '
Chris Townson, drummer with John's Children

The Who were Britain's premier pop art group, with a stage act which often ended in a mess of smashed guitars, microphones, drums and howling feedback. These frenzied climaxes were, on the one hand, celebrated as wanton destruction, but fully justified on the other by band leader Pete Townshend, who claimed a direct link with the teachings of artist Gustav Metzger. Metzger's Ealing College lecture, where he illustrated his theory of auto-destructive art by destroying a bass guitar, had a significant effect on Townshend. He was interested in the relationship between violence and creativity, not least because the visual (and publicity) potential for introducing the idea into public performance with his beat group was enormous. He was right. Crowds flocked to see the Who in concert, even though their record sales never quite matched their on-stage reputation.

In April 1967, several thousand young West German pop fans crowded into the large Rheinhalle venue in Ludwigshafen to witness the Who sacrificing their equipment in the name of auto-destruction. Few had even heard of John's Children, the English support act and the Who's label-mates on Chris Stamp's and Kit Lambert's newly formed Track Records. There was probably more interest in the two local bands, including the Rattles, who went on to have a Top Ten British hit with 'The Witch' in 1970. The audience never got to see the Who, but they did get more than their fair share of destruction.

The memory of the events that evening remain firmly etched into the minds of all involved, including John's Children vocalist Andy Ellison. 'Most of our gigs ended in some form of disarray,' he smiles, 'but that one was way over the top. We'd only played about three or four longish numbers, and then the customary feedback, thunderous drumming and vocal chants took over. Marc began to whip his guitar and amplifier with a heavy chain. Meanwhile, I'd jumped into the audience, started stirring the crowd up and throwing feathers everywhere. Before long, the whole place was covered with them.

'People tried to pick fights with me, but I scrambled back on to the stage and had the preconceived battle with John, the bassist, complete with fake blood capsules. I think that's what sent the audiences mad on that German tour. At the Ludwigshafen date, the crowd started picking up chairs and throwing them through windows. Everyone was fighting and there was a hideous noise from the audience. I remember thinking that it had all gone berserk. While this was going on, the feedback continued and Chris carried on banging away on his drums.'

John's Children's act often closed with Chris Townson alone on stage pounding hell out of his kit, but on this occasion being last to leave nearly cost him more than a few broken drum-skins. 'It was very dangerous,' he recalls, 'it was almost like mass hysteria. I remember John laughing like a maniac out of fear, I think, not because he was enjoying it. At one point, the audience surged on to the stage, including this huge guy who looked like a Viking. He wore an RAF roundel T-shirt like the one Keith Moon always used to wear. I'd just decided to make a run for it, when this guy bore down on me. I really thought my time was up, but instead of beating me up, he gave me this huge wet sloppy kiss. Eventually, I got away from him, kicked my kit towards the crowd and ran.'

Andy, John and Marc had already beaten a hasty retreat from the unwanted attentions of bouncers and officials who, having been forewarned of the band's on-stage antics, had turned out in force. 'All the bouncers in those days were left-overs from the old Nazi regime,' maintains manager Simon Napier-Bell. 'They only went to rock concerts so they could bang people's heads together. These were the most vicious people you could ever meet, so when we tackled the gig in what was more or less our customary way, they felt justified in responding like that. The whole place just went mad.'

There was no time to listen to the Who's angry protestations, or those of their manager Kit Lambert, whose patience with John's Children had already been stretched by milder controversies on previous nights. In a scene reminiscent of an adventure movie, Napier-Bell and his young charges, with a group of enraged concert stewards at their heels, escaped through a maze of backstage corridors, leaving their equipment and personal belongings behind. As they raced towards Napier-Bell's limousine, water cannons arrived outside the hall and began firing through the windows in a last resort to quell the crowd. Once inside the vehicle, the musical agitators swerved out of the car park, hit the nearest *autobahn* and sped off in the direction of Munich. Under the well-lit freeway, they began to assess the damage. Chris had a massive jackboot mark on his chest. Andy, who had already dislocated his neck by falling off stage a few nights earlier in Düsseldorf, sat in the tattered remnants of his stage clothes. Marc and John remained silently shell-shocked, picking off the feathers from their white uniforms. The Who didn't play that night, and John's Children were kicked off the tour. They weren't too surprised.


John's Children provided an unlikely vehicle for the poetic ambitions of Marc Bolan. A group that had to resort to shock tactics on stage and session musicians on record didn't quite match the artistic integrity Marc envisaged for himself. But for a few months, he was John's Children's guitarist and chief songwriter, a somewhat estranged member of a group of nearly pop stars who had become the latest project of Simon Napier-Bell. When the manager offered him the chance to join, Marc's acceptance obliged him to compromise his isolationist position. If he had previously been an island, and one with very few visitors, John's Children welcomed him on to the mainland. Or, more accurately, the peninsula.

Shortly after the release of 'Hippy Gumbo' at the end of

1966, Marc had returned to the studio to record 'Jasper C. Debussy', which was intended as the follow-up. It was another portrait song, this time concerning a mischievous character whose 'kinda fun' was tying people to railroad tracks, and signalled a marked shift in style from the serious tone of his previous work. The song's humour, although a dark shade of grey, was underscored by an upbeat boogie-woogie tempo, and lightened further by Nicky Hopkins' distinctive bar-room piano-playing. Interestingly, 'Jasper C. Debussy' employed a 3/4 fairground-style motif between the verses, paying lip service to the quirky musical spirits which were increasingly infiltrating British pop. (Bassist John Paul Jones and 'Big' Jim Sullivan on guitar were among the other backing musicians.)

In the wake of the failure of 'Hippy Gumbo', Simon Napier-Bell decided to shelve 'Jasper C. Debussy'. He had a much better idea. At his fingertips was a songwriter whose voice was so abrasive that nobody would listen, and a band that couldn't write decent songs. Why not combine his assets into one perfect pop combination?

John's Children had been playing, in one form or other, for at least as long as Marc Bolan. They started life as the Clockwork Onions, and after losing the likes of Louie Grooner and Martin Sheller, the nucleus of the group, Chris Dawset (bass), Geoff McClelland (guitar), Andy Ellison (vocals) and Chris Townson (drums), soldiered on as the Few, before revealing their art school origins by adopting the conceptually more intriguing name of the Silence. In spring 1965, they began gigging with a noisy brand of Who and Kinks covers, interspersed with blues/R & B standards like 'Smokestack Lightning' and an endless version of Booker T. & the MGs' 'Green Onions'. Chris Dawset was the next to leave, and his place was taken by the then decidedly unmusical John Hewlett. The rest weren't much better and to compensate for their technical inadequacies, the Silence, dressed in moody dark clothing, began to turn on the volume. Meanwhile, Andy Ellison developed a stage act which started with him shaking the maracas furiously and ended with him diving into the audience.

Although Ellison still lived in Finchley, north London, the group's base was in Leatherhead, Surrey, some ten miles outside the city. There, the Silence became regulars at the Chuck Wagon based at 22a Bridge Street which, by early 1966, had been

renamed the Bluesette Club. One night, pop impresario Don Arden,
then handling the up-and-coming mod band the Small Faces, saw
the Silence and immediately offered them work through his
agency, often placing them on the same bill as his prize act.

Andy Ellison describes the group's early days as 'a load of
fun and a good way of picking up birds', and it was with similar
intent that Chris Townson, John Hewlett and Bluesette co-owner
Gordon Bennett spent a few summer days in San Tropez in
August 1966. It didn't quite turn out the way they'd expected,
and after Bennett mysteriously vanished the two band members
also went their separate ways after a dispute with members of
the local population. Also holidaying in the area was Simon
Napier-Bell, who was introduced to Hewlett in a club one lunchtime. Hewlett suggested that the young manager should check
out the Silence on his return to England, while Napier-Bell
offered Hewlett the fare home.

True to his promise, the young entrepreneur drove down to
Surrey to catch the Silence at an outdoor party at the Burford
Bridge Hotel, just off the A31, where the group had set up
dangerously close to a swimming pool. By this time, they had
developed into a semi-competent, Who-influenced R & B-type
band, but the element of performance remained an integral part
of the Silence's act, and sometimes threatened to take over. 'We
couldn't afford to smash up our amplifiers every night like the
Who,' recalls Ellison, 'so we used to destroy ridiculous things
like maracas – in fact anything that just happened to be on stage
that wasn't ours. We excelled ourselves at that open-air barbecue.
Some of the amplifiers ended up in the pool, and I can clearly
remember being up on the diving-board singing, and then diving
into the water with the microphone. I think Simon was quite
taken aback, but he must have seen something in the band,
probably complete madness.'

'My motivations were primarily sexual,' explains Napier-Bell.
'Like most people in the sixties, I was very hedonistic, and here
were three attractive boys. Brian Epstein only signed the Beatles
because he fancied them. What did I have? The Yardbirds who
were the straightest bunch ever. I thought, it's all very well
learning about this business and making money, but I'm not
having any of the fun out of it.

'The reason there were so many gay people in management
was because in those days, pop music was selling mainly to

teenage girls, and a gay man has the ability to see the artist from the perspective of a teenage girl and a businessman. That was a very valuable property to have. Pop management seemed to me the ideal way to mix business with pleasure. It was the modern equivalent of being the choirmaster, but in the sixties, instead of being arrested for the nasty little things you did round the back of the church, they gave you a million pounds and made you a hero.'

As it turned out, Napier-Bell's massive investment in John's Children didn't bring the financial rewards he might have expected, but he had a lot more fun with them than he had had with the Yardbirds, whose scholarly approach and disagreements over 'musical differences' always threatened to break them apart. John's Children provided the perfect antidote. 'They were one of the most intelligent and fun groups I ever met,' maintains Napier-Bell, 'but they weren't very good. Andy couldn't sing but he looked great on stage. Chris could only just play the drums, though he was the best musician of the lot. When I saw them, I thought they were probably the worst group I'd ever seen, but it was just too tempting. I jumped in quickly, ignoring the fact that they weren't good musicians. I then realised that I had to do something with them. The worst of the lot was Geoff the guitarist, not necessarily musically, but in terms of rapport. I decided to put Marc in the band instead.'

When Napier-Bell took the band under his wing in autumn 1966, his first move had been to rechristen them after the tone deaf bassist who had introduced him to the band. Then he dressed the newly named John's Children in clean white outfits, hung gold medallions around their necks and recommended smart, boyish mod haircuts. John Hewlett, who went along with it all at the time, regrets the band's naïve willingness to be manipulated. 'I seriously think we were on the way to hell,' he says. 'It was the frustration of youth. We wanted to express ourselves, but the truth was that we were not in touch with what we really wanted to achieve.

'I think Simon had a real gift for sensing talent, but he responded to the fun element and the sexual aspect, and tried to manufacture something out of that. I can never recall him addressing our talents or encouraging us to work at it. All I can recall is negativity, the feeling that we could con the world, which later became part of the punk ethos. The difference was that

during the punk era, bands were far more aware than they were
in the sixties. The punks clearly understood what they were
saying and doing. We didn't have a clue.'

At a time when pop musicians were starting to take themselves very seriously, spending weeks rather than hours on their
songs, 'composing' albums instead of churning out three-minute
tunes, and seeking to acquire a degree of control over their
destiny, the idea of a manufactured, blatantly hyped group who
didn't always play on their records was repugnant in the new
'rock' climate. You couldn't even call John's Children Britain's
failed reply to the Monkees. Their recorded legacy is minimal,
often badly played, full of strange edits and produced in a way
that is best described as eccentric. Yet this peculiar brand of
apparently fabricated mayhem, when coupled with the mythical
status afforded the group due to Bolan's involvement, has
secured an unexpected place in rock history for John's Children
– an inconsequential aberration in 1967, yet a mini-legend twenty-
five years later.

Prior to Marc's joining towards the end of February, John's
Children had issued two singles and recorded an album for
release in America. Napier-Bell's clout at EMI, which had recently
placed Marc's 'Hippy Gumbo' on Parlophone, secured a deal
with Columbia in the UK for John's Children, while overseas
outlets were also found in Canada, America and Germany. The
début 45, 'Smashed Blocked' (retitled 'The Love I Thought I
Found' for the more reserved British market), was a monstrous
freakbeat classic, opening with thirty seconds of pulsating weird-
ness over which a crazed voice intones, 'Please . . . I'm losing
my mind . . . Help me . . . ' The remainder of the song, which
had been recorded in Los Angeles using session musicians, was
vaguely reminiscent of the Turtles, but its odd character was due
in part to Simon Napier-Bell's passion for editing the tapes. 'After
we recorded something,' recalls Andy Ellison, 'Simon always
took the tapes away and cut them about. There are edits all over
the John's Children's recordings. It was probably a legacy from
his background in film editing, and it made life very difficult for
us. We'd rehearse a number in a certain way, and then find that
Simon had chopped the last chorus and put it somewhere else,
or had dropped in a middle section from another track completely. We had to re-rehearse our own songs to make them
sound like the finished records.'

'Smashed Blocked' enjoyed enough localised success in parts of America to creep into the *Billboard* Top 100 singles chart, and this encouraged the independent White Whale label to commission an entire album from the group. John's Children had yet to play to screaming audiences, but that didn't stop Napier-Bell conceiving the idea of a faked 'in concert' LP. The band played their set at Advision Studios, New Bond Street, Napier-Bell drowning out their incompetence with a tape loop of screams lifted directly from the Beatles' *A Hard Day's Night* film. Journalists often commented on the damp seats left in the wake of rock 'n' roll and pop concerts, and the manager, always seeking to create controversy around his perfectly formed pop band, came up with a title for the LP that crystallised that excitement – *Orgasm*. It wasn't even presented to Columbia in the UK; and after complaints from the reactionary Daughters of the American Revolution pressure group, the White Whale release was cancelled. (It eventually appeared in 1971, indicating that a significant shift in morality had occurred during the interim.)

A second John's Children single, 'Just What You Want, Just What You'll Get', released in February 1967, again suffered from awkward production, but it at least proved that the group was capable of writing a song without the guiding hand of their manager. However, the flip, 'But She's Mine', a blatant recycling of the Who's 'I Can't Explain' riff, was a strong indication that they soon ran out of original ideas, although unbeknown to the public, Ellison, Townson, McClelland and Hewlett wrote and played almost everything on the shelved *Orgasm* album.

By this time, it had become obvious that guitarist Geoff McClelland, whose job it was to faint when the band had run out of songs to play, thus giving them a perfect excuse to cut their concerts short, didn't really fit in. Simon Napier-Bell had impressed upon the band the need to create outrage. He liked the contrast between the quartet of innocent-looking pretty boys who walked out on stage dressed in Persil-white outfits, and their wild act which found them scrapping and generally running amok, against a background of discord and a heavily amplified wall of sound. 'At first I wanted to be a good drummer,' says Chris Townson, 'but there was a transition after Simon took over. In the end, playing well didn't really matter: the performance was much more important than what we sounded like.

'Simon encouraged the mayhem, the more outrageous the

better. And we were happy to go along with it. It was rather like saying to a child, "Go and smash that kitchen up", and he'd do it with glee. We were like that, but Geoff couldn't carry it off. He looked unconvincing. When Pete Townshend smashed up a guitar, you knew he meant it. When Geoff did it he looked awkward which was really not what we wanted.'

Some say that Simon Napier-Bell issued Marc Bolan with an ultimatum: either join the Yardbirds or John's Children. The very thought of finding a place for Bolan's rudimentary guitar style in the virtuoso R & B band is preposterous. In John's Children, though, his lack of expertise mattered little. Yet for someone who, since the early sixties, had envisaged himself as a solo singer – whether it be in the Cliff Richard or the Bob Dylan mould – becoming part of a group effort was a partial admission of defeat. The decision provided the acid test between Marc's desire to pursue the undiluted path of the Romantic artist in isolation, or to take the opportunist route and become part of something that could nudge him closer towards stardom. Bolan opted for the latter.

Simon Napier-Bell believes the decision wasn't a difficult one. 'Marc was obsessed with being in a band,' he says. 'He really wanted to be a rock 'n' roll star, and so when I put the idea to him, he was immediately taken with it. It was rather manipulative of me, but I knew John's Children were about to succeed and I knew that I couldn't sell Marc's voice to the public. If Marc was a backing singer behind Andy, and the band had some hits, I figured that the public would soon get used to his voice. Then I'd take him out of the group again and he'd re-emerge as a solo artist with a ready-made audience. That's what I really had in mind when I put Marc in John's Children. We made "Desdemona" with exactly that in mind.'

The manager prepared the way for Bolan's entry into John's Children by casually leaving his photographs lying around, playing his demos and enthusing about his songwriting talents. Sometimes, Marc would sit almost unnoticed at the group's evening sessions at Advision. Perhaps understandably, only Geoff McClelland seemed to be aware of Marc's presence. One night at Advision, 'there was this little guy there,' said McClelland. 'Actually, I wasn't too sure if it was a guy. He was sitting, playing an acoustic guitar, very influenced by Dylan and Donovan. At around 10.30 p.m., he suddenly leapt up and said, "Look, I've got to go now otherwise my parents will be really mad at me." And he ran out. That was Marc Bolan.'[1]

Eager to forge the union, Simon Napier-Bell next drove Andy Ellison to Marc's home in Summerstown, and left hoping that the pair would strike up a rapport which would ease Marc's entry into the band. On that day, Bolan raved about the book he'd been reading, Günter Grass's *The Tin Drum*, played several Bob Dylan records, and cooked mushrooms on toast for Ellison, one of Marc's few culinary specialities. Then he picked up his acoustic, ran through some ideas, and almost immediately the pair started working on a new song of Marc's called 'Midsummer Night's Scene'. 'I was really impressed with his songs,' recalls Ellison. 'They were great and simple – exactly what John's Children needed.'

The coup was complete. Geoff McClelland was out of the band, John's Children got their potential hit songwriter, Marc Bolan had an outlet for his creative talents and Simon Napier-Bell now had all his delicious young things together. 'We were all about the same size,' Ellison says, 'and Simon must have known that he could market us as four pretty boys.' John Hewlett feels that Bolan's recruitment into the band was somewhat wasted. 'He was probably the one person who could have made John's Childen more than just a band of drinkers and womanisers. He'd been around longer than us, was more streetwise and had his heart set on success, whereas we were more loony. He was definitely the right person for the band, and I think the combination, short-lived and poorly guided as it was, showed signs of working really well.'

Hewlett sensed a lack of focus in John's Children, but there was a camaraderie among the three original members which Marc found difficult to penetrate. If his natural instinct was to start issuing instructions and redesigning the group in his own self-image, the lackadaisical attitude of the other three, combined with the control exerted by Napier-Bell, worked against him. Kit Lambert had agreed to sign John's Children on the proviso that Bolan be incorporated into the group as a Pete Townshend-type figure, writing the songs, providing the musical direction and guiding the musicians forward. John's Children certainly benefited from his songwriting, but Marc never managed to carve out a role for himself as the group's mentor. 'He entered into this really wild, over-the-top band and he was flabbergasted,' suggests Ellison. 'That Townshend-type relationship was never given a chance to develop, because we worked on the material democratically. I never once heard Marc say, "This is how you play the song." We used to work at it together.'

Ellison's contention may be true – but only to a point. A couple of John's Children recordings exist featuring Marc on lead vocals, namely 'Hippy Gumbo' and 'Sally Was An Angel' (the latter shared with Andy Ellison), while other Bolan titles covered by the group stuck closely to his original demos. These include 'The Perfumed Garden Of Gulliver Smith', 'Hot Rod Mama', 'The Third Degree', 'Sara Crazy Child', 'Lunacy's Back', 'Jasper C. Debussy' (re-recorded as 'Casbah Candy') and 'Mustang Ford' (re-recorded with non-Bolan lyrics as 'Go Go Girl').

Simon Napier-Bell's irreverent attitude towards the band's tapes extended beyond his customary edits to wiping instruments and voices off at random. With this in mind, it is possible that other Bolan songs were taped during his months in John's Children. What is certain is that more work was undertaken with Marc Bolan in the band than was once thought. Even 'Cornflake Zoo', which appeared on the B side of Andy Ellison's April 1968 solo single, 'You Can't Do That', started life as a Bolan demo: Napier-Bell simply added Andy Ellison's voice, wiping off Marc's original vocal line. Although the song still retained Bolan's acoustic guitar playing, the melody was completely different. Further evidence of the group's wholesale appropriation of the Bolan songbook extends to live performances of 'Catblack', and possibly even Marc's second single, 'The Third Degree'.

The rejigged schedule of record releases in the wake of his joining the band confirmed Bolan's central role in John's Children. 'Not The Sort Of Girl (You'd Take To Bed)', the group's planned follow-up to 'Just What You Want, Just What You'll Get', was immediately cancelled. The title alone had been enough to alarm the executives at Columbia/EMI and Napier-Bell had no reservations about accepting Kit Lambert's offer to team up with Track Records. With a proper songwriter in the band, the decidedly odd stop-start arrangement of the planned 45 – which resembled nothing more than Dave Dee, Dozy, Beaky, Mick and Tich attempting to cover a track from Captain Beefheart's *Safe As Milk* – was shelved in favour of a new Marc Bolan composition.

That song was 'Desdemona', the nearest thing to a hit single the band ever committed to tape.

The prospects for John's Children were now looking good. They had a potential hit in the can; had purchased the Bluesette club in Leatherhead, allegedly on the proceeds of the American success of 'Smashed Blocked' (though Napier-Bell cannot recall any money finding its way back from White Whale into the group's account); their new record label, which had been launched with the Jimi Hendrix Experience's 'Purple Haze' (itself enough to tempt Bolan into the fold), was enthusiastic about the group; and they had a brief but prestigious short promotional tour of Germany scheduled for April with label-mates the Who.

Although drummer Chris Townson was the only technically competent band member, eyebrows were raised when Marc plugged in the Gibson SG he had purchased from Trevor White, guitarist with another Leatherhead-based band the A-Jaes. From his first rehearsal, held as usual at the Bluesette (by this time retitled the John's Children club), it was obvious that John's Children with Marc Bolan wasn't necessarily a musical advance on the old line-up. To compensate for his inadequacy on a solid-bodied guitar, Bolan's distinctive, almost percussive rhythm style was rendered almost unrecognisable at the volume he chose to play at; but he wasn't simply masking incompetence. The Who had Pete Townshend, the Experience was led by Jimi Hendrix, and now John's Children had Marc Bolan. In a typical gesture, he detected the most obvious manifestation of what he aspired to be and homed in on it. In this case – to be an electric guitar hero – the required device was volume.

With the amps turned up full blast, Marc Bolan didn't think it mattered if his guitar was slightly out of tune. Chris Townson disagreed, and tuned it up when Bolan wasn't around. One day, he was caught doing so and was severely reprimanded. 'He found it insulting and unnecessary,' says Townson. 'With Marc in the band, we'd swapped a little chinky noise for a huge indistinguishable blurge. There was no way that John's Children could ever get a feel or tick. It was just a manic thrash.'

Bolan's ego, partially bruised by the failure of three consecutive solo singles, was on the mend. He continued to write songs at an alarming rate, but he was less eager to return to the stage. Before making his concert début with John's Children at a hall in Watford, he got totally drunk. To make matters worse, the band were told to stop playing after two songs, and Marc broke down and cried. Once again, his rock 'n' roll dream had been rudely awakened by an unmitigated disaster. Things improved in the weeks leading up to the start of the German tour early in April, though Marc continued to quell his nerves with a bottle of wine until matters came to a head one night when he was advised to go out stone cold sober.

His social integration into John's Children also came slowly. The on-stage lunacy wasn't just an act for Andy, Chris and John, who pursued a vigorous social life, chasing women, clubbing in Soho after recording sessions round the corner at Spot Studios in Bruton Street and engaging in wild nights at the Lotus House restaurant in Edgware Road. 'Marc sometimes joined in,' says Andy, 'although when we were on the road, I remember him staying in the car and writing in one of the notebooks he used to carry round with him. Generally, he was quiet, very shy and rather nervous. We had to force him to be a nutter on stage, and eventually he got into it, going over the top with his chains and playing the guitar above his head.'

The idea of Marc Bolan being some kind of reluctant showman is somewhat incongruous, and this period of pre-concert trepidation didn't last long. But, in a sense, Marc was holding something back. He was unwilling to subsume the whole Marc Bolan into one quarter of John's Children and, by remaining slightly aloof, he was still able to envisage his own destiny without having to depend on others. He made no bones about it, telling *New Musical Express* writer Keith Altham that, 'Although I still hope to record independently as a solo artist, as far as this group is concerned Andy is the lead and sings on the discs.'[2] Joining this potentially successful band just days earlier had done nothing to quell his burning ambition to succeed in his own right.

Maintaining this sense of apartness unsurprisingly extended into the realm of visual styles. Marc only partially adhered to John's Children's striking all-white image, and continued to break the rules by wearing T-shirts with embroidered motifs, and draping scarves or cravats around his neck. His newly fringed hair fell into line with the rest of the group's, but this style had been suggested by Simon Napier-Bell prior to Marc's joining, and had been captured in a session by photographer Gered Mankowitz. Although John's Children's stage act owed much to the violent example of the Who, Kit Lambert's enthusiasm for them, now that Bolan was writing the songs, outweighed any common sense calculations about the potentially disastrous consequences of billing both acts together. He was soon to be disappointed on both counts.

The April 1967 tour of Germany turned, somewhat inevitably, into a battle of the bands. Reports of the first couple of nights filtered back to the UK music press in the form of a letter from an outraged English serviceman stationed in Germany, who caught the tour in Düsseldorf. He described John's Children as 'the most atrocious excuse for "entertainment" I have ever seen . . . the lead guitarist kicked his equipment, beat the stage with a silver chain, and sat in a trance between his speakers producing deafening sounds on his guitar. It was sickening . . . Britain was shamed on that stage!'[3] Bolan, the offending guitarist, had obviously settled in, and had joined in the fun by manufacturing his own stage prop. He purchased a pair of folding vanity screens from a junk shop, coverd them in silver foil and stood them in front of his amplifier. The idea was to reflect the sound so that he could produce piercing feedback – and, by all accounts, it seemed to work. Unfortunately, he got carried away during the early stages of the tour and the sound reflector screens were destroyed.

The group's almost immature appetite for destruction aggravated the Who. In terms of material and musicianship, John's Children paled when held up against their peers, but the sheer unpredictability of their performance made them a difficult act to follow. Determined to get his share of fun out of rock 'n' roll, Simon Napier-Bell encouraged the group to push their stage act to the limits, and had imported some Jordan amps and speakers – the loudest equipment available – in a bid to upstage their rivals. Andy Ellison remembers one night when the Who asked to borrow the John's Children backline and drum-kit and then proceeded to demolish it. Keith Moon did untold damage to Chris's drums, but the sturdily built Jordan gear proved invincible, even to Pete Townshend's well-practised amp-ramming tactics.

Relations rapidly deteriorated between the two groups, and Kit Lambert warned Napier-Bell before the Ludwigshafen concert that John's Children's antics created a highly charged atmosphere among the crowd, which made it difficult for the Who to play. Napier-Bell's response was to encourage his boys further – with near-catastrophic results. 'Kit told me, "If they do that again, they're off the tour'',' he remembers. 'I thought, if we don't do it, there's no point in being on the tour, and if we do it, we're off. So let's do it.'

That decision cost Simon Napier-Bell in the region of £25,000 in terms of lost equipment – and with it his dream of making John's Children successful. The group arrived home weeks before the release of 'Desdemona', their first single with Marc, but they all cite Ludwigshafen as the turning point in the band's fortunes. 'They came back from the tour and Marc never played anything else with John's Children,' says Napier-Bell. 'By that time, the relationship with Kit and Track Records had soured, we'd lost the equipment, I'd wrecked my car, and I don't think they even recorded again.'

There can be no greater testament to the devastating effect of the German tour than that all those involved seem to suffer from a collective amnesia about the events immediately following it. In fact, Bolan didn't bow out on the band's return to Britain. He appeared with John's Children at the 14-Hour Technicolor Dream benefit concert at Alexandra Palace on 29 April, and made a final appearance with them at the John's Children club on 19 May. They also released 'Desdemona' to a publicity fanfare that put the group on the cover of *New Musical Express* and in record shops for signing sessions. In May, they recorded a follow-up, 'Midsummer Night's Scene', which was pencilled in for a July release.

While on tour, Marc had written to his girlfriend Terry enthusing about the trip. In a letter dated 13 April 1967, he wrote, 'the tour's going OK. The Who are a drag but we were going down quite good . . . we were out-playing the Who in most shows . . . ' It also bore many of the usual Bolan trademarks – poems, prose and drawings, all dedicated to Terry. Other letters revealed a more effusive style. 'I love you my sweetness lover,' he wrote in one, a sheet of paper adorned with hackneyed hearts pierced with the love arrow. 'I see with my eyes your facial un-tai clinic face & I'll desolve [sic] happy as a sandgirl into your belli & remember YOU ARE MY ANGEL love Marc xxxxxxxx.' If you take the sexual metaphor at face value, Marc may still have been confused about his sexuality, but the rest of the band remember Terry as his regular companion throughout this period.

By the time of the Alexandra Palace all-nighter, a couple of weeks after the tour, Marc's attitude had changed considerably. 'It was all a bit of an anticlimax,' says Chris Townson. 'There was definitely something odd going on by then. Marc didn't play at all that night. He was there, but he didn't play. He plugged in, let his guitar feed back, and wandered around the stage with it on his head. I pounded out a beat on the bass drum, occasionally throwing bits of the kit around. I don't think we even pretended to play any numbers: it was minimal even by our low standards. That performance was the equivalent of throwing buckets of paint around. We did that using noise.' The response from the audience was in marked contrast to the *Sieg Heiling* and acts of violence they had encountered in Germany. The 14-Hour Technicolor Dream concert was London's first major hippie event where thousands congregated to celebrate the 'anything goes' spirit of 1967.

Another guitarist went on stage that night and behaved in much the same way as Bolan did. Pink Floyd, whose reputation among the fast-blooming underground was second to none, beat a hasty retreat after just three or four numbers, when they realised that their guitarist, singer and chief songwriter, Syd Barrett, wasn't going to touch his instrument. It is quite possible that Marc had seen Syd's performance earlier that evening and decided to follow his example. His future wife June Child has said many times that he adored the Floyd front man, and one of Andy Ellison's final memories of the Bolan-era John's Children is of the group sitting round a jukebox listening to endless plays of 'The Scarecrow', the B side of Pink Floyd's 'See Emily Play' single.

Appearing at Alexandra Palace may have been an opportunist attempt to court a new freaky crowd, but it was obvious that the band's desire to succeed had waned. It was unfortunate because 'Desdemona', released in May, was their most likely opportunity to find success, but again, this tendency to shoot themselves in the foot was accompanied by mitigating circumstances. The song's lyric, or at least the phrase 'Lift up your skirt and fly' (which Marc claimed was an innocent evocation of a witch clambering onto a broomstick), proved too risqué for the BBC, and despite picking up airplay on pirate radio, 'Desdemona' was never going to emulate Hendrix's 'Purple Haze' and the Who's 'Pictures Of Lily' and make it three consecutive Top Five hits for Track Records.

'Desdemona' was a relative failure, but it marked an important step in the development of Bolan's songwriting style. Unlike the three-chord trick employed on his earlier pop material, or the tentative finger-picking on the Napier-Bell sessions, it hinged around a single chord which moved up a key at the beginning of each verse. It was tightly structured, contained more hooks than he had previously used, and was the first of Marc's songs to evoke the music of his fifties' idols, in this instance Gene Vincent's 'Rollin' Danny'. It was also the most professional-sounding record of John's Children's career. 'Desdemona' conformed perfectly to the scenario envisaged by Napier-Bell when he had first introduced Bolan into the band. Andy Ellison took the lead vocal, complete with Marc's cherished references to Paris, youth, and exotically named artists (on this occasion, Toulouse-Lautrec), while Marc piped up during the chorus answering Ellison's invocation of the song's subject with his own 'De-de-de-Desdemonaaah'. It was a notable interjection, providing a much-needed touch of exoticism to the band's usual cluttered wall-of-sound, as was his brief burst of pseudo-Hendrix-isms during the guitar break, which was an acutely restrained piece of mayhem.

Had the single succeeded, John's Children could well have become England's answer to the Velvet Underground. Featuring a lyricist with literary pretensions, musicians who liked to (or couldn't help but) flout the rules, a producer who paid scant attention to achieving anything like a clean, regular sound, and a stage show that was as much about visuals as it was music, the John's Children attitude was in marked contrast to the infatuation with technique which had begun to seduce rock musicians. The difference was that the Velvets' rock 'n' roll excursions were knowing flirtations with form, drawing from John Cale's extensive knowledge of avant-garde music and Lou Reed's college grounding in literature. John's Children were in it for the fun and the fame. (Incidentally, touring American and British groups operated on an exchange basis back in the sixties, and the two bands were coupled for one projected swap. *New Musical Express* reported a week-long visit by 'psychedelic leader' Andy Warhol and the Velvet Underground, who were scheduled to appear at the Alexandra Palace all-nighter, with John's Children flying out to the States on 4 September for a week-long tour. As it turned out, neither group – excepting a phoney Velvets' line-up – ever made the crossing.)

BBC Radio may have taken exception to half a dozen words in the group's latest single, but they still invited John's Children to record a four-song session for *Saturday Club*. If 'Desdemona', with its vastly improved production and tight performance, showcased a proficient John's Children working on the cusp of the beat-psychedelia crossover, this 17 June 1967 broadcast was a more accurate statement of the group's musical anarchy. Two of Marc's songs, 'The Perfumed Garden Of Gulliver Smith' and 'Hot Rod Mama', were coupled with the pre-Bolan 'Jagged Time Lapse', plus a cover of 'Daddy Rolling Stone' (popularised by the Who) thrown in for good measure. Marc's guitar remained blissfully out of tune throughout as he thrashed his way through the songs, letting Townshend-like power chords resonate over Townson's impressive drumming. Bolan overdubbed a second guitar track to the songs, but the atonal squeals and piercing single notes bore little trace of Hendrix's skill or Syd Barrett's intuition. The version of 'Hot Rod Mama', featuring Bolan and Ellison on alternate verses, reinforces the belief today that John's Children were nothing less than Britain's premier garage band.

The radio session was probably Marc's last recording with John's Children, but there is a memorable coda to his time with the group which, he later claimed, precipitated his departure. 'Midsummer Night's Scene', a title that neatly encapsulated Bolan's desire to become a rock 'n' roll Shakespeare, was readied for release in July and a few dozen copies had been pressed for distribution among the group's followers at their club in Leatherhead. But despite the aural advances achieved on 'Desdemona', 'Midsummer Night's Scene' marked a return to the muffled cacophonies created by Simon Napier-Bell back in the days of 'Smashed Blocked' and *Orgasm*, and the group weren't happy with the finished record. Bolan always maintained that the basic track was fine, and insisted that when the band left the studio, 'All of us were in tears because we knew we had a Number One record. We were so happy. Next day, we went back into the studio and listened to it, and the guy who was producing had totally destroyed the song, so much so that I walked out and never came back.'[4]

There is an element of fantasy in Marc's explanation. The sound was poor, but no one else recalls any big bust-up over it. Anyway, Marc's commitment to John's Children had been on the wane ever since they returned from Germany. The parting of the ways probably came peacefully and gradually, with him slowly drifting out of the picture, though the apocryphal tale obviously appealed to Marc's compulsive sense of drama.

Rhythmically, 'Midsummer Night's Scene' contained the slightly awkward, plodding feel that was to be expected as the band tentatively sought to break out of the basic pop format. No one instrumentalist was prepared to anchor the song, and its individual parts were as disparate as on any purportedly mainstream rock record made before or since. Even Beatles producer George Martin, who created works of art from a band who – on the evidence of their *Let It Be* jams – couldn't improvise their way out of a paper bag, would have been stretched by this eccentric opus. The 'petals and flowers' vocal refrain lost time with each successive verse, Marc jettisoned rock 'n' roll guitar in favour of freaky fretboard fun with a bottleneck, while Townson's manic percussive flurries gave Keith Moon a run for his money. (During John's Children's lean, post-Ludwigshafen period, Townson deputised for the injured Moon on a few British Who dates.) As if to prove the confused claustrophobia of the A side wasn't an accident, there was more of the same on the flip. 'Sara Crazy Child', another Bolan original, also lacked the economical approach and the commercial appeal of 'Desdemona', with Marc again using his guitar decoratively rather than rhythmically, eliciting strange, piercing, single notes that paid no respect to the key of the song. Unfortunately, 'Midsummer Night's Scene' was cancelled before any more copies were pressed (it is now one of the most sought-after records ever released in Britain). In its place the Bolan-less John's Children substituted the A side with a new version of 'Remember Thomas A'Beckett', which had previously been coupled with 'Desdemona', retitling it 'Come And Play With Me In The Garden'. The remaining trio appeared naked behind some strategically placed flowers for the publicity shots, but once again, the only real effect of the hype was to boost advertising revenue.

John's Children reshuffled in the wake of Bolan's departure, bringing in an old friend Chris Coville on drums, with Townson switching to guitar. The group returned to Germany, where they played the Star club in Hamburg and appeared on television, but new internal tensions developed between John and Chris, which came to a head in a particularly angry confrontation at the Flamingo club in Redruth, Cornwall. Chris Townson finally walked out. Simon Napier-Bell maintained his interest in Andy Ellison's career for a while, where the spectre of Marc Bolan – already apparent on John's Children's reworking of 'Mustang Ford' for an October 1967 single – continued to shadow the singer's work. Neither Ellison nor Napier-Bell could get on with the musical climate of the late sixties, and both dropped out of the music industry for several years.

'One day,' recalls Chris Townson, 'Simon, Marc and I played a game in the back of the Bentley after we'd broken down in a German town. I was Marc's manager and Simon was the big record company magnate, and I had to convince Simon that this new protégé of mine was going to be a big star. It was a funny idea for a game. I remember us all doing it in Jewish accents. But Marc really took off.

'I "introduced" him to Simon and then we both just sat back and listened as Marc outlined everything he was going to do, and it was the truth. He had the confidence to come out with it because it was all in the context of a game, but it was obvious that, to him, it was serious play. It struck me then that he knew exactly what he wanted and where he was going. I remember thinking that it sounded completely feasible.'

Townson was right. Bolan did know exactly what he wanted, but developments in rock music were happening at such a fast pace that he was unsure of the best means to attain it. He knew John's Children had outlived its usefulness, and he had learned some very important lessons during his stay with the band. He had also grown in confidence, both as a songwriter and performer. Perhaps too much so. His first instinct now was not to pursue the solo career he had bragged about to Keith Altham three months earlier. Buoyed by his experiences, he now wanted to front his own band, over which he could exercise complete control. On 11 June 1967, the following advert appeared in *Melody Maker*. 'Freaky lead guitarist, bass guitarist and drummer wanted for Marc Bolan's new group. Also any other astral flyers like with cars, amplification and that which never grows in window boxes. Phone WIMBLEDON 0697. 9 a.m.–3 p.m.'

Loaded with coded references to the hippie movement, the advert inevitably yielded a few hopeful travellers. In the meantime, though, Bolan continued to work with Simon Napier-Bell, and that same month recorded 'The Lilac Hand Of Menthol Dan' at Advision. Known to John's Children as 'Dan The Sniff', this song occasionally found its way into the band's live shows, complete with much demonstrative sniffing into the microphones. Bolan's version, his first completed new solo recording since the aborted 'Jasper C. Debussy', gave full reign to what was increasingly becoming known as his 'Larry the Lamb' voice, particularly noticeable as he pleaded 'Dan, Dan, Dan, you don't understand' in each chorus. It was a nonsensical song that once again celebrated a male character, which could easily have been himself – a cautious person 'with the face of an angel and the mind of a man', who moved from his monastic cell, fell into 'the art of truth' and understood everything. It sounded very much like someone who had made the trip from Summerstown to 'Subterranean Homesick Blues'. Musically, it ranged from the rock 'n' roll style opening that was a direct lift from Eddie Cochran's 'Something Else', to a guitar break that brought to mind the impassioned playing of Janis Joplin's backing band, Big Brother and the Holding Company.

'Menthol Dan' remained in the vaults, while Marc rehearsed his new band – in public. 'He got this gig at the Electric Garden in Covent Garden,' recalls Napier-Bell, 'and I think it was on the Wednesday night of the same day that his advert in *Melody Maker* appeared. I asked him where he was going to rehearse, and he said, "Who needs a rehearsal when you know you've got the right musicians." At three o'clock he was auditioning; by five o'clock he had the musicians, including drummer Steve Peregrine Took and pipe-smoking guitarist Ben Cartland, and by eight o'clock they left to make their début. I refused to go.

'From what I heard, the gig was just what you'd imagine it to be like – five people who'd never played together before, together on stage with no songs. It was a disaster. The experience wrecked his ego for ever. He came straight back from that gig and said he would never use an electric instrument again. He was booed off and thrown out. Marc always had this fantasy that things just happened, and if you got it right, things would come together without any effort. But he hadn't even picked good musicians. He only chose those who looked good or who had interesting names.'

This notorious concert is still shrouded in mystery, not least because all of the stories passed down over the years have come from Simon Napier-Bell who wasn't even there. The existence of archive posters seems to indicate that it did take place, but over a month later, in mid-July. There is a possibility that the line-up made a preliminary appearance at the noted underground venue UFO the night before.

Three months earlier, in mid-March, Marc encountered a musician who not only looked good and had an interesting name, but also appealed to his craving for the exotic and the unusual. On the way home from Germany, John's Children had taken a scenic diversion through Luxembourg and ended up at a concert in the capital city's town hall. 'It was a Ravi Shankar performance of Indian music,' remembers Napier-Bell, 'which was an incredible contrast to what we'd just experienced on the John's Children tour. This man played to a hushed, reverential audience in the simplest of ways imaginable – seated on a carpet and surrounded by joss sticks which filled the air with a pungent smell. That really tripped Marc's mind. I think, from that moment on, he realised that's what he should be doing. But he did give it one more try with that electric gig before he went the whole Ravi Shankar way.'

# CHAPTER SIX

'You'll laugh at this but I left John's Children because I
thought they were getting too commercial.'
Marc Bolan to Spencer Leigh, 1976

'Nowadays, people consistently ignore the hippie thing about
the group in the early days. Tyrannosaurus Rex was a
completely different concept from what T. Rex is now. I
guess for a while Marc was a good hippie. Like, we used
to sit around and rap about what needed changing.'
Steve Peregrine Took, *New Musical Express* magazine, 1972

'Marc wasn't a hippie. Most hippies practised free love and
took a lot of drugs like acid. He abhorred drugs in those
days, and he certainly wasn't into free love. He was a mod
dressed up as a hippie.'
Tony Visconti

Marc Bolan hungrily absorbed many ideas and influences during
his life. Some, like his devotion to Bob Dylan and his compulsive
need to invent and inhabit fantasy worlds, were deeply felt;
others were whims to satiate the perennial quest for novelty. All,
however, were put to good use in the hope of achieving his
ultimate goal – stardom.

That concept sat uneasily with the hippie movement which
blossomed during 1967. In many ways, the hippie idea was an
extension of the Romantic disposition which, in pop terms, had
been prompted by Bob Dylan's arrival from the folk margins.
Dylan had shown pop stars, both actual (the Beatles, the Rolling
Stones) and aspiring (Donovan, Marc Bolan), that the commercial
medium of popular music was a valid vehicle for social comment
and for unique personal expression too. Now, by 1967, the form
– not to mention the medium itself – was being stretched further
as a new post-Beatles, post-Rolling Stones, post-Dylan generation
of musicians looked beyond the simple three-minute pop song.

This tendency towards new musical freedoms was a reflection of the growing sense of social liberation, and the hierarchical star system to which Marc Bolan aspired began to look decidedly uncool.

Since he started writing his own material in 1965, Marc had seen his songs in terms of genuine personal expression rather than as pure pop cant. His position as part of the manufactured, manager-led John's Children was always ambiguous; by the summer of 1967 it had become untenable. With Napier-Bell rapidly losing interest, the rest of the band demoralised by the loss of their equipment, and with the failure of 'Desdemona', it was obvious that the group wasn't going to provide a launching-pad to instant stardom. Marc had little to lose by pursuing a new direction. Within weeks, he re-emerged clutching a beat-up acoustic guitar, joined by a long-haired, bongo-wielding partner who called himself Steve Peregrine Took.

Took was a year younger and had no experience of the music industry when he responded to Marc's advert in the music press. Before he changed his name shortly after meeting Bolan, he had been Stephen Porter, born in the south east London suburb of Eltham on 28 July 1949. Unlike his new colleague, Porter had not enjoyed a gregarious and self-assured childhood. Eczema and asthma, conditions which are both related to a nervous disposition, plagued his youth and, predictably, the schoolboy with the bandages soon attracted the cruel taunts of 'leper'. He found solace by withdrawing into his own world, and his happiest childhood moments were spent leafing through animal books and inventing stories for the younger children in his street. Stephen was dealt a further blow when his father left home, leaving his mother to fend for him and his brother, a traumatic event that contributed further to his growing introspection.

When Porter gravitated towards the emerging hippie scene after leaving school, he was at last able to rejoice in the sense of apartness that had once been unwelcomely foisted upon him. Growing his hair long, dressing in fashionable silks and velvets, and changing his name to Steve Peregrine Took (after one of the central characters in Tolkien's *The Lord of the Rings* trilogy) endeared him to Bolan and the pair spent much of the summer together. Marc, too, had let his hair grow, and had exchanged his white John's Children clothes for second-hand girls' school blazers and crumpled, loose-fitting trousers. This was all part of the prevailing 'culture of poverty' ethic, which was in marked contrast to what had motivated the aspirant Mark Feld during the early sixties. The ideal hippie was very much the inverse of the classic mod – anti-materialist, anti-urban and anti-social. Instead, the counter-cultural 'freak' celebrated a pre-industrial order: the unspoilt countryside, mystical sites, stories and experiences, personal communication, and creative rock – as opposed to commercial pop – music.

Marc Bolan played the part to perfection. He had begun to grow his hair into a massed crown of corkscrew ringlets, conjuring up visions of Medusa, the beautiful Gorgon sister of Greek classical mythology. With dark curls cascading around his face, the emphasis shifted from the assured jaw-line to his cutie-bow Theda Bara lips, large eyes and broad smile. His short stature only served to emphasise the impression of an elf that had walked straight off the pages of a children's story. The late sixties' Marc Bolan was, suitably, a picture of wide-eyed innocence and beautifully androgynous with it.

Right from the start of his recording career, with songs like 'The Wizard' and 'Beyond The Risin' Sun', Bolan had dealt with the kind of imagery that now threatened to become over-used. Donovan provided a much more immediate, quintessentially British influence on Bolan than Dylan could. Although Marc's 'The Wizard' was a very early example of pop mysticism, it was Donovan who had pioneered the interest in myth and legend among pop musicians, although his songs were more firmly steeped in the folk tradition than Bolan's ever were. Donovan cites the interaction between the popularising of the Celtic ballads and the art school sensibility as providing a firm foundation for the British hippie movement. 'Many of us saw ourselves as painters and artists, and we dressed ourselves in our dreams,' he says. 'The interest in the ballad tradition seemed quite natural because it was in direct contrast to the materialistic world that we grew up in. I think we were searching for our own indigenous religion, which is Celtic, but which had disappeared in the face of the Christian teachings. We looked to the East, because we felt that we could enter the secret world only through meditation, which wasn't taught in the West.' It was a secret world in which Marc Bolan also liked to believe.

In turning his back on chauffeur-driven cars and the endless search for a hit single, Bolan homed in on a cult hippie audience willing to celebrate the strange, and open to the simplicity of an acoustic, mystical style, similar to that pioneered by Donovan. The post-John's Children Electric Garden concert had suggested that his first choice was to front an electric band in the mould of the Who, the Jimi Hendrix Experience or perhaps an underground act like Syd Barrett's Pink Floyd or Tomorrow. Its reception proved that this was beyond his capabilities. Nevertheless, the underground's openness to new sounds and styles meant that Bolan could take control of his destiny once more, play his songs without having to compromise with managers or multiple band members, and do so without any great expense. The value of his acoustic guitar and Took's bongos barely exceeded the price of a cab into the West End.

This dramatic turnaround from would-be pop idol to laid-back hippie musician placed additional strain on Marc's relationship with his manager Simon Napier-Bell, who failed to share his enthusiasm for the trappings of hippie culture. He has his own reasons as to why Marc's transformation occurred. 'Initially, I was surprised,' he says, 'because I knew what he really wanted. Everything he did as a hippie was not what he wanted, but he didn't want to make a fool of himself again, like that Electric Garden gaffe. He sensed that the hippie attitude, which was totally prevalent then, would not accept a glossy rock star, and because that had become the flavour of the day, he was going to have to go with it. It was obvious to him that becoming a hippie was the right thing to do.'

It probably wasn't quite such a cynical decision. The trappings and the collective interests of the hippies were an extension of the Romantic quest Marc had been pursuing since encountering that personal crisis back in 1963 and 1964. In his eyes, hippie culture provided the perfect meeting-place of the flamboyant fashions and intellectual aspirations that had dominated his teenage life.

Even Marc's return to an acoustic style presented no problem – after all that was his forte – but he wanted to retain a harder stylistic edge that would avoid him being miscast as a meek and humble folkie. His pop-star looks and defiantly untraditional voice were obvious pointers towards something that reached far beyond the beer-and-sandwiches circuit, and to hammer the wedge home he chose the name Tyrannosaurus Rex. According to the books he shared with Harry back in Stoke Newington, this most terrifying dinosaur of all destroyed anything and everything that got in its way. That sounded powerful enough. Marc had a stockpile of songs, and once Steve had been familiarised with the material, Tyrannosaurus Rex were soon ready to record. Napier-Bell booked the duo into the studios for two sessions, one with an unknown bass player and Marc's girlfriend Terry in attendance. The songs recorded ranged from slimmed-down versions of material John's Children had been using ('Sara Crazy Child', 'Hot Rod Mama', 'Sally Was An Angel', 'Lunacy's Back' and 'Jasper C. Debussy'); 'Rings Of Fortune', 'Highways' and 'Beyond The Risin' Sun' from the Decca era; and the hitherto unheard 'One Inch Rock', 'Sleepy Maurice' and 'The Beginning Of Doves'. The sessions blueprinted the basic Tyrannosaurus Rex sound that was vigorously pursued for the next couple of years.

Although Bolan's speaking voice had by now substituted East End laziness for a softer, more cultured tone, he made little pretence at maintaining perfect diction when he sang. Instead, he punctuated his slurred, poetic lines with the occasional lapse into Hollywood-inspired Bronx-speak ('at da time') and plenty of in-fill as the voice took on the role of a solo instrument ('da-da-da da-da-da-da') with a whole host of bleating, childlike interjections. There was little trace of the ersatz Dylan of the Decca recordings, give or take the odd lyrical scan on 'One Inch Rock'. In its place was a preciously cultivated vocal style which was so strongly foregrounded that any 'message' Bolan may have sought to convey was hopelessly lost – not that it mattered much. It was the remarkable strangeness of his voice that did his talking for him.

The flurry of bongo beats and handclaps, the drone of panpipes and whistles, and the richness of an occasionally struck gong, coupled with a guitar-style that now flirted with Eastern scales, created a spontaneous-sounding backdrop perfectly suited to Bolan's endless lyrical romps through fairylands peopled with a series of unlikely characters. It was the flight from the cerebral hemisphere manifesting itself as the human voice which captivated John Peel who, for the next four years, became Marc's most vociferous supporter. 'I liked Tyrannosaurus Rex initially because I've always been drawn to extreme voices,' he says, 'and I really liked the noise of Marc's "Larry the Lamb" stuff. I also liked the lyrics which read terribly, but when they were sung, took on another dimension. You could only ever pick up the odd isolated word.'

At the time of his first meeting with Marc Bolan, Peel was still broadcasting his late-night *Perfumed Garden* show from the *Galaxy*, home of the off-shore pirate station Radio London. His reputation as the DJ of the underground won him a committed audience, and a postbag which contained its fair share of strange mail. One envelope, marked 'To John Peel at the *Perfumed Garden*', and decorated with what looked like a child's drawing of a castle, promised no more than the familiar 'Thanks for playing . . . ' response, which gave him the strength to continue during those lonely all-night shows. However, it was to spark off a close friendship, during which time the fortunes of the correspondents were to change dramatically.

> John. *Thanks* for playing Hippy Gumbo, it gave me a real high knowing you turned on to it. I did a session on Monday night and we (tyrannosaurus rex = steve porter on tablas and assorted auxilliary) are diping our hearts in the sounds and trying to xtend our musical hi over the twitchy hangups
> of the *hard* world and get the communication of a BE IN into everything we do. The twelve things we did are for White Whale in the States and are being put out in late September
> – its a real heart hang up about *The Garden* vanishing but it really is a bopping concern. Thanks again for coming thru' for hippy and I'd truly like to talk or turn on or something. I'm on the phone at WIM 0697 so maybe we'll talk.
> So long keep hi
> Truly   Mark bolan

In fact, there were no plans to release the Tyrannosaurus Rex demos on White Whale: this was just typical Bolan exaggeration. So was the reference to 'turning on', because most of Marc's friends and associates from the late sixties remember him as one of the few long-hairs who didn't have an abiding interest in drugs. He rarely took acid or smoked, and with only Simon Napier-Bell able to recall some casual drug-taking, it is likely that – together with references to 'Be-Ins', which took place in the psychedelic centre of the universe in San Francisco – Bolan was heavily laying on his counter-culture credentials. In the polarised climes of 1967, you were either on or off, in or out. Marc was keen to prove that he was both turned on and tuned in.

The pair met when Peel returned to London and, discovering that they shared similar hippie culture ideals and an unquenching thirst for old Gene Vincent and Eddie Cochran 45s, they struck up an immediate friendship. Marc gave John Peel some acetates and ensured that he had a complete collection of his recorded work to date, and the enthusiastic DJ liberally sprinkled his final few Radio London broadcasts with examples of Bolan's work. On his very last show, which ran from 12.00 a.m.–5.30 a.m. in the early hours of 14 August 1967, he included no less than six Marc Bolan compositions: 'The Wizard' and 'Hippy Gumbo' solo singles, John's Children's 'Sara Crazy Child' and 'Desdemona', and two unreleased recordings from the first Tyrannosaurus Rex sessions, 'Rings Of Fortune' and 'Highways'. The closing down of the pirates signalled the end of an era, but with BBC producer Bernie Andrews earmarking Peel to present the *Top Gear* programme on the nation's new Radio 1 station, the change in the broadcasting law was a mixed blessing for both Peel and Bolan. The new Broadcasting Act effectively silenced the pirates, but state radio would guarantee a much wider audience for John Peel and the music he championed. Tyrannosaurus Rex was among its earliest beneficiaries.

Marc Bolan now moved in circles where the boundless energy and straight business-like manner of Simon Napier-Bell was regarded as distinctly unhip. 'There was no place for me in Marc's new world,' recalls his ex-manager. 'I told him that if you want to get gigs on the hippie circuit, you'd be better off without a manager. At first, he wanted me to call up and get the contract and the money sorted out, but I said, "I can't do that if you're going to sit on a prayer mat and play surrounded by joss sticks." It was an incredible feeling that swept through the country for a year or so.'

John Peel, then DJing at Middle Earth (previously known as the Electric Garden, site of Marc's electric shock), ensured that Tyrannosaurus Rex started appearing on the Friday and Saturday all-night bills. 'Trip softly with Denny Laine's Electric String Band, the Piccadilly Line, Tyrannosauras (sic) Rex and John Peel' ran one advert that autumn. The duo were certainly playing there by the end of September and were Middle Earth regulars for several months to come. This wasn't entirely down to John Peel's patronage: Marc had another champion from within. Jeff Dexter, his old mate from the Lyceum days, was another mod-turned hippie. 'I'd heard that Tyrannosaurus Rex were about,' he recalls, 'and I remember John talking about this incredible guy called

Marc Bolan. He said you gotta meet this guy. I was also MCing at Middle Earth by that time, but I think I met Marc in Hyde Park. We took one look at each other and it was like . . . aaaaarrghh! There was a slightly nervous reaction from him at first because he knew I was DJing all the underground live shows, but it was great to see him again. He wasn't busking that day, just standing around looking great. Pete Sanders, who I'd known from the Orchid Ballroom, Purley, was also there.

'A lot had happened since we'd last met, which had been in the audience at *Ready, Steady, Go!* a couple of years earlier. We'd all been chained up by all that competitive mod stuff and now we were freeing ourselves, blowing away the cobwebs. It was a totally different world, particularly after coming into contact with LSD, but I don't know how much Marc truly let himself go. I immediately assumed by his look that he was into the same thing, and I never realised until a few years later that he wasn't really into acid. Marc was very careful.

'I went back to Middle Earth and said to the owners, "You've got to see this band. They're great looking . . . old mates . . . " and he was on about two days later. I loved it because it was so different, although I found it difficult to come to terms with the idea of Marc singing. I was also a bit taken aback by the fact that this East London Face I'd known was now so wordy. He must have really worked at it, researching everyone else's lyrics and reading absolutely everything to find out what was going on. And he was into the spiritual path. We all were.'

Bolan was reading a lot, and in 1967, it was the fantasy worlds of C.S. Lewis and J.R.R. Tolkien, followed by the mystic poetry of Kahlil Gibran which nourished his capacity for escape. Yet when it came to pursuing his musical career, his mind would work in wonderfully practical ways, sniffing out deals and contacts like a psychedelic James Cagney. While Marc was still with John's Children, Simon Napier-Bell had taken him to see David Platz, head of Essex Music, the international music publishing company, which already had several deals going with Kit Lambert's Track label. Having watched him sign a publishing deal, leave John's Children and form Tyrannosaurus Rex all in the space of a couple of months, Kit Lambert began to question his own faith in Marc Bolan, whom he had envisaged as a big pop star in the way Cat Stevens had recently become. Like Simon Napier-Bell, Kit was equally perplexed by the acoustic hippieness

of Tyrannosaurus Rex so he sent for Joe Boyd, then running
Sound Techniques Studio in Chelsea.

Boyd had already worked with several of the top names
among the British underground, including Pink Floyd and the
Incredible String Band. The Floyd mixed cosmic instrumental
jams with short nonsense songs that were almost rock nursery
rhymes, and their influential début album, *The Piper At The Gates
Of Dawn* (a title chosen by Syd Barrett from a chapter heading in
Kenneth Graham's children's novel, *The Wind In The Willows*),
made a strong impression on Marc. Barrett's songwriting style
wasn't far removed from his own, snatching phrases, twisting
events and images to fit in with his own world-view seen, more
often than not, from the vantage point of a playpen. Ancient
wisdom, in the form of the *I Ching*, found its way into 'Chapter
24'; 'Mathilda Mother' invoked medievalism and 'The Scarecrow'
a charming rusticity, while 'The Gnome' simply told a story. The
similarities between the two were uncanny – and the affinity
could be stretched further. Both were dark-haired beauties, pin-
ups of the Aquarian Age; both exuded an air of untouchable
innocence; and both became transfixed by June Child. There was
one important difference. Within a year, Syd's diet of acid and
Mandrax had detached him from his pop responsibilities, and he
was quietly coerced out of Pink Floyd. Marc Bolan, meanwhile,
had no such distractions to knock him off course.

When Joe Boyd first met Took and Bolan, he remembers the
pair being keen Incredible String Band fans, although the producer admits that he was slightly condescending in his attitude
towards the pair. 'Marc seemed like someone who had decided
that being a hippie was the "in" thing, and switched from taking
black bombers to smoking good Afghan hash,' he suggests.
'There was no real conviction in his acoustic-ness. It was just a
musical change that went along with the change of drug and the
change of dress.' Despite some obvious similarities, any comparison with the Incredible String Band, a Scottish duo of multi-
instrumentalists with a profound feeling for indigenous folk and
music from around the world, would be unduly crude. Whereas
Bolan usually worked within the standard A/B/A/B pop song
format, the String Band wove intricate melodies around a progressive, linear A/B/C/D structure. The main point of reference
was the use of acoustic instruments not generally used in rock
(bongos, bells, toys) and the general aura of Eastern-tinged

exoticism. In months to come, Marc often invoked the Incredible String Band, if only to catch a ride on the tide of popularity created by the duo's 1967 album, *The 5000 Spirits Or The Layers Of The Onion*.

'The Incredible String Band approached their music on a much more deeply spiritual and intellectual level,' insists Joe Boyd. 'They came to the music via a genuine fascination for ethnic sounds, and there was a depth to their approach which I related to. Marc's approach was to take what were essentially pop tunes and play them in an acoustic, folksy way. It didn't have the musical signposts that I was looking for, but I have to confess that I saw the appeal and the potential there, even if I wasn't struck on the music.'

The String Band's Mike Heron agrees. 'I don't think our styles were ever that close,' he says. 'Although Tyrannosaurus Rex were acoustic, Marc's songs were always rock-orientated.'

Bolan and Took were invited round to Joe's flat, sat themselves down in front of the fire and proceeded to play their basic repertoire. Despire his reservations, Boyd was sufficiently intrigued to accept Lambert's commission and arranged to work with the pair at Sound Techniques. But Marc's and Steve's lack of any conventional musical ability worried him, so he called on ace session bassist Danny Thompson to provide an anchor. 'I think Marc seemed pretty unsure of what he wanted at that session,' maintains Thompson, 'though I was immediately struck by his nature, which was an endearing mix of gentleness and shyness together with an aura of confidence.' Perhaps the prospect of playing with a technically gifted musician made him feel insecure, but Bolan boldly informed Thompson that he had done his vocal training with the Westminster School Choir.

The session with Boyd and Thompson was taped and mixed in a single evening, and just one recording is known to survive from the liaison. This is 'Chateau In Virginia Waters', a gentle piece of lazy psychedelia awash with a swirling sound, created by the George Martin/Beatles trick of running the bass through a Leslie speaker. As John Peel has suggested, lines such as 'Her one rich wish is to write a book about/A Venetian mother's problems on a barge in Little Venice' didn't necessarily translate well on to the page, but Bolan's barely decipherable trill sent Peel raving about the demo in his column for *International Times*, the newspaper of the British underground. In his piece, the DJ also mentioned other songs recently recorded by Tyrannosaurus Rex for Track Records – 'Dwarfish Trumpet Blues', 'Child Star' and 'Highways' – which probably bears out Danny Thompson's recollection that several tracks were taped that evening. Boyd can only recall 'Chateau', although this may mean that it was the only one to make it to the mixing stage.

Boyd harboured hopes of establishing a working relationship with Track, but soon after the session, these fell through and Marc was obliged to hawk the acetate around with a view to getting a deal elsewhere. John Peel originally floated the idea of forming his Dandelion record label around this time and told *International Times* readers that if he had the cash, he'd sign Tyrannosaurus Rex immediately. He didn't get the backing, but Essex Music, Marc's publishers, stepped in and paid Boyd's studio bill as they had their own plans for Tyrannosaurus Rex. Peel did arrange a photographic session for the group late in the year with Ray Stevenson, who remembers seeing Tyrannosaurus Rex in concert at one of Peel's *Perfumed Garden* evenings at the Marquee. Bolan suggested Holland Park as a location, claiming that the painted *Magic Roundabout* figure of Dougal on a fence would provide an appropriate backdrop for the pictures. Marc, dressed in a striped blazer with collar upturned, hair furiously backcombed but not yet a dense mass of curls, stared directly into the camera, as Steve Took, looking towards him, fell straight into a secondary role. The group's internal politics were revealed at a stroke, but Bolan rejected the photos: he thought he looked too much like Bob Dylan. Turning his back on the ethos that had governed John's Children, he was determined to take firmer control over the sounds, images and politics of Tyrannosaurus Rex.

In the meantime, the group had received their first national exposure, again courtesy of John Peel, who had convinced *Top Gear* producer Bernie Andrews to feature them in a specially commissioned session – the first unsigned band to do so. On 30 October 1967, Bolan and Took recorded six songs for their trial broadcast, five of which went on the air on 5 November. Of the six, 'Child Star', 'Dwarfish Trumpet Blues' and 'Scenescof' (literally, 'to scoff at the scene' – Marc regarded any spoilers of his late sixties' idyll as scenescofs) were recent additions to Bolan's repertoire. When Marc made a live appearance on *Top Gear* during Peel's rebroadcast of the session weeks later, he described

his new character as 'a villain in all the songs', a relative of the
'people who are hung up with outward things' on 'Pictures Of
Purple People'. The BBC's selection panel inevitably sensed the
group's potential cult status, describing Tyrannosaurus Rex as
'very far out' and 'very way in', though one member was less
generous, calling it 'crap, and pretentious crap at that'. Nevertheless, he was in the minority, and with the immortal words 'OK
for *Top Gear*, I suppose', the group were passed for further sessions. By the time Marc heard the news by letter on 15 February
1968, Tyrannosaurus Rex had received an even bigger boost.
They had signed a record deal and had begun working on a
début album.


Brooklyn-born Tony Visconti began his musical career as one half
of the husband-and-wife harmony duo Tony and Siegrid, and
had been a songwriter/house-producer for the Richmond Organisation before producer Denny Cordell, on a scouting trip to the
States looking for an assistant, brought him over to England. It
was June 1967 and Procol Harum's 'A Whiter Shade Of Pale',
produced by Cordell, topped the British charts. Having established his reputation as a producer with the Moody Blues' 1964
hit 'Go Now', he was enjoying considerable success with Harum
as well as the Move. He had also established a unique relationship with Essex Music whereby, in exchange for the publishing
rights and copyright ownership of his New Breed productions,
Essex put up the money for his studio time.
   The relationship had been further cemented in July 1967,
when Cordell joined forces with Essex boss David Platz to form
the Straight Ahead/New Breed independent record production
company. Within a month, they had secured a deal with EMI,
commandeering the near-dormant Regal Zonophone label
(excepting the odd Salvation Army release) as an exclusive output
for Cordell's productions. These had previously been released
through Decca's Deram subsidiary, and one reason for the new
deal was Deram's Ken East's defection to EMI, and the fact that
he wished to take Cordell with him. Consequently, Procol Harum
and the Move ended up on Regal Zonophone, the oddball label
that would also provide a home for future Straight Ahead sign-
ings. Straight Ahead operated out of Essex Music's Dumbarton
House base in Oxford Street, with the main part of the building

concerned with music publishing and the smaller production company occupying a few rooms at the front. Denny Cordell, his new assistant Tony Visconti and secretary Richard Kerr shared a small office and it was their job to seek out and nurture new talent for the ambitious company.

Visconti's first job was to produce Manfred Mann's 'So Long Dad' single, but his real break came when he was asked to attend the Move's 'Flowers In The Rain' session. Just as it looked as if the song was going to be dropped, he suggested embellishing the track with a woodwind quartet. At once, spirits were raised and 'Flowers In The Rain' went on to become another massive hit for Straight Ahead.

In September 1967, while 'Flowers In The Rain' threatened to top the UK singles chart, Tony Visconti caught Tyrannosaurus Rex in concert at UFO, the leading haunt of the underground. 'I'd been working with Denny for a while,' recalls the producer, 'and he thought it was time I found my own group. It was my very first night of talent scouting, and I walked round the corner from Oxford Street into Tottenham Court Road where UFO was, and saw a poster for this group called Tyrannosaurus Rex. When I walked in, there were around three hundred people sitting around the stage in silence, watching this strange little person seated on the floor singing in what I thought to be something other than the English language.'

The producer was immediately mesmerised but, imagining the charismatic singer to be somewhat unapproachable, introduced himself to percussionist Steve Took. 'Marc gave off an air of being very precious, very special and powerfully charismatic. I fell in love with him. Whereas Steve just looked like a hippie, Marc resembled an exotic gypsy, with his curly hair, his tiny waistcoat, a tattered silk shirt and a scarf tied to his arm. Steve Took mumbled something about Marc being "the leader", so I finally approached him and said I'd like to work with him. "Oh, man, you're the eighth producer that's come up to me this week," he told me, in perfect English of course. "John Lennon came up to me last night." That was the first of many lies Marc told me!'

Undeterred, Visconti gave Bolan his number. When he arrived at the Straight Ahead offices the next morning, his telephone was already ringing. It was Marc Bolan. Visconti immediately invited the duo down to play for Denny Cordell. 'I told Denny about Marc's great voice and strange songs. I thought everything about them was extraordinary. An hour or two later, Marc and Steve showed up with the oriental carpet under their arm, the guitar with the missing peg on the G string and the bells, pixiephone and one-string fiddle. They did the entire set from the previous night, uninterrupted. Denny was agape and I just glowed with pride. As soon as Marc and Steve were out of the door, Denny said, "I don't understand them at all, but we'll sign them as our token underground group." '

Cordell then went to see David Platz. 'There was no question that it was Tony's enthusiasm that carried the day,' recalls the music publisher. 'My first impression of what Marc was doing was total uncertainty, but whatever convincing I needed was soon complete when I saw the audience reaction to him.

'I was also struck by his utter determination to succeed. He knew he would, but he put it across in a way that was completely disarming. It was absolutely charming. Most artists at the outset of their careers usually come across as rather shy and diffident, but that was never the case with Marc. I think that confidence had a lot to do with his later success. He was overjoyed at the signing and I remember him saying to me, in front of Tony and several other people, that he guaranteed he would stay with me for ever if I could make him successful. Of course, that didn't happen.'

Immediately before the deal with Platz and Cordell had been finalised, Tyrannosaurus Rex rehearsed their material with Tony Visconti at his flat at 108 Lexham Gardens, Earls Court, coinciden- tally just yards away from the rooms Marc once shared with Allan Warren. The producer, eager to make the most of his first major assignment, ran a two-track tape recorder so that he could familiarise himself with the material. The tape, which still exists, reveals that all the songs which eventually made their way onto the début album were already in place, although at this early stage, 'Hippy Gumbo', 'Lunacy's Back' and the evocatively titled 'Puckish Pan' were also being considered. Despite the income generated from a string of Move and Procol Harum hits, Straight Ahead Productions hedged its bets and offered Visconti and Tyrannosaurus Rex a minuscule budget of £400 – which gave them only four days in Advision Studios, where a brand-new eight-track recorder had recently been installed. This meant that any lavish production ideas envisaged by Visconti had to be scotched; only one track, 'Strange Orchestras' (topped and tailed with a bizarre vocal that conjured up sounds at a Punch-and-Judy show), sounded as if it had much time spent on it. Also recorded during the album sessions was one of Marc's most recent songs, 'Debora', which had been worked out in Visconti's flat and sung down the telephone to John Peel immediately afterwards. It was chosen to precede the album as the duo's first 45.

Tunes apparently inspired by women clogged up the charts in April 1968 – the Monkees' 'Valleri', the Hollies' 'Jennifer Eccles', Tom Jones' 'Delilah', Scott Walker's 'Joanna', and a couple of catch-alls in the Union Gap's 'Young Girl' and Bobby Goldsboro's maudlin ballad 'Honey'. 'Debora', the first official Tyrannosaurus Rex release, was an obvious choice for a single, though describing the subject's 'sunken' face as 'like a galleon' and as mysterious as the 'Spanish main' may not have immediately struck the right chord with the Debbies out there in Radioland. The song won some favourable reviews in the pop press, but the general feeling was summed up by *New Musical Express*, which concluded that it was 'All very clever and intricate – probably too complex to register.' This was quite a compliment for a producer who had hardly produced, a percussionist who had only recently taught himself to play, and a songwriter who rarely strayed beyond three chords on the guitar. In fact, 'Debora' was Bolan's songwriting at its best, giving the impression of being more musically intricate than it really was. Its structure, complete with oddly positioned verses, chorus and bridge, played tricks with the usual pop format and was one of his most ambitious constructions to date; and yet almost every line was a hook. Marc's habit of suspending the lyrical onslaught and breaking into pure vocal noise ('nah-nah nah-nah-naaah') was fast becoming a trademark, too. It maddened many listeners, but enough enjoyed its originality, or at least its obvious novelty appeal to take 'Debora' to within four places of the Top Thirty.

More BBC radio sessions on John Peel's *Top Gear* show promoted the cause: three were broadcast between March and May 1968, familiarising listeners with the bulk of the duo's forthcoming LP and giving a further plug for 'Debora'. It was hardly surprising when the album repeated the success of the single, elevating Tyrannosaurus Rex from Hyde Park buskers to moderately selling recording artists in a matter of months. By the end of July, it was outselling the latest albums by Pink Floyd and the

Jimi Hendrix Experience. The LP, from its wordy title (*My People Were Fair And Had Sky In Their Hair . . . But Now They're Content To Wear Stars On Their Brows*) to the children's story towards the end of the second side, struck a chord with the more precious inclinations of the British underground. John Peel, who narrated Marc's 'Woodland Story' about Kingsley Mole and Lionel Lark ('Marc probably thought he was doing me a favour by letting me recite that on the LP,' he says), contributed a sleeve note which recounted the group's brief history in flawless English hippie vernacular.

> Tyrannosaurus Rex rose out of the sad and scattered leaves of an older summer. During the hard, grey winter they were tended and strengthened by those who love them. They blossomed with the coming of spring, children rejoiced and the earth sang with them. It will be a long and ecstatic summer.

'The whole hippie thing had very little grasp of reality,' Peel explains, 'but I think Marc had more of a grasp of it than I did. I can't think of anybody alive who didn't: I was quite astonishingly naïve. We all wanted things to be true so much that people would blind themselves to a lot of what was really going on.' While Saigon was learning some truths about American democracy in practice, indigenous Rhodesians hanged as Ian Smith desperately clung onto minority white rule, and students and workers united to bring down the de Gaulle government in Paris, British alterna- tive society was flat on its back, fraying its jeans and frying its minds with a mixture of hallucinogenics, hash and hippie hedonism. Everything was Beautiful, at least to those wearing psychedelic blinkers.

Tyrannosaurus Rex epitomised the idyllic yearnings of the British underground which, more than its European or American counterparts, tended to look towards inner truth at the expense of material realities. The *My People* album was its perfect musical companion. The sleeve, painted by George Underwood, an old colleague of David Bowie's, garishly depicted Took and Bolan amid an underworld peopled with stock fantasy figures – gallop- ing horses, maidens with flowing, blonde hair and full breasts, bearded figures from antiquity, winged messengers and serpents, in their various shades of lilac, metallic blue and green. The song titles were spot on too – 'Afghan Woman', 'Weilder Of Words',

'Chateau In Virginia Waters', 'Dwarfish Trumpet Blues', each one an invitation to take flight from the straight world on a search for all things strange and wonderful.

If the overall sound was painfully thin (something Marc often complained about when the subject came up), the songs and arrangements were unique, even by the standards of 1968, when pure pop acts like Dave Dee, Dozy, Beaky, Mick and Tich, and the Herd were trying to sound 'weird'. But there was little improvisation or space to 'freak out', in the manner of contemporaries such as Pink Floyd, Cream or Hendrix, except for a short burst during 'Weilder Of Words', when Bolan issued forth an extended burst of baby-like wailing as the pair treated their respective instruments with a healthy disrespect. 'Hot Rod Mama' and 'Mustang Ford' (a title that must have its origins in Chuck Berry's 'My Mustang Ford' or Donovan's offer to 'buy you a Ford Mustang' in 'Hey Gyp', both from 1965), which opened each side, employed the basic three-chord trick, though the combination of Bolan's voice and Took's expanding inventory of percussion instruments (including a pixiephone, used to good effect on 'Scenescof') and inventive harmonies, belied the simplicity of the material. Rounded off with a sleeve dedication to the C.S. Lewis characters, 'Aslan and the Old Narnians', the album answered the hippies' need for an imagined, happy, innocent community, so much so that even Bolan found something to praise in fat Sheba, the odorous, gluttonous, meat-cleaver-wielding subject of one of the album's more gentle songs ('Graceful Fat Sheba').

'Do not adjust your record players,' wrote Allen Evans in *New Musical Express*. 'This is how Marc Bolan and Steve Peregrine Took sing – as if they are about to break out crying.' The press, if not always supportive, were intrigued, and by the middle of 1968, through the group's regular concert and radio appearances, most people involved in the pop business had at least become aware of Marc Bolan and Tyrannosaurus Rex. With Jeff Dexter, John Peel, and a young reporter/Peel protégé called Bob Harris on his side, Bolan's name had spread rapidly among the underground. Behind him was a powerful music publisher, a successful production company and, more recently, new management.

The days of playing the Middle Earth for free or for a nominal sum soon subsided once Tyrannosaurus Rex had established a marketable profile and, through Tony Visconti's connections, Bolan had managed to place the group with hip management

*Above left:* Private Mark Feld, victim of a tragic killing in 1946. A year later, Simeon and Phyllis named their second son after him. *(Private collection) Above right:* Bolan's parents, Simeon Feld and Phyllis Atkins, on their wedding day in January 1945. *(Private collection)*

*Above left:* Mark *(second row up, second from right)* pictured near his home during celebrations for the Queen's coronation in June 1953. His brother Harry is in the top row *(second from left)*. *(Private collection) Above right:* One of the earliest surviving pictures of the infant Mark Feld. *(Private collection)*

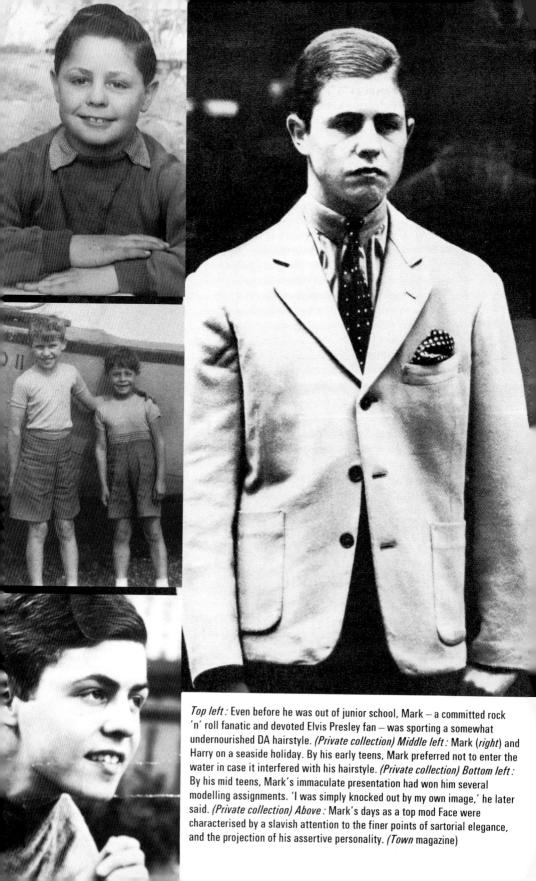

*Top left:* Even before he was out of junior school, Mark — a committed rock 'n' roll fanatic and devoted Elvis Presley fan — was sporting a somewhat undernourished DA hairstyle. *(Private collection) Middle left:* Mark (*right*) and Harry on a seaside holiday. By his early teens, Mark preferred not to enter the water in case it interfered with his hairstyle. *(Private collection) Bottom left:* By his mid teens, Mark's immaculate presentation had won him several modelling assignments. 'I was simply knocked out by my own image,' he later said. *(Private collection) Above:* Mark's days as a top mod Face were characterised by a slavish attention to the finer points of sartorial elegance, and the projection of his assertive personality. *(Town* magazine)

*Top left :* John's Children, spring 1967. The group inspired riots and gave Marc his first glimpse of pop stardom. *Left to right :* John Hewlett, Chris Townson, Andy Ellison, Marc Bolan. *(Private collection) Above :* Mark Feld, now Marc Bolan, pictured in November 1965 at the time of his first single, 'The Wizard'. *(David Wedgbury/Deram Group Records) Left.* Bolan formed Tyrannosaurus Rex in 1967 with Steve Peregrine Took (*left*) and quickly became a leading figure on the British underground circuit. *(Tyrannosaurus Rex Appreciation Society/ Ray Stevenson)*

*Top left.* Tyrannosaurus Rex pictured at the first Hyde Park festival in the summe of 1968. *(Tyrannosaurus Rex Appreciation Society/Ray Stevenson) Top right :* As the group's sound became more electric, bassist Steve Currie *(right)* was recruite to the line-up. *(Barry Plummer) Above :* Marc rejected this photograph, taken in the winter of 1967, because he thought he looked too much like Bob Dylan. *(Tyrannosaurus Rex Appreciation Society/ Ray Stevenson) Left :* By 1970, Bolan had found a new partner, Mickey Finn, and abbreviated the group's name to T. Re *(Barry Plummer)*

*Main picture:* Bolan was the architect of T. Rex and the newspapers were happy to project him as the first pop hero of the seventies. *Above:* 'T. Rextasy' reached a dramatic climax at the Empire Pool, Wembley concerts on 18 March 1972, where Bolan's exhibitionist tendencies reached new heights. *(Barry Plummer) Left:* The classic T. Rex line-up of Currie, Legend, Finn and Bolan, pictured during a 1971 television appearance. *(Barry Plummer)*

*Top left:* Mickey Finn (with camera) and Bolan, together with some snappily dressed EMI press plant workers. *(Barry Plummer) Above:* Bolan's warbling singing style, together with his cascade crown of corkscrew curls, made him a unique fi in pop. *(Barry Plummer) Left:* Elton John and Ri Starr, together with Marc at the première of the *Born to Boogie* film, on 14 December 1972. *(Ba Plummer)*

*Above:* T. Rexcessive: when the group returned to the British stages in January 1974, fans were shocked at Marc Bolan's physical transformation. *(Barry Plummer) Top left:* When girlfriend Gloria Jones gave birth to a son, Rolan Seymour Bolan, in September 1975, Marc was inspired to pull back from the excesses of the rock 'n' roll lifestyle and began to work at his career again. *(Barry Plummer) Middle left:* Tony Visconti with his first wife Mary Hopkin. As Bolan's producer between 1968 and 1973, Visconti's role was crucial to the success of Marc Bolan and T. Rex. *(Barry Plummer) Left:* By the time of the December 1972 T. Rexmas shows, Bolan was beginning to take more interest in the fruits of his success than in his guitar-playing. *(Barry Plummer)*

*Above :* Marc, pictured during a soundcheck on final T. Rex tour, where they were supported b Damned. *(Erica Echenberg) Top left :* Perhaps appropriately, Bolan resembled a faded movie glamour queen on his 1976 *Futuristic Dragon* t *(Barry Plummer) Middle left :* By the end of 19 the old mystic had resettled in London and had revived his creative juices once more. *(Barry Plummer) Left :* 'Listen, guys, I really *am* the Godfather of punk rock,' explains Marc to his look T. Rex in spring 1977. *From left to right :* Miller Anderson, Herbie Flowers, Bolan, Tony Newman and Dino Dines. *(Barry Plummer)*

company Blackhill Enterprises. Run by Pete Jenner and Andrew King, a pair of London Free School renegades who fused hippie sensibility with entrepreneurial acumen, Blackhill managed Pink Floyd and was in a formative stage of empire building. The pair had been to see the group perform a lunchtime concert at Ealing College, together with office helper June Child, and were impressed enough to invite Bolan back to the company's Alexander Street office in Westbourne Park. June Child was particularly spellbound.

Meanwhile, Marc's love affair with Theresa Whipman had blossomed over the months, and the bisexuality of his late teens apparently subsided as he consolidated his relationship with her. Terry coped well with Marc's occasional lapses into self-pity (at the end of 1967, he signed one card with love from 'a Christmas elf metamorphosed into a sad little flower'), and when they fought, he apologised with palpitating poetic flourishes. On 17 January 1968, he wrote to 'My Dearest Teresa':

Just the thought of your Torqauy smile + your ballerina body brings tears from so deep within me I qauke . . . I'm ever so sorry that we fight but all close people seem to have to endure them, a divine error or a purifacation for a blissful after life. I love you coz your unique Teresa of the childhood dancing nights, Truly Mark x

A second letter to Terry is somewhat more revealing:

Here's to the gates of my very own castle happy
where I'll live with foxes and ponys and my true love.
Here's to my true love who live with me when I'm me.

The city dweller's dream of solitude in the country is, perhaps, to be expected, but it's the 'when I'm me' reference which lays bare the tension at work in the heart of Bolan's quest. At first glance, the phrase seems to look towards a time when the role-playing is over; the 'me' referring to Mark Feld, devoid from 'surface' pretensions. On the other hand, it suggests a continued sense of becoming, of being only partially complete, something which, in acknowledging the reality of the surface, could only be resolved by attaining stardom – and with it the financial means to retire to his 'castle' retreat.

R.D. Laing's fashionable book *The Divided Self*, published in 1960, suggests a similar dichotomy at the centre of his study of schizophrenia, where he states that attempting to sustain the split between the real self and the invented personality is the motor behind what is referred to as 'madness'. Since then, the post-Freudian psychologist Jacques Lacan, in his theory of the subject, has bypassed Laing's old categories of 'invented' and 'real' and instead stresses the role of social experience in the construction of self. Lacan suggests that a child becomes aware of a difference between 'self' and 'not-self' during what he calls the 'mirror stage', a metaphor for the moment when the child first recognises itself and constructs its own ego.

According to this idea, self-awareness is intrinsically bound up with image, and an idealised one at that. Any concept of 'self', therefore, is said to rest upon a misrepresentation, thus making a mockery of any abstract division between 'invented' and 'real'. Marc Bolan, who spent much of his life exercising his own formidable ego with a series of playful character-hops, seemed to have an instinctive grasp of this apparent delusion.

It doesn't really matter whether Bolan's concept of 'when I'm me' refers to the removal of 'false' identities or the acquisition of a 'complete' one. What is important is that his search for self, whether through adopted personae or a gradual acquaintance with the 'real', amounts to much the same thing. There is nothing necessarily 'false' about self-image, just as there is nothing particularly 'real' about an 'intrinsic' self. Marc, perhaps more than most, was acutely aware of the 'reality of the image', though during the late sixties he was drawn into the collective search for the inward, authentic personal experience. Mark Feld was Marc Bolan as much as Harry Feld has continued to be Harry Feld. But Marc's greater range of experiences and insatiable quest to enrich his knowledge gave him the skills which he thought would enable him to find 'me' more quickly.

One of the things Bolan had learned was that he couldn't find 'me'/stardom alone. John Peel, who describes Marc as his 'best mate' during the late sixties, is realistic about their relationship. 'He obviously saw me as a means of promoting Tyrannosaurus Rex and getting his music heard,' he admits. 'Of course, I knew he had a hard side to him, as we all do, but in the early years, I really didn't see it very often. Marc was a more practical person, but I don't think he was being cynical and manipulative. That's not the Marc I remember. He had his eye on something in the distance but he didn't work towards it in any kind of obsessive way as far as I was aware.' Maybe not, but people who would become vitally important in Marc's career were beginning to fall into place, while others less crucial started to drop out.

The sheafs of flowery prose in which Marc proclaimed his love for the mild-tempered Terry came to a halt in the spring of 1968. Credited as 'Euterpian dancer' on the sleeve of the début album, Terry 'Mosaic', the girl once destined to share Marc's castle, was displaced overnight after the odes to love started flying in the direction of Blackhill Enterprises' June Child. The pair fell in love almost as soon as Bolan set foot in the Alexander Street office, and by the time he had returned home, his passion burned sufficiently enough for him to telephone and invite her over. On her arrival, Marc presented June with a romantic poem, and over a shared bowl of ultra-hip muesli it was clear that a strong bond was forming between the pair. Strong enough, in fact, for both to leave their respective partners (it marked the end of June's four-year relationship with jeweller Mick Milligan) and set up home on Wimbledon Common for four days in June's van, furnished with a mattress in the back.

So intense was the union that June quickly found a cold-water attic flat at 57 Blenheim Crescent, Ladbroke Grove, close to the Blackhill offices and in the heart of the capital's freak community, so that they needn't be apart. Bolan's record and publishing deals and his regular concert appearances didn't provide for an opulent lifestyle, because there was still little money coming in. The £2 8s. 6d. rent they had managed to scrape together for the love-nest yielded a two-ring gas cooker and the use of a shared bathroom.

Pete Sanders, a close friend who photographed the following four album sleeves, is one of several who points to the important role June played in laying the foundations for Marc's later success. 'She was the person who kept his feet on the ground,' he says, 'or should I say enabled him to float in his own world while she took care of all the day-to-day business – money, gigs and getting from A to B. She obviously loved Marc a lot, gave him encouragement and was very loyal to him.' Jeff Dexter agrees. 'June was wonderfully organised,' he acknowledges. 'She had a little van, worked at Blackhill, knew everyone, had access to a telephone and could make things happen. She made a lot of difference.'

June, five years Marc's senior, was the soulmate he had been

looking for, and their immediate sexual chemistry was com-
pounded by the compatibility of their chosen roles. Bolan's
creative desires demanded further nourishment, while his career
aspirations needed support from the industry men who mattered.
June, who was both literate and instinctively skilled in PR, was
able to fulfil both needs, introducing Marc to new writers and
poets by night and selling him to a number of sceptical men in
suits during the day.

Unsurprisingly, living out the role of the Romantic artist and
winning people over with his songs, poems and general air of
innocence and sensitivity, while at the same time creating his
own luck, inevitably meant that two public faces of Marc Bolan
were on show. Today, June seems keen to play down the mythology that has sprung up around Marc's artistic aspirations, maintaining that he was a 'businessman' who regarded his fellow
musicians as mere 'wage-earners', and whose motivation for
organising cut-price concerts was simply that he would reach
more people, who in turn would go out and buy his records. It
wasn't so much that Marc Bolan was Janus-faced: his twin drives
towards creation and stardom were nothing more than two contrasting sides of the same shiny coin, a currency in widespread
use in the world of the modern-day commercial artist.

It was his love of escape, mystery and sense of wonder at
the world around him that had drawn him into the hippie culture.
He could dress up, laugh at the mundaneness of the 'straight'
world, and discuss Poon with friends who showed every sign of
taking him seriously. Poon was Marc's muse. Marc often spoke
of exterior forces governing his life, and words such as 'reincar-
nation' and 'destiny' often found their way into his vocabulary.
By 1968, this sense of a spiritual path had been extended to
embrace the idea that his creativity came to him from an icon
called Poon, which was symbolised by a statue of a fairy on his
mantelpiece at Bienheim Crescent. Regular visitors recall seeing
handwritten notes to Poon, in Bolan's unmistakably runic hand-
writing, placed around the statue.

It was a sign of the times that, during the late sixties, an
aspiring pop musician could entertain a Tibetan lama for tea, but
that is what happened after Tony Visconti, a student of Buddhism
and meditation, introduced Bolan to his teacher, Chime Rinpoche. 'I said to Marc, "You're into mysticism, this guy's a real
mystic. You should meet him." After a while, he agreed, and so

Chime and I went round to his flat. It was the only time I ever saw Marc in a humble posture. They were seated cross-legged facing each other, and Chime, dressed in his splendid gold waistcoat, the maroon robes of a monk and with a crew cut, said to Marc, "Tell me about yourself." Marc bowed his head, had his hands clasped tightly and I heard him say, "Well, I'm very young . . . " I thought I shouldn't really hear such a private conversation, and so I joined the others at the other side of the room. But I'd have loved to have heard the rest of the story. Marc was very impressed with that meeting.'

Buddhism seeks to eradicate vices such as greed and self-delusion, but Marc's interest in personal enlightenment didn't convince everyone. John Peel preferred to ignore the 'harder side', but some, like Steve Sparks, Ilford's 'Ace Face' who went on to become a rock executive, believed Bolan's ego was intolerable. 'I knew him from when he was a mod, when he was Mark Feld,' he told Jonathon Green. 'He was a shit, a cocky little shit.'[1] Journalist Keith Altham, who was also aware of Marc's determination, is more measured – and convincing – in his assessment. 'Marc had that inner drive, that intuitive and instinctive feeling to do something that was a bit special, a bit magical. He was intrigued by some of the trappings of hippie culture, but I don't think he appreciated the likes of Tolkien in a deep, literary sense. He was a chameleon, a butterfly, taking what he wanted out of something and then moving on.'

If Marc was the innocent abroad in the midst of hippie culture, then his role-playing was impeccable: his ambition appeared restrained rather than naked. Tyrannosaurus Rex almost had a hit single in the summer of 1968 with 'One Inch Rock', a simple blues-based tune about a 'Liquid Poetess' who tempts a young man back to her flat, offers him a drink which reduces him to one inch in height, and places him in a bottle with a similarly sized woman. It strayed into the Top Thirty, but Bolan chose to bide his time, continued to play the club and festival circuit, and made no attempt to capitalise on its success with a quick commercial follow-up.

'One Inch Rock' was drawn from the duo's summer sessions for the second Tyrannosaurus Rex album, titled, somewhat more succinctly, *Prophets, Seers & Sages The Angels Of The Ages*. Unlike the single, which had been knocking around since the Simon Napier-Bell days, *Prophets* (with the exception of 'Eastern Spell') contained new material composed since the spring, but still employed the minimal production, excepting 'Deboraarobed', a re-recording of the single which reflected its palindromic title in music by reversing the tape midway through the song. The format of acoustic guitar and assorted percussion instruments remained the same, as did the blend of simple but strange melodies of its predecessor. If anything, it represented a further retreat from brash urbanism, rejoicing in the mysticism of the East and the innocence of childhood. In one of the interviews conducted to promote the album, Marc stated that he disliked cities and modern life, and if there was a moment when striving for success took a back seat to more critical concerns, the summer of 1968 was probably it.

*Prophets* was dedicated to 'the memory of Kahil [*sic*] Gibran, the hill of Youth and Dandy the Beano-Seller', which was probably as openly critical of contemporary society as Marc Bolan ever got. Talk of revolution was in the air that summer – Lennon wondered whether he could be counted 'in' or 'out', the Rolling Stones celebrated the 'Street Fighting Man' and the full force of the British democratic process came down on the heads of anti-war demonstrators outside the US Embassy in Grosvenor Square. There was a considerable blurring of the children of Marx and those of Coca Cola and, for a brief moment, the rock world almost questioned which side it was on. But as revealed by Columbia Records' 'Revolutionaries Of Rock' campaign earlier in the year, it was all too obvious what was really being sold and, despite the upheavals of the time, rock music – in Britain at least – was near silent when it came to supporting the radicals' cause.

This stems back to the break in the mid-sixties, when the Romantic search for self pronounced itself beyond left- or right-wing politics and priority was instead given to the goal of personal liberation. The *International Times* crowd apparently liked to say, 'Politics is pigshit', which was reflected in the editorial content of the magazine, the central thrust of which was devoted to a rabid libertarianism. *Challenge*, the broadsheet of the Young Communists, was sceptical of this bourgeois yearning for the ultimate personal statement, summing up the mood of the time by attacking its most visible icon. 'Sgt. Pep-Ups Phoney Thoughts Club Band', it chortled. The triumph of Romantic individualism was encapsulated by Elektra Records' boss Jac Holzman in 1969, when he proclaimed, 'We think that the revolution will be won by poetry not politics, that poets will change the structure of the world.'

Kahlil Gibran, invoked on the *Prophets* sleeve, was one of the founding fathers for the hippies' poetic revolution. He was an early twentieth-century Lebanese mystic whose best-known work, *The Prophet* (1923), was a book of proverbs, which nestled comfortably in every freak's rucksack, alongside the obligatory Tolkien and C.S. Lewis titles. Bolan probably didn't know it but Gibran never learned to spell, had little formal education, and even had his own 'wizard', Selim Dahir, who encouraged him in his search to attain higher knowledge. Sharing Gibran's biblical and Blakean influences, Bolan was captivated by his work, which preached a gentle message of love and peace in imagery already familiar to Marc. Gibran's world was populated by mighty and lofty wise men with swords, eagles and minstrels, where the moon always shone brightly and the trees swayed majestically, and where Beauty, Love, Life and Death all warranted capital letters. But did he realise that Gibran also believed in the purity of mind, and felt that success and power could only be gained at the expense of compromising one's integrity?

Like many old friends, John Peel remains sceptical about the depth of Marc's understanding of Gibran and similarly fashionable writers: 'The idea of sitting down and studying anything would have been anathema to him,' he says. 'Most people used to get their ideas from reading the backs of paperbacks in W.H. Smith. You'd leave books by Gibran and Hesse and *The Tibetan Book of the Dead* lying around because they were part of the uniform. You could lie on the floor, smoke dope, listen to the new Donovan album, talk a load of shite and it was all rather pleasant.' Tony Visconti cannot recall Marc reading a book in his life, but maintains that Marc was acutely aware of where his influences lay. Early on in their friendship, Marc said to the producer, 'If you're gonna record me, you gotta read these', and handed him copies of *The Lord of the Rings* trilogy and *The Hobbit*.

The image of Marc and Steve on the cover of the *Prophets* album, photographed by Pete Sanders, depicted two long-hairs in a park unconventionally dressed (Took had a full-length cloak around his shoulders) and with a jester's puppet in the foreground. The combination of the strange camera angle and the duo's assertive gaze seemed to belie any preciousness imparted by songs like 'The Friends', 'Our Wonderful Brownskin Man'

and the aphorism on the rear sleeve that celebrated innocence –
after stating that in the head of a man is a woman and vice
versa, Bolan asks 'what wonders' roam in the head of a child?
Tyrannosaurus Rex liked to play, but their game was taking on
an increasingly serious tone.

Despite Bolan's hidden agenda and Took's increasing
involvement with the more out-to-lunch set of the Ladbroke
Grove hippie community, Tyrannosaurus Rex concerts were reverential gatherings of the flower children, one year on from the
summer of love but no less convinced of the sanctity of their
mission. John Peel, who had made it a condition of his university
and college gigs that Tyrannosaurus Rex be allowed to perform
on the bill, travelled the length and breadth of the country with
the duo and remembers that even by the standards of the time
they were seen as 'elfin to a degree beyond human understanding'. The effect was enhanced by Bolan's tendency to sit cross-
legged on a mat on the floor, while Took caressed his bongos
seated on a stool. It was a striking contrast to the conventional
pop concert. Keith Altham was surprised at the transformation
of the ex-mod, ex-Dylan-styled beatnik, ex-John's Children hus-
tler. 'I saw Tyrannosaurus Rex at the Albert Hall and they bored
me to death,' he recalls. 'I remember thinking that Marc's guitar
playing had improved dramatically, but that the whole affair was
terribly insular. Nevertheless, I think he learned a lot during that
period, especially about the business.'

Throughout 1968, Marc was too busy cultivating his audience
to get deeply embroiled in management deals and complicated
business arrangements. He seemed like the child out of time,
guaranteed to bring last year's hippies out of the woodwork
whenever Tyrannosaurus Rex visited the provinces. Few took
much notice then, but his pixie-like good looks had also won him
the beginnings of a female fan following. By February 1969, a
Tyrannosaurus Rex fan club had been established, and a month
later, was forced to plead in its newsletter that, 'Because so many
of you have requested locks of Marc and Steve's hair, they are
now beginning to go a bit thin on top, so please, all you adorable
fans, no more requests for locks of hair.'

Marc's private life reflected his public image during these
early months of minor pop stardom. There were trips to Glastonbury Tor and Stonehenge with June, John Peel and Sheila, John's
new girlfriend. The passionate commitment to music was further
cemented as Marc and John made endless journeys round the

London circuit of record shops, from obscure stores in Wimbledon to the popular Musicland in Berwick Street in the heart of Soho, where they indulged their shared enthusiasm for rare Donovan imports or obscure James Burton solos on Ricky Nelson B sides. Marc Bolan, once a brash Cockney kid, was now the soft-spoken hippie offspring of the English middle classes, with a face that exuded sincerity and whose songs and poetry elicited a mixture of wonder and joy.

The climax of this period of unbridled Romanticism came with the publication, in March 1969, of *The Warlock of Love*, a collection of Bolan's richly descriptive blank verse in a slim hardback volume. There weren't many published rock poets at that point, although Dylan's example had encouraged a whole host of writers to embrace rock, and vice versa. Marc's talent in stringing attractive-sounding words together was instinctive, if untroubled by intellectual concerns, but his florid, precious style, so perfect for its time, quickly became unfashionable, and its lack of obvious content – emotional or political – gives it little relevance outside the culture from which it sprang. But in many ways, Bolan's poetry accurately reflected his attitude towards himself. Cloaked in the highly imaginative language of the Romantic, the stream of seemingly unrelated images and characters leapt out from the page (or the lyric sheet) almost screaming to be noticed.

Proclaiming oneself a poet in the sphere of popular music was acceptable if you were called Bob Dylan, because he brought with it a hitherto unheard-of intellectual and social dimension to rock lyrics. There were few qualms when award-winning Canadian poet Leonard Cohen transposed his rhymes to music, or when Pete Brown, who had been a regular face on the British poetry scene since the early sixties, began writing rock lyrics for Cream. Bolan's words, regarded as suitable only for a few months in 1967 and 1968 during a mass flight of teenage fancy running on acid and Tolkien, were rarely taken seriously. Even comparisons with Syd Barrett failed to stand up in the eyes of his peer group. 'Syd was much more convincing,' says Pete Brown, 'because he was much less self-conscious about his poetic content. The thing that Syd actually did was address British subjects and he made it work. He had been through that whole art school background which gave him a greater sophistication. When Dylan used mysticism, it more often manifested itself in biblical imagery and was much harder-edged than anything Bolan did.

'There was a lot of phoniness about the hippie thing, and

the whole business of the twee side of things always annoyed me. All that Tokien stuff which was co-opted by the hippies was bullshit. They felt they recognised something in it – fantasy, Utopias, good and evil. To me it was an abomination and it fucked people's heads up. The combination of that stuff and acid was lethal. It sent people off to a kind of numskull Cloud-cuckoo land.'

Bolan's aptitude with words was better confined to song lyrics, where any pretensions – or portentousness – was rendered redundant by his obscure vocal delivery. John Peel – himself credited as 'poet' on the sleeve of the Idle Race's début album – regards Marc's poetic aspirations as being very much a product of the time. 'He did regard himself as a poet or, at least, he was encouraged to do so,' he remembers. 'As much a part of the corrupting process are the fans and people like me who tell musicians how wonderful they are. So few have a steadying hand on them to say, "Frankly, that is shite." A lot of people would benefit enormously from such a figure in their lives, although I don't think Marc would have taken kindly to such criticism. Marc liked words, and sometimes he'd ask me what a particular word meant. When I told him and its meaning seemed inappropriate, he'd say, "Well, it doesn't fit but I like the sound of it", and so in it would go.' Throughout his career, Bolan had no doubts about his poet status, a claim that was laughable to those with preconceived notions of literary greatness. But in time, when he had moved into the mainstream of popular music, his words were readily identifiable, a constant talking-point among both fans and detractors. And they were undoubtedly *strange*, opening up a new perception of the pop lyric to a distinctly non-hippie generation. In that respect, their meaning was far more important than any discussed in the rarified atmosphere of the lecture theatre.

In September 1968, plans were afoot for an album's worth of rock poetry, read by none other than John Peel. Contributions were solicited from Bolan, Arthur Brown, Tim Rose, Syd Barrett, Roger Waters, Chris Wood, Keith West, Captain Beefheart and, oddly enough, the Move's Carl Wayne. It would have been a remarkable curio from the hippie era had it not been aborted in its early stages. 'What an awful idea that was,' recalls a horrified John Peel. 'I'm glad we had the wisdom to pack that in before it got too serious. I think I got as far as taping Syd Barrett's "Effervescing Elephant" and "Baby Lemonade", but not Marc's piece.'

By the end of 1968, the dream – which had been little more than a fashion accessory for those in the right financial, social or artistic circles to enjoy – was already over. The arrival of the less committed 'weekend hippies', the continued use of acid wreaking havoc with some of the best minds of the generation, and the desire for even greater musical sophistication signalled the death knell for the Love Crowd. Just as it wasn't conjured up out of thin air, the wide-ranging ideology that underlay the hippie life-style didn't subside overnight either, though its leading musicians increasingly sensed that the mood of the audience was changing as the hippie subculture began to fragment. This diffusion was reflected in the music. Hard rock began to replace the soft, poetic Eastern influences which had wafted over Western pop music; musical gurus like Dylan, the Beatles and the Rolling Stones embraced a new rock simplicity, while another generation of art rock groups prised open the divisions between élite and mass musical tastes still further. Bolan sensed the changes too, but he moved much more slowly. Many of the trappings of hippie culture – clothes, cliques, escape – had neatly coincided with his own interests, and the movement had offered him the opportunity to sample his first taste of real success. 'Marc was just an amiable lad who was quite ambitious and enjoyed the fashion aspects of life,' insists John Peel. What close friends like Peel and Pete Sanders failed to appreciate was just how consuming that ambition was. Neither did his fans. It wasn't until two years later that they saw a different Marc Bolan, one who was able to jettison the cult status he always seemed destined – and happy – to inhabit. But the signs began to show through considerably earlier.

# CHAPTER SEVEN

And now where once stood solid water
  stood the reptile king,
Tyrannosaurus Rex, reborn and bopping.
Marc Bolan, *The Warlock Of Love*, 1969

'The credibility of the band was lessened by the fact that
people associated us with Flower Power, and that was a
long gone era. I wanted people to look at the thing in a new
light, and the only way to do that was have a label change,
and change the music, and change the name, but not lose
any identity either way.'
Marc Bolan, to Charles Shaar Murray, *Cream* magazine, 1972

'I think our time for singles may come again.'
Marc Bolan, spring 1970

Because Tyrannosaurus Rex seemed to personify the exuberant
mood of 1967 and its immediate aftermath, the group's appeal
was perceived to be limited when what was claimed to be the
real world invited itself back into youth consciousness. *Prophets,
Seers And Sages* failed to capitalise on the success of the first
album, and those not immediately smitten by the duo's work
found the music one-dimensional, boring and *passé*. Lacking the
profound, psychedelic appeal of Pink Floyd or the eclectic musicality of the Incredible String Band, Marc's and Steve's Tyrannosaurus Rex, far from being a powerful monster of a sound,
became typecast as lightweight and anachronistic.

As early as June 1968, in an *International Times* review of their
prestigious gig at the Royal Festival Hall, their set was described
as too long and too unvaried, which contrasted unfavourably
with the praise heaped upon bottom-of-the-bill David Bowie.
Kenneth Pitt, who had toyed with the idea of managing both
back in 1966 but plumped for Bowie, secured a supporting slot
for his artist on several Tyrannosaurus Rex dates in February

1969 and, although Bolan had enjoyed some success while Bowie's career was still to flourish, Pitt insisted he had made the right choice. 'There was something shallow and crude in Marc's performance,' he wrote later, 'and it gave me no reason to believe that it would ever be otherwise, but David invested his work with a couth intelligence that held great promise for the future.'[1]

There was no middle way with Marc Bolan. For every manager or industry executive who had fallen in love with his voice, his songs and his charm, there were dozens who had laughed him out of the office; and it was the same story with audiences. Bowie learnt a lesson and began to spread his appeal more widely. Marc maintained his 'purity': he let his heart rule his head, brushed aside criticism and pursued his magnificent obsessions ever more doggedly.

He did listen to advice on one rare occasion, when he was encouraged to release 'Pewter Suitor' as a single in January 1969. Singer Barry Ryan, reviewing the disc wrote: 'I should imagine if you were in a stoned state at a party, you'd think this record was fantastic',[2] and perhaps there was a grain of truth in his sideswipe. The song, which possessed little of the usual Tyrannosaurus Rex charm, featured a briskly played two-chord hook that seemed more designed to irritate than enchant. 'Pewter Suitor' only really came to life towards the end as it disintegrated into a glorious mess of percussion and some near-hysterical wailing from Bolan. The flip, 'Warlord Of The Royal Crocodiles', marked something of a new departure, with Bolan's voice effectively multi-tracked and Took's percussion dressed up in studio trickery. In terms of maintaining the singles profile established with 'Debora' and 'One Inch Rock', Bolan had been ill-advised and 'Pewter Suitor' was doomed to failure. Despite encouraging – if not overwhelming – concert appearances at reasonably sized venues, even Bolan himself was beginning to question seriously the direction being taken by Tyrannosaurus Rex.

At the same time that he was apologising to his friend John Peel for not visiting him lately ('I've had strange wrestles with the gaolers of my destiny causing much upset in my usauley [sic] sweet calm life', he explained), EMI's pressing plant was busy churning out copies of Unicorn, the third Tyrannosaurus Rex album, which reached the shops in mid-May 1969. It was a notable departure in that the amateurish, guitar-and-bongos-in-the-park feel of their earlier work had been unshackled by a considerably more produced sound. A barely disguised Phil Spector touch could be detected (particularly on 'Catblack [The Wizard's Hat]' and 'She Was Born To Be My Unicorn'); the basic guitar/bongo/percussion/vocal line-up was augmented with Tony Visconti's rudimentary piano skills on 'Catblack' ('Thankfully it was in the key of C,' he recalls), a full drum-kit on 'Chariots Of Silk' and 'Catblack', and a wider range of instrumentation including harmonium, bass and fonofiddle; and Marc's brand-new Suzuki acoustic rang with exceptional clarity as Visconti's mastery of the control board enriched the duo's overall sound. Marc was particularly proud that there were twenty-two different overdubs on 'Romany Soup', a nine-word mantra to a dish he and June discovered during a short holiday in Cornwall in December 1968. Meanwhile, his melodies were becoming ever more intricate, as evidenced on 'The Seal Of Seasons' and 'Iscariot'.

As if his songs weren't already overflowing with Romantic and fanciful notions, Marc proudly stepped outside the pop discourse and chose to reveal some of the sources for his inspiration when being photographed for the album sleeve. The *Unicorn* photo session took place at one of his regular meeting places, 2 Park Square Mews, just off Upper Harley Street in Central London. The flat had originally been occupied by Pete Sanders who, in struggling to build up a career as a photographer, had met John Peel and begun taking shots of Tyrannosaurus Rex at venues such as Middle Earth. Finding the pressure of rent too much of a burden to cope with alone, he invited Peel to share the flat (conveniently close to Broadcasting House, home of BBC Radio) and before long the place was buzzing with all manner of British underground luminaries and visiting Americans like Buddah Records boss Artie Ripp.

'Marc had very strong ideas about what he wanted,' recalls Sanders. 'He brought some of the objects over for the session, which took place in our kitchen. I think the Gibran books were his, as were the *Children's Shakespeare* and Blake's *Complete Writings*, but the Singer sewing-machine and the photo book of the Cottingley fairies, which has since been proved a fake, were mine. On some of the shots which weren't used, Marc and Steve held sparklers to create a more wizardy effect. He was very generous because I wasn't a very good photographer then, but we worked well together. He was always meticulous about the sessions and was incredibly very aware of the power of image.

'Not long after that session, I decided I wanted to live on my own again, and as John could afford the flat outright, I let him have it. By this time, Marc and June had moved out of the attic at 57 Blenheim Crescent down to the more spacious floor below, and so I moved in above them.'

John Peel, who had recited a second 'Woodland Story' on *Unicorn*, continued to champion Tyrannosaurus Rex, even though he was increasingly committed to seeking out new acts for his own Dandelion record label, which he had finally managed to get off the ground at the start of 1969. (The label and its publishing arm were named Dandelion and Biscuit after Peel's two hamsters, gifts from Marc and June.) Nevertheless, Peel, who had attended most of the band's appearances in 1968 including festival appearances at the Isle of Wight and Kempton Park, continued to MC for them, and was still firmly committed to the shared Utopian philosophy as his 'John Peel proving the existence of fairies' billing at the Queen Elizabeth Hall on 13 January 1969 indicates. Lower down on the bill that night were sitar player Vytas Serelis, and a new American singer called Melanie, who, like Bolan, sang with a strong vibrato and polarised audiences in a similar fashion. 'A pretty evening of wafer-thin material,' chided Chris Welch in *Melody Maker*.

Tyrannosaurus Rex continued to feature heavily on Peel's radio programme and their May 1969 session was the sixth in eighteen months. During that time, Bolan had also joined Peel live on air to discuss his work and read his poetry. Predictably, there had to be a backlash. Peel's manager Clive Selwood recalls that 'John got a letter from the Controller of Radio 1 which actually ordered him to stop playing Tyrannosaurus Rex, on the basis that listeners were complaining that John had a financial interest in Marc's affairs, which, of course, was not true. John ignored it, but at least one other Radio 1 DJ was playing records by artists with whom he actually shared the same agent. John rightly told them it was madness.'

'I used to get a lot of critical mail,' Peel recalls, 'and of all the artists I used to play regularly, Tyrannosaurus Rex was always the name that used to be mentioned. "C'mon, you can't *really* like all that stuff, all that bleating!" And, of course, the more people react like that, the more I'm drawn to it. Another

thing was that people used to say that I liked the band because
I fancied Marc, and they also thought that was why I moved in
with Pete Sanders, because he was immensely beautiful as well.
Actually, I didn't fancy either of them.' John Peel had found his
soulmate (and future wife) in Sheila, whom he had met on the
set of Tony Palmer's *How It Is*, BBC television's alternative pop
show. Meanwhile, Marc's relationship with June blossomed as
she actively campaigned on his behalf, giving businessmen like
music publisher David Platz some hard times in the process. But
Marc's and June's shared love affair with Blackhill Enterprises
soon came to an abrupt halt. According to photographer Ray
Stevenson, in late spring 1968, prior to the release of the first
Tyrannosaurus Rex album, Marc had suggested to Blackhill
Enterprises the idea of holding free concerts in London's Hyde
Park. A couple of months later, on 29 June, an audience of some
7000 enjoyed a summer's day chasing bubbles and boating down
the Serpentine to the sounds of Roy Harper, Jethro Tull, Pink
Floyd and Tyrannosaurus Rex. It was the hip management company's heyday, and one which planted the seed for the following
year's mammoth presentation of the Rolling Stones to around
250,000 non-paying fans. Blackhill's Pete Jenner had initially
warmed to Marc at the start of the year, but before 1968 was out
his partner Andrew King, apparently returned home one day to
find Marc and June in his bed and abruptly severed the relationship. Marc took Tyrannosaurus Rex to the Bryan Morrison
Agency which, by December 1968, also handled Pink Floyd, Captain Beefheart and His Magic Band, the Pretty Things and
Aynsley Dunbar's Retaliation.

Morrison's offices at 16 Bruton Place in Central London (also
the base for his Lupus Publishing Company, which was responsible for *The Warlock of Love*, also provided a home for the Tyrannosaurus Rex fan club, which was established when a keen fan
named Suzy advertised in the music press for members. Most
underground acts sought to distance themselves from the star/
fan divide, but Marc and Steve happily went along with the idea
when Annabel Butler and a colleague called Maxine, who both
worked for the Morrison agency, took over running the fan club
early in 1969. The hundred or so members, which included four
from Germany, three from France and two from Norway,
received a monthly newsletter and 'Life Lines' – personality profiles of Marc and Steve. Among the round of typical questions

and answers (height; colour of eyes; favourite clothes, pets, drinks), were comments which revealed that Steve Took was the real Syd Barrett fan (Marc plumped for the Beach Boys) while Bolan played the perfect hippie (living in a 'château in the west', vegetarian, lover of C.S. Lewis, the music of Dvořák, the dawn, and whose favourite costumes were 'elfin and medieval').

The newsletters offered nuggets of information such as the equipment used by the band (which, impressively, included their own WEM 200 watt PA with Shure microphones, purchased with the proceeds of their record sales); the reactions of their peer group ('Steve and Marc are a gas,' said Pink Floyd's Dave Gilmour as all four Floyd members enrolled in the club, 'they play such beautiful music and make terrific records'); little-known details such as Marc's visit to the Robin Ross School in Wimbledon in March, where he gave a talk on drums and other subjects to a class of five- and six-year-olds; and endearing insights into the nature of the hippie duo. 'I have never heard either of them raise their voices above their normal talking voices,' sighed Maxine in February 1969.

Nevertheless, the gentle sounds and good karma which surrounded Tyrannosaurus Rex began to dissolve as the year progressed, and the process seemed to accelerate with the purchase of an electric guitar in March, towards the end of the *Unicorn* sessions. For several months, Bolan had been picking up Tony Visconti's electric while at the producer's flat listening to the Beach Boys, where he had occasionally shared tips with Visconti's other protégé David Bowie. Having augmented the sparse Tyrannosaurus Rex sound with more ornamentation on the latest album, Marc's return to electricity was the result of imagining himself in the role of an Eric Clapton, a Jimi Hendrix or a Pete Townshend. Rock was undoubtedly getting harder.

Unlike the blues-infected rhythms of up-and-coming names like Led Zeppelin, Jethro Tull, Humble Pie and the US-based Creedence Clearwater Revival, Bolan chose to unveil the electric Rex with a doomy, descending guitar line that would become something of a trademark in later years. The song, 'King Of The Rumbling Spires', forsook Marc's usually strong melodic sense and instead hung on a Gothic-style riff which, with the introduction of Mellotron half-way through, owed more than a little to the new classically inspired British rock groups like King Crimson and the Nice. It sounded self-important (a strong feature of

Bolan's later work), but this rather plodding fusion of hard rock with progressive intent was uncharacteristically dense and dark.

It was a brave move, as Marc felt his way around the new fretboard and Took pounded hell out of a full drum-kit and provided the anchor with his own bass-line. It prompted a prophetic 'Electrified Teenybop!' headline in *Melody Maker*, sales were up on 'Pewter Suitor' but 'King Of The Rumbling Spires' failed to open up Tyrannosaurus Rex to any new markets. The flip, 'Do You Remember', with its opening line, 'Her face was like a cult to me', easily misheard, plodded along with similar austerity, and in many ways the single disappointed those expecting Bolan to capitalise on the bright, upbeat *Unicorn* album. Lyrically, 'King' was more streamlined than before, consisting of just two repeated verses, neither of which conjured up much about the obscure subject of the song. Photographer Pete Sanders had taken a picture of a tramp who was a regular sight in Oxford Street, and when Marc saw the picture, he immediately wanted it for the sleeve which accompanied the first few hundred copies. 'He said it seemed to go with the title,' recalls Sanders.

In the same month that the Tyrannosaurus Rex newsletter announced that Marc had purchased an electric guitar came news that the group were to tour America, hopefully in May. It wasn't the first time such a visit had been planned. As early as August 1968, the music press had reported a projected Pink Floyd/Tyrannosaurus Rex link-up for some dates on the US college circuit a month later, but nothing came of it. Instead, the duo made a couple of European trips, appearing on French and German television and the inevitable festival circuit.

The May 1969 tour was set in motion by Steve O'Rourke from the Bryan Morrison Agency, supposedly supported by Blue Thumb, the group's new American outlet, which also provided a home for fellow Peel favourites Captain Beefheart and Love. In fact, the original intention was an exchange visit whereby Tyrannosaurus Rex, Pink Floyd and Aynsley Dunbar's Retaliation went to the States, while Love, Captain Beefheart and His Magic Band and the Byrds toured Britain. Instead, Marc and Steve were eventually sent to America on the basis of an exchange with Bob Dylan, who was due to fly in for the Isle of Wight Festival at the end of August.

In a recorded interview with John Peel used to promote the band on air in the States, Marc outlined his aspirations for the tour. 'I want to play to people there with a quieter thing,' he said in his soft, precise manner, 'with an excitement which equals rock 'n' roll but doesn't have any of the violent feelings. If people dance or move about or scratch at the air, it's because they want to and because they're enjoying the music as music, not as a theme to violence.'[3] America, the home of so many of Marc's childhood fantasies, from Mighty Joe Young to Elvis Presley, Davy Crockett to James Dean, was, by 1969, in the midst of a violent upheaval. Sections of the nation's youth attempted to pierce the mores of Middle America, exposing it racism, its imperial ambitions, its material greed and its spiritual wastelands. Assassinations, riots and fierce demonstrations had been ripping the country apart. Marc, who seemed quietly to exorcise politics from his mind after his brief flirtation with CND and protest songs in the mid-sixties, naïvely imagined he would bring some good British vibes to a country in deep crisis, and hoped to emulate the success that Donovan had enjoyed there a couple of years earlier.

Once the work permits had been sorted out, the duo, together with June and Ron the roadie, flew out to San Francisco on 6 August for a lengthy stay that kept them away until late September. The tour began ominously as Steve Took, in his customary early-morning daze, only just caught the flight after Ron had to force his flat window open to rouse him. Marc described San Francisco as 'lovely' in a postcard to a friend, but he was less enamoured of the country by the time the group were encamped at the Drake Hotel (after finding the infamous Chelsea Hotel too grubby) in New York a couple of weeks later. 'John, we're terribly homesick,' he wrote to his DJ friend. 'It's such a strange alien country. The gigs are going well and in time I think it will be very big . . . We hate New York.'

While in America's cultural capital, the duo played the Café Au Go Go on Bleecker Street in Greenwich Village, home to the American folk movement. Unfortunately, the date coincided with the start of the Woodstock Festival which, according to one report, Tyrannosaurus Rex were at one time scheduled to play, and the mass exodus to Yasgur's farm meant that the New York clubs were left virtually empty. By the time the festival ended, Marc and Steve were already in Chicago, where they visited a temple and stayed at the Tides Motel, before moving on to New Orleans to appear alongside many of the top American West

Coast bands at an open-air festival. Marc was disappointed with some of the big names like Jefferson Airplane, Grateful Dead, the Byrds and Janis Joplin, although the lesser-known It's A Beautiful Day and Santana made a favourable impression.

Tyrannosaurus Rex supported It's A Beautiful Day on their final date, at the Grand Ballroom, Seattle, but, despite a vague musical affinity with the mystically inclined San Franciscan outfit, it was a post-concert party in Detroit with headliners the Turtles which provided the only lasting friendship from this début transatlantic tour. Fronted by the twin vocal force of Howard Kaylan and Mark Volman, the Turtles started out as Byrds-inspired folk-rockers before crossing over into pure pop during 1967 and 1968 with a string of hit singles including 'Happy Together', 'She'd Rather Be With Me' and 'Elenore'. Musically, the groups were poles apart, although the Americans had belatedly made an attempt to 'go psychedelic'. Nevertheless, Kaylan and Volman promised to look up Marc and June when they were next in London. Kaylan later explained the basis of the friendship by saying, 'Marc isn't one of the most humble guys we've ever met, but neither are we, so that gives us a really good rapport.'[4] Tony Visconti recalls a surfeit of Jewish humour whenever the pair were around, which Marc appreciated, and it appears that the two Turtles were the first to describe their London-based friend as a 'cosmic punk'.

Their enthusiasm greatly outweighed that shown by the group's US record company Blue Thumb, although that problem paled into insignificance compared with Marc's rapidly deteriorating relationship with Steve Peregrine Took. David Platz describes Took as someone who 'floated more than walked'; certainly, he accepted the hospitality of the American underground with his mouth wide open, eager to consume each and every joint and acid tab that came his way. Took's love of excess contrasted wildly with Bolan's restraint, but it was the resulting lack of professionalism which most bothered Marc who, in spite of the cool hippie demeanour, was sufficiently 'showbiz' to encourage fans to clap along at concerts ever since an early performance at the Royal Albert Hall in June 1968. (He could be partially excused: it was to help him keep time during an a cappella performance of 'Scenescof Dynasty'.) Took, despite his strange yet compelling harmonies, flurries of inventive percussion and expanding role as a multi-instrumentalist, had been continually undermined by Bolan's determination to keep a tight rein on the group. All of the Tyrannosaurus Rex material was conceived in Toadstool Studios, the suitably named patch of floor-space Marc had cordoned off in his flat to enable him to write and play undisturbed. While Bolan composed the songs, it was Took's job to add the percussion and harmony parts after he had been presented with the basic melody and tempo. This subordinate role wasn't a problem during the early stages of the group (prompting Simon Napier-Bell to recall Took as 'a bit of a yes-man, he got the hash, lit the joss-sticks, carried the carpet'), but the novelty began to wear off as Took realised that his own songwriting ambitions would find no outlet within the group. One of Steve's friends recalls that, 'Marc seemed to be some kind of power maniac who only wanted his own songs recorded. I think Tony Visconti tried to encourage Steve to contribute more but Marc wouldn't have it.

'At one time, Marc and Steve were incredibly close and, despite the bitterness, you could still sense that years later. When Steve talked about Tyrannosaurus Rex, it was always with a mixture of real love and a feeling of hurt and anger at being rejected; but it was largely his own fault. Basically, he took too many drugs, and during that disastrous tour of the States, he was constantly supplied with acid and was really out of it. Having said that, I think he functioned better on acid than most people. Because he took so much of it, he became slightly immune to its effects. He's often cited as the quiet one of the group, but Steve was very charismatic. People either loved him or hated him. He'd get right up people's noses so they'd end up wanting to kill him. Marc and Steve could both be difficult people, so it's no wonder that they clashed.'

Visconti remembers Took's aspirations, but maintains that he was 'a supporter not a creator. He worked out his own backing vocals and they were chromatic, really quite ingenious. His voice was probably more sophisticated than Marc's. He slept over at my place on occasion and we'd do some of his songs, but they were awful. He wanted equal say on the albums, and I think Marc was quite justified in sacking him.'

With Marc staying close to June, and Steve pursuing a nomadic existence, the two unequal halves of Tyrannosaurus Rex rarely saw each other socially. Their early companionship had waned but, in the months leading up to the US tour, the relationship hadn't totally soured. On one occasion, after Steve was busted for possession of drugs, Bolan and his girlfriend immediately came to his side. They hired a top lawyer, and did their best to hide their friend's hippie demeanour for the court appearance, kitting him out in a blue pin-stripe suit and stuffing his long hair down the neck of his shirt. In spite of the moral support and image managing, however, Steve was packed off to a remand home for a few weeks, an institution which was not wholly suited to sensitive, vegetarian types. 'Marc treated Steve with great love,' says Visconti, recalling the drugs bust.

Steve was ostracised yet again when Marc and June returned home from the States without him, leaving him to recover from his hallucinogenic holiday. He had disturbed some of the group's concerts by removing his clothes on stage and performing acts of musical sabotage.

It became obvious that if Marc Bolan was to fulfil his dream of pop stardom, he wasn't going to get very far with this musical companion. The great love had turned to disappointment and, on his return, Took was told his services were no longer required. Three years later, he recalled the split. 'I was a flower child,' he said, 'and there are things that a flower child can't do. Being a natural-born rebel, I wanted to do all the things I was meant not to do. That caused a lot of raps with the management and a lot of raps with Marc.' An air of innocence and freedom may have surrounded the group, but Took sensed little of it, finding himself shut out by Marc's ego and hemmed in by ground rules laid down by management. 'I was getting really shat on by them,' he said. 'A typical thing was when I used to go out and jam occasionally with the Deviants and the Pretty Things, the management would come and say, "Boy, don't go and jam with this group, it's bad for the image." And I'd go, "What image? I'm Steve Took, well-known drug addict."'[5]

Bolan wasted no time in looking for a new partner. On 4 October 1969, a boxed advert simply headed 'Tyrannosaurus Rex' appeared in *Melody Maker*: 'Wanted to work with T. Rex – a gentle young guy who can play percussion, i.e. bongos and drum-kit, some bass guitar and vocal harmony. Photos please. Box 8679.'

The advert yielded some 300 replies, all of which remained undisturbed in a pile. Meanwhile, through Pete Sanders in the upstairs flat, Marc had been introduced to a good-looking young painter/would-be musician – with the equally appealing name of

Mickey Finn. In his world inhabited by various *noms de plume* (John Peel, Steve Took, even Jeff Dexter), Marc was amused to learn that this was his genuine name.

Born Michael Norman Finn in Thornton Heath, Surrey on 3 June 1947, Mickey had attended All Saints' Primary and Rockmount Secondary schools, neither of which had dampened his enthusiasm for rock 'n' roll music or art. Like Marc, he had progressed from idols of the fifties like Elvis and Gene Vincent to the group sound of the Beatles and the Rolling Stones. After leaving school, he attended Croydon College of Art, spending the weekends at the Orchid Ballroom, Purley, where he first met fellow music fiends Pete Sanders and Jeff Dexter. Mickey also developed a passion for motorbikes, and quit college after his first year in the hope of raising some cash for a machine of his own.

In an echo of Mark Feld's teenage aspirations, Finn enrolled with Mark Palmer's English Boy model agency, which put him in touch with some of the fashionable London crowd, but by 1967 formal modelling was out. The streets – King's Road and Portobello Road in particular – provided the new catwalks for the hippie look, and instead Finn found part-time employment with Michael English and Nigel Waymouth (trading as Hapshash and the Coloured Coat) helping to paint an art-nouveau-style mural at their Granny Takes A Trip boutique in the King's Road. It is also possible that he contributed something musical to Hapshash's occasional ventures into rock, although it is unlikely that he appears on either of their albums.

Finn's entry into Tyrannosaurus Rex was suitably gentle. 'I think Mickey was coming round to visit me,' says Pete Sanders, 'and somehow he got introduced to Marc, told him he liked getting quietly stoned and banging away on the bongos, and the next thing I knew, he was part of the band and they were practising away together downstairs.' Jeff Dexter corroborates the story, and pinpoints exactly why Mickey Finn was drafted into the band. 'He looked great and was very agreeable. He had a wonderful character and a great feel for what Marc was doing at the time.'

Bolan greeted his new partner dressed in a patched multi-coloured waistcoat with long tassles hanging from it, green girls' shoes and a full head of Pre-Raphaelite hair. The five foot eight Finn had long straight hair and the incipient stubble of a beard. From the stalls, it probably looked as if nothing had changed, just as Marc had hoped. Tyrannosaurus Rex were still a duo: one played bongos, the other played guitar. But musically there were differences. Finn's vocal harmonising was unexciting, and his proficiency as a percussionist unremarkable. 'Mickey Finn was instantly likeable,' recalls Visconti, 'had a great sense of humour and was a breath of fresh air after Steve, who was very heavy. But I immediately assessed that he wasn't as good as Steve.' Bolan was unconcerned. By the end of 1969, he was more interested in altering the structure of Tyrannosaurus Rex, disregarding the relatively minor inconvenience of technical proficiency.

If the sacking of Steve Took brought with it a new world view, it was one which took many months to filter through. Bolan's history of shifting styles and musical fads had found a degree of stability in the tolerant climes of late sixties' hippie culture, where his poetic and musical fantasies were allowed to flourish, and where there was a ready-made audience to receive it. The end of the sixties was weeks away; the underground was in retreat; and the musical free-for-all, unleashed by *Sgt. Pepper*, four- and eight-track studios, and uncritical, stoned audiences, was beginning to coalesce around new formulas. The contradiction between individual expression masquerading as a collective one (the Beatles' 'All You Need Is Love', the Youngbloods' 'Get Together', and the empty rhetoric of Jefferson Airplane's attempt to tap into revolutionary politics on 'We Can Be Together') had broken down by the end of the decade. Instead, the 'sincerity' demanded by hippie audiences was transmitted to intensely personalised statements from a new breed of singer-songwriters, many of whom followed the lead of Bob Dylan's work. Riding high among this new breed of tortured troubadours were Cat Stevens, Leonard Cohen, Joni Mitchell, James Taylor and Neil Young.

Closely linked with this continuing desire for the 'authentic' statement was the discovery of a new set of roots – country music. Whereas black American working-class music had set in train the motor that eventually transformed 'Rock Around The Clock' into Jimi Hendrix's rendition of 'The Star Spangled Banner', the sound of country, the forgotten element in early Presley and Jerry Lee Lewis records, had been revived by Bob Dylan (whose duet with Johnny Cash in 1969 on *Nashville Skyline* symbolised his return from art-rock wilderness into a 'tradition'), transformed by the Band, and taken up by a host of American groups who had overdosed on stoned improvisation and sought a soft landing.

While American rock artists sought to find truth in themselves or in a traditional musical form, it was technique that reigned supreme in Britain. Gifted players formed supergroups, hard rock acts begat a whole host of guitar (and bass and drum, for that matter) heroes, while everyone raced to be the most 'progressive', a word that combined prowess with classical pretension. The categories weren't mutually exclusive, and Bolan had a veneer of 'authenticity', a conceptual purity and had built up enough goodwill through his records and concerts to ensure there was still a place for Tyrannosaurus Rex in the rapidly shifting musical order. He had changed styles almost overnight years before, but he was unwilling to gamble with sales of around 20,000 per album just yet. After his return from America, and prior to the recruitment of Mickey Finn, Marc played safe when he told Chris Welch, 'There won't be a new direction . . . Tyrannosaurus Rex is still a very young thing and although it has gone electric, it will still be much softer and more harmonious than most groups.' He was also clearly frustrated with the singles' market. 'Forget England for singles,' he complained. 'People keep telling me to make singles and we always get good reviews. But John Peel is the only DJ who will play us here, and Alan Freeman.' As a contrast to his own aspirations, he mentioned his former partner Steve Took 'wanting to get into this heavier group thing with Twink from the Pink Fairies'.[6]

Marc and Mickey escaped to the west coast of Wales for a short holiday to rehearse, so that they could complete work on the album Marc had started with Steve, and prepare for a short tour kicking off at Manchester Free Trade Hall on 21 November. It wasn't the first time Marc had been to Wales, the land of mystery and Celtic legends which still incorporated a red dragon on its national flag. He and June made occasional visits to an old house up in the north-west corner of Wales not far from Portmadoc and Harlech. Other visitors to the house were Lord Harlech's daughters, including Alice Ormsby-Gore. While he was there, Marc was temporarily seduced by the lifestyle: with no electricity, he chopped wood for the open fire and sang his songs to the silent sheep on the foothills of Snowdonia. 'People wear peace, deep green peace as a halo here,' he wrote on a postcard to one of his friends during a holiday in June 1969.

The friendship with Ormsby-Gore extended to visiting the

house in Surrey where she lived with her fiancé, ex-Cream guitarist Eric Clapton. Bolan was photographed in the garden with his Les Paul guitar, but tales of receiving formal lessons from Clapton, once regarded by his audiences as 'God', have been grossly exaggerated. Marc, who told Tony Visconti, 'I sat at the feet of the Master', was certainly in awe of the British blues player, and seemed to have substituted arrogance for careful study whenever Clapton picked up his instrument.

Having spent a week in the studio completing work on the new album with his electric guitar and Tony Visconti – Mickey Finn in a largely passive role – Bolan decided it was time to remind the London rock journalists that Tyrannosaurus Rex were still around. Reborn maybe, but not yet bopping, for despite the higher volume levels that Visconti had to deal with during the recent sessions at Trident, and Bolan's increasing tendency to dig out his old Ricky Nelson singles (specifically for the James Burton guitar licks), Marc turned up at the *Melody Maker* offices with his acoustic in hand and proceeded to play a selection of his new songs. Mickey Finn's inexperienced bongo playing went unnoticed because he left his instruments behind, preferring to tap out a beat with his hands on a table.


David Bowie celebrated the arrival of his twenty-third birthday on 8 January 1970 at Trident Studios by working on a follow-up single to 'Space Oddity'. Among the musicians with him that night was Marc Bolan. Despite rumours of several prior collaborations, this was the first time that the pair had worked together in a professional capacity – in fact 'together' is probably overstating the case. In recalling the session, David Bowie has said, 'There was quite a lot of rivalry between Marc and myself. We had a sparring relationship. We both knew we were going to do something in the future, but he was a few rungs up – he was really starting to happen . . . I don't think we were talking to each other that day. I can't remember why, but I remember a very strange attitude in the studio. We were never in the same room at the same time. You could have cut the atmosphere with a knife.'[7] There are many parallels between the pair's fortunes, and their paths had often crossed since the days when Bolan was Mark Feld, and Bowie was plain David Jones from the south-east London suburb of Bromley. Like Marc, David had been an image-conscious mod, who had played some skiffle in his early teens and was determined to become a singer after leaving school. He, too, started his professional career at Decca during the mid-sixties, fronting the Maidstone-based R & B group the King Bees, before securing a contract in his own right with its Deram subsidiary towards the end of 1966. By this time he was known as David Bowie, taking his new surname from the knife that was hurled across screen in so many Hollywood westerns, including, of course, those early Davy Crockett movies.

Neither Bowie nor Bolan allowed rejection and failure to dent their determination and self-belief and, by 1966, both had found managers with whom to share their aspirations. While Simon Napier-Bell listened attentively as Marc dreamed aloud, Bowie was being well catered-for by Kenneth Pitt. Napier-Bell managed to get Bolan's 'Hippy Gumbo' published by Campbell-Connelly, but it was Bowie's songwriting deal with Essex Music, signed around the same time, on 7 December 1966, that looked much more promising. Essex had already successfully published Anthony Newley, and Bowie – then writing in Newleyesque, cheeky Cockney style (his best-known song from this era is 'The Laughing Gnome') – was keen to share the same publisher as his idol.

It wasn't a lucrative deal – he received an advance of £500 for the first year, rising to £1500 a year later – but the association with Essex had put Bowie in contact with Tony Visconti, who befriended the young songwriter after Denny Cordell turned him down as unsuitable for Straight Ahead/New Breed. Visconti recorded Bowie's 'Let Me Sleep Beside You' and 'Karma Man' at Advision on 1 September 1967, for a projected single, but the idea was quickly shelved.

There were no more David Bowie records until 1969, though his growing repertoire did find a welcome outlet on sessions for BBC's new Radio 1 station. Bowie used Tony Visconti as musical director on some of these recordings. (The producer continued to work with Bowie up to 1970's *The Man Who Sold The World* album and 'Holy Holy' single, and the pair re-established their ties towards the end of 1973, after Visconti's relationship with Bolan had ended.) John Peel recalls the Bowie of the late sixties as, 'a chap who was full of extraordinary ideas and notions, none of which seemed very likely ever to come to fruition'.

The Visconti connection soon brought Bolan and Bowie

together socially. 'I started inviting them round to my flat,' he has said, 'because I had a gramophone and they didn't. They were both living at their mums' at the time, actually. They used to jam together but what we mainly used to do was listen to Beach Boys and Phil Spector albums.'[8] Little love was lost between the pair, though, as Visconti remembers: 'Ray Stevenson took some photos at Hermione's house in Edenbridge, Kent (Bowie's girl-friend at the time, and immortalised in his song 'Letter to Her-mione'). I set it up and Marc, Steve, Ray and June all drove out there. But they never even spoke to David or thanked Hermione for the use of her parents' garden. The rivalry was always there.'

George Underwood, one of Bowie's closest friends since pre-teen days, recalled that, during the mid-sixties, he and his Bromley friend 'were never into drugs and booze – we were stoned on imagination'.[9] Several years later, Bowie – who fully embraced the Romantic notion of the creative artist by also taking up mime, dance and acting, and was prompted by the counter-culture's anti-materialism to look East, taking an interest in Tib-etan culture and philosophy – was praising Bolan for his ascetic restraint and single-mindedness. 'Marc has been a great influence on me,' he said at the end of 1969, 'not so much with his music, but with his attitude to the pop scene. He shuts himself off from the destructive elements and prefers to get on with his work. That's how I intend to be.'[10]

Until the night when Visconti brought Bolan and Bowie together at Trident for 'The Prettiest Star', there had been no real musical link-up of note, though Steve Took did appear on one of Bowie's BBC Radio 1 sessions. 'Steve sang some of the backing vocals on the 26 May 1968 Top Gear session,' recalls Tony Visconti. 'He slept on my floor the night before and came along to the session the next day for the fun of it. I have a clear vision of David, Steve and myself standing around a microphone and adding various "oohs" and "aahs" and handclaps on those tracks.' Keen-eared fans who have heard the archive recording will spot Took singing the high 'slow down' harmony on 'Karma Man', and droning on the introduction to 'Silly Boy Blue'.

Kenneth Pitt may have been assured that he made the right decision after witnessing his protégé supporting Tyrannosaurus Rex on several dates early in 1969, but even he must have been surprised by the manner of Bowie's sudden ascendancy from abstract mime performances to television guest appearances. The singer caught the atmosphere of that summer's moon landing with an unusual song called 'Space Oddity', though few listened carefully to the lyric which ended with the astronaut floating away into oblivion and an inevitable death. When Bowie played the demo to Marc, the response was apparently ecstatic: 'It's going to be a hit, Davie!' enthused Bolan. Visconti was less enamoured of the song and passed up the opportunity to work on it, allowing fellow New Breed producer Gus Dudgeon to step in. If Marc seemed genuinely excited by 'Space Oddity', its surprise success gave him something to think about. 'If he reminds you of anyone,' wrote Penny Valentine in October 1969, 'it is a gentle mixture of Bob Dylan and Donovan with 90 per cent pure (himself). He says he sings like Dylan would have done if he'd been born in England – and he's an absolute charmer. His charm is so overpowering that it has given him more freedom to achieve his ideals than you would have thought in this day and age.'[11] It was actually a perfect description of Bolan, except, annoyingly for Marc, it was a portrait of David Bowie.

This kind of press may have contributed to the air of bad feeling which Bowie remembers at 'The Prettiest Star' session. Tony Visconti has said that 'Marc was in rivalry with everybody. He simply couldn't stand attention going in anyone else's direction. He was a total megalomaniac, God bless him. David, on the other hand, is a very gregarious, open-minded person, and apart from a normal, healthy type of rivalry, he was never obsessed with Bolan. David always liked Marc. He liked to be with him. He would come home after a social session with Marc feeling quite hurt after Bolan had taken too many digs at him.'[12] Meanwhile, the ever-loyal June Child stood by her man, and walked out of 'The Prettiest Star' playback session claiming that Marc's guitar line was the only worthwhile thing on the song. Bowie must have wanted to swallow his recently sung words which, while probably directed at his new girlfriend Angie, also appeared to eulogise his guest: 'One day, tho' it might as well be someday/You and I will rise up all the way/All because of what you are/The Prettiest Star'.

David Bowie wasn't the only friend of Marc's suddenly thrust into the public gaze. A young, black American student named Marsha Hunt had taken time off from her studies to visit London in 1966, became embroiled in the underground music scene and had, by the autumn of 1968, landed a part in the

controversial rock stage show *Hair*. Kit Lambert coaxed her away
from the Shaftesbury Theatre with the promise of a career as a
rock singer, signed her to Track in March 1969 and promptly
assigned Tony Visconti to the case. While looking for material to
fill a projected album, Visconti decided to put forward some of
Marc's material. Eventually, the production of Marsha's singles
and her *Woman Child* album was split between Visconti, Gus
Dudgeon and Kit Lambert, though she did record and release
four Bolan songs in all. 'Hot Rod Mama' (retitled 'Hot Rod
Poppa') was the first to appear, on the flip of the début single –
her impressive version of Dr John's 'Walk on Gilded Splinters',
a song which conjured up much of the Creole menace of 'Hippy
Gumbo'. She courted controversy when one of her breasts fell
out on a *Top Of The Pops* appearance, and while the record was
only a minor hit, her strong image – fringed jacket, leather pants,
thigh-length boots, hula-hooped earrings and wild Afro – made
a considerable impression on the rock world during 1969.

Marc Bolan was similarly captivated. 'Marsha loved "Hot
Rod Mama" ', recalls Visconti, 'and she showed up one night
while we were recording *Unicorn*. By chance, it was the one night
June wasn't there. The two of them just looked at each other and
it was like magic. You could see the shafts of light pouring out
of their eyes into each other. They were eating each other up
alive. We finished the session unusually early, and Marc and
Marsha walked out into the night hand in hand. He said, "See
you tomorrow, Tony", and gave me a wink. He'd never behaved
like that before. It was a total shock to me.'

Although the affair only lasted a matter of weeks, it became
dramatised in Marsha's recording schedule. 'Desdemona' and
'Hippy Gumbo' were earmarked for her next single, and 'Stacey
Grove' (where the woodwind mimicked Marc's voice) for her
forthcoming album. Marc himself made a rare guest appearance
when he sang a brief line from a nursery rhyme ('Hickory Dickory
Dock, the mouse ran up the clock') on her version of the
Supremes' 'My World Is Empty Without You'. Marsha recalled
the liaison in her *Real Life* autobiography. 'I personified things
which Marc rejected,' she explained. 'He was reclusive, macrobiotic, and professed aversion to success. He had no money and
acted as though he was opposed to it on social grounds. Maybe
his choosing to be with me was an indication that he was changing.'

While his mates were still deliberating on which spiritual path to follow, Marc and Marsha discussed success. 'He teased me about my success,' she recalled. 'I almost believed he spurned it, except he brought it up too much . . . To Marc, my visibility was commercial, and this wasn't appropriate to the serious art of music which he implied was validated by obscurity. His undercover enthusiasm for the Ronettes and Melangian girl-group vocals made his protestations about pop and rock success seem hypocritical.'[13]

In the face of the success of his friends and rivals, Bolan's adherence to hippie cool and sincerity was beginning to weaken. He had begun to venture out from Toadstool Studios (now soundproofed with dozens of egg cartons), mix with the scene and break the precious, unspoken bond with June by conducting an affair. On the surface, it was little more than a childish exploit, quickly patched up when June found out and paid a visit to Marsha, reprimanding her man/child when she got back home; but the breach of trust was symbolic of a growing impatience on Marc's part. June was forgiving, Marc full of remorse. He also knew just how important June was to his career. In an act of unbridled passion, the pair turned their back on *à la mode* sexual freedom and got married.

It was a spur-of-the-moment decision and, having notified the local Kensington Register Office a couple of days earlier, Marc and June took their matrimonial vows on Friday 30 January 1970. Just five close friends were invited – Mickey Finn and his girl-friend Sue Worth, Jeff Dexter, Alice Ormsby-Gore and resident photographer Pete Sanders – and the revellers celebrated by going out for a meal and getting drunk. Sid and Phyllis Feld didn't know anything about their son's marriage until some time after the event, but a treasured photograph of an impishly delighted Marc, his hair flecked with confetti, became a regular fixture on the family mantelpiece as a reminder that they were learning to live with the knowledge that their second son did things very much his own way.

The events of the previous six months had drawn Marc Bolan out of his insular existence and given him a new-found worldliness which reacquainted him with his original dream. Musically, this was reflected in the first recordings with Mickey Finn and aired on John Peel's *Top Gear* show in November 1969. Finn's obviously rudimentary skills, coupled with Marc's economical writing style – simpler structures, more hooks and increasingly audible lyrics – reflected a noticeable shift, even if the performances were rather erratic.

The full-blown electric guitar sound of the 'King Of The Rumbling Spires' single did not immediately unleash the half-expected onslaught that would have brought Tyrannosaurus Rex into line with rock's recent obsession with volume and power. Marc valued his present customers. Instead, his sinewy lead lines, softened with regular use of a wah-wah pedal, were mostly ornamental. However, when the duo agreed, at short notice, to fill the bill for Radio 1's new rock concert programme, *John Peel's Sunday Show* (later known as *In Concert*), Bolan unveiled himself as a guitar hero on 'Elemental Child'. This new number, which contained almost all of Marc's favourite electric chords – E, D, A minor, C and G – in one song, consisted of two short verses, followed by a lengthy – and loud – lead guitar passage. Compere John Peel, speaking between the songs, was obviously excited about this new development. 'Once or twice a week, Marc comes round to Peel Acres to listen to Ricky Nelson, Gene Vincent, Elvis and James Burton's guitar work,' he told the audience at the Paris Studios. After 'Elemental Child', Peel paid him the ultimate compliment by invoking Elvis Presley's legendary sideman: 'Scotty Moore would be proud of you,' he said.

The broadcast was followed by a single, 'By The Light Of A Magical Moon', released in January, and the album, *A Beard Of Stars*, issued a couple of months later, but neither did much to alter the group's fortunes. *Beard* was grandly dedicated to 'the Priests of Peace, all Shepherds and Horse Lords and my Imperial Lore Liege – the King of the Rumbling Spires', and its subject matter was much the same as before. 'Great Horse' (originally recorded with Took whose contribution was subsequently wiped: 'Marc was terrified of paying Steve any royalties,' says Visconti), 'The Woodland Bop', 'Dragon's Ear', 'Dove' and 'Lofty Skies' were all titles that could have walked off the previous trio of albums, yet there were significant changes. Marc now kept the lyrics to a minimum, the songs were more immediate (if, on occasion, somewhat more sophisticated) and Visconti's production was crystal-clear and uncluttered. The group's musical parameters had been widened to embrace the guitar-pyrotechnics of 'Elemental Child' and a more plaintive acoustic sound than aired before. One song, 'Dove', almost fell into the realm of the conventional love ballad and, as a sign that his musical expression was taking on a life of its own, two titles – 'Prelude' and 'A Beard of Stars' – contained no lyrics at all.

David Bowie's 'The Prettiest Star' fared worse, failing to make any impression whatsoever, despite Bolan's memorable lead guitar contribution (which Mick Ronson adhered to closely when the song was re-recorded for the 1973 *Aladdin Sane* album). Meanwhile, Bowie had tired of using pick-up musicians for his recordings, and formed the Hype, with John Cambridge (drums), Mick Ronson (guitar) and Tony Visconti (bass). This new outfit followed Tyrannosaurus Rex on to *John Peel's Sunday Show* in February for a rather shambolic performance, which was repeated at the Roundhouse that same month. The show was musically erratic but memorable, if only for its visual impact. 'I remember John Cambridge was a cowboy and Tony Visconti wore a Superman outfit,' Bowie recalled a couple of years ago. 'I can't remember what I wore, but it was very spacey and there was a lot of Lurexy material in it. Bolan was there and he was open-mouthed that we had the balls to camp it up so much.'[14] Bowie still has a series of photographs to prove it, showing Bolan leaning against the stage watching attentively with a floppy hippie hat on his head. 'He wasn't into his glam thing yet,' recalls Tony Visconti. 'We were!'

Bolan's and Bowie's musical uncertainties were merely reflections of crises in their careers. Bowie had been the one-hit wonder while Bolan enjoyed a more substantial cult audience. Both had relished the freedom to indulge extra-musical creative passions (poetry and mime respectively) which had been tolerated by underground audiences, but with the music industry rapidly hardening up all around them, there increasingly looked like being only winners and losers in 1970. The long boom of western capitalism appeared exhausted; mean-spiritedness gradually supplanted open-mindedness; hopes gradually mutated into fears, and the Conservative Party under Edward Heath was voted in as a reflection of that change. Pop was not immune to these cultural shifts, and 1970 brought with it its own share of tragedy. The Beatles imploded under the weight of lawsuits; Jimi Hendrix, Janis Joplin and Canned Heat's Al Wilson all followed ex-Rolling Stone Brian Jones into rock 'n' roll heaven;

and the pungent aromas of 1967 had turned stale, as did any real belief in the anti-heroes of the counter-culture. Audiences changed too, hardening around the twin pillars of the recently enlarged student population and a growing body of teenagers. With no underground to pledge allegiance to any more, both Bolan and Bowie (the latter had always managed to maintain a distance from it anyway) were prompted into making some kind of a response.

The fashionable notion of the counter-cultural 'anti-hero' was always a misnomer. The artistry of Dylan, Hendrix, Joplin, and even Frank Zappa was what seemed to matter – and that all had colourful personalities and identifiable images which translated well into poster form was largely overlooked. Dylan's arrogance, Hendrix's crotch, Janis's empty Southern Comfort bottle and Zappa's dry humour were all inextricably entwined with their art – indeed, their entire lives were perceived as art. By 1970, record companies were gradually latching on to the fact that this kind of credible 'star' was a better long-term investment (via the booming and extremely lucrative album market) than a good tune sung by faceless one-hit wonders. Musicians like Dylan, Lennon and, to a much smaller extent Bolan, expressed something far greater to their respective constituencies – though by now Marc was keen to extend his.

The sleeve photo for *A Beard Of Stars*, taken by Pete Sanders, was the most blatant selling of Marc Bolan yet. 'He had very strong ideas about what he wanted,' recalls the photographer. 'Image was very important to him. At the time, Marc was a very gentle character and the *A Beard Of Stars* cover shot really personifies that for me. That's how I like to remember him. What you see is just a small part of a negative with Marc dressed in a velvet coat and ruffled shirt. He and June went through the contact sheets and came up with the idea of enlarging this small portion of the photo. It gave the image a nice, grainy effect and a slight Pre-Raphaelite feel with all those wispy curls, which I think worked well. It made an impression on the fans, too, because I started receiving letters that said, "I've looked at the photo through a blue filter, and discovered the heads of Dylan and the Beatles in Marc's hair. How did they get there?"!'

In 1966, Simon Napier-Bell had been laughed out of record company offices when he played bemused A & R men Bolan's demo for 'Hippy Gumbo'. There was no strident beat to it, but worse still, they said, was the voice. Hippie audiences, willing to court the weird and wonderful, had generally warmed to it, and as time went on, Marc had softened its abrasive edges. Then, during the summer of 1970, it was as if the whole of Europe suddenly discovered vibrato. The irritatingly infectious pop song on everyone's lips was Mungo Jerry's 'In The Summertime'.

'What really made Marc a star was Mungo Jerry, not Marc Bolan,' insists Napier-Bell. 'He could not make any headway with his voice other than as a hippie act playing to 300 people in universities for £20 a night. His albums were selling in reasonable quantities but he wasn't really going anywhere. Ray Dorset sang in a similar fashion and put it into a super-commercial song, got a hit, and suddenly that voice was acceptable. I don't know what Marc must have thought when he heard that voice: it must have been terrible for him. But it was a turning point.'

Marc's individual singing style had been an influence on others on several occasions. 'I couldn't get that voice,' John Lennon says at the end of 'Cold Turkey' on the *Live Peace In Toronto* album (released in December 1969), before emitting a brief bleat to illustrate the point. Then again, he could have been trying to mimic his wife's strange vocal emissions. However, there was no mistaking Ray Davies's usage of the vibrato on 'King Kong', the B side of the Kinks' April 1969 'Plastic Man' single. 'Everybody wants to be King Kong,' he forecast, in blissful ignorance of both Bolan's ambition and his earlier Mighty Joe Young fixation.

As he watched from the sidelines while someone else scored a massive hit on the back of his voice, Bolan sought solace in the latest Bob Dylan album, *Self Portrait*, issued in July 1970 while 'In The Summertime' still topped the singles chart. Many thought the shapeless, erratic twenty-four-track double LP was Dylan's idea of a joke, and it was savaged by the critics. Bolan was similarly outraged – but by the press, not Dylan – and wrote a genuine plea to *Melody Maker* defending an artist's right to pursue his own path. The letter was published in the paper's 11 July 1970 edition.

I've just listened to Dylan's new album, and in particular 'Belle Isle', and I feel deeply moved that such a man is making music in my time.

Dylan's songs are now mainly love ballads, the writing of which is one of the most poetic art forms since the dawn of man. 'Belle Isle' brought to my memory all the moments of tenderness I've ever felt for another human being, and that, within the superficial landscape of pop music, is a great thing indeed. Please, all the people who write bitterly of a lost star, remember that with maturity comes change, as surely as death follows life.

Coming from someone who was about to thrust himself into pop stardom it is a remarkable document, full of the contradic- tions which make pop music – and Marc Bolan's place in it – so contentious. Dylan had turned in a sprawling set, which included three instrumentals, a cover of an old standard ('Blue Moon'), and a few lukewarm live recordings of material from his cata- logue. Worse than that, the vibrant imagery of his past work was nowhere to be found; and most of the record seemed to have been aimed at an audience that preferred to listen easily rather than actively. Marc, who was fiercely competitive when it came to his close contemporaries, remained loyal to Dylan. If the singer had moved towards a new style, then there must have been something in it. More than that, perhaps, Bolan's interjection on behalf of such a great – if changing – talent was an astute piece of self-elevation by association.

Bolan was right about the fate of the love ballad. When rock separated from pop, this well-trodden form was left behind, unless it was couched in medievalism (Donovan's 'Guinevere') or psychedelia (Country Joe and the Fish's 'Grace' or 'Janis'). Dylan's error was complacency in the face of the new school of up-and-coming singer-songwriters, who brought with them new melodies, new arrangements and a frank personal style. Marc, who was acutely aware of the human capacity for adopting differ- ent personalities and attitudes overnight, stuck by his idol, just as he hoped his supporters would stand by him, should a similar transformation occur.

No one suspected a thing when, in August 1970, a single crept out on the Bell label credited to Dib Cochran and the Earwigs. Since 1967, many rock musicians had been keen to throw off the simple requirements of a pop song, and a spate of British groups (some little more than session musicians masquer- ading as a collective unit) cashed in on the rising tide of what was called 'bubblegum' – easy on the ear, immediate, and instantly disposable. Marc Bolan and Tony Visconti decided they too could knock out a tune like Edison Lighthouse, White Plains, Picketty-witch or the Pipkins had done earlier in the year. They came up with two similarly 'throwaway' songs, which Visconti sang while Marc played some lead guitar, and gave them unmistakably 'pop' titles – 'Oh Baby' and 'Universal Love' – while Visconti added sprightly string arrangements to ram the melodies home. The result was nothing less than a blueprint for the future T. Rex sound. The important missing ingredient was the image and the auteurship of Marc Bolan.

'David Platz got me some free time at a TV studio,' recalls Visconti, 'and I went in and recorded a song as Yankee Dayglo, which was a play on my Italian-American background. Steve Took was on that too, as Skinny Rose, and Bowie loved it. It was a funny version of Tyrannosaurus Rex. Then Marc said he had this song, "Baby, Baby", which he wanted me to sing. We got in John Cambridge and Rick Wakeman to help out, and as Platz wanted nothing to do with it, I set up the deal with Bell. It was definitely the precursor of T. Rex.'

The record didn't sell. No one expected it to: it received no record company promotion or radio airplay. But the exercise, playful though it was, provided more than just a therapeutic distraction from the business of furthering Marc's bona fide career. It pointed the way.

Around the time of the split with Steve Took, Bolan had again switched management, and having approached Chris Blackwell at Island Records, he was referred to the ambitious new EG management company. EG, founded by David Enthoven and John Gaydon, who had met while working for the Noel Gay organisation, already had King Crimson on their books and were in the process of breaking Emerson, Lake and Palmer. The switch meant the end of the Tyrannosaurus Rex fan club, though a new one was promptly formed by Carol Oliver from Hornchurch. Many of the old fans stayed, but some, alarmed by the sight of Bolan strapping on his white Stratocaster during the group's occasional appearances in recent months, began to lament the passing of an age. Marc, meanwhile, continued to immerse him-self in fifties rock 'n' roll. He attended a Rock Revival Show at the Roundhouse in March, where Marty Wilde, Joe Brown, Tommy Bruce, and the original king of the fumbling wires Bert Weedon appeared on the bill. He enthused about the vocal virtues of Frankie Lymon and the guitar-playing of Lonnie Mack and Link

Wray; and told reporters, 'It's nice to get back to the originals.' Bolan insisted that he, like Dylan, wasn't going to be strait-jacketed. 'We were thinking of going on at the Festival Hall with 400 watts each,' he said in March 1970, 'and freak 'em out! All the kids will come to see freaky Bolan quietly doing his thing and then NEARH!'[15]

Tyrannosaurus Rex played the summer festival circuit for the third year in succession, and can be seen in the *Stamping Ground* film of the Kralingen festival in Rotterdam, Holland, per-forming 'By The Light Of A Magical Moon'. The first half of the set usually consisted of acoustic versions of 'Debora', 'Hot Rod Mama', 'One Inch Rock' and 'Wind Quartets' from the Took era, plus 'Organ Blues' (with Marc on his £6 keyboard from Woolworths). The second half consisted of electric numbers, including 'Pavilions Of The Sun', 'By The Light Of A Magical Moon' and 'Elemental Child' from *A Beard of Stars*, before climax-ing with a lengthy reworking of 'The Wizard', which bore little resemblance to the original 45 from 1965. A new song, 'Jewel', also started appearing in the set. If 'Voodoo Chile' marked Jimi Hendrix's acid-tinged resurrection of the blues, 'Jewel' was Bolan's own psychedelicised return to blues-based rock 'n' roll, a mesmerising fuzz guitar extravaganza which found him stumbling, glorious and barely coherent, into guitar-hero territory.

There was a considerable difference. Much of Hendrix's music inhabited the netherspace which had been unlocked by acid, constantly peaking and troughing, and endlessly worked and reworked in mammoth studio sessions in a bid to recreate the experience. Bolan's music provided a richly tapestried back-drop to the psychedelic age, rather than a mirror to it, which wasn't altogether surprising. Hallucinogenic excess didn't auto-matically ensure a career of psychedelic improvisation, as Syd Barrett's solo work amply illustrates, but it did tend towards a breakdown of old twelve-bar formats. Bolan picked up on some of the stylistic nuances of psychedelic music because of his pro-digious talent for absorbing influences, but it never threatened to become anything other than a passing acquaintance.

In 1976, Bolan confirmed that 'None of the [Tyrannosaurus Rex] albums were written under drugs. I came into drugs very late and I never wrote under any kind of stimulant. I took acid about four times in 1970 but I didn't like it. I was spiked with

STP (an extremely potent hallucinogenic drug) and was under sedation for two weeks. I came out and wrote "Ride A White Swan".'[16] As usual, Bolan's chronology was slightly askew – several months separated the event of his unfortunate spiking and the writing of 'Ride A White Swan', but the main thrust of what he had said was true. Marc liked to remark that acid only confirmed a way of viewing the world that he had experienced since an early age, but the truth was probably less romantic. 'I think he was slightly afraid of dropping acid,' says Jeff Dexter. 'He read all the books, knew all the words, but I don't know if he actually learned the song.'

Dexter was with Marc on the night of the infamous spiking. The pair had attended a party for the short-lived British-based version of *Rolling Stone* magazine in Hanover Square, just off Regent Street in Central London. June, who had been working late, arrived to collect Marc, only to find him dazed, confused and mumbling something about wanting to eat himself. According to June's account in Jonathon Green's *Days In The Life*, she intended to drop Jeff off at his place in Haverstock Hill, but Bolan was so out of control, screaming and salivating, that the only way she could get him home was if Dexter returned with them to Blenheim Crescent. With Marc rooted to his seat in the car, June called a doctor friend, Bernie Greenwood, who managed to talk him up to the flat. Once inside, he gave the unsuspecting patient a large dose of Largactil which put Bolan to sleep. This process continued for the next day or two, until Marc finally 'came down'. 'He was absolutely petrified and he made me promise that nobody would ever give him acid again,' recalled June.

'Ride A White Swan' didn't come out of this experience. Instead, the song marked the culmination of months spent pursuing a career as a musical archaeologist, digging out old rock 'n' roll records, combined with the growing realisation that a return to a simplified electric twelve-bar style would be timely and well received. It appeared to be an expertly judged calculation, but because success depends on a combination of so many factors, the decision to release 'Ride A White Swan' as the next single was nothing more than a well-executed gamble that paid off. Nevertheless, the impression was that Marc, his management and his record company were doing everything they could to pave the way for its success, short of physically forcing people into shops to buy the record.

It was undoubtedly the most overtly commercial song Bolan had written to date, bolstered by a simple string section and Marc's own bass guitar part, but there was no certainty that anyone would pick up on it. Months earlier, Marc claimed that he had written several single-type songs but was reluctant to release them because of the attitude of BBC radio. This time round, the record secured one daytime airplay, which prompted enough sales to force the BBC to include it on its much-resented playlist. Tyrannosaurus Rex had been regarded as little more than a joke at Broadcasting House; and many people lacked confidence to ask for their records over shop counters for fear of stumbling over the name. Calling themselves T. Rex (the abbreviation used by Bolan in the advert to find a replacement for Steve Took and one also utilised by Tony Visconti when he filled in the Trident Studio session sheets) emphasised the sense of rebirth projected by the group in autumn 1970.

Even the familiar Regal Zonophone labels were missing. 'Ride A White Swan' was the first release on the newly formed Fly label, set up by David Platz after New Breed's three-year contract with EMI had expired. Having built up the subsidiary label from archaic purveyor of Salvation Army records to a strong force in British pop music, with names like Procol Harum, the Move and Joe Cocker charting regularly, Platz wanted a piece of the action himself. With the partnership backing of Track Records' Kit Lambert and Chris Stamp, and the expertise of Malcolm Jones, who had been responsible for the day-to-day running of EMI's progressive Harvest label, Platz decided to place all his contracted artists on Fly.

Having been a production company which licensed its material out, functioning as a fully fledged record label in its own right meant that, in its early stages at least, Fly could not afford to back many losers. 'Ride A White Swan' had to kick-start Bolan's career in a new direction *and* get the entire operation off the ground. 'When we heard what we got,' recalls Platz, 'it was simply so exciting that we knew we had a potential superstar on our hands. It had such a different sound, and was exactly right for that particular time.'

Tony Visconti puts the sudden success down to two things. 'The image changed, and we had a string section in there. I had to beg David Platz to use four violins for the single and a couple of *T. Rex* album cuts. Fly had very little to do with Marc's success.

T. Rex was a legacy from the old days. I felt that we were almost
an embarrassment to the company.'

There was considerable activity in the weeks leading up to
the launch of the label. A distribution deal with Chris Blackwell's
Island was scuppered, but not before a handful of acetates of
'Ride A White Swan' were pressed up bearing the OCTO 1
catalogue number (Malcolm Jones had originally named the label
Octopus). Interestingly, the hard-hitting 'Jewel' was planned to
appear on the three-track single at this stage, and some have
insisted that it was once touted as an A side itself, which would
have pitched T. Rex at an entirely different audience. Then Lambert and Stamp became involved, the former suggesting the Fly
name. Eventually, the company returned to EMI for a distribution
deal and, in a bid to get the single out on time, a logo was quickly
knocked up by the Track designers and the pressing plant given
the go-ahead. Meanwhile, a moody Pete Sanders' portrait photo
was prepared for the group's first mass-produced picture sleeve
(uncommon in 1970; earlier Tyrannosaurus Rex sleeves were only
printed in very small quantities, and rarely found their way past
DJs and record pluggers).

'The business as such was at a very low ebb at that point,'
said Marc, months later, 'there was nothing really going down.
And we put it out. I was well prepared for it to bomb. I expected
to get a lot of aggravation from people saying, "It's too electric",
or whatever, and it was a hit in three weeks.'[17] Everyone had
hoped for some kind of impact, but the record took off so quickly
that Malcolm Jones had difficulty in meeting the demand. 'I was
so busy trying to get records pressed and sleeves printed,' he
recalled, 'and if you look at the record itself, you'll see that it
appeared on brown or lilac labels. That was because I purchased
Immediate Records' lilac paper after they'd gone out of business
– simply to get records pressed quickly at any cost.'[18]

'Ride A White Swan' did not conform to the pure pop/
bubblegum of Dib Cochran and the Earwigs' 'Oh Baby'. Rock 'n'
roll, the missing ingredient from 'Oh Baby', provided the basis
for 'Swan', and the sense of rock's former glories was reinforced
by the inclusion of Eddie Cochran's 'Summertime Blues' on the
B side. Hinged round a precise guitar riff which echoed James
Burton's work on old Ricky Nelson 45s, 'Swan' neatly tailored
many of the old Tyrannosaurus Rex trademarks towards an audience that preferred its pop more clearly defined. The voice was

restrained by Marc's usual standards but still recognisably unique; the lyrics conjured up the same magical/natural imagery, but had been pruned down and made understandable (or at least audible); the handclaps, percussion and minimal bass provided a more pronounced beat; and the falsetto backing vocal restricted itself to one simple note. Once the track had been completed, Visconti added a string arrangement, fleshing it out by echoing the melody line without swamping it. What sold the song was its simplicity, Bolan's voice and – when the duo started appearing on *Top Of The Pops* – the image.

The co-ordination of the push to break T. Rex was completed by the organisation of a tour of major British venues, kicking off a week after the single's release with all ticket prices pegged to a maximum of 50p. It was the final masterstroke in a well-prepared campaign, although the ramifications of sudden success had not been thoroughly thought through. B.P. Fallon, who first met Marc at the December 1966 *Ready, Steady, Go!* appearance, and had become his publicist after Tyrannosaurus Rex signed to the EG management company, began to feed phrases like 'The Last of the Great Underground Groups' to the music press, invoking a word that had long been usurped by 'progressive', but which was still rich in mystique. More than that, it sparked off a debate in the press that continued to rage, particularly in its letters pages, for the next two years: had T. Rex 'sold out'?

They certainly sold out their string of concerts, which kept the duo busy right up to the end of the year. The press made the most of the transition from night-time to daytime radio, and Bolan responded by giving them informed and entertaining interviews. T. Rex also began to pick up more than warm applause from audiences who, since an appearance at Sheffield in mid-October, were now increasingly inclined to mob them. Marc lapped up the attention. Meanwhile, the first appearance on *Top Of The Pops* early in November – a subdued mimed performance with Mickey seated with a bass guitar and Marc shirtless in dungarees with his black Les Paul strapped around him – made it all too obvious that T. Rex had outlived its two-man format. A nervous Tony Visconti appeared with the group on bass for a couple of concerts, including a performance at Oxford Town Hall on 12 November, but Marc was keen to find a permanent bassist. The group took ten days out of the hectic schedule to redress the situation.

Bolan once said, 'I have no time for tension in groups,' and having ousted the troublesome Took for the more flexible Mickey Finn, he wanted a third member who would cause him few problems. Steve Currie had no great ambitions other than to pursue a musical career without too much material hardship. When he was offered the job after an audition in south London, he accepted immediately, even though he wasn't wholly enamoured of the group's music, at least not the pre-'Ride A White Swan' material. But he sensed that the old sound wasn't going to be around for much longer.

Born on 20 May 1947 in Grimsby, Steve Currie had been playing in groups since the mid-sixties, starting out in a jazz band called the Rumble on Friday nights at the local South Bank Jazz Club. By day, he worked in a shipping office, and after three years, had become a qualified ship broker. But music was his first passion, and when the Rumble uprooted to London in the hope of stirring up some record company interest, he gambled on his professional career and went with them. The sojourn ended in disaster, with the group returning home to Grimsby in debt, though Steve, whose girlfriend had a steady job in the capital, decided to stay. He had joined a band called the Meteors, but an advert in *Melody Maker* led him to the T. Rex rehearsal at a school hall near the Elephant & Castle. Having proved immediately acceptable to Marc, Steve had such confidence in the future success of T. Rex that he celebrated his new status with a bottle of whisky, ordered a special licence from Willesden Register Office, and married his girlfriend Hazel the next day.

The addition of Steve Currie was announced in the news pages of the music press on 12 December 1970, and ten days later he played his first London gig with the group at the Roundhouse, where T. Rex were further augmented with the Turtles' Howard Kaylan on backing vocals. The announcement coincided with the release of the first album bearing the group's truncated name which, in marked contrast to the verbosity of the previous titles, was simply called *T. Rex*. It wasn't exactly the new beginning it purported to be, and in interviews around the time of its release, Bolan maintained a distance from it, saying it had been recorded months ago and regretted that it hadn't been heavier-sounding.

*T. Rex* offered a similar balance of electricity and gentle acoustic material to that featured on *A Beard of Stars*, though both styles had been further refined. Bolan's voice was effectively double-tracked, and the percussion was more upfront and given added weight by simple bass lines on several songs, providing a more commercially acceptable vehicle for the catchy melodies Bolan had been peddling to a minority audience for several years. The major difference was that *T. Rex* included no less than four traditionally based rock 'n' roll tunes – 'Jewel', 'Is It Love?', a reworking of 'One Inch Rock' and 'Beltane Walk'. The latter was a direct steal from Chess R & B star Jimmy McCracklin's 'The Walk', recorded in 1957, which McCracklin later said he wrote to show how easy it was to have a rock 'n' roll hit. Its origin goes back further than that, though, because Chicago slide guitarist Hound Dog Taylor was playing an approximation of it as 'Taylor's Boogie' a couple of years earlier.

Bolan came into his own as a guitarist on the *T. Rex* album, displaying some subtle touches on 'Seagull Woman' and some distinctly unsubtle sub-Hendrixisms on the concert highlight 'Jewel'. Most notable was his increasing tendency to use the descending single note guitar riff on several songs, on 'Seagull Woman' (which featured inaudible guest backing vocals from Marc's old American friends Kaylan and Volman) and on the lengthy reworking of Bolan's first single, 'The Wizard', in particular. The latter, which proved that the wild wailing of the early Tyrannosaurus Rex days had not been fully exorcised, also employed a heavy string section, but even this couldn't mask the fact that the song cried out for some flamboyant Steve Took percussion and harmonies.

Intriguingly, the album was topped and tailed by short excerpts of symphonic rock titled 'The Children of Rarn' which, Marc told interviewers at the time, would provide the basis for a full-length concept album. Set in an imaginary age when the earth was known as Beltane, it appeared to be based around the usual leitmotif of the fantasy genre: namely the battle between good and evil. Bolan first laid out his grandiose ideas for it in November 1970, when he envisaged it spread across two LPs, complete with a spin-off book. It seemed a perfectly feasible idea at the time. Marc Bolan, who toured everywhere with a notebook, pencil and tape-recorder by his side as an aid to formulating the constant stream of ideas in his head, had already created a full repertoire of otherworlds, Utopias and invented characters. He only had to put them into some kind of order . . .

The *T. Rex* album was packaged in a semi-fold-out sleeve

which doubled as a poster of Marc and Mickey looking every inch the well-scrubbed, good-looking hippies they hoped audiences would think they were. The cover of *A Beard Of Stars* masqueraded as art; the sleeve of *T. Rex* promised nothing more than a pin-up, selling the world a sanitised version of the long-haired cult, crucially, at a time when the greater social threat seemed to come from the skinheads, whose total opposition to everything the hippie stood for was clearly expressed in their number one crop cuts and proletarian image. In the face of this new brutalism, T. Rex went for a more androgynous, beatific image than ever, and Pete Sanders was on hand to take the pictures. 'We went down to my mother's house in Sussex and did the session in the garden,' he remembers. 'Marc and Mickey wore white make-up, which gave their faces a porcelain-like effect. It was all part of the new electric image Marc was trying to create. That's why he wanted to be pictured with his electric guitar.' Marc Bolan had become the 'Bopping Elf'. One hit doesn't make a star, but the scenes surrounding the winter tour, the extended chart run of 'Ride A White Swan' (which was cruelly denied a top spot by Clive Dunn's 'Grandad'), and the willingness of the press to allow Marc free reign to become the new spokesman of pop signalled that there was more to come.

# CHAPTER EIGHT

'I've suddenly tuned into that mental channel which makes
a record a hit and I feel at present as though I could write
Number Ones for ever. Let's face it, the majority of pop hits
that make it are a permutation on the twelve-bar blues and
I've found one that works.'
Marc Bolan, *Disc* magazine, November 1970

'He aspired to being a rock 'n' roll idol. He'd have done
anything to be a success. People said he sold out when he
made the transition from Tyrannosaurus Rex into T. Rex, but
he wanted to be the Marc Bolan of T. Rex from the time he
was fourteen. He wasn't really interested in being the
esoteric, underground cult figure that had emerged from
Middle Earth. He played that role and did it well, but he
always wanted to be the Star.'
Keith Altham

'The record industry really needed someone at that point
and Marc was just the right person. With bands like ELP,
Yes and Led Zeppelin around, it wasn't hip to be making
singles any more and that part of the market had suffered
as a consequence. I really loved what Marc was doing in
1971, but because he'd come in the opposite direction,
from the underground to Number One in the charts, he was
such an easy target for the critics.'
Bob Harris

Marc Bolan had spent thirteen years fantasising about pop stardom: as 1971 began, he sensed it was within his grasp. 'Ride A
White Swan' was in the Top Ten and still on an upswing; the
British tour had generated increasingly ecstatic audiences; Marc
had refined his musical formula and was writing songs faster
than ever; and he had decided to enlarge T. Rex to a four-piece.
Just weeks earlier, the group had still begun their concerts cross-

legged on the floor beating out minor hippie anthems like 'Debora' and 'Wind Quartets' on bongos and acoustic guitar. Now they had become a fully fledged rock band. The rock 'n' roll beat had never been completely erased during the Tyrannosaurus Rex era, though the years of restraint – latent frustration, even – found a perfect vent in the newly constituted T. Rex.

The quietly confident, but usually gentle demeanour of Marc Bolan also began to alter with the first whiff of success. Marc, who had always insisted that songwriting came easily to him, began to claim that he could write a hit single in ten minutes, maybe five, thereby offering journalists the chance to conclude either that he was a swell-head, or else that his songs were essentially rewrites of others. With each successive single, and the inevitable clutch of press interviews which accompanied them, Marc's motor-mouthing shifted up a gear. Ringo Starr, one of his closest friends over the next few years, said that Marc had a catchphrase: '300,000 in five days, Number One in two weeks.' Some lapped it up, but many of the old guard, who had been through the same cultural changes as Bolan (and took them considerably more seriously), saw it as a betrayal of all that the counter-culture stood for. The debate – which centred on Bolan's style and his music but was about something much bigger – raged in the press for the ensuing months, and for the next two years, Marc Bolan was the most visible, successful and controversial musician in Britain.

At the peak of his commercial powers, in June 1972, Bolan sold magazines by the truckload, and even the mainstream press grappled for a slice of the T. Rex phenomenon. One such publication, *The Weekly News*, decided to hinge a competition around one of Marc's latest records, and asked, 'What are the qualities that make a top pop star?' Of course, there was no mention of the co-ordinated industry backing that helps make such a seemingly overnight transformation possible, but its simplistic breakdown of the individual parts at least revealed that Bolan did have much on his side: good stage presence; great singing voice; good looks; sincerity; brings something new to the pop scene; belief in himself; warm personality; sense of timing; individual sound. His old comrades may have questioned the veracity of his sincerity, though to his new fans, offering three tracks per single, attractive picture sleeves, and fixing maximum prices for concert tickets were much appreciated gestures. No one could really doubt that

Bolan possessed all the other qualities in abundance, although
the apparent 'newness' of his sound was hotly contested. More
than that, he wrapped up all the essential ingredients in a mystique that was commonplace in the worlds of literature or fine
art, but far less so in the pop world. Unlike past teen idols
like Peter Frampton and Steve Ellis, Marc's face cast a series of
intriguing, multi-faceted shadows.

The most important step in consolidating the success of 'Ride
A White Swan' was finding the right follow-up. Marc had been
concentrating on writing material based around the standard
twelve-bar format, and the best and most immediate of the new
batch was a song called 'Hot Love'. Structurally, it differed little
from, say, 'Hot Rod Mama', the opening cut on the début
Tyrannosaurus Rex album: but the finer points had been altered
dramatically. Measured electricity had replaced the awkward
acoustic rhythm; the voice and its message ('and I give her Hot
Love' – sex) was clear; the beat was simple and pronounced; and
the full if uncluttered production, boosted by tuneful backing
vocals and supportive strings, made it perfect for daytime radio.
Marc pulled out all the stops, utilising Presley's 'uh, uh, uh'
vocal affectation from 'All Shook Up', the guitar riff from 'Heartbreak Hotel' for the break, and added a 'Hey Jude'-type singalong
for a lengthy coda. A month after its release, 'Hot Love' was the
Number One record in Britain, and remained there for six weeks.

After years spent enduring managers, agents, journalists and
friends advising him how to improve his act, Bolan quickly settled
into the role he had been waiting to play for so long. Any change
in him was not immediately recognisable to his long-standing
friends, but the new faces in his circle saw a rather different Marc
Bolan. The generosity of spirit that oozed from Tyrannosaurus
Rex record sleeves, their ever-so-slightly precious concert appearances and the magical quality projected by the songs, didn't
extend to business practices within the T. Rex organisation. But
as Keith Altham stresses, this wasn't unique in the rock world.
'A lot of young artists get ripped off in various ways,' he says,
'and they realise that the most self-protective way of looking after
that situation is to do everything yourself. I think it was more a
defensive mechanism than being about control.'

The *putsch* to achieve total control was several months away,
but the new musicians in T. Rex soon found that regular television appearances, massive record sales and frenzied concert

performances didn't quite reap the rewards they'd imagined. Bassist Steve Currie, together with future drummer Bill Legend, was placed on a mere £40-a-week wage which rose to £50 in 1973.

Bill, who was born Bill Fifield in Barking on 8 May 1944, grew up in east London, and began drumming while still a pupil at Mayfield School in Ilford. Having started out tapping along on a school desk to rock 'n' roll numbers played and sung by a friend, Stewart Tanner, he soon progressed on to a Boys' Brigade drum and brushes. In the early sixties, Fifield and Tanner formed the Teenbeats, then the Zodiacs who, at the height of Beatlemania, became the Epics. (Another Epic, lead guitarist Vic Elmes, went on to find fame with bubblegum group Christie.) When the Epics secured a season in Scandinavia, Bill chose to put his job as a design artist at Bryant & May in east London's Bow district first, and was replaced by Mike Blakely, brother of Alan in the Tremeloes. Even after joining the prototype pub rock band Legend, with whom he recorded a self-titled album and a couple of singles, Bill remained only semi-professional. After all-night sessions with the group at Advision Studios, the bleary-eyed drummer would make his way down to Bow for his day job, while the rest of the band returned home to bed. It was a dedication that extended to his work in T. Rex, though it wasn't always appreciated.

Bolan had decided to introduce drums into T. Rex for 'Hot Love', which was his re-creation of the classic rock 'n' roll format that had excited him as a child, refined and tailored to suit the early seventies pop world. 'I know it's exactly like a million other songs,' he said at the time, 'but I hope it's got a little touch of me in it too. It was done as a happy record, and I wanted to make a twelve-bar record a hit, which hasn't been done since "Hi-Heel Sneakers" really.'[1] In fact, many songs had employed the twelve-bar formula since Tommy Tucker took 'Hi-Heel Sneakers' into the charts in 1964, but few spoke in the rock 'n' roll vernacular as succinctly as 'Hot Love'. Bolan even furnished journalists with a name for his new brand of rock 'n' roll. Drawing on the interstellar aspirations of Jimi Hendrix, and the late sixties' fascination with the creation of other worlds, he described it as 'Cosmic Rock'. It was Tony Visconti, producer of the Legend album, who alerted the T. Rex camp to Bill Fifield's suitability to join the band's first session as a four-piece. 'Tony came up to me in the pub one night,' Bill remembers, 'and asked me if I wanted to sit in for T. Rex. I didn't really know too much about the group, but he told me that they were working in the studio and wanted to try out drums for the first time. I went straight up to AIR Studios, met Marc – who I remember as being fairly flamboyant in a green suit – Mickey and Steve, and recorded "Hot Love" and "Woodland Rock" [a hybrid of Presley's 'Jailhouse Rock' and Little Richard's 'Long Tall Sally']. Those recordings ended up on the next record.'

Marc hedged his bets before plunging in and reconstituting T. Rex as a permanent four-piece, but when 'Hot Love' showed immediate signs of following 'Ride A White Swan' into the charts, and with an American tour on the horizon, the decision was made for him and he auditioned extensively for a drummer. So many candidates were considered that Bolan left the jamming up to Mickey and Steve. No one seemed immediately suitable.

Bill Fifield, who got a kick out of hearing his drumming on a record that was now receiving considerable airplay, received a call at Bryant & May from June Bolan inviting him to audition at the small Gooseberry Studios in Soho. He begged, bought and borrowed some of Marc's old albums, though, in retrospect, he says, 'I needn't have bothered because it was all rockin' and rollin'. He was on another kick by then. The chart success had really whetted his appetite.' They ran through a set made up of standards like Eddie Cochran's 'Summertime Blues' and 'C'mon Everybody', and Bolan's cosmic rockers like 'Ride A White Swan', 'Hot Love' and 'One Inch Rock'. Fifield, who had recently backed British rock 'n' roll idol Billy Fury on some London dates, tossed in every drum cliché he could remember.

He may have had an instinctive feel for the group's new direction, but Bolan's reaction at the rehearsal left him puzzled. 'We rarely got any feedback from Marc,' Bill says. 'My status wasn't clearly established at all. Tony asked me how it all went, and I told him that Marc had mumbled something about getting the gig in a rather low-key way. I didn't realise that was his way of saying I was in. There was no big introduction. We spent the next few days rehearsing in a cellar in Victoria and two weeks later, towards the end of March 1971, I was playing my first concert with T. Rex in Detroit.' Bill saw no need to maintain his day job.

The enthusiastic scenes on the recent UK dates were by no means repeated in America, where the group opened for hard rock acts like Humble Pie and Mountain. Instead, the five-week tour, which climaxed in New York with four nights at Bill Graham's Fillmore East, was regarded by Bolan as very much an exploratory mission. *Unicorn* and *A Beard Of Stars* may have been in the shops, and the 1969 tour had at least established the group's name in American rock circles, but with a shortened title, and a new sound and line-up, T. Rex were testing the water – and finding it slightly uncomfortable.

If the stage performance paled in comparison to that of the more experienced musically accomplished bill-topping acts, the group started to gel in the studio as they began to fit sessions around their taxing schedule. Recording while on tour or on short breaks between dates, which became the norm over the next couple of years, served three purposes: it was convenient; ensured that the results wouldn't be over-laboured, and was relatively cost-efficient. Since *Unicorn*, Tyrannosaurus Rex had spent considerably more time in the studio, perfecting takes and overdubbing. These American sessions, which took place at Wally Heider's in Los Angeles (a studio used by Jefferson Airplane) and Media Sound in New York, saw a considerable change in Marc's attitude to recording, which harked back to the thinking behind all those great fifties' sides cut at Sam Phillips' legendary Sun Studios in Memphis. His 'progressive' period was over.

Modern recording technology precluded a truly authentic Sun sound, but as the group rarely knew what they were about to record when they entered the studio the forthcoming *Electric Warrior* album acquired a primitive quality, which flew in the face of rock's increasingly highly polished sheen. 'I think we did well to remember the songs,' maintains Bill Legend (who had quickly assumed his new stage name while on tour). 'We used to run through the song three or four times and then we'd go for a take. I used to invent my drum breaks as I was playing. It was all done so quickly. Nothing was well prepared, but it did give an edge to those records: they were really powerful.'

There were occasional exceptions, and Legend was privy to a sneak preview of the song which is regarded by many of Bolan's associates as his best, 'Get It On'. 'He called me into his room while we were on tour,' recalls the drummer, 'and asked me to bring a snare drum along. We sat on the bed and he played it through, giving me a rare opportunity to work out all the stops. He told me, "I'm thinking about using the song as a follow-up

to 'Hot Love', and we're gonna record it when we get to Wally
Heider's in LA". And we did.'

The decision to record while on the road was not conveyed
to producer Tony Visconti. 'I wasn't invited,' he remembers. 'It
was a risky period because he was just going to make those
recordings in America without me there. It was only by chance
that we really hooked up again. "Hot Love" was already a hit,
so I decided to go home and see my mum. It was my first holiday
since coming over to England in 1967.

'We met up again in New York, and recorded "Jeepster",
"Monolith" and maybe "Lean Woman Blues" in Media Sound
Studios. Then he flew me out to California where we worked on
more songs. That was the only time Marc tried to usurp me, but
the recordings turned out so successfully that I was kept on. I'm
sure the album wasn't quite conceived until we took all the tapes
back to London.' Bolan worked hard to sustain the momentum
of 'Hot Love', adding finishing touches to the new recordings at
Advision and Trident in London before embarking on yet another
tour of a dozen or so well-chosen major British locations in May.
Once again, there was a noticeable shift in the audiences, with
a younger, mainly female following ousting the remnants of any
stragglers from the Tyrannosaurus Rex days. 'People used to tell
him, "As soon as you're on telly, Marc, it'll be fantastic. You're
bound to happen",' recalled Jeff Dexter. The conditions were
right for Bolan's arrival, Marc was more than ready for it when
it happened, but it was the impact of a solitary appearance on
*Top Of The Pops*, which planted the seed that turned the new star
phenomenon into something akin to an entire musical movement.


As the personality machine got under way, a poster/programme
was manufactured for the May tour. For it, Boland wrote the first
of many short poems of gratitude to his new-found audience,
which ended: 'Now I know you, and like it.'

Marc Bolan had the determination, the charisma, and the
musical intuition to capitalise on his recent successes, but he was
only able to lead audiences so far. The slightly hesitant début on
*Top Of The Pops* for 'Ride A White Swan' had given way to cooler
performances for its follow-up, and the snap decision to stick
some glitter on his face sent sales of the stuff sky high, as young

teenagers responded quickly and chose to wear their new affiliation outwardly. Like Johnnie Ray, the Beatles and the Monkees before him, Bolan found himself invested with a strange power that made audiences copy his style and scream at him. At first he draped eye-catching jackets from Alkasura and Granny Takes A Trip over his blue dungarees, but by the summer he had transformed himself into a radiantly sparkling star, and the stalls began to shimmer with the new 'glam' trappings. Bolan popularised satins, lurex and velvets, wore silver glitter on his face and women's tap shoes from Anello & Davide on his feet. It wasn't only his audiences that sought to emulate him. Increasingly, groups like Rod Stewart and the Faces, Slade, Sweet and, in time, David Bowie and Gary Glitter began to be passed off as glam rock idols; but in mid-1971 Bolan had the field to himself.

Marc Bolan's tireless reconstruction of himself had – ever since he was plain Mark Feld – always been played out in the field of subcultural style. His guises – mod, Bohemian, hippie – all went against the grain of mainstream culture but, more important than that, they offered him the opportunity to sensationalise his own life. None of these styles was unique: he followed tendencies that were being played out worldwide, from the suburbs of Southend to the streets of San Francisco – but because being different was so central to subcultural needs, he always gave the respective 'uniforms' his own nuances.

By the time glam rock began to harden as a visual style, Marc not only had all the drama and acclaim he had long striven for, he was now cast in the role of head of a new movement which was regarded as musically retrogressive and far too dependent on style. It was time for a backlash. His next single, 'Get It On', fanned the flames of controversy, not least because of the 'meanwhile, I'm still thinking' kiss-off over the fade, which was an obvious nod in the direction of Chuck Berry's 'Little Queenie'. The glam style was too glitzy and 'showbiz' for the new rock establishment, which preferred to hang on to the authentic, sincere, and anti-commercial ethic espoused by the counter-culture and Bolan was challenged by the rock press to defend himself. During 1970–71, the press had altered dramatically: *Sounds* magazine was launched in October 1970 to cater for the growing interest in 'serious'/progressive/album-orientated music; *New Musical Express* drafted in names like Charles Shaar Murray and Nick Kent, who had cut their teeth on magazines like *IT* and *Oz*, to offset the threat from the margins. Not only did the creation of Bolan as Star help see these papers through a period of uncertainty, but his switch in allegiances made him a perfect vessel with which to invest the whole pop/rock debate.

There was a lot of Chuck Berry in 'Get It On'. Marc also paid homage to Eddie Cochran by name-dropping *Untamed Youth* (a Cochran film), and there was more than a little of Cliff Richard's 'Move It' about the rhythm too. But for someone who was generally regarded as second division festival fodder to dress up the simple rock 'n' roll style of a bygone age in bright clothes, and have success heaped upon him from new quarters was too much for the serious rock press to take. Where were the originality, virtuosity, conceptual rigidity, and prerequisite blue jeans and lumberjack shirts? they asked. What they couldn't bear was the idea that rock 'n' roll, which had travelled so far since Bill Haley and the Fab Four, remained essentially a teenage phenomenon. Marc Bolan, the sensualist who lived his life as if in a perpetual teenage universe, found that working on such a basic, instinctive level was far more satisfying – and real – than in the rarified, and at least as contrived, world of the cult artist. 'If there is going to be any revolution in pop,' he said, 'it must come from the young people and if you ignore them, you are cutting yourself off from the life-supply of the rock music force.'[2] That didn't mean his pretensions towards an older audience were very far away. During 1971, as he pulled out all the stops to secure his pop stardom, Bolan compartmentalised these into one project: *The Children Of Rarn*.

Like Dylan before him, Marc delighted in taunting his adversaries. If Dylan was Judas in 1966, Bolan saw himself playing the traitor's role five years later. There were further parallels. Bob Dylan didn't just create art, he lived it, as a rock 'n' roll Shakespeare whose waste-bins and fluffed on-stage lines were just as revealing as 'Like A Rolling Stone' or 'Mr Tambourine Man'. Marc saw himself very much in that tradition, as a prolific, wholly creative personality who lived his life in public because he had the talent to get there. He, too, was worthy of close inspection.

Five years earlier, Dylan had also left behind an audience wary of commercialised pop music, and had 'crossed over' using a similar musical source to that now tapped by Bolan – electric twelve-bar rock 'n' roll. 'Subterranean Homesick Blues', for example, was little more than a restating of Chuck Berry's 'Too

Much Monkey Business'. In turn, Chuck Berry, regarded as the father of rock 'n' roll, whose riffs have been aped by every living guitarist in the world, has described his own music as 'nothing new under the sun', and openly admits to drawing his style directly from Charlie Christian, T-Bone Walker and Carl Hogan. (By the mid-sixties, he was even plagiarising himself – 'No Particular Place To Go' was a direct rewrite of his 1957 hit 'School Day'.) Beyond that, Elvis Presley and Jerry Lee Lewis drew their repertoires from already proven country and blues material, while Woody Guthrie and the whole spectrum of American blues owe their existence to tunes borrowed from their Celtic or African forefathers.

Both Bolan and Dylan built on past traditions, both paid homage to their musical antecedents, and both sought to transform their respective worlds in their own image. Dylan may have been the better poet, Marc the better melody writer. But in 1971, as rock continually strived for art status, it was the poetry – preferably without the shiny jackets – that appeared to matter.

With the clarity of mind that hindsight offers, John Street (in *Rebel Rock*) has argued that we should play down the tendency to see each musical genre obliterating the last, concluding that much remained the same in the transition from hippie to glam. He wrote: 'Glitter replaced the rhetoric, sequins replaced beads, and decadence replaced politics . . . The search for sensations continued, while the styles and the tastes changed.'[3] The distance between a puzzled expression in an ashram and trying to negotiate a set of stairs in a pair of four-inch platform boots wasn't always as great as it purported to be. Hippies shunned artifice: glam rock simply exposed it and celebrated it.

If there was cynicism in what was most certainly unashamed opportunism in Marc's public transformation, then this also appeared to infect his private life. On the back of the success of 'Ride A White Swan', the Bolans had moved from Blenheim Crescent into a spacious flat in Clarendon Gardens, in upmarket Maida Vale, a residence more suited to their growing need for privacy and better equipped to cater for Marc's growing battery of guitars, home recording equipment and record collection. Sometimes, the pair took the short trip to London Zoo at nearby Regent's Park, where memories of Mighty Joe Young would be reawakened by Guy the Gorilla. More often, though, during the spells when T. Rex weren't touring, Marc increasingly spent his time socialising with the rock aristrocracy at clubs like the Speakeasy or Tramp. When it came to upgrading June's car, the couple opted not for one of the big American models that Marc liked to celebrate in song, but a white Rolls-Royce, the classic symbol of British wealth and respectability.

The new status wasn't without its casualties among Bolan's close circle of friends, most of whom had shared the aspirations and frivolity of the hippie years with him. 'He was obviously interested in spiritual things, but as the materialistic side took off, all that took a back seat,' remembers Pete Sanders. 'I was seriously searching and had gone off to India, and when I asked him about it when I came back, he said, "I'm gonna make it first, and then when I'm rich, I'll buy an island and then get into the spiritual thing." It was like something he decided to shut off until later.

'In a way, I suppose he did betray something, because he had the possibility of finding out a lot more about himself; instead he turned into something I didn't imagine him to be. No one minded him being successful, and I think he dealt with the fame in the early days very well. I remember visiting him in that block of flats off Edgware Road, and while it was all very nice – I think we had tea or something – I felt there was a door closing, that we were both pursuing totally different goals. I think the fame really got to him, he began to believe the myth and moved away from the person he once was.'

The most public indication that it wasn't just music that was changing in Marc's life came when his close relationship with John Peel ended abruptly. At the end of 1970, Marc joined *Top Gear* stalwarts like Rod Stewart and the Faces, Curved Air's Sonja Kristina, Ivor Cutler and a couple of Soft Machine members for a seasonal airing of Christmas carols. This was Bolan's final appearance on Peel's show. His profitable relationship with BBC radio had been an important factor in the success of 'Ride A White Swan' – Marc had re-recorded the song on no less than four separate sessions for broadcast between October and December 1970, the last being a second *In Concert* for Peel. That show's producer, Jeff Griffin remembers Marc thanking Peel, Bob Harris and himself in front of the audience at the BBC's Paris Theatre for their role in helping him achieve his success.

While the group were on tour during the early months of 1971, there was little time to return to the BBC studios, with the exception of a three-track session for the daytime *Radio 1 Club*, taped before the American tour. There was no doubt that T. Rex had become a fully fledged electric outfit by then, but contrary to popular opinion, neither voltage nor Marc's new-found fame seemed to bother John Peel. Under a music press headline that read, 'Peel cried with joy when he heard "Hot Love" was Number 1', the DJ was wholly supportive of Bolan's success. 'The great thing about Marc,' he said, 'whom I regard as a dear friend, who comes round, plays rock 'n' roll records, watches TV, drinks tea and keeps the hamsters company, is that he has stayed completely true to his principles. People say he's sold out by having hit records, but that's just because they like to be part of a cult.'[4]

Pete Jenner, who, as co-founder of Blackhill Enterprises, had sensed Marc's ambition back in 1968, had no doubts about Bolan's motives. 'Bolan was a complete arsehole,' he said. 'Quite clearly he was just a very ambitious little kid who wanted to become a pop star . . . He'd sussed that the way through for him was by being a little hippie. He used me and he used John Peel.'[5]

Peel is more charitable about the hiatus which, he admits, was prompted by his decision not to play 'Get It On' when Bolan sent him his customary advance copy. 'I said to myself, "If this wasn't Marc I wouldn't play it; so I mustn't play it." It seemed to prompt a fairly sudden rupture. I phoned him up and someone else answered the phone and it was, "Hey man, Marc's busy. He'll phone you back." And he never did. I was disappointed, because Marc had been somebody I liked and spent a lot of time with.

'This is not a criticism of Marc but he did have this harder side to his character, and there's nothing that's more calculated to activate this kind of dark side of people than success. There aren't that many people who survive it. Most people become monsters. Marc didn't become a monster but he didn't have to be Mr Nice Guy any more. I suppose it was rather like the electorate's rejection of Churchill after the war. They associate you with the difficult years, and so they move on to someone else.'

By this time, Bolan had a second reliable ally at Radio 1. Bob Harris first met Marc when he turned up to interview John Peel in 1967 and discovered Bolan in tow. The pair built up a friendship over the next few years, and when Harris, as Peel's understudy, secured his own *Top Gear* slot on Radio 1, Marc began to record sessions for his shows too. Unlike Peel, who quickly tired of Marc's electric work, Bob Harris's enthusiasm for the new recordings flourished with each release. 'I think that Marc was desperately underrated, particularly once T. Rex got going,' he recalls. 'I still think the early T. Rex records match any of the great pop that we've heard over the past thirty or so years, but at the time they were dismissed as mere fluffy pop singles. He really peaked with "Get It On". That was a magnificent record.'

After taking most of June off for a much-needed rest and to complete work on *Electric Warrior*, Bolan began July with the release of 'Get It On' and a short series of concerts. One night, at a gig in Boston, Lincolnshire, he received a surprise visit from an old mate. *Frendz* magazine decided it would be great fun to see the ex-underground hero playing to a hall of screaming girls and organised a coach trip to the concert. Among the entourage was Steve Took. 'Steve said to me, "Do you think I ought to go to his dressing room and see him?",' remembers a close friend. I said, "Yeah", so we trotted round and knocked on the door. Marc nearly fainted. They just fell into each other's arms, hugging each other tightly. At an instant, you could see there had once been this really close relationship.'

The contrast between the fortunes of the old musical buddies was now greater than ever. Since leaving Tyrannosaurus Rex, Steve Took had fully immersed himself in the politics of ecstasy, occasionally getting himself together enough to make half-hearted attempts at finding rock stardom. The most notable of these was as a founder member of the Pink Fairies, together with ex-(Social) Deviant Mick Farren and one-time Pretty Things drummer Twink. The band débuted at Manchester University in October 1969, and Twink recounted the occasion to Fairies' archivist Nigel Cross. 'I sat down on the drums and started banging away. Mick was trying to sing, Steve Took was playing guitar and my girlfriend Silver Darling was on the keyboards, even though she'd never played them before. There was no music as such, and the concert ended up with us standing in the middle of the audience, just talking to people, pulling down our trousers, farting in their faces. It was unbelievable!'[6]

The close friendship formed with Twink during this period was cemented on the drummer's *Think Pink* solo album, which included two Steve Took compositions, 'Three Little Piggies' and 'The Sparrow Is The Sign'. Steve contributed guitar throughout, and also made a notable appearance on Mick Farren's solo album,

*Mona: The Carniverous Circus*, credited as Shagrat the Vagrant. One track, 'Carniverous Circus Part II', featured Took reciting his unpleasant experiences inside the Ashford Remand Centre, where he had spent time after his drug bust.

After the Pink Fairies hardened into something more than a drinking club intent on wrecking concerts, Took soon fell out with Mick Farren. In spring 1970, he split to form Shagrat with Larry Wallis and Tim Taylor, lead guitarist and bassist respectively with the Entire Sioux Nation, together with drummer Phil Lenoir. Took had again ventured into Tolkien's *The Lord of the Rings* to find a name for the group though, revealingly, it was not a hero hobbit but an evil orc captain which spawned Shagrat. Among the songs recorded by this line-up was Wallis and Took's 'Peppermint Flipstick', apparently inspired by an intriguing combination of Pink Floyd's 'Astronomy Dominé' and the Cadbury's Flake television advert. It was five and a half minutes of stoned aggression, and with its doom-laden chords and malevolent vocal, represented the obverse of the hippie coin flipped by Tyrannosaurus Rex.

A more representative example of Took's songwriting ability was 'Amanda' where, in spite of his near hero-worship of Love's Arthur Lee, he sounded a dead ringer for the lazy San Franciscan drawl of Quicksilver Messenger Service's vocalist Dino Valenti. This was recorded later in 1970, with the more gentle backing of Wallis on bass and ex-Chicken Shack drummer, the late Dave Bidwell on tambourine. The group were short-lived, and Took next embarked upon a series of solo concerts, including an appearance at the Pink Fairies' Christmas party at Chiswick Town Hall in the summer of 1971, where he sat on a stool, accompanied himself on acoustic guitar and mesmerised the crowd. But still there were no takers for a record contract.

Meanwhile, Marc Bolan, with two successive Number One hit singles behind him, and an album recorded and ready to go, wanted to see his new-found stardom more adequately reflected in financial terms. Despite his early promise to David Platz that he would stay if the publisher/record-company boss could make him famous, Bolan reneged on a new contract worked out with Fly. 'We'd thrashed the renegotiation of Marc's contract out at the Venezia restaurant in Soho one Friday,' recalls Platz, 'and after four hours, everyone – Marc, David Enthoven and ourselves – was happy.

'But over the weekend, I received a phone call at home from

Tony Secunda, who told me, "I've taken over as Marc's manager and Marc tells me you're renegotiating the contract." And I said, "As far as I know, we've negotiated it and it's being typed out ready for his final approval and signature." Secunda said, "Listen, I'm in charge now, and what I require on Marc's behalf is not what you've negotiated." He asked for a royalty figure that exceeded what we got from EMI, and I told him that was impossible. He was also seeking to restrict the territories so that we would have England, while he and Marc would "own" the rest of the world, so to speak. We discussed it at length and it got more and more difficult. I told him, "You don't seem to understand. What you're asking is something that would actually cost us money." We may have been getting something like 15 per cent from EMI and he was asking a figure higher than that. I said, "How the hell are we going to negotiate a deal whereby we are going to lose money?" '

Johnny Rogan, in *Starmakers and Svengalis*, his study of pop management, describes Tony Secunda as 'one of the great sensationalists of the sixties'. Like Andrew Oldham before him, Secunda had courted scandal during a management career that had seen him launch the Moody Blues and the Move. Not content with encouraging the latter to smash up televisions on stage, he produced a postcard to promote the 'Flowers In The Rain' single which offended Prime Minister Harold Wilson, and was successfully sued for libel. The settlement involved the song's royalties being donated to charity, and the prankish manager lost the Move to Don Arden.

Tony Secunda first met Bolan and Took in the Essex Music/ New Breed offices around the time that Tony Visconti first stumbled across the duo. His management of the Move brought him into close contact with Denny Cordell and David Platz, but in time, both Cordell and Secunda fell out with the publisher, which partly explains Secunda's aggressive stance when he was enlisted by Bolan in 1971 to negotiate a new deal for him. 'I never felt that Tyrannosaurus Rex were really worth managing at that early stage,' he says. 'After all, I had the Move and Procol Harum, two top chart acts. Marc took up with David Enthoven and Mark Fenwick, two rich kids who wanted to get in on the music business. After a few run-ins, he ran his course with them. He had a class complex and though he liked to be around that middle-class stuff, it used to get up his nose at the end of the day.

'After he'd decided to do a Dylan – stand up, uncross his legs, and go electric – and had a couple of hits, I found out he'd been trying to get in contact with me. I went to visit my ex-wife Chelita one night, and he was there. She'd set it up in her typically Machiavellian way! Marc was with June, and then some crazy French guy appeared with some pure amphetamine sulphate which he laid on the table for our pleasure. Marc and I did some of this stuff and we sat and talked for something like fourteen hours. He knew I'd be the ideal person to go in and sort out his business affairs for him.'

After a second meeting over lunch, Marc gave Secunda some demo copies of 'Get It On' to pass on to his influential contacts like DJ Murray the K in the States. In the meantime, he toyed with the idea of using Chas Chandler, then in the process of breaking Slade with 'Get Down And Get With It', before flying out to New York for some promotion and formally enlisting Secunda's services. 'All the agreements had run out,' recalls Secunda, 'so it was a perfect situation for me to walk into and really do what I do best – negotiate good deals. I cut out the middleman, which is basically what Platz and Fly Records was, and went straight to the top of the mountain, EMI Records.' By the end of 1971, Secunda and Bolan had formed the T. Rex Wax Co. label, the Wizard Artists and Warrior Music Projects Ltd publishing companies, and struck a tape-lease deal with EMI which gave Marc control over what could be released under the T. Rex name. In America, a new deal was signed with Warner/ Reprise, while Secunda negotiated separate deals elsewhere.

Bolan had no real concept of what to do with a record label of his own – he never used it for anything other than his own releases – but in following the Beatles, the Rolling Stones, even the Moody Blues, the main motivations were money and prestige. 'It was to make the most mileage out of his life,' recalls Secunda. 'We grossed something like six million dollars in six months on worldwide record deals alone,' he claims, 'and most of that was upfront. It was one of the great rock deals of all time, and we had great fun doing it. We did a deal with a German company, and it reached the point where we were almost ready to sign. And I said to the guy on the phone, "Naah, it's still not enough. We need more, in cash and upfront. And we want it in a suitcase – today!" This was around eleven in the morning. He called back fifteen minutes later and said, "I'm getting on ze twelve fifteen from Frankfurt and I'll be here by two o'clock viz

ze money in ze briefcase.'' It was like a fucking Bugs Bunny
movie, man! By three o'clock he was there with all the money
laid out on the table with Prince Wilhelm de Earwig's face on it.
It was a wonderful moment.'

Faced with the wrath of Secunda and an artist who had
conveniently forgotten his promise of loyalty once the money
started to roll in, David Platz did something he had never done
before: he decided he didn't want any further involvement with
his artist and pulled out of the negotiations. 'That literally ended
my association with Marc,' he says. 'I never saw him again, he
never contacted me again. Whether it was a guilty conscience I
don't know. It was ironic that he ended up signing to EMI, the
very company we had a deal with. I remember talking to one of
the heads there and said, "How could you do that? Couldn't
you, as a matter of decency, have told us that you'd been
approached to sign Marc Bolan?" But that's not the way the
music industry works. Highest bidder wins.'

With lucrative new deals either in the bag, or at least nearing
completion, Bolan was ready to promote *Electric Warrior*, the first
T. Rex album recorded as a four-piece. He was in ebullient mood
when he discussed the eagerly awaited record with the press,
comparing its energy and spontaneity to vintage rock 'n' roll. 'As
far as I'm concerned,' he told one writer, 'it's the first album I've
ever made. The others were just ideas, but in this one I spoke
about me and you and all of us.'[7] It was true: several of the
songs, most notably the acoustic-based 'Cosmic Dancer', 'Girl'
and 'Life's A Gas', seemed more private while at the same time
spoke in a more universal tongue than had his previous work.

At the same time, Marc's compulsive need to create fantastic
vistas and characters in his earlier songs was pursued to satisfy
a hunger for otherworldliness, where it could displace his dissat-
isfaction with the commonplace. Beautiful words created impossible worlds. Fantasy for Bolan was not a search for attainable
Utopias, did not offer a critique of contemporary society in any
constructive manner, nor did it suggest any real insight into
character development. It was an impulsive flight of fancy that
denied any real space to self-reflection.

*Electric Warrior* wasn't Marc Bolan's answer to John Lennon's
*Plastic Ono Band* album, an intimate and revealing coming of age
where the ex-Beatle reappraised his childhood, his stardom, his
idols, in short, his whole life. But it did share Lennon's desire to

return to basic truths, couched in a simple rock 'n' roll style and with concentrated, pointed lyrics. The memorable Aubrey Powell-designed hipgnosis sleeve portrayed Marc in outline, an apparition complete with solid-bodied guitar and large twin speaker stack – the Electric Warrior. Electricity raged throughout the bulk of the album, but it was by no means a complete transformation. Only the blues jam, 'Lean Woman Blues', and the proto heavy-metal 'Rip Off' were vaguely unexpected.

Nevertheless, *Electric Warrior* was a near-perfect summation of all Bolan's aspirations – fronting his own pop band, singing three- and four-chord anthems of decadence and desire, and finding favour with a massive public. One track in particular, 'Jeepster', found Bolan brilliantly rewriting rock music in his own image. Basing the verses on a riff that had done the rounds of Presley ('My Baby Left Me'), Howlin' Wolf ('You'll Be Mine'), and one of Marc's lesser-known rockabilly idols Sleepy La Beef ('I'm Through', 'All The Time'), 'Jeepster' marked the climax of Bolan's nonsensical-yet-sensual singles when lifted from the album in November (against his wishes), although the characteristic overdose of seasonal quirkiness meant that sales of Bennie Hill's 'Ernie (The Fastest Milkman In The West)' narrowly prevented a hat trick of T. Rex Number Ones. That fans already had the song on the album probably made all the difference for, despite being on the shelves for just three and a half months, *Electric Warrior* was among the Top Five best-selling albums of 1971.

After a couple of European dates, T. Rex promoted the album with another month-long British tour, where they were accompanied by the soft-rock band Quiver and the soft-spoken Bob Harris as MC. The tour opened at the Portsmouth Guildhall on 19 October 1971, a month after the release of *Electric Warrior*. With the exception of an appearance at the Weeley Festival, where reaction to the band that had allegedly 'sold out' was somewhat divided, it was the first date since the massive success of 'Get It On' in the summer.

The response of the by now almost exclusively teenage audiences, which one journalist dubbed 'T. Rextasy', stunned Harris, who had seen Marc progress from Middle Earth to the festival circuit. 'On that tour, the entourage travelled in five big, gas-guzzling Vauxhall Crestas,' he recalls, 'and after the gig at Portsmouth, we waited backstage for a while, enjoying a drink and meeting one or two of the prettier girls that had been chosen by the roadies to join us. When we headed for the stage door, the attendant said, "I'd wait if I were you. There are quite a few people out there." When we opened the door, we were absolutely stunned. It was as if the entire audience had shifted from the auditorium round to the back! The local police were on hand to ease the situation, but the most frightening aspect was that so many of the girls were armed with scissors hoping to get a lock of Marc's hair.

'By the time we'd edged our way to the cars, everything had been ripped off them and taken as souvenirs – registration plates, windscreen wipers, hub caps, the lot, all gone. After getting into the vehicle, we began to edge forward, despite there being a mass of faces pressed up against the glass and people on the bonnet and on the roof. Then there was this almighty crunch as the whole suspension gave way under the weight. Three of the five cars were written off that evening. That was the night they came up with the idea of letting the last guitar chord resonate while the band made their getaway before the crowd could get at them. Otherwise, it would have been complete madness.'

The scenes on the *Electric Warrior* tour far exceeded anything witnessed earlier that year or, for that matter, since the heyday of the Beatles during the mid-sixties. The entourage needed police escorts in and out of every town and Bolan's claim that he had become the 'Prophet of the New Generation' began to ring true. There was nothing particularly new about the collective response witnessed at T. Rex concerts which, by most accounts, could be summed up as 'damp seats, shrill screams and sweet wrappers', but there was a difference in the range of his appeal.

By winter 1971, *Jackie* magazine was receiving some 800 letters a week from Bolan fans, many of which expressed concern that he was dying of a rare blood disorder. Although similar fears were expressed over doe-eyed Paul McCartney several years earlier with the 'Paul is dead' rumours, the pop star phenomenon surrounding Bolan was much more intensely focused. The Beatles' following was spread over four individuals, and while Mickey Finn was acquiring a substantial fan following, almost all the attention centred on Marc. His unashamed self-publicity increasingly aggravated the rock press, but bypassed the growing army of younger fans whose own uncertain sexuality was perfectly mirrored by Bolan's convoluted image as dismembered cock-rocker, the thrusting, pouting star who only really wanted to read you his poems. Mysterious tales from his past (the wizard, the hippie years), began to fill the increasing number of teenage magazine titles (*Popswop*, *Music Scene*), and the strangely dressed elfin figure with the mop of corkscrew curls and a penchant for inventing words like 'Jeepster' suggested much more than the usual pretty-boy pop singer.

Marc Bolan fell in love with what he created and his followers reciprocated. All fans identify with stars to some extent, but outside Presley and his old friend/adversary David Bowie, Bolan has inspired a fiercely loyal devotion unprecedented in the pop world – although the star phenomenon has been more fully exploited during the eighties, elevating Madonna, Prince and Kate Bush to similar heights of worship. (A good measure of the strength of this identification is the number of fanzines on the market: interestingly, though both have sold many more records than Bolan, very few are produced in the name of Queen or the Rolling Stones.)

At the height of his popularity, Marc told *Jackie* magazine, 'I don't see Marc Bolan of T. Rex. I see a little boy of a year old. In a sense, I am still waiting to grow up. I am still waiting to be a man and see some hairs on my chest.'[8] It is this sense of being an innocent adrift in the incredibly important world of pop and rock that was Marc's trump card. If his unquenchable drive for success had left a few casualties along the way, and the business matters were kept firmly under control, this doesn't mean that the apparent naïvety was bogus. 'He was intuitively very bright,' explains Keith Altham, 'and he had an instinctive understanding of music. There was always an air of innocence about him, a childlike quality that made it very powerful and very honest. A child's vision can be much clearer than an adult's. Sometimes I found it quite disturbing. He could express a profound truth very simply.' Previously, Marc's intuition had kept him rooted to his chair in Blenheim Crescent, where he practised his guitar playing, dipped into reading matter that would fire his imagination and wrote reams of poetry. Now his instinct told him to maintain his high public profile with endless tours and interviews and keep a close watch on his business interests. His 'magical' aura remained, but there was little time to pursue less lucrative projects, such as further books and *The Children Of Rarn*.

'It was going to be our *Tommy*, our *Sgt. Pepper*, our big rock opera,' recalls producer Tony Visconti, 'but Marc never saw *The Children Of Rarn* through.' The idea was initially conceived during 1970, and despite several later attempts to reactivate it, only the basic theme and a skeletal fifteen-minute demo have ever seen the light of day, for what was originally conceived as a double album/book/film/concert project. *The Children Of Rarn* was to have been the culmination of Bolan's imaginative thinking, but his new-found status as a teenage fantasy figure increasingly meant there was no place for such a release.

In October 1971, before taking off on the UK *Electric Warrior* tour, the idea still excited Bolan. He set down several ideas for the song cycle while at Tony Visconti's London flat, in an unprepared session, as evidenced by his use of the producer's nylon-stringed classical guitar. As the tale of the Dworns and their Lithon adversaries unfolded onto Visconti's two-track Brenell tape recorder, both musician and producer envisaged the sounds of Mellotrons, strings, and percussion on the finished suite, which was also planned to incorporate instrumental and narrative passages.

Marc's concept was set in a prehistoric era, when the earth was Beltane, where Dworns drove around on 200 m.p.h. motorcycles and where advanced beings known as Peacelings stood seven feet tall. Out of the inevitable battle between the conflicting forces of good and evil step the Children of Rarn, though a Lithon egg hatches in the heat of the sun to form a new enemy – the dinosaur. It was sentimental and escapist, and unlike the legends of King Arthur or Beowulf which Marc had read, there was little possibility that the tale bore any resemblance to reality – metaphorical or otherwise.

Bolan did attempt to resurrect *Rarn* between 1973 and 1975; first returning to it late in 1973 while on holiday in Marbella, before the script was lost on his return to the States. Around forty minutes of a studio rehearsal exists from 1974 covering the same themes as the 1971 tape. Just how much further Bolan got with the script and character development (if any) is not known. Marc's original demo, which Tony Visconti had built into a full-blown piece with added Mellotron, recorders, percussion and bass, appeared posthumously in 1978. Bolan's music has been re-mixed and re-edited several times since his death, but Visconti's treatment of *The Children Of Rarn* is, perhaps unsurprisingly, the only instance of its having been done with any real insight or empathy.

After he had recorded the initial demo in October 1971, Marc realised that such a project would be lost on his new audience who screamed for three-chord, three-minute anthems so it was shelved. Instead, his attentions turned to America, where 'Hot Love' had failed to create much impression, but where Mo Ostin and Bob Regehr at Warner/Reprise, who had just renegotiated a new deal with Secunda, had high hopes for the follow-up, 'Get It On'. The label had already invested in the new breed of singer-songwriters such as Randy Newman, Neil Young, Joni Mitchell, Van Morrison and James Taylor. Now they had the biggest Dylan protégé of them all.

After a short promotional visit in December 1971, when Marc made several high-profile radio appearances, things looked set for a breakthrough. 'Get It On' entered the US Top Ten in January 1972 and went on to sell a million. It might have sold even more had Warners not shied away from controversy by altering its title to 'Bang A Gong (Get It On)'. A euphemism for 'fuck', 'Get It On' was also deemed too close to the title of a recent hit, 'Get It On In The Morning' by Chase. Marc, June and Tony Secunda apparently celebrated the imminent conquering of America by dropping handfuls of dollar bills from their seventh-floor terrace of the City Squire Hotel in New York. With rumours of world-wide T. Rex record sales amounting to 14 million, December 1971 certainly was a time to savour – and to build on.

# CHAPTER NINE

'Initially when you make it big it's a gas. Success is always very exciting and it's nice to have. The downers and the pitfalls that go with it happen whether it's at the Labour Exchange or the London Palladium – that's life.'
Marc Bolan to Caroline Boucher, *Disc* magazine, December 1972

'I'd have thought he was in much more of a fantasy world during the period when he was a star than he was in the Tyrannosaurus Rex days.'
John Peel

'It's very important for me to keep in contact. That's why I send the roadies out to buy all the music papers.'
Marc Bolan to Keith Altham, *New Musical Express*, August 1972

'The whole thing was Marc Bolan. It was never T. Rex. He was T. Rex.'
Steve Currie, T. Rex bassist

Having achieved the fame he had consistently striven for, and with his financial future secured in a series of lucrative deals, Marc Bolan sought to capitalise on both by patenting an irresistible T. Rex sound. *Electric Warrior* and the singles taken from it were masterful strokes of good-looking, slightly rough-edged rock 'n' roll, and had made him the most successful musician in Britain. But Bolan was aware of the fickle nature of the young pop audience, and had spied potential rivals like Rod Stewart and Slade on the ascendant by the end of 1971. With memories of the Phil Spector hit factory and the 'Motown sound' lodged firmly in his mind, Marc, together with producer Tony Visconti, aimed to transform T. Rex from just another fly-by-night pop group into something much larger and longer-lasting. They constructed their own wall of sound based on past pop glories, into which they fed songs celebrating the claustrophobic, pop art fantasy world of their creator. It was a brilliant combination, resulting in a string of intensely personalised pocket symphonies which ensured that the name of Bolan would continue to dominate British pop music for many months to come.

'Telegram Sam' and 'Metal Guru', the first T. Rex singles of 1972, and the first to bear the distinctive new blue and red T. Rex Wax Co. labels and sleeves, weren't necessarily Bolan's best songs or Tony Visconti's most technically perfect productions. Yet both embody the purest expression of the T. Rex sound, a sound untrammelled by its underground origins and untainted by any hint of desperation that inevitably sets in when trying to maintain a formula that has outlived its usefulness.

Recorded in Copenhagen, Denmark, before the US tour, 'Telegram Sam' was propped up by another Chuck Berry riff, and secured by one of Bolan's characteristic runs of passing tones. Once again, this weaved itself behind the chorus which, like 'Jeepster' before it, hung on one short phrase, 'Telegram Sam, you're my main man.' (There's considerable controversy surrounding the characters in that song. Some have cited 'Sam' as the band's drug dealer, although Tony Secunda maintains otherwise. 'It's about me,' he says, 'I was his main man. "Jungle Faced Jake" was Sid Walker, my assistant, who was a black guy.' No one bothered to question the identity of 'Bobby', the 'natural born poet' who could only be Dylan.)

'Metal Guru', which reverted back to the most important character in the T. Rex repertoire – Bolan himself – threw off the mantle of the funky rock 'n' roll riff and highlighted the familiar three-note descent which always inflected Marc's joyous teenage anthems with a tinge of melancholy (mirrored perfectly by his occasional tight-lipped, down-in-the-mouth expression that always threatened to break into tears). There was no chorus as such: the entire song, which hinged around its oft-repeated title, was akin to being locked into two and a half minutes of verseless paradise. Many critics found what appeared to be lyrical inanity and the rudimentary musical form too much to take, and even Marc's staunch supporter Bob Harris was forced to rethink his own attitude towards his friend's music in the wake of the single. 'I never actually told Marc that I didn't like "Metal Guru",' he remembers, 'but that was the record which made me think, "Hang on, what's he doing?" I was never that keen on his music after that one.'

Bolan knowingly swam against the tide of critical opinion, believing that his art – for he surely still saw his music as such – was at its most potent when it was kept simple and continued to be consumed in massive quantities. Whereas in the past he had been received with cool indifference, now his every move, utterance – sung or spoken – and mode of dress was actively digested by an audience that was, despite what critical snobbery dictated, far from passive. Poet Pete Brown, who was sceptical of the whole notion of hippie culture anyway, remains a dissenting voice from the frowning underground. '"Metal Guru" sounds far more honest to me than his published poetry or his lyrics with Tyrannosaurus Rex,' he says. 'It had an identity, a very strong identity, which seemed perfectly valid and entertaining. At least it wasn't pretentious. Everyone who's been really successful in British rock'n'roll has assumed a persona, and the lyrics Bolan wrote later on support that persona.'

Several years later, Marc explained his thinking behind the repetition that underlay his lyrics and music, and which had peaked during this period. 'I wasn't deliberately trying to be obscure,' he said. 'It's just that I think in an abstract way. My songs fit my personality and my lyrics are very important to me. I like my songs to be durable to the ear and exciting to the mind. Repetition comes into my songs a lot because I think my lyrics are so obscure that they need to be hammered home. You need to hear them eight or nine times before they start to make sense. I don't see anything wrong with that. Some artists repeat the most simple lyrics about forty times over. Look at "I Want To Hold Your Hand" or "All You Need Is Love".'[1]

During 1972, each successive T. Rex record brought with it further debate and backbiting as to the 'originality' of Bolan's music. His return to electric rock 'n' roll in 1971, which had been partially accepted by the rock cognoscenti, was now seen to have been replaced by a cynical and formularised sound that employed little musical skill and some brief lines of lyrical nonsense that an imaginative eight-year-old could have written. Such a combination was, and remains, essential to pop music, but it was deemed an unwelcome contribution by those critics who sought to elevate rock culture. Charles Shaar Murray who, like Pete Brown, was not a fully paid-up convert to Bolan's earlier work, offered a partially dissenting voice from that of the outraged rock 'scholars'. 'T. Rex's music is not derivative,' he wrote, 'because though you can see where it's coming from, it is a synthesis, and all creative rock music has been a synthesis.'[2] After invoking some of Bolan's chief influences – Berry, Tolkien, Spector, Cochran, Hendrix, Holly, the Ronettes, Brian Wilson, Syd Barrett and David Bowie (the latter arguably influential only in a competitive sense) – indicating just what that synthesis consisted of, he then stated that Bolan's music only worked in the singles market. The great divide, which had been set in motion by *Sgt. Pepper*, had continued to widen, and even a vaguely sympathetic critique read like a put-down.


However much Marc brought his songs into line with that aspect of himself which he sought to project, the Bolan persona was predominantly visual. When Ringo Starr heard that the forthcoming T. Rex shows at the Empire Pool, Wembley, were due to be filmed, he contacted Bolan with a view to documenting the concerts for a forthcoming Apple Films project. Ringo had been the ex-Beatle least likely to succeed on musical talent alone, and despite a surprise hit in 1971 with 'It Don't Come Easy', he had already capitalised on his greatest asset – his sense of humour – and branched into films with parts in *The Magic Christian* and Frank Zappa's *200 Motels*. More importantly, he was now also the self-appointed managing director of Apple Films Ltd. His original idea was for a series of television documentaries profiling celebrities like Elizabeth Taylor, George Best and Richard Burton, but after talks with Bolan and Secunda, the project soon grew too large for the small screen. But Tony Secunda didn't stay around to see it develop far beyond a basic outline thrashed out in Ringo Starr's office.

After a short jaunt around Europe at the end of January 1972, T. Rex had flown out to Seattle on 10 February for a two-week tour of the US. For the first time, they were the headline act, and with 'Get It On' still fresh in the memory, many hopes were pinned on the visit. 'T. Rex are the new Beatles. The teen idols of the seventies and the biggest pop sensation in years,' screamed one concert programme. As it turned out, the tour did break the group – not commercially, but in terms of spirit. Everyone was on a high as they touched down in Seattle, but the response to the tour was depressingly lukewarm. The audiences, who were generally several years older than their British counterparts, remained seated for much of the time, and expected large helpings of technical proficiency with their rock 'n' roll. They were disappointed. With no budding Ginger Bakers or Jack Bruces in the group, and Bolan, who was used to spending more attention on duck-walking and pouting than on doing anything more than strum out a basic rhythm, couldn't compete with the likes of Mountain's Les West or the twin-guitar assault of Humble Pie's Peter Frampton and Steve Marriott, both of whom appeared alongside T. Rex in America. The concert-going audiences in the nation constantly searching for its roots remained po-faced, and returned home to seek solace in Bob Dylan or country rock or black music or whatever else they could find to exorcise the demon of British artifice that was T. Rex.

Playing sets that lasted for just forty-five minutes including encores didn't help, and Mick Jagger, who saw the group at the Hollywood Palladium in Los Angeles, told Bolan so after the show. Nevertheless, he summoned up the enthusiasm to dance in the wings in his white suit, and attended the post-gig party back at the band's hotel, where he discussed cricket with Bill Legend and signed an autograph for Steve Currie. Marc Bolan had only been two years behind the Stones in his attempt to break into pop music, but to the old guard he was still merely a novice.

One highly publicised concert took place in Chicago, where T. Rex were supported by British hard rock group Uriah Heep and the regular opener Jackie Lomax. Leaving aside the obvious antagonisms between 'progressive' Heep and 'pop' T. Rex, Bolan's proposal that Uriah Heep should be placed at the bottom of the bill was misjudged, not least because he hadn't figured on the following they had in the audience (their US label, Mercury Records, was based in that city). According to Heep's main man Mick Box, 'It was an unfortunate night for Marc Bolan because his decision not to allow us to do an encore upset the audience so much that they continued to shout throughout the entire T. Rex set. Their management locked us in our dressing room so that we couldn't come back on, but we could hear the uproar in the hall because there was a speaker in the room. Marc went out there and was greeted with a bit of booing and jeering, but he found a good way round it. He said, "What about Jimi Hendrix?", and a big roar went up. "What about Eric Clapton?" Same again. Then someone shouted out, "What about Uriah Heep?", and the place went mad. He really had a hard time that night.'

The climax of the tour came with two performances at New York's prestigious Carnegie Hall, the scene, many years earlier, of protests when the Beatles were booked to appear at this hallowed shrine to the arts. When Marc returned home to Britain, he told reporters that his performance was 'incredible', and that even Paul Simon was spotted dancing in the aisles. Eye-witness accounts and contemporary reports indicate otherwise, though it does seem to have been the second show which provided most of the controversy. Dressed in his sequined white satin suit with two silver stars beneath his eyes (not a wise move in the States: the image alone was enough to court instant disapproval from the denimed hordes), Marc opened with a poor-sounding 'Cadillac', a new song which had been performed in concert since late 1971. It received only mild applause – and that was for one of the harder-edged songs in the group's repertoire. As 'Jeepster' died a similar death, Bolan sought to distract the audience by dancing wildly. After his customary three-song acoustic interlude, which included the as-yet unrecorded 'Spaceball Ricochet', the group returned and roused the audience sufficiently with a fifteen-minute 'Get It On' to win an encore of 'Summertime Blues'. But it was hard work.

Some generously described the band as exhausted, but manager Tony Secunda rests the blame more firmly on Marc's shoulders. 'Carnegie Hall was the final straw,' he recalls. 'It had been pretty much the worst tour I'd been on in my life, and Marc just wasn't the same guy any more. Cocaine had become fashionable and he'd started using it. I think it was getting to him – he was using very bad quality stuff in America – and he'd become almost impossible to communicate with. I'd taken him to the hall several weeks earlier and I'd stood at the back and had a conversation with him just to show him how acoustically perfect the place was. I said, "When you play here, you're not gonna need that Marshall stack, baby."

'We set up this hot media blast for the gig, searchlights lit up the Manhattan skyline, heavy faces there to see the concert, and what does Marc do? Locks himself in the toilet with two bottles of champagne and gets out of his brain. He walked on stage wearing a T-shirt of himself and fell flat on his face during the opening number. And it was so loud that no one could hear a damn thing – it was awful. I walked out and sat on the steps outside, and Paul Simon came running out after me and gave me shit and then he walked off into the night. I thought, this is where it comes to a close. I went off and stayed the night with friends.

'The next day, I took off with Mickey Finn, who was more embarrassed than anybody, because he had to stand next to Marc on stage, and a friend for a holiday in Acapulco where we tried to pretend it didn't happen. Mickey then flew on to Paris, where T. Rex were due to start recording *The Slider* album, and I followed a few days later. But I knew it was the end of the line and told him so in no uncertain manner. The embarrassment was just too extreme. Still, I made a lot of money and got a nice Ferrari out of it.'

Although Secunda's name appeared on the initial advertising for the 18 March 1972 Wembley concert, he had gone by the time it had been redesigned to incorporate the announcement of a second show at 5.30 p.m., and the news that it was 'being filmed for posterity!'. Ringo and his Apple Films camera crew set up with a view to capturing both Marc's stage charisma and the frenzied audience scenes, and the results, which can be seen on the *Born To Boogie* film, reveal the potency of the relationship formed between Bolan and his fans. The crowd appear blissfully unaware of the cameras and Ringo Starr, who, just a few years earlier, had been a recipient of similar acts of worship, now went largely unrecognised.

Bolan, dressed in a sparkling pink jacket and his favourite Marc Bolan T-shirt (at least for the second show), strutted and swaggered across the stage, letting out a stream of whoops and shrieks, all of which elicited an even greater response from a crowd already at fever pitch. He played the part of the smiling, lovable guitar-hero-cum-entertainer to perfection. A massive ten-foot-high cardboard cut-out figure of himself (a throwback to his John Temple modelling days) provided the backdrop, while many of the – predominantly female – audience waved scarves bearing his name and decorated their faces with stars and glitter, even though Bolan had dropped the idea by that time. This strong identification with a single star became an overriding feature of what was fast-becoming known as the glam rock era, set in motion by Marc several months earlier.

The newly conceived notion of the 'superstar' was quickly adopted by magazines, and reinforced by the coterie of 'new' names that sprang up in the wake of Bolan's success. In fact Rod Stewart, David Bowie, Elton John, the Sweet, Slade, and the token American, Alice Cooper, had all been making records for several years. They had all begun to frequent boutiques such as John Lloyd's Alkasura and Trevor Miles's Mr Freedom/Paradise Garage shop in London's King's Road, where the apparently retro sounds of glam rock were mirrored in costumes that pastiched the styles of the post-war decades, with a touch of Hollywood glamour thrown in. So had singer Paul Gadd who, as Paul Raven, had been an unsuccessful home-grown rock 'n' roller, and was at one time the warm-up man for *Ready, Steady, Go!*.

Gadd buried Paul Raven in a much-publicised stunt on the river Thames and, with Marc's ex-arranger Mike Leander behind him in the capacity of songwriter/manager, sought to challenge Bolan's supremacy by rechristening himself Gary Glitter, and going several steps further in terms of stage presentation and reductionist musical appeal. 'Marc didn't go as far with it as I did with Glitter,' says Leander, 'but what he did with the eye make-up and looking sharp was fantastic. A lot of the styles can be attributed to John Lloyd, whose whole thing was satins, sequins and Lurex, materials that looked sensational when you saw them on television. All those multi-coloured satin suits with giant flares, and the platform boots came from his Alkasura shop.

'It was a time of great spectacle. That was what it was really about, and the records were geared to that. In the seventies, the music was constructed to be seen, whereas during the previous decade, it was made to be heard, preferably with a joint dangling from your lip. The audience became part of the show too: they dressed up the way the star dressed. Every show was like a party.'

Had Marc Bolan not had tiny feet, he would never have been able to shop at Anello & Davide for the dancer's tap shoes which, together with his girlish features, feminine long hair and small frame, helped create the overall aura of androgyny that was central to his appeal. (Incidentally, the shop capitalised on Marc's patronage in 1972 by marketing 'Bolan shoes'.) And just as small feet led him to women's footwear, a similar mix of pragmatism and sense of distinction lent a peculiar air to his music in the minds of his massive young audience which, in numerical terms, peaked that spring.

Throughout 1972, more seasoned observers continued to

depict Bolan as a cynical manipulator, milking the rejuvenated star system for all it was worth and churning out hits like Ford make cars. But from the perspective of his fans, now almost exclusively in the eleven-to-fifteen age bracket, his name, his look and his music combined to create a world beyond pop music. T. Rex didn't exist to prove that pop musicians could compete on the same level as classical musicians; nor did it matter if Bolan's lyrical conundrums sat uneasily when held up against conventional literary expectations.

The transformed realities of LSD, combined with the anti-materialist adventures undertaken by the late sixties' counter-culture, had a climactic effect on people's willingness to accept reality at face value. Religion had long ceased to offer spiritual nourishment for the young, but the post-war revolution in the media industries – typified by the fact that sound and vision could miraculously appear out of a box in the corner of a room – provided a magical restatement of wondrous stories through consumer goods. For Bolan, who concluded in song that life was, at various times, 'strange', 'a gas' and 'an elevator', the world really did resemble one great big dream factory, just like they told it in the movies; and his eventual success only strengthened his belief in Samuel Goldwyn's oft-quoted dictum that, 'God makes the stars – it's up to the producers to find them.'

Bolan's 'magical' relationship with the world extended to his attitude towards music-making. During this period, he told *She* magazine, 'It's up here floating around, and if I don't pull it out of my head and make the record, then it won't exist. Whereas in one second I can pull it out, tape it and it exists, and you sell one million records. If I don't pull it out of my head, if I don't weave that dream, nothing will happen.' As fans trawled through his rubbish bins at Clarendon Gardens, and as countless magazine, television and newspaper interviewers sought his views on everything from sex to science fiction, Bolan's wish to turn himself into a complete work of art had not only been fulfilled, it had also been recognised. Unfortunately, the 'magic' of the relationship between a pop star and a notoriously fickle teenage audience also tends to vanish rather quickly.

Marc Bolan's sense of his own divine inspiration goes some way towards explaining the haste with which T. Rex songs were recorded during 1971 to 1973. It was an attitude that harked back to the early days of rock 'n' roll when the likes of Elvis, Johnny

Cash and Jerry Lee walked into the small Sun Studios, gave all they'd got for three minutes, and walked straight out again. (Incidentally, researchers are now continually disproving this myth of apparent spontaneity, and many different takes of songs like 'I'm Left, You're Right, She's Gone' and 'Whole Lot Of Shakin' Goin' On' have since seen the light of day.) This reliance on 'feel' can be borne out by his decision to recruit musicians on the basis of compatible personality, rather than exceptional musical skills.

Although such a no-nonsense attitude made a refreshing change to the overblown progressive rock experiments of the era, it contributed to the frustrations of the backing musicians – Steve Currie and Bill Legend, in particular, who were both kept on a basic wage plus £26.50 per recording session. 'We were hired hands, really,' admits Legend. 'Steve and I were in the same boat, though he resented it more than I did. He was always on the verge of leaving. I think Tony Visconti's insight in managing to hold it all together was marvellous, under the circumstances.'

Visconti's trick was to get the basic rhythm section down on tape, add several layers of Bolan's rhythm guitar, and then spend a considerable amount of time perfecting the vocal line. This was usually double-tracked – something Marc was particularly skilled at – a technique that gave a greater intimacy to the voice than simply slapping on a bit of studio reverb. After the addition of a lead guitar line, Visconti would add the string section he had scored and backing vocals, if required. Marc and Tony would then spend as much time again on the mixing of the individual tracks (in the case of most T. Rex recordings, sixteen), ensuring that any gaffes – and the haste with which most sessions were conducted meant there were many – were hidden to all but the most acute ear.

*The Slider*, the long-awaited follow-up to *Electric Warrior*, was recorded with characteristic speed. Ever since T. Rex began to earn big money, early in 1971, Marc had preferred to record while on the road. This made sense, not only because the group were already together in one place and fired up from the nightly concert schedule, but recording abroad was also beneficial from a financial point of view. On the recommendation of Elton John, who'd recently dedicated the title of his next album, *Honky Chateau*, to the French studio where he recorded it (the Château D'Hérouville, also known as the Michel Magne Studios), situated

just outside Paris, Bolan and T. Rex had decamped there for
three days early in March, soon after the Carnegie Hall débâcle.
Once the basics had been recorded (some preparatory work had
already been done in Copenhagen towards the end of 1971),
Bolan and Visconti took the tapes to Elektra Studios in Los Angeles, where they overdubbed the unmistakable falsetto voices of
Kaylan and Volman.

By the time *The Slider* appeared in late July, the tide of T.
Rextasy had been maintained as magazines rushed to serialise
the Marc Bolan Story, and the group undertook a short series of
concerts in June. Bolan expressed concern over his own safety at
one of the dates and within days, the inevitable 'BOLAN to quit
tours?' headlines began to appear. (As it turned out, there were
no more UK tours for the next year and a half.) The appearance
of *The Slider*, somewhat appropriately, marked the pivotal
moment in Marc's career. Despite the immediate rush of sales,
reputed to be 100,000 copies in the first four days, the album was
unable to sustain the momentum of *Electric Warrior*, and as sales
quickly tailed off, it failed to find a place on the end-of-year Top
Ten best-sellers' lists.

Although savaged by several critics for producing an album
that largely consisted of a mixture of first- and second-rate single
material (Charles Shaar Murray described it as 'close to a total
artistic collapse'), Bolan counterblasted with the claim that *The
Slider* was the first record on which he had been truthful and
written songs about himself, in contrast to the fictions of the
Tyrannosaurus Rex days. Certainly, the overtly sexual material
of *Electric Warrior* had diminished (though not completely, for
instance 'Buick Mackane' and the title track) and been replaced
by a surfeit of portrait songs, some self-mythologising, others
typically obscure but full of name-drops (Bob Dylan, John
Lennon, Alan Freed, New York street-musician Moondog and
Italian film director Pier Paolo Pasolini all got a plug).

Once past the two singles, 'Telegram Sam' and 'Metal Guru',
disappointedly placed at the start of each side, it soon became
apparent that the main facets of T. Rex – the familiar boogie
machine, the slower electric ballads and the gentler, acoustic-
based songs – had been closely adhered to. There was even
another token heavy rock number thrown in, just to prove to the
sceptics that the group had some guts, with 'Buick Mackane'
sounding every inch the bastard offspring of the as-yet-unre-

leased 'Children Of The Revolution' and Deep Purple's 'Black Night'. 'Baby Boomerang', which reactivated 'The Walk' riff and overlaid it with some 'Subterranean Homesick Blues' Dylan-like scanning, was definitely T. Rex boogie-by-numbers without the customary sprinkling of magic.

Bolan was right: it was the 'personal' songs which made *The Slider* worth listening to. 'Spaceball Ricochet' (its title an uncanny echo of Tony Visconti's Tibetan lama friend Chime Rinpoche – the song may have resembled the tale Bolan had told back at the Blenheim Crescent flat), with its measured acoustic strums and vocal hum, opened as if in answer to David Bowie's 'Space Oddity', before Bolan delivered eight verses with such conviction that even lines like, 'With my Les Paul/I know I'm small/But I enjoy living anyway', start to sound as if he's reading from a book of Zen truths. 'Main Man', the answer song to 'Telegram Sam', put the singer back in the driving seat once occupied by Tony Secunda, and after the self-referential 'Bolan likes to rock now/Yes he does', Marc openly expressed a vulnerability that had never been far from his music, but which he rarely declared in song. 'I've never cried so much in my whole life as this last year', he said around the time of the album's release, revealing a growing sense of doubt reinforced by the title track which ended, perhaps prophetically, with the words, 'And when I'm sad I slide/Watch now I'm gonna slide.'

When the record appeared, Bolan's media profile had never been higher. The memorable monochrome image of *The Slider* – Bolan playing twenties' Hollywood star Theda Bara playing the Mad Hatter – seemed to be everywhere; each successive T. Rex record topped the charts; and there were still hopes that the success would be repeated in the States and the Far East later in the year. Meanwhile, Ringo Starr's film project had been further developed into a full-length cinematic feature, and it looked as if the self-styled 'Cecil B. De Bolan' was widening his creative powers at just the right moment in his career.

Having carefully observed the vicissitudes of the pop world as stars like Billy Fury and his old friend Helen Shapiro, then Fleetwood Mac and the Bee Gees became *passé* overnight, Bolan knew that his time at the top was limited unless he could take his audience with him into new musical territories, as the Beatles had done several years earlier. Unfortunately for Bolan, youth culture had already become far too fragmented to repeat the mass 'growing up' achieved by both musicians and audiences during the sixties. While he made a concerted effort to repeat the initial burst of excitement generated by fifties rock 'n' roll – and had succeeded – maintaining that success wasn't going to be easy. On the one hand, a large proportion of his young audience would, in months to come, inevitably ditch the fantasy of Marc Bolan for a real boyfriend; while any attempt to regain credibility as a 'rock' artist provided him with an almost insurmountable task, bearing in mind the fracas over his alleged defection in 1971.

It wasn't only the *Born To Boogie* film that consumed much of Marc's time during 1972. Business matters had begun to weigh down heavily upon him ever since he had set up the T. Rex Wax Co. and related companies at the end of 1971, complete with a complicated tax structure that involved registering some of the businesses in the Bahamas. The situation became considerably more acute after the departure of Tony Secunda, particularly when Bolan decided he could do without a manager at all, once the deal with EMI was in the bag. After several disappointing experiences, he had dropped the romantic notion of finding the perfect manager – which, in his eyes, was someone willing to adopt the role of a hopelessly devoted parent, but one with great ambitions for the child. June came closest: she did much to ensure that the day-to-day running of Bolan's life and T. Rex in general went as smoothly as possible, so in March 1972 the pair took charge of the entire business operation too.

After the split with Secunda, the Bolans moved the T. Rex offices into temporary premises at 16 Doughty Street, just off Gray's Inn Road near Holborn. Both Marc and June were directors of Warrior Music Projects Ltd, while the striking Chelita Secunda, ex-wife of Tony, was made merchandising PR and personal assistant to Marc Bolan, which meant that she ran the office and the newly reconstituted T. Rex fan club.

'A man that doesn't look after his own affairs is basically a fool,' commented Marc at the end of the year. 'You owe it to yourself to have some idea of what's going on. I like to know what's going on, but it doesn't mean I can't have people working for me. But I can't get behind the conventional management bit because it was built for puppets and Pinocchio didn't do too well, did he?'[3] The analogy wasn't without a certain poignance. Walt Disney's *Pinocchio* featured a puppet figure brought to life by the ineffective father figure of Geppetto. Despite the advice of Jiminy

Cricket, Pinocchio succumbs to the temptation of a career in showbusiness, and ends up on Pleasure Island where his every whim and fancy is fulfilled. Unfortunately, the Island exists merely to ensnare the weak-willed, who become destined to spend the rest of their lives in servitude as donkeys. Thankfully, Jiminy Cricket reappears and delivers Pinocchio back to Geppetto, whereupon the puppet is transformed into a real boy. Pleasure Island had proved irresistible to Marc, too, and as the year progressed, he further indulged in its instant gratification showing no desire to harness his new-found hedonism. And with Secunda gone, there was no budding Jiminy Cricket close at hand with a will strong enough to pull him back from immersing himself wholeheartedly in his fantasy.

When publicist Bernard P. Fallon, who had successfully worked with Bolan for the past two and a half years, was the next to leave (announcing his departure in verse, paraphrasing Dylan, 'It's Alright Marc, I'm Only Leaving'), it became clear that something had changed in the T. Rex camp. Bob Harris also began to drop out from the inner sanctum around this time: 'Marc was a strong self-promoter and was extremely astute in terms of where he placed himself,' he recalls. 'But I think this ability evaporated during the 1972–3 period as he increasingly began to believe all the publicity and lose sight of where he sat. It was a shame because I really liked Marc a lot. He was so energetic, and never less than interesting to be with. You'd forgive the moments when you saw the harder, nasty streak coming through because that had always been outweighed by the enjoyment of being with him.

'Suddenly, Marc saw himself as the most important thing in pop music and a great poet too, and I found it all rather unpleasant and unnecessary. I thought the records stood on their own merits without Marc having constantly to remind everyone just how great he was. The posing really did get out of hand, whereas before it had only been limited to the concert stage or photo sessions. I'd go round and suddenly I found I wasn't talking to Marc any more. He'd be sitting back pouting his lips, and I thought, "No! Remember me?" '

Further disruption to his life occurred when a national newspaper published Marc's and June's private address. The couple were inevitably besieged by fans and were forced to set up home in a high security rented flat at 47 Bilton Towers, Great

Cumberland Place, just behind Marble Arch. The protective trio of roadies-cum-minders Mickey Marmalade, Mick O'Halloran and Marc's chauffeur Alphi O'Leary, provided a buffer between Bolan and his public, but this also ensured that real privacy – solitude – was kept to a minimum. Already, Pleasure Island was starting to show disturbing signs and the Bolans took a break from the chaos around them by joining Ringo Starr on a star-studded cruise on his yacht in the south of France.

It wasn't long after their return that the strain of trying to marry artistic temperament with a businesslike mind proved too much, even for Bolan, who had the desire to assume control of T. Rex's commercial affairs, but neither the head nor the stamina. The catalyst was the news that Track Records were planning to release a twenty-song collection of demos dating back to the Simon Napier-Bell days, titled *Hard On Love*. It wouldn't have been the first time archive material had been released without prior consultation. Fly had already compiled *Bolan Boogie*, a collection of single and album material, including some Tyrannosaurus Rex recordings, which was carefully timed to appear on the same day as 'Metal Guru'. Prior to this, the first two Tyrannosaurus Rex albums were issued together as a budget-price double LP set in the wake of the reissue of 'Debora', which managed a Top Ten placing in the singles chart at the end of April. Marc was getting an acceptable artist and composer's royalty for all these releases, so his reaction to them was inevitably double-edged; but he drew the line at hastily recorded demos which were never intended to be released in the first place.

The *Hard On Love* saga made Bolan aware of the limitations in trying to take on every aspect of his career at once, particularly as he was scheduled to fly to America shortly to make arrangements for an autumn tour. The T. Rex office needed more clout and Tony Howard, who had previously worked for the NEMS agency, was recruited, initially as a freelance, though the arrangement eventually proved to be the longest-lasting in Marc's career. This was partly due to Howard's ability, in Bolan's eyes, to adopt the role of adviser as opposed to manager: certainly the battle of wills that characterised earlier relationships seemed to subside during the Howard era. They got off to a good start. On 22 June 1972, Track and its Polydor distributors were successfully injuncted, preventing either company from manufacturing, distributing, selling or broadcasting any of the songs slated for

*Hard On Love*. (Two years later, when Bolan's circumstances had altered considerably, the release trickled out to a largely disinterested public as *The Beginning Of Doves*.)

With *The Slider* and the most pressing business matters out of the way, Bolan again switched his attentions back to *Born To Boogie*, by now his most favoured project. The end result was a typical product of Bolan's sensualist approach to his work – if it feels good, do it. As a devoted fan from an early age of rock 'n' roll cinema, he was profoundly aware of the impact of the star on the screen, and he milked that for all it was worth: there's rarely a frame in the movie where Bolan is not featured. From its title, and the opening still of the eight-year-old Mark Feld, with a guitar strapped, Presley-like, around him, *Born To Boogie* captured Marc Bolan as he'd always imagined himself: the pop hero who was different than the rest.

The press release, written by the widely respected PR man Les Perrin, quoted Bolan as saying, '*Born To Boogie* is a film with surrealistic overtones.' In truth, there probably wasn't an ounce of genuine surrealism during its entire sixty-five minutes, but there were some entertaining moments aside from the concert footage, which spoke for itself. The central sequence was a variation on the Mad Hatter's Tea Party (filmed in the garden of John Lennon's Tittenhurst Park estate at Ascot), where a white-faced Marc performed an acoustic medley of 'Jeepster', 'Hot Love', 'Get It On' and 'The Slider', backed by a string quartet conducted by Tony Visconti. Meanwhile, Geoffrey Bayldon (better known for his role as the children's television character Catweazle) recited some Bolanic verse (who else would write 'Beatles, Stones, Rex'n'all/Keep on rockin' at the Union Hall'?), June and Chelita got to dress up as nuns and chew beefburgers, while a vampiric Mickey Finn gorged himself on a blood-red delicacy.

It was Bolan's heart, not his head, which allowed the inclusion of the scenes with Ringo Starr on a runway, where the pair tried unsuccessfully to deliver a line each from Elvis's 1957 hit, 'Party'. Not only was its presence in the film a symbol of the friendship between the two pop heroes: it also injected a much-needed spark of spontaneity into the proceedings, as the pair spent several tiring weeks editing down some fifty-two hours of material at Twickenham Film Studios. At the other end of the scale, *Born To Boogie* included a super-session consisting of T. Rex jamming in Apple Studios with Ringo Starr on a second drum-kit and Elton John at the piano. (Like Bolan and Bowie, Elton John had struggled to find a niche during the late sixties, but took off around the same time as T. Rex after the success of 'Your Song'. Bolan joined him in concert at the Fairfield Hall, Croydon, in December 1971 for a rock 'n' roll jam, which included versions of 'Get It On', 'Whole Lot Of Shakin' Goin' On' and 'My Baby Left Me'.) The supergroup are depicted running through Bolan's latest composition, 'Children Of The Revolution', and a rip-roaring version of Little Richard's 'Tutti-Frutti', though among the acres of footage consigned to the cutting-room floor was a unique Elton/Bolan version of 'The Slider'.

With the film in the can, Bolan and T. Rex prepared to take on the elusive but lucrative American market once more. In contrast to *Born To Boogie*, which had been an exciting venture into new territory, the idea of the regrouped T. Rex had already become a chore to Bolan, who had recently begun to make discontented noises about expanding the line-up. While Marc's business frustrations had started to subside with the arrival of Tony Howard, this was replaced by an increasing creative restlessness. He may have made the front cover of *Rolling Stone* magazine in March, just as the band's first bill-topping tour came to a close, but despite some reasonable record sales figures, the reception in the States had been disappointing. Even *Rolling Stone* wasn't sure how to depict Bolan, opting for a mix of sex and sorcery, and ensuring that his music was placed firmly in the background. When the group returned in September, after some projected warm-up dates in France had been hastily scrapped, T. Rex met with the same old muted response.

The opening night's performance took place over the Canadian border in Montreal, where Marc openly revealed his impatience by telling the audience, 'I feel that we're working damn hard up here and not getting much response.' Backstage, he confided in a reporter after the show, 'We're not hoping to achieve anything from this tour . . . Basically we came here because we want to work . . . We want to get in shape for our Christmas gig in England.'[4] He had been defeated before he'd barely started. Bolan's US label, Warner Brothers, assisted by publicist Gary Stromberg, continued to invest heavily in T. Rex, taking the unprecedented step of paying for around 150 local television adverts to tie in with the group's concert appearances. There were pockets of committed fans at many venues but, in the main, audiences remained to be convinced. Meanwhile, critics took a similar, cynical line to that touted by the rock press in Britain. 'T. Rex is undoubtedly the worst excuse for a rock 'n' roll band to hit Toronto since the golden days of the Monkees . . . Rock music could be set back five or six years,' warned Ian MacDougall of the *Toronto Star*. Before long, the Doobie Brothers, who had been booked as the group's support act, began to headline the bill, although T. Rex received top billing when the show arrived in New York. For this performance, Bolan recruited three black backing singers in an attempt to fill out the group's sound, including one by the name of Gloria Jones.

It is said that this Cincinnati-born singer first encountered Marc Bolan during the 1969 Tyrannosaurus Rex tour, when she was a member of the Los Angeles *Hair* cast and the group were in town for a concert. They exchanged a few words at a party thrown by Miss Mercy of the infamous all-girl groupie rock band the GTOs (Girls Together Outrageously), where Marc and Steve had been invited to perform, but the meeting had little significance. By the summer of 1972, their fortunes had changed dramatically, with Gloria now established as an in-house Tamla Motown songwriter, writing material for many top artists. She had been over in England in June as one of the Sanctified Sisters, part of the entourage for Joe Cocker's European tour which rolled into London for the Crystal Palace Garden Party. It was during this visit that Marc first noticed her. 'Joe took the four of us to the Speakeasy,' Gloria recalled, 'and when we arrived there was this big Rolls-Royce parked outside. It was Marc's car. As we went in, he was coming out, and seeing Joe with these four black American chicks on his arms, he says, "Hey, man, can I help you, I mean, can I help you?!" So I let him have it. "Yeah, Joe's with these chicks from California, darlin". Marc gave me one of those looks, "Shall I kick her ass or what!" '5 It was a look that changed dramatically over the course of the next twelve months.

Joe Cocker, another Denny Cordell discovery, was one of New Breed's top artists and, following a memorable appearance at the 1969 Woodstock Festival, had enjoyed massive success in the States. But his achievement had taken its toll, and after the gruelling *Mad Dogs And Englishmen* tour, Cocker retreated into the Hollywood hills of Laurel Canyon where he stayed until the early months of 1972. Whereas Marc Bolan had definitely added an American flavour to the quaint Englishness of his vocals (particularly noticeable on 'Telegram Sam'), Cocker possessed a joyous foghorn of a voice that caused some to dub him a white Ray Charles. To the Americans, Cocker had soul, a quality that was apparently missing in Bolan's music. The rock 'n' roll roots of T. Rex may have been sound enough, but dressing this style up in sequined suits and trying to hype audiences into concert halls gave Americans the impression that Bolan was nothing more than Vegas Presley meets the Monkees.

By employing a trio of black American backing singers, Marc Bolan was responding to the myth that his music was more artificial than, say, Cocker's, and a second myth that black musicians necessarily add a sense of authenticity. Nevertheless, both misconceptions were widely held at the time, particularly in the States, and Bolan, desperate to break into the US market, felt it was a gamble worth making. In America, he'd be a different kind of pop artist.

Before taking off for the first T. Rex tour of the Far East, Marc dropped into London to promote the new single, 'Children Of The Revolution', to tie up the Christmas release of the *Born To Boogie* movie and complete the purchase of a country residence found by June on the Welsh borders. The Bolans' new rural retreat was an old, thirteen-roomed vicarage in Weston-under-Penyard, near the Forest of Dean, bought for the considerable sum of £67,000 in mid-October. While June was the motivating force behind the purchase, Bolan – perhaps mindful of a time when his teen idol days would pass – could envisage a creative life in the wilds, with his own home studio and peace and quiet for his writing and painting. But by the end of 1972, there was no question of the Bolans spending much time there in the immediate future, and a Mr and Mrs Stapleton were employed to look after the residence, complete with stables and outbuildings, where a pack of lurcher dogs, a pony called Spotted Dick and Colin the hedgehog basked in the tranquillity of country life, awaiting their absentee landlord. Like the fans who constantly stalked the building, they were to be disappointed.

The new three-track single, which included an electric version of 'Sunken Rags', previously recorded in acoustic form and donated to the *Glastonbury Fayre* benefit album, had been taped at a short session at the Château in August, and its reception showed the first signs that the T. Rex phenomenon may have peaked. 'Children Of The Revolution', propelled by a delightfully crude two-chord motif straight from the 'Louie Louie'/'You Really Got Me' school of riff rock, invoked a sixties' concept, applied it to Bolan's 'children', but said so little that no one was any the wiser as to the song's meaning – despite the unprecedented use of some of the lyrics on the striking full-page ads in the press. But that wasn't the reason why it failed to top the charts: Slade and David Cassidy were to blame for that.

Since the summer, the rest of the glam pack had arrived in earnest, alongside a new set of pre-teen idols imported from America. Bolan, somewhat unfairly, was seen as the catalyst for both, and when the hastily conceived 'Solid Gold Easy Action' appeared in time for the Christmas market, the knives were again out in force. 'That was written while we were recording at the Château,' recalls Bill Legend. 'We'd stopped what we'd been doing and Steve and I started playing around with that shuffle beat. Marc came along, asked us to play it again, scribbled down some words, and within ten minutes, we had "Solid Gold Easy Action" in the bag.' There wasn't much of a song to be found once you looked beyond the riff, and had it not borne the T. Rex name on the label, the track might have struggled to find the Top Thirty. But when you'd just enjoyed a year like T. Rex had, the luxury of one aberration could be afforded. It's a pity Bolan hadn't used the opportunity to release something more radical.

There was little sign of waning Bolanmania when *Born To Boogie* opened in several suburban cinemas on the last day of 1972, although critics claimed that tickets for the two live London 'Rexmas' shows had taken almost a month to sell. Yet the audience reaction was no less subdued than at Wembley earlier in the year, and the festivities were heightened by several minutes' worth of fake snow, the addition of three English backing vocalists, a sax player, and a neon sign that flashed the group's name. Most welcome though, were the addition of 'Buick Mackane' and 'Chariot Choogle' to the increasingly formularised set.

The Bolan backlash had been further fuelled towards the end of the year when two of his ex-associates teamed up and won some publicity on the back of Marc's success. In the summer, Tony Secunda broke with his tradition of only working with successful acts and paid for Steve Peregrine Took to record some demos at Olympic Studios. Took was particularly anxious to counter Bolan's recent claims that his old partner was 'in the gutter somewhere', but the ensuing press coverage gave little indication that he was anything other than the idle dreamer most imagined him to be; and Secunda's tutelage wasn't about to alter that. 'Steve used to call him Tony Suck Under,' remembers a friend. 'That relationship didn't really do Steve much good at all. So much cocaine went up his nose during that time, and Steve became so paranoid that he ended up a total recluse living in a flat behind Secunda's office in Mayfair. He became convinced that, because he was with Secunda, Marc's lot were going to have him kneecapped or run him over. He sat in the flat and listened for noises all day long. Nothing came of the association, though Secunda was useful when he issued all kinds of threats to David Platz at Essex Music when they tried to get some royalties out of him.'

Mick Wayne, ex-Junior's Eyes guitarist and future Pink Fairy, had known Took and Bolan since the Blackhill Enterprises days. 'Those Secunda sessions were much more rock-oriented,' he remembers. 'There was Russell Hunter on drums, Duncan Sanderson on bass, me on guitar and Tookie on guitar and vocals. He was trying to re-record "Amanda", but the trouble with all that dope-induced thinking was that he was always questioning the results. Nothing ever got finished.'

Little else was heard of Took, apart from the odd rumour concerning his appetite for self-destruction. 'He knew he had the talent,' remembers a friend, 'and so did we. He was an extraordinary performer and it broke my heart that he couldn't just get up and do it without getting out of his head. It was as if he never could believe that anything good would ever happen in his life. It was a total death wish trip, and he eventually achieved it.' It was one of Took's rare royalty cheques that finally killed him. He invested part of the money in some morphine and a bag of magic mushrooms, and on the night of 27 October 1980, he awoke from his stoned slumber, reached for a cherry and swallowed it. The effect of the mushrooms had numbed his throat, the cherry got stuck and Steve Peregrine Took choked to death.

Back in October 1972, at the time of the Took interviews, the lonesome figure of Marc's former colleague contrasted wildly with that of his own, but it wasn't just falling chart positions and marginally less fanatic audiences that provided harbingers of mounting problems. Bad Bolan vibes were beginning to filter through to some of his most eager fans. 'You have knocked Marc Bolan, criticised him and abused him,' complained 'A T. Rex Fan' to *New Musical Express*. 'He has now been driven to drink and if it wasn't for his wife, June, he'd be dead by now . . . Yes, he's going to die soon. It'll be YOUR fault.'

From the time they had first met, early in 1968, June Bolan had been a powerful force in Marc's life. She nourished his appetite for creative work by introducing him to new writers and the fine arts; she had been his roadie, driving him, Steve Took and their PA system round the country in her van; she made sure he met the right people; did his business for him, including the dirty work he found too uncomfortable to do himself, and even corrected his appalling spelling. Most important of all, she believed in him. Publicly, Marc Bolan draped himself in the cloak of self-belief, but having the unqualified devotion of a close female ally strengthened that belief immeasurably. June, by no means a sycophant, was able to heal Marc's private moments of doubt with a convincing show of support and constructive criticism.

As evenings spent indoors plotting his future success began to give way to nights out with the boys, who by the early months of 1973 included hardened drinkers like Ringo Starr, Harry Nilsson and – when he was in town – Alice Cooper, June's role tended to fade. Her faith in Marc was such that she'd stopped accompanying T. Rex on their worldwide tours and overseas recording sessions, though she invariably discovered any misbehaviour that occurred. More often than not, her informant was Marc himself, who openly confessed to the Marsha Hunt episode and, while on the spring 1971 US tour, an affair with the New York-based artist Barbara Nessim, a good friend of Tony Visconti's.

If June was disappointed by these occasional infidelities, she must have been equally, if not more disturbed by the gulf between Marc's public claims to be 'leaving the image behind . . . I'm becoming more like the old Marc Bolan', and the private descent into an existence where cognac, cocaine and champagne began to oust Poon, Marc's totemic well-spring of creativity, from his mantelpiece. The sternly self-denying ascetic of the late sixties had become, in the words of Jeff Dexter, 'a monster', a description verified by several of Bolan's close friends.

Tony Visconti's realisation that the cocky but likeable character who once brought him Tolkien's *The Lord of the Rings* trilogy ('you must read it if you are going to produce me', Marc had told him) was being transformed into an unappealing power junkie by the scale of his fame suddenly dawned on him when the group travelled to Paris to record *The Slider*. 'We were on our way to the Château in a limo,' he remembers. 'I'm sitting in the back with Marc and Mickey, and Steve and possibly Bill too. Marc is drunk. He's swigging from a bottle of cognac, and this is in the morning. All of a sudden, he breaks into a song, "I'm an old boon dog from the boon docks." He tries to get us to sing. There's an element of fear in the air. The leader is out of control.

'I was often confrontational with him, but I knew this was the wrong time. "C'mon, everybody, sing!" he says. "C'mon, Mickey, you cunt." Marc's howling like a dog and he's slobber- ingly drunk. It's like a scene from *A Star Is Born*, or Elvis. To keep the peace, Mickey starts singing, and Marc puts his arms around him. That's how *The Slider* began.

'When we arrived at the studio, it turned out that Marc was not able to have the master bedroom. The owner's clothes were in there, although he wasn't around himself. While we were having dinner, Marc instructed his roadie Mickey O'Halloran to throw the guy's clothes out. Mickey showed some reluctance, so Marc shouted at him, "Do it now!" Mickey's a big guy, and before long, he returns and he's furious. "You're not gonna talk to me as if I'm a fucking animal, and I'm not gonna treat other people like they're fucking animals. I'm not gonna do it," he says. They ended up nose to nose, before Marc says to him, "Let's talk this over." He was really embarrassed at losing face in front of all of us. And after all that, when Marc returned with the situation resolved, he turned to us and said, "Don't worry, guys, it's just an ego thing." '


'20th Century Boy' didn't have quite the element of mystery that surrounded the equally self-mythologising 'Metal Guru', but it was a convincing restatement of Bolan's pop ingenuity. From its electrifying burst of a brace of blocked E chords onwards, the song immediately washed away any misgivings that the Bolan Boogie was beginning to recycle itself with undue regularity. Its two-note riff was a hook straight out of the Rolling Stones' songbook, albeit polished with a hard rock feel. Saxophonist Howie Casey and a quartet of backing vocalists – Sue and Sunny, Vicky Brown and Barry St John – bolstered an already strong production, and the signs were that Bolan and Visconti had successfully answered the critics by developing the T. Rex sound without necessarily jettisoning the entire formula. But three weeks later came proof that all of Bolan's musical soul-searching since the previous summer had not provided any lasting answers.

The *Tanx* album betrayed a more 'rock' feel than *The Slider*: pop cool had been replaced by tentative moves into new musical territories. The heavily stringed 'wall of sound' had been dismantled and replaced by an increasing reliance on gadgets ranging from Mellotron to vocal phasing. Both were heavily featured on the opening 'Tenement Lady', part of which had been written during a high-spirited evening with Ringo Starr and writer Terry Southern at the Park Lane Hotel in New York, after the unsuccessful performances at the Academy of Music on the autumn 1972 US tour. In fact, the whole album was probably conceived that way: *Tanx* had jet-lag, coke and brandy, together with a large helping of musical uncertainty, written all over it. That Marc had better songs lying around – 'Over The Flats', 'City Port' and the inspired 'Is It True' (which, if developed, could well have provided him with the ideal solo single he was now searching for) – but failed to use them is ample proof that his judgement was becoming impaired. Even rough acoustic demos for 'Broken Hearted Blues' and 'Life Is Strange' were far better than the finished versions.

Attempts were made to mask the dearth of good material, recorded during hurried sessions in Copenhagen and Château D'Hérouville, by fleshing out the instrumentation, but it wasn't convincing. 'Shock Rock' and 'Mad Donna' maintained the hard rock posturing of the single, 'Born To Boogie' was simply T. Rex-by-numbers, 'Highway Knees' and 'Life Is Strange' were vaguely reminiscent of past glories, while the rest of *Tanx* was filler. A considerable amount of Americana was scattered throughout the album, particularly on 'Electric Slim & The Factory Hen' (originally taped in Tokyo) and 'Left Hand Luke', both of which probably account for Bolan's misguided idea that it was a gospel album. 'Frozen feet on a winter street, man that ain't your fate/ Greased in the sun, California fun, man that's more my style', he enthused on the former, as an indication of where, geographically at least, Bolan was heading. But one of the highlights, 'Left Hand Luke' (which, by offering the line, 'Myxomatosis is an animal's disease', at least provided some light relief) was probably a more accurate indication of where he was at, climaxing with a hideously drunken scream that zeroed in towards the mike, before tailing off with a loud, final groan as if he'd just passed out on the studio floor.

Marc wrapped his feather boa round his neck, hid behind his mass of hair and slapped-on eye-liner, and blatantly asserted his sexuality with the aid of a suggestively placed tank (gun-barrel pointing outwards) for the cover photo, but nothing could distract from his tell-tale bloated features. To insiders, it was an announcement that T. Rex were beginning to fuck up; cynics sniggered that Bolan was shafting his audience who, in turn, noticeably began to stay away from the album. Even early pressings of the record contained a manufacturing fault towards the end of 'Mister Mister', piling on the misery.

Bolan's fans were, indeed, growing out of him. Historically, circumstances were against him, although he did his best to pretend that it was he who was outgrowing them by making tentative lurches beyond the pop audience. Very few artists managed to bridge the divide between the pop and rock markets during the seventies (Bowie and Roxy Music excepted), and to add to the mounting scepticism, Bolan was becoming increasingly guilty by association, responsible for the rising tide of 'fun' stars like Gary Glitter, Slade and Sweet. Just as the teenage Mark Feld had constantly sought out new styles with which to impress his friends, so the many thousands of T. Rex fans started to 'progress' onto more sophisticated musical terrain, or else shift their allegiances to the next round of glam idols. Slade's 'Cum On Feel The Noize' and Donny Osmond's 'The Twelfth Of Never' kept '20th Century Boy' off the top of the charts, and Marc Bolan never again enjoyed another Top Three hit.

The controversy stirred up by Bolan when he deserted his underground audience to play halls crammed with screaming girls left a deep incision, open sores that would take years to heal. By investing all his faith in his young audiences, Marc had placed himself on a time-bomb. He knew it, but by the time the fuse was ready to ignite, he was too busy chasing lines of cocaine with bottles of cognac to care. In interviews, he still made all the same grand old claims but, increasingly, neither the quality of his music nor the sales figures could back it up. His only possible re-entry into the rock market would have required a rethink of his whole strategy, and reshaping his music as he had done a couple of years earlier. But Marc was reluctant to drop out of the scene completely, particularly with an old adversary making enormous inroads into the crossover market he ought to have been striving towards.

Although it had been Marc Bolan's defection which had symbolised the irreparable prising apart of the pop and rock categories, it was David Bowie who turned out to be the greatest beneficiary. As Dave Thompson has observed, Bolan's fall-out had been extensive. 'The people who followed could not help but take his lead,' he wrote, 'and with it a facet of his own personality. Gary Glitter took the primeval stomp, Slade took the terrace chant simplicity, the Sweet took the pre-pubescent awareness and David Bowie took the sex.'[6]

Having largely disappeared from view after the surprise success of 'Space Oddity' in 1969, Bowie finally began to forge a strong musical direction around 1971, dropping his quirky Englishness for the inspiration of American mavericks like Iggy & the Stooges and the Velvet Underground. He made his first play for stardom on the back of Marc's success by taking Bolan's androgyny a few steps further. 'I'm gay,' he told the press in January 1972, five months after *Pork*, the Warholesque freak show complete with transvestite Jayne/Wayne County and plenty of outrageously camp costumes, had enjoyed a short run at London's Roundhouse. The declaration provoked front-page headlines in the rock press, which easily accepted hippie unisex values but maintained conventional codes whenever the sexual politics turned serious. Bowie was news, and with the *Hunky Dory* album already out, and *The Rise And Fall Of Ziggy Stardust* on the way, his timing was impeccable. Within a year, 'The Jean Genie' and *Ziggy Stardust* had enjoyed lengthy chart runs, and Bowie had outshocked and outplayed his rival. Marc tried to dismiss his most talented challenger by telling journalists that Bowie was 'only a one-hit wonder', and that Mott The Hoople were bigger. But it wasn't convincing and Bolan knew it. The words of Bowie's 'The Prettiest Star' had begun to look prophetic, although the prettiest was also beginning to look the most exhausted.

Glam rock provided a marketable tag for a variety of eager pop acts, but it was at its most potent when, in the words of critic Ian Chambers, it was 'a sensationalist aesthetic of the strange'. Smiling, vaguely camp Marc Bolan had been the prototype. Odd-eyed Bowie, with his bisexual declarations, painfully gaunt features, skin-tight costumes and dyed, lavatory-brush hairstyle, provided its most extreme manifestation.

There was a sense of mod individualism run riot as Bolan

and Bowie competed for magazine covers. The exaggerated pres-
ences of the pair marked the fruition of years spent cultivating
themselves as spectacular works of art. Revelling in the idea of
the star, they represented a refusal, both of late sixties' enlightenment and of working-class puritanism. While glam has often
been denigrated as representing an escape from reality, it was
probably more about accepting the reality of the façade. Bowie
understood this more clearly than Bolan, who, while immersed
in the artifice of self-construction, still believed in the divine right
of the artist. 'It's much more of a realism for me to think that
this [clothes, hair, gestures, the room] is all me, that there's
nothing else in here. It's all outside. I prefer that way of existence',[7] said Bowie in an impeccable example of Warhol-speak.

The rampant, self-congratulatory individualism of the early
seventies extended to the music of the new stars. Elton John
wrote 'Teenage Idol' ('I sit cross-legged with my old guitar/Going
to get an electric and put a silk suit on') about Marc, while his
'Rocket Man' was inspired by Bowie, who in turn used to perform
'Lady Stardust' ('People stared at the make-up on his face/
Laughed at his long black hair, his animal grace') on stage with
an image of Bolan as a backdrop. Bowie also name-checked T.
Rex on 'All The Young Dudes', which became a hit for Mott
The Hoople. Marc, too, often name-dropped in his songs: comic
characters like the Silver Surfer or idols like Dylan and Lennon
appeared sporadically, but he was careful never to give publicity
to the names of his close competitors.

After a rare onstage jam with the Electric Light Orchestra at
Watford Town Hall in April 1973, Bolan chose to make the break
and virtually bowed out of the British music scene for several
months. It was getting congested at the top, and by venturing
abroad he could distance himself from the glittering parade of
home-grown impostors and finally conquer the world stage. It
offered an easy way out, avoiding any real confrontation with
the new rising stars, and gave Bolan the chance to return, having
discovered a fresh musical model to wash away the remnants of
second generation glam rock. 'Glam Rock is DEAD! says Marc',
ran the *Melody Maker* headline shortly before T. Rex left the
country. It was one of the last major front-page stories in his
career.

# CHAPTER TEN

**'Whatever happened to the Teenage Dream?'**
'Teenage Dream', Marc Bolan, 1974

**'What was popular yesterday is not today, for the people today are not what they were yesterday.'**
Bertolt Brecht, quoted in 'Against George Lukács', *New Left Review*, 1974

**'It was like Elvis on a bad trip.'**
Jeff Dexter

Gloria Jones has said that she fell in love with Marc Bolan on their third meeting, soon after Marc's manager Tony Howard had recruited her as vocal director for T. Rex. It was several months, though, before any mutual admiration developed into a fully fledged romantic liaison. Gloria's first task was to assemble a backing trio to join the group on stage in New York during the September 1972 US tour. The pair didn't meet up again until early in 1973, when T. Rex returned to the States to film 'The Groover' and 'Jeepster' for an ABC-TV *In Concert* programme. By the time this was broadcast in June, Bolan was in Munich for an eight-day recording session, where he was openly flouting Gloria Jones as his new partner. Not long afterwards, his five-and-a-half-year relationship with his wife was over.

For many months, Marc Bolan had been able to stamp his foot and reduce a room to silence. If hoteliers or air stewards dared cross their flamboyant customer, he would invariably cause a scene, often boasting that he could afford to buy the property or the airline outright. In the face of Marc's waywardness, June Bolan had come to the conclusion that she wanted a life of her own outside of T. Rex. This meant that while she could avoid some of her husband's worst excesses, she was also failing to provide Marc with the solid foundation which had given him the scope and confidence to build his career – and had therefore become expendable.

The long weeks on the road without June by his side certainly contributed to Bolan's increasing bouts of loneliness. Male camaraderie was fine up to a point, but Marc thrived on the close interaction of a one-to-one relationship, a need that was as much psychological as it was sexual. June's continued absence was a constant reminder that they were growing apart. Her idea of success was sitting in the garden of Eric Clapton's house, basking in the relaxed lifestyle of the English rock aristocrat; Marc's career uncertainties rendered him unable to settle so easily. Gloria Jones, who thrived on the excitement of life on the road, was much more in tune with Bolan's current state of mind. Marc, by now describing himself as a 'street punk', had no immediate wish to retire to the Welsh borders and return a year or two later with the kind of pastorally induced concept album then currently in vogue, which was why *The Children Of Rarn* kept being shelved. That he had grown contemptuous of his own past was confirmed in an incident recalled by John Peel's manager Clive Selwood, who'd known Bolan since the early days of Tyrannosaurus Rex. 'I was with Bridget St John at Television Centre and bumped into Marc and Harry Nilsson there,' he recalls. 'Both of them were having great difficulty remaining vertical, and Marc introduced Bridget to Nilsson as "You know, one of those Peel protégées". The whole affair was a bit of a downer because Marc had become quite fat and was obviously drinking too much by that time.'

The contents of his fridge were a further indicator that Bolan was in the midst of another significant transformation in his life, as Tony Visconti discovered. 'He was coked out of his brain a lot,' says the producer, 'and he was drinking. Around the time June left him, I went up to the Bilton Towers flat one day, and he said to me, "Get some champagne out of the fridge." I opened the fridge door, and there were, like, ten bottles of champagne and one big, cold boiled chicken, which was a staple Jewish dish. I said, "What's this?" because I was still a vegetarian, and he said, "I'm into chicken now, man. June says I need chicken." Marc thought it was immoral and unhealthy to eat flesh from a dead animal, but drugs make your body and your soul very dense. There's no capacity for subtle thinking any more. Marc was super-conscious for most of his career; now he's a step away from being asleep from the booze, the coke is doing something to his nervous system, and he's eating greasy chicken. He was talking gibberish too.'

It was probably Bolan's final break with the self-denial that had become fashionable as part of the late sixties 'alternative' philosophy. A couple of years later, he stated that it was impossible to remain a vegetarian in the States because 'everything has got meat in it there'. He then attempted to rationalise his decision: 'I didn't object to eating animals because, given the chance, I'm sure they'd eat us. It was just that I didn't like the thought of putting something of a lower intelligence inside myself. You are what you eat and all that. However, I may have been wrong. I'm much more perceptive now than when I was in a macrobiotic state. I can't explain that at all.'[1]

In 'Working Class Hero', John Lennon took a barbed swipe at bourgeois morality (and, perhaps, at his own 'Beatle John' days) when he advised those who wanted to be 'like the folks on the hill', that 'first you must learn how to smile as you kill', advice that Marc Bolan never really needed. But by 1973, Bolan didn't even bother to smile any more. As he had told Radio Luxembourg's Mark Wesley a year earlier, his message was a simple one: 'Just freedom. I came from a working-class background, a straight sort of background. And if nothing else, I've proved that someone from that environment can get a Rolls-Royce or whatever.'[2] Bolan had spent the past decade trying to win his 'freedom', and the self-belief it inevitably took to maintain that determined course spilled over into gross exhibitionism off stage as well as on. Keith Altham, who had taken over from B.P. Fallon as Marc's PR in mid-1972, maintains that he saw little sign of the ogre. 'He was obviously a very self-centred person,' he recalls, 'but if he hadn't been, he wouldn't have been a star and he wouldn't have got where he was. All stars have to be selfish to survive.' Unfortunately for Marc Bolan, his selfishness – or, more correctly, his self-centredness – was a vital factor in why he couldn't hold on to his success, if by success we mean keeping up with contemporaries like Rod, Elton and Bowie.

As at every important point in his life, once Marc made a decision, he pursued it in earnest, and in the summer months of 1973, he entered into his affair with Gloria Jones with all the unbridled passion of a teenager. That she was both black and American represented a further distancing from the confused state of his current lifestyle, and an embracing of the psychological Other he had been pursuing since his childhood. The only constant during this stage of his career was his absolute passion for music which never left him. (On his return from trips to the

States, it wasn't uncommon for Bolan to have a couple of thousand records in his packing cases.)

Marc was fascinated by Gloria's deep understanding of musical form, and by her contrasting background. If his early heroes had been good old white boys like Presley, Cliff Richard and Ricky Nelson, black music was never far away. He understood its pivotal place in rock history, was aware of the close affinity between his own voice and those of blues legends like Bessie Smith and Robert Johnson, and admired its fusion of raw 'authenticity' and gregarious showmanship. He also saw in contemporary black music a powerful force on the ascendant which could offer him a route out of his current creative malaise.

Gloria Jones had been born into an Evangelical family in Ohio on 19 September 1947, and had grown up to the sound of gospel music. By her early teens, the minister's daughter began to skip the services at her father's church to sing with her own friends, and formed a group with Billy Preston, Blinky Williams and Edna Wright. The latter pair appeared on her 'Heartbeat' and 'Tainted Love' singles of the mid-sixties – unsuccessful at the time, but subsequently rediscovered by Northern Soul enthusiasts several years later. Gloria also sang demos for other artists and guested on many sessions, including 'Silent Night' for *Phil Spector's Christmas Album*. She also harboured ambitions of becoming an actress, which took her to Los Angeles and a part in *Hair* by the end of the decade. (She subsequently appeared in Jack Good's rock *Othello, Catch My Soul*.)

While in Los Angeles, Gloria formed a trio of backing singers with Brenda and Patrice Holloway, before she was spotted playing piano by the British-born lyricist Pam Sawyer. For the next couple of years, the pair became in-demand songwriters (Gloria writing under the pen name LaVerne Ware), freelancing for Jobete Music Co., the music publishing wing of Motown. Their work was covered by many big names including the Jackson Five ('2468'), Gladys Knight and the Pips (the Grammy-nominated 'If I Were Your Woman'), Diana Ross and Marvin Gaye ('My Mistake [Was To Love You]') and the Four Tops ('Just Seven Numbers [Can Straighten Out My Life]').

It was an impressive pedigree and, almost immediately, Gloria became Marc's most trusted musical confidante. However, the new T. Rex sound, which he described on some Munich work-in-progress studio sheets as 'Spaceage funk/interstellar super soul', remained his concept – and his alone. Gloria returned to the States after the sessions to work on her own album, *Share My Love*. Marc remained in London to promote the latest T. Rex single, 'The Groover'.

As part of the promotion, he strengthened his rock 'n' roll animal credentials by appearing on all fours in the double-page adverts and, confident that he had finally found a new musical direction, he insisted in interviews that 'The Groover' would be the last single to feature the familiar T. Rex sound. This time round, there was no stinging riff as with '20th Century Boy', although the characteristic T. Rex boogie was noticeably harder than on the previous year's singles. The subject matter stayed the same, though, with Marc name-dropping his own 'Jeepster', and confirming his reputation as a stud and a star, at whom 'the kids yell for more, more, more'. While 'The Groover' reached the Top Five, Slade's 'Skweeze Me Pleeze Me' leapfrogged above it with ease to go straight to the top, as did Bowie's 'Life On Mars', an old song excavated from his back catalogue. Bolan was no longer public property number one.

If the plan was to compensate for falling UK sales by strengthening interest in the States, then this clearly wasn't working either. The five-week American tour, which kicked off early in August, was notable on three counts. It failed to break T. Rex in the States at the fourth attempt; the growing bond between Marc and Gloria was allowed free reign to flourish into something more meaningful; and the rest of the group became irrevocably alienated from its leader. The band members had always been promised a greater share of the earnings once T. Rex became established as a regular chart act, but by the summer of 1973, success had come, now looked like it was about to fade – and Steve Currie and Bill Legend were still on a wage of just £50 a week.

Bill was aware that he, together with Steve and Mickey Finn (who enjoyed a somewhat more lucrative arrangement), owed his livelihood to Marc, so he was able to accept that he travelled economy class on international flights and stayed in smaller hotel rooms. What was more difficult to reconcile was the contrast between his high media profile and the meagre financial reward, though another source of disappointment centred around the recording studio. 'I don't think Marc was a good tactician,' insists Legend. 'We all wanted to contribute more, but it was so frustrating when we spent so little time working on things in the studio. He tended to take everyone for granted and didn't really know how to motivate people. I always gave him my best but it wouldn't have taken much for him to give us the occasional word of encouragement. When Marc started to talk about going solo, I took his comments literally and that also affected me badly.'

With his music and his personal life in transition, Bolan increasingly took his frustrations out on the group members, and matters came to a head at a concert in Portland, Oregon, near the end of the US tour. 'It was a disaster,' recalls the drummer. 'I think he was coked up or speeding, and in the middle of "Jeepster", he stopped playing and began to tune up, just as the dry ice engulfed the stage. All of a sudden, Marc fell to the floor, still trying to tune his guitar at full volume. Steve and I cut our losses and prematurely ended the song. Meanwhile, these whining notes could be heard coming out of the dry ice, though nobody could see where from. Then Marc got up, walked towards Steve and me and said, "You're fired! FIRED!" He walked off stage, up a gangway that led to a dead end, threw his guitar off and got down on his knees. It was a terrible night.'

The following day, Bolan was all sweetness and the incident was never mentioned. But the increasingly erratic behaviour rattled Bill Legend, who preferred a strife-free existence. He stuck it out for the following tour of the Far East, before calling it a day after the Australian dates early in November. There was no big bust-up: the drummer simply asked Tony Howard for his passport after the final concert at Brisbane Festival Hall and took the next flight home to a quiet life in Essex, where he has remained ever since. Like so many former associates, Bill never heard from Marc Bolan again.

T. Rex played some large venues on that confused tour, where they were paired with Three Dog Night (though the American group soon took top billing), but they were always regarded as a poor second in the eyes of the US audiences. This was despite the addition in July of a second guitarist, Jack Green, in a bid to fill out the sound. Green, who had previously played the part of Woof in Sunshine, the rock group featured in the London cast of *Hair*, did very little recording during his spell with T. Rex but he joined them on US television's *Midnight Special* in September, where they performed 'Hot Love', 'Get It On', and 'Squint Eyed Mangle'. Unsurprisingly, Pat Hall, Gloria and a third singer, Stephanie Spruill, were also in the line-up, lending spirited backing vocals to the set, but the frills were over-shadowed by Bolan's attempt to redesign himself as a guitar hero. Rough demos recorded earlier in the year showed that Marc's desire to prove himself as a lead guitarist extended to overdubbing additional guitar parts all over his new songs, a lack of restraint that perfectly mirrored his attitude to most things during this period. And the craftily released 'Blackjack'/'Squint Eyed Mangle' single released that summer, and credited to the entirely fictitious Big Carrot, was nothing more than a T. Rex instrumental showcase for Bolan's playing, with some small input from Pat and Gloria. His sweat-soaked American performances on this latest tour often climaxed with Marc furiously hammering on his wah-wah pedal, before dropping to his knees agonisingly bending notes on his Les Paul, and were in marked contrast to the good-natured, featherweight shows served up for British audiences. He had even reactivated his old John's Children on-stage trick of whipping his guitar with a belt, but still the States wouldn't submit. To make matters worse, Alice Cooper and David Bowie had both completed successful tours there during the year.

The picture painted by the somewhat gleeful British press was one of total disaster, but it hadn't been all doom and gloom in America. In fact 'Telegram Sam' and *The Slider* both followed 'Get It On' into the charts, but there was no full-scale routing of the market as both Bolan and Warner Brothers had hoped. The label had invested heavily in British acts since the start of the decade, and one by one, they had been dropped as sales figures failed to match up to expectations. It was a great disappointment when T. Rex couldn't capitalise on their early promise, and in the spring of 1974, they, like Back Door and Roxy Music before them, were dropped by their US label. A spokesman for Warners is reported to have said, 'Promoting Marc in the States cost a fortune, what with press, radio and television adverts every-where he played, and having to take on additional people to work on his publicity. We just haven't made enough money off him to justify what we were having to spend.'[3]

After completing the Far East tour, Bolan stopped off in Los Angeles to pay Gloria Jones a fleeting visit before returning to London. By the time he arrived back, June had made up her mind to leave him. Marc was initially distraught, before emerging from the split shorn of his lengthy curls, as if in symbolic recognition that he had broken with yet another past. With June's departure went the last line of defence against the continued assault on Bolan's conscience. Now he could enjoy the fruits of Pleasure Land guilt-free. June understood this, and the further damage that Marc was likely to inflict upon himself, but even her loyalty had been stretched beyond repair by Marc's unsubtle behaviour. She decided to let him get on with it.

The new image was something of a blessing. His now puffy features no longer complemented the old corkscrew image, whereas the substantial trim gave his hair more body and took the emphasis away from his face. When Gloria eventually arrived in London, the pair moved into a rented apartment in St John's Wood and prepared to unveil the new-look T. Rex with a forthcoming album and tour. After an absence of almost eighteen months, Marc Bolan was taking the group out on the road again in Britain, hoping to cut the losses of the failed American adventure.

Things had deteriorated further since T. Rex left the country in the summer. EMI, wanting to capitalise on the group's success before it was too late, requested a hits collection for the autumn. Bolan decided it should be called *Great Hits*, the hopeful message being that there would be plenty more to come, and the record was hastily stuck inside a sleeve that was probably intended for a soundtrack album from the *Born To Boogie* film. It included no less than six Top Five hit singles, and a smattering of memorable B sides, but still couldn't persuade enough buyers to hoist it into the Top Thirty. Worse still, that winter's 'Truck On (Tyke)' single was the first officially released T. Rex 45 to fall outside the Top Ten, and any attempt at breaking the mould with the female backing vocalists sharing the limelight was overshadowed by the need to repeat the song title no less than sixty-three times during its three minutes and eight seconds duration. Promoting it on Granada's *Lift Off With Ayshea* in December, Marc looked uncomfortable without his guitar (Jack Green held the Les Paul on this occasion), his short, stocky stature now nearer to that of his old Regal Zonophone label-mate Joe Cocker.

With June out of the picture, only Tony Visconti now survived from the early Ladbroke Grove days, but even that friendship had been under considerable strain for many months. From the moment Bolan and Secunda set up the T. Rex Wax Co. with

EMI, Marc's relationship with the producer changed from that of near equal partners (they had both been employees of David Platz, though Visconti had been freelance for several months) to one which reflected Bolan's new entrepreneurial status. Marc, who had not forgotten the years of hardship and bad deals, was reluctant to give anything away. Now that he called the shots, his initial reaction was to match the fee paid by David Platz for recording sessions, a fee that both knew was below the going rate. Visconti was unhappy with the arrangement and was referred to Marc's lawyer who told him, 'At this stage in his career, Marc feels he doesn't have to pay a royalty to anybody.' Visconti continued to press for a royalty, but instead was offered a flat fee of £10,000 per year. He recalls, 'To top it all, the lawyer then asked me, "What does a producer do anyway, Mr Visconti?" I went home very upset, and later received a call from a sobbing June, who came over to smooth it out. She explained that the most Marc could afford was one per cent. Bullshit! My manager couldn't get it any higher than that, so I actually dropped my earning power by fifty per cent.' Visconti worked on *The Slider*, *Tanx* and *Zinc Alloy* albums under those terms.

Eventually, the combination of the financial snub and Bolan's inability to progress musically forced Visconti to end their six-year association. 'After "Truck On", I saw that the writing was on the wall,' he recalls. 'His songs weren't getting any better and he couldn't break free from the formula. It took half an hour to mix T. Rex songs. I'd EQ the drums in a certain way, compress the bass, put a slap-back echo on Marc's voice or ADT it to make it sound like two voices (in the end he was too lazy to double-track his vocals). I remember mixing a song very quickly one day, and Marc turned to me and said, "Cheap, isn't it?" We both laughed, but that was the sad truth. It was getting very cheap, it was easy to do, and it was no fun any more. We were drinking more than we were working.'

Back in 1972, Marc had complained about his lifelong musical idol's apparent inertia in the showrooms of Las Vegas. 'I don't want to hear Elvis singing live now,' he said. 'I'd just like to see him walk on stage – and walk off again before the performance. I'd hate to be disillusioned.'[4] The early-morning tequila with lemon and salt may have had something to do with it, but Bolan was fast slipping into exactly the Presley-like decline that so disturbed him. His life had become so detached, and the Bolan myth had taken such a hold, that he failed to notice his own slump into caricature.

At the end of 1973, Marc sidestepped any doubts about his commercial clout by declaring that he didn't want to be a 'plastic idol. I want respect as a musician.' Always the master of saying one thing and doing another, he was caught out when he invited several journalists to the second night of the six-date *Truck Off* tour, at the Apollo Theatre, Glasgow on 22 January. The notices he received ranged from disappointing to downright mocking. Marc had promised a show that would live up to the group's new Zinc Alloy and the Hidden Riders of Tomorrow name (another indication that Bolan felt compelled to break with the immediate past), but critics hoping to see a recharged T. Rex were presented with a group that hadn't really moved on at all.

Bolan could never let go of the idea that he was anything less than what the teen magazines liked to call a 'superstar'. Having reached that point, he couldn't see that, by adhering rigidly to the ground rules he had already established, he was jeopardising the very status he sought to maintain. Having been widely quoted as saying that glitter was dead, he continued to use the same old flashing 'T. Rex' neon backdrop, and made his entrance on a star-shaped dais which raised him, god-like, from the ground. Dressed in flared white trousers bearing a musical motif that conjured up visions of the gates to Presley's Graceland residence, a sparkling dark cape, and an open-fronted shirt which revealed more than it should have, Marc Bolan couldn't have been closer to Gary Glitter if he had tried (a fact emphasised by the enlarged twin-drum and sax line-up). Worse still, at the showcase Apollo concert, he took an ungainly leap onto the star-shaped prop, fell on his back and had to be helped off stage by Mickey Finn and his two roadies.

As a hideously powerful parody, or just plain kitsch, the tour worked a treat. But that wasn't Bolan's intention. He believed in the power of the formula. In retreading his past – only one new song, the forthcoming 'Teenage Dream' single, appeared in a set devoted almost exclusively to old hits – Bolan seemed content to live off the memories of 1972. There was no hint of Bowie's detached or ironic stance towards the pop game. 'Marc thought that whatever he did was great,' recalls Jeff Dexter. 'He never felt he was stuck. No one could ever question what Marc did because *he* was doing it, and he *knew* he was right. If you questioned Marc, you'd be frozen out.'

June Bolan, Tony Visconti, Bill Legend, B.P. Fallon, John Peel, Bob Harris, even Chelita Secunda were just some of Marc's closest allies who had either been given the frosty stare, or else decided to cut their losses and let him party alone with the sycophants. They had heard about the likes of Judy Garland and Marilyn Monroe succumbing to the pressures of stardom; and June and John Peel had first-hand experience of early pop casualties like Syd Barrett and Gene Vincent. Now, early in 1974, Marc Bolan, once the most determined, astute pop musician in the country, appeared to be out of control. And he had even written a song that seemed to summarise his current malaise.

'Teenage Dream' was less a lament than a lordly glimpse out of the prison bars of an increasingly detached existence. In the song, which asked whatever happened to that dream, Bolan surveyed the debris of his past ('the Silver Surfer and the Ragged Kid/Are all sad and rusted boy/They don't have a gig') in a mocking tone that began with a cackle and ended in a crescendo of effusive strings and chorus. If Bowie played with irony as an artistic device, then here was the evidence that Bolan was actually living it. The difference between the two ex-mods was that while Bolan was serious about his stardom, but had become less so of his art, David Bowie was using the star system to further his creative ambitions. Bowie, who had been so in awe of Marc's self-discipline, had achieved control over his career at its optimum moment. Marc was fast losing it, and the song's aura of melodramatic resignation indicated – quite brilliantly, it must be said – that he really couldn't give a damn.

Bowie was also more ruthless about who he took with him. Marc's on-stage conservatism (he always preferred to please rather than lead audiences) extended to his inability to reassess his own artistic needs, and the capabilities of his surrounding musicians to help him fulfil them. Since 1970, Mickey Finn's role had diminished within the group; Steve Currie was in a constant state of demoralisation; and Bolan had recruited Jack Green and replacement drummer Paul Fenton with no real regard for future musical plans.

Ace session bassist Danny Thompson, who had worked with Tyrannosaurus Rex on the Joe Boyd session towards the end of 1967, was called in to play on some of the material that ended up on the *Zinc Alloy* album. 'There was a problem with some of the bass parts,' he recalls, 'so Tony Visconti, who I'd worked with on a Tom Paxton album, invited me up to Advision. The

tracks were almost completed by that stage, and they gave me a
free hand to improvise bass for the songs.'

Although the evidence overwhelmingly suggests otherwise,
Thompson does offer an alternative perspective to the notion that
Bolan was spinning hopelessly out of control by the end of 1973.
'I saw quite a bit of him around that time,' he recalls, 'and we
had a lot of fun baby-sitting for Tony [Visconti] and Mary
[Hopkin]. When he shut that door, he forgot all about that star
trip. I thought he was really sweet and I remember him laughing
about Gary Glitter and all the hype. Of course he used to brag
about writing fourteen songs a day, and I loved that about him:
I don't think he really believed it. To see him as an egomaniac
is to totally misread him. If anything, he seemed a bit lonely at
the time.' The image of a sad little elfin character, adrift in a
fantasy world entirely of his own making, may be a difficult one
to swallow, but there was undoubtedly a private hell that coexisted alongside the increasingly public displays of megalo-
mania. A tape exists of Marc reading poetry into his ever-present
cassette recorder, words that gave no real indication of his
emotional state, but which ended up with a telling verbal signature: 'Marc Bolan. 1973. And I'm lonely.' It was further evidence
that Bolan's muse had departed him. The creative animal of
the late sixties, who had happily shut himself away in his own
makeshift Toadstool Studios, had achieved what he set out to
do, but had become exhausted in the process. Finding Gloria
Jones eased his loneliness but, despite her avowed musical skills,
the pair were intent on celebrating their new-found togetherness
before putting them to any real creative use. Between February
and September 1974, there were no tours or significant recording
schedules. Marc Bolan finally took his first real holiday – or 'lost
weekend' – in years.

David Bowie was always perceived as an *auteur*, inventing characters like Ziggy Stardust whom he could pension off at a later
date. Marc Bolan, even when he became Zinc Alloy, always
remained Marc Bolan. 'Teenage Dream' may have been an
inspired choice as a single, but its relative failure suggested that
the mass audience hadn't just tired of the T. Rex sound; it was
fed up with Marc Bolan too. When the record appeared at the
end of the tour, in February 1974, it sparked off much debate as

to its meaning. One teenager furnished *Melody Maker* with his own conclusions. 'Bolan's talking about himself,' opined Randolph Angel from Glasgow. 'He thinks he is the teenage dream. Years after he's been forgotten, he's trying to make a comeback.' (Today, 'Teenage Dream' sounds like nothing less than the perfect embodiment of post-glam melancholy – and Bolan's desperate attempt to stand above it. It carries the same hallowed ring that 'An American Trilogy' does for the Presley legend.)

To reflect the musical changes he was making, Marc wanted the new album to be called *A Creamed Cage In August* and credited to 'Zinc Alloy and the Hidden Riders Of Tomorrow'. EMI disliked such a risky tactic, particularly in the light of the group's falling record sales, and chose to add a 'Marc Bolan & T. Rex' flash across the corner of the sleeve, thus tarnishing the overall concept. Sessions for the LP had taken place in Copenhagen, Munich, London and America (specifically Georgia and Los Angeles), and before jetting off to Japan in October 1973, Marc had the unprecedented luxury of sifting through over thirty tracks from which to select the best material. The sessions may have been chaotic, proving the last straw for Visconti and Legend, but the finished album had a consistency that had been lacking from *Tanx*. Before settling on 'Teenage Dream', Bolan had toyed with the idea of releasing 'Venus Loon' as a single, a track that clearly drew its influence from the soul stations he had consistently tuned in to while driving through America stretched out with Gloria and Pat in the back seat of his limousine. The song, which opened the album, still retained an essence of T. Rex about it: much of *Zinc Alloy* didn't.

'He'd really got into black music by the time of that last American tour,' remembers Bill Legend, 'but I think he tried to force it unnecessarily. Marc was so bloody impatient and trend-conscious. I loved tracks like "The Avengers (Superbad)", "Liquid Gang" and "Carsmile Smith & The Old One" but I don't think those influences always worked. I sensed that Gloria started to take over.' It was probably Bolan's impatience, rather than any apparent takeover, which led him into territories that John Lennon, David Bowie and Elton John would all later exploit with considerable success. The presence of black music had never actually left mainstream pop and rock. Even Pink Floyd, those founding architects of the European classical rock tradition, had used black singers on their art-rock extravaganza, *The Dark Side*

*Of The Moon*. In altering the T. Rex sound, Marc gambled by venturing way beyond mere tokenism and, via what one insider calls his 'Black Queen', bought into the black musical culture wholesale. It proved too radical a move for the bulk of his dwindling audience: even on the back of the tour and the 'Teenage Dream' single, the album only managed a paltry two-week stay in the chart.

If Bolan's timing had been impeccable during the winter months of 1970–71, it was one of the factors which worked against him on *Zinc Alloy*. The album found him in fine lyric fettle, unleashing a stream of characters and entertaining wordplays in a way that he hadn't done since 1969's *Unicorn*, although that record's underlying mood of rusticity had since been replaced by streetwise jargon. Cosmic Rock had given way to Interstellar Soul, and produced some of Bolan's most genuinely personal statements to date (several songs celebrated his new-found love), but from the half-caste image fashioned for the gatefold cover inwards, *Zinc Alloy* was pronounced a fake and was quickly forgotten.

While Pink Floyd, Led Zeppelin and David Bowie fulfilled the music industry's desire to channel hip respectability into huge capitalist spectacle, Marc Bolan spent much of 1974 gorging on his own, smaller slice of the cake in the exotic playgrounds of Los Angeles and Monte Carlo. In his absence, British pop had seen the original old guard of glam replaced by the likes of Mud, Alvin Stardust and Showaddywaddy, revivalists every one of them, but none was able to take pop beyond its usual referents in the way Bolan had done. Instead, the screamers opted for the wholly safe Bay City Rollers, who offered a cutesy boys-next-door image gift-wrapped in tartan. Stripped of their costumes, Les, Eric and the guys could easily have been apprentice car mechanics, and like Sweet and Slade before them, brought pop stars back into line with their public once more. Bolan's more serious competitors, Bowie and Roxy Music also had a relatively quiet year in 1974, and it seemed as if mainstream pop's loving embrace with the peculiar had been no more than an illicit flirtation.

As Marc Bolan sipped brandy from the veranda of his South of France *pied-à-terre*, the class struggle, which he had sought to displace by becoming a 'classless' artist, raged in his absence. When the oil-producing nations decided to double their prices in autumn 1973, the West was plunged into deep recession. A three-day week, prompted by a successful miners' strike, brought down the Heath government, and Harold Wilson returned to Downing Street, albeit with little of the optimism of his first administration in 1964. With Labour back in power, there was no good news for those in high income brackets: Marc was happy to remain abroad – and felt no shame in stating why when he flew into London towards the end of the year, midway through his self-imposed exile. Like most artists, Marc believed he had worked hard for his success, and though always proud of his working-class origins, the fact that he had succeeded only strengthened his belief in the fairness of the system that produced him.

As he divided his time between a spacious residence in Del Resto Drive in the hills of Benedict Canyon, California, and a flat along Avenue Princess Grace in Monte Carlo, Marc's decision to move abroad was his equivalent of Bob Dylan's 'motorcycle accident'. Like his hero, Bolan used the much-needed lay-off to wrestle with personal demons, though very few 'Basement Tapes' of his own have since surfaced from the period, indicating that for the first time since the mid-sixties, Marc was genuinely idle – or so it seemed after the hectic schedule of the previous years.

Having announced that 'Teenage Dream' was effectively a solo single (it was billed as Marc Bolan & T. Rex), Bolan also began to harbour great notions of himself as a producer and gave himself a co-credit with Visconti on *Zinc Alloy*. His first real activity in this field was producing a solo album for Gloria's partner Pat Hall, recorded in Hollywood during the winter months, but his extended cognac honeymoon in the sun took the heat out of the project and the album was shelved. (Several Bolan titles were among the dozen songs recorded, including 'Ghetto Baby', 'Jitterbug Love', 'City Port', 'Sailors Of The Highway', 'Sunken Rags', though the intriguingly titled 'When I Was A Child' seems to have been a Gloria Jones original.)

Marc also claimed to have produced an album by John Stevens, leader of the improvised jazz group the Spontaneous Music Ensemble. He also expressed a desire to pursue free-form music himself, but he must have realised that his strengths (songs, hooks and melodies) lay in an entirely opposite direction, because nothing more was heard of that idea. Bolan had been in Japan when the finishing touches were being put to Gloria's *Share My Love* LP, and while he claimed that 'It's a very nice album, although I'm sure I could produce a better one for her,' the nearest he got at that stage was producing three tracks for her singing brother, Richard Jones (who had been part of the 'Cosmic Choir' on *Zinc Alloy*). Instead, he hoped that Gloria's vocal and keyboard talents would help resuscitate T. Rex.

Paul Fenton and Jack Green had been dropped after the January 1974 tour, leaving the second drummer Davey Lutton (ex-Eire Apparent, Heavy Jelly and Ellis), Mickey Finn and Steve Currie. A second organ player, Peter 'Dino' Dines, was picked up by Bolan while he auditioned backing musicians for David Bowie's June 1974 US *Diamond Dogs* tour, by which time T. Rex had already taped several tracks at Gary Ulmer's Music Recorders Inc. Studios in Hollywood during the initial stay in Los Angeles. Marc and Gloria then took off for Monte Carlo, leaving the next T. Rex album only partially completed, although the signs were that EMI weren't in a hurry for any new product.

The guardian angel which Bolan believed protected him in times of duress arrived this time in the shape of Neil Bogart, boss of the newly established Los-Angeles-based Casablanca record company. A deal was negotiated, allowing the label to borrow three of the strongest tracks from the *Zinc Alloy* album (which Warner Brothers had passed on), and these were combined with the new material as the *Light Of Love* LP and released in September. An extensive American tour was scheduled for the autumn to tie in with its release.

Now that the expanded *Zinc Alloy* touring group had been pruned down to a six-piece, T. Rex should have fitted more comfortably on the stages of the smaller nightclub venues that formed part of their US itinerary. But Marc, who had been dubbed 'Porky Pixie' and the 'Glittering Chipolata Sausage' after the British dates at the start of the year, emerged from the months of seclusion looking bloated and ungainly. It was difficult to imagine him enduring the rigours of the extensive cross-country jaunt, which ran from September through to November. Yet images only tell half a story. Paunch and chins aside, the truth was that the twin-keyboard line-up, bolstered by strong clavinet and support vocals from Gloria Jones, provided a solid wall-of-sound backing, which gave Bolan the freedom to show off his by-now considerable lead guitar skills. Interstellar, indulgent soul it may have been, but as Bolan's performance moved closer than ever to vaudeville, it was obvious that it wasn't simply the music that was taking him higher. The tour, on which T. Rex were billed with the likes of Blue Oyster Cult, Black Oak Arkansas and a quartet of home-grown glam-influenced heavy rockers called Kiss, closed the four-year quest to conquer the US market. Bolan had failed dismally, but for the first time in his life, he was too wasted to care.

The absence of T. Rex from the British scene for much of 1974 inevitably hastened the decline that had been on the cards since the final months of 1973. 'Light Of Love', issued in May, the first 45 released during Marc's period of exile and promoted by a film shot in Paris, signalled the much-needed break with the old sound in terms of the singles market. But as proof that the mass audience had grown tired of Marc himself, the record sold to the faithful for a couple of weeks before quickly dropping into obscurity. Strings, which had bowed out in such dramatic fashion on the closing bars of 'Teenage Dream', had been replaced by a lightweight funk-pop backing, where handclaps and clavinet were brought to the fore and the subject matter appealed more to Bolan himself than to the dreams of his teenage audience. For a man in the formative stages of a new love affair, the apparent yearning of 'Light Of Love' ('Won't you shine for me?') didn't quite go with the finely matched fusion of Bolan's melody and Gloria's dance music influence.

There was no doubting that the new material on Casablanca's *Light Of Love* album, which eventually appeared in Britain in February 1975 as *Bolan's Zip Gun*, complete with three recently recorded songs taped with Dines in the line-up, was an extended love letter to Gloria. Bolan expressed his devotion in the most economical terms yet with little of the sensuousness or the floridity of 1968's ode to June, 'Juniper Suction'. Tracks like 'Solid Baby', 'Precious Star' and 'Space Boss', hinged round simple one-line refrains, reflected a retreat from the dense arrangements of *Zinc Alloy*, but were a far cry from the opulence of 'Telegram Sam' and 'Metal Guru'. Months later, Marc stated that the album was over-produced, something that was perhaps to be expected as he sought to forge a new sound in a post-Visconti world. But from the vantage point of the 1990s, *Bolan's Zip Gun*, the most disastrous Bolan album of all in sales terms (though this was

partly explained by the availability of the *Light Of Love* album
on import since the autumn), remains the most contemporary-
sounding record ever produced under the T. Rex name. The
slightness of some of the material was largely compensated for
by the directness of its production, which was the true legacy of
the months spent listening to the American soul stations.

Bolan had a potential winner on the album in 'Think Zinc'
but, sadly, this only appeared on single in Spain and Germany.
Britain and most European countries had to settle for 'Zip Gun
Boogie', which parodied both T. Rex and hard rock in one stilted,
three-minute romp. In the end-of-year singles tables compiled by
the music press, T. Rex scored fewer points than acts like the
Pearls, Andy Kim and Peppers. Things had reached a new low.

British audiences had overdosed on Marc Bolan for the best
part of three years, so Marc's decision to take himself off the
market early in 1974 had suited both his commercial and his
personal life. But when he returned with *Bolan's Zip Gun*, there
was no reservoir of nostalgia for the Bolan boogie, even if T. Rex
had attempted to take on board the sounds of contemporary
black music. It looked like Marc had backed the wrong horse.

By 1974, the highly polished and heavily stringed Philadel-
phia sound created by songwriters Gamble and Huff had become
the Motown of the seventies. Marc once believed the string
arrangements on T. Rex records fulfilled a sort of talismanic
function, an aural good-luck charm, but since Visconti's departure, he had ditched them in favour of a tight, funkier style. It
was David Bowie who decided to immerse himself fully in the
new style by recording his *Young Americans* album at Sigma
Sound Studios, heart of the 'Philly Sound'. He was rewarded
with his biggest US success to date. Bolan had been less decisive
in following the trend according to the rules, partly because his
understanding of black music was noticeably broader. He loved
the fluid voice of Al Green, but knew he couldn't emulate him.
He had even tried his own full-blown gospel song several months
earlier, but 'Sky Church Music' (a nod in the direction of another
idol, Jimi Hendrix, who often used the phrase during 1969 as he
searched to find *his* new musical direction) contained very little
Marc Bolan at all. Instead, he had fashioned his own unique pop
blend of the distinctly British T. Rex sound and American black
music, but it led him into a commercial cul-de-sac by proving too
marked a shift for his old audience, while lacking a fresh enough
identity to appeal to a wider public.

There were only two T. Rex singles to show for the whole of 1975, but this didn't mean that Bolan hadn't rediscovered his zest for recording. He had a follow-up to *Bolan's Zip Gun* in the can by the spring, and recorded many home demos and studio tracks throughout the year in the hope of stumbling across a new winning formula, or at least a hit single. The wealth of out-takes from this period suggest a sense of floundering, but when the next album eventually appeared early in 1976, it was probably his most satisfying since *The Slider*, maybe even *Electric Warrior*. EMI, though, weren't so sure, and stalled its release. Privately, Bolan may have been more committed to forging ahead musically than his critics gave him credit for, but the aura of Marc Bolan, which had once been such a major selling-point but now looked jaded, prevented audiences from taking his new music seriously. He was increasingly perceived as a spent force.

His commitment to T. Rex as a musical entity seems to have almost totally vanished during 1975. After the autumn 1974 US tour, the group had remained in the States and cut several songs, including 'Casual Agent', 'Chrome Sitar', 'Sparrow', 'All Alone' (which was originally hatched during the *Zinc Alloy* sessions as 'Saturation Syncopation') and 'New York City'. Marc told the press he had been working on a solo album. In fact, all except 'Sparrow' were eventually released as T. Rex recordings, but the departure of Mickey Finn in February 1975 severed an important tie with the band of old, leaving only Steve Currie from the group's heyday.

Finn had been an onlooker for much of his career as T. Rex percussionist. His chief role was as a visual foil to Marc during the height of T. Rextasy, though his near-silent presence beside Marc added a touch of vaguely camp glamour. But now another previously well-balanced relationship had soured beyond repair.

When Bolan checked into the Carlton Towers Hotel in London early in 1975, a portly frame balanced on a pair of American moon boots, and with an early-morning beer in his hand, seasoned rock writers like Roy Carr from *New Musical Express* sensed another fallen star. Carr reported one incident when Bolan caught sight of himself and uttered, 'Oh, God, just look at the state of me,' a recognition that after a three-year diet of brandy, cocaine and leapers – not forgetting calorie-laden meals – he was able, at least on occasion, to see himself as others saw him. For a brief moment, the invincibility that his excessive lifestyle had given him was pierced.

In the months ahead, events conspired to force Bolan to confront the 'T' that stood for Tyrant in T. Rex. Like most individuals who shelter behind a strong will, Bolan had an answer for everything. At the height of his success, he used popular approval as the yardstick with which to judge his work. Now, in the darkest days of his career, the delusions of grandeur he harboured seemed to fly in the face of popular opinion, but he still claimed victory. He told Carr that his fall from grace had been deliberate: he was bored, he said. His failure to break in America was blamed not on poor performances but on over-hyping. What did it matter anyway? Marc was going to be big in the movies, and in March was due to start shooting a film called *Obsession* with David Niven. Apparently, he was in line to play the part of a drug-selling psychotic with sexual problems, who ends his days behind bars after murdering three people. The film was never made – Niven apparently knew nothing of the project – though tapes exist of Marc reading from a film-script with what is probably a voice coach. Whatever happened, he clearly didn't get the part.

Bolan had stressed that 'T. Rex no longer exists' while he was in Britain during the early spring of 1975, but by May the established line-up of Currie, Dines, Lutton, Marc and Gloria Jones flew into the Château D'Hérouville, Paris, to complete work on material which had been started at the end of 1974 – and also to lay down plans for a new project. Having attempted to revive *The Children Of Rarn* in the late summer of 1974, Marc had shelved the idea yet again in favour of what he was now describing as his 'teenage punkoid opera'. This was *Billy Super Duper* (which bears no resemblance to the posthumous album of the same name), a tale loosely based on the life of a street kid living in the twenty-fifth century – I say loosely, because Marc only spoke of the project in very general terms, and the songs which are known to have been intended for it ('Brain Police', 'Metropolis', 'Dynamo' and the title track) gave away very little in terms of narrative structure.

With most of a follow-up to *Bolan's Zip Gun* already recorded back at MRI in Los Angeles, the decision to return to the Château was a further indication that Bolan had decided to retreat from America. In the coming months, London began to figure in his life again, an influence that would reacquaint him with his childhood and alter the tenor of his forthcoming rock spectacular.

*Billy*, which had been conceived as a pseudo-religious spaceage fantasy ('Maybe us and God will truly meet,' he sang on the 'Dynamo' out-take, intended as part of the climax to the rock opera), was ousted over the course of the next year in favour of what Marc grandly titled *The London Opera*.

During the summer of 1975, two tensions were clearly evident. While he continued to enthuse about his enlarged musical projects, Bolan found himself enjoying his first real success since 'Teenage Dream', eighteen months earlier, with 'New York City', a delightfully inane 'boogie mind poem' based around the same riff that had once given Tyrannosaurus Rex a minor hit with 'One Inch Rock'. Its poetic qualities rested on just three lines – 'Did you ever see a woman/Coming out of New York City/With a frog in her hand' – taking Bolanic minimalism to dramatic new heights. The presence of Flo and Eddie (alias Howard Kaylan and Mark Volman) as backing vocalists on the record marked a further reacquaintance with Bolan's past, which had been all but erased during the lengthy absences in Los Angeles and Monte Carlo. Marc embellished the song's subject matter with a typical mix of fantasy and name-dropping. 'I was walking with David Bowie in New York City,' he said, 'and we saw this ninety-year-old lady who is part of Andy Warhol's Factory and who claims to be a witch. She was walking down Park Avenue with this enormous toad in her hand.'[5] Other sources close to Bolan suggest that the inspiration for the song came from a toy Kermit the Frog he had given to Gloria.

The frog appeared with the group for the first T. Rex British television appearances since Bolan promoted 'Teenage Dream' alone at the beginning of 1974. By now, the revival of showbiz values during the glam glory days had blossomed into full-blown camp, as Bolan pouted gaily and pirouetted through the song, leaving the macho guitar-hero posture of the previous year far behind him. There was definitely a sense of mischievous fun in him again. America had finally passed through his system, though it had left him overweight, psychologically dependent on drink and drugs, and musically in a state of abeyance. In the process, he had lost much of his audience in his own country. Mindful of returning to half-empty venues, Marc decided to test the water by playing a mini-tour of dates at four holiday resort towns that summer: Douglas on the Isle of Man, Great Yarmouth, Hastings and Folkestone. It was a low-budget venture, but while the group arrived at their destinations in a minibus, Marc and Gloria Jones turned up in a black limousine. Once inside the hotel bars and foyers, though, fans discovered that Bolan was the most approachable he had been since the early days of T. Rex.

As with Bowie, much of Marc's appeal resided in the character he had created, an exaggerated presence, which fulfilled the desire to look at least as much as the beat of his music demanded a physical response. Now he was back and conversing with the faithful. From this point on, Bolan enjoyed greater contact with his fans, and, such was the strength of the persona he had created, this did nothing to diminish his star appeal. T. Rex concerts now took on a carnival atmosphere, still providing a fetishistic celebration of the image, even if that image was looking a bit worn round the edges. The parade of top hats, glittering costumes and ringleted hair mingled with a smattering of genuinely curious holiday-makers as Bolan and his new-look T. Rex appeased the loyal fans by performing short sets of almost exclusively familiar material, 'Jeepster', '20th Century Boy', 'Teenage Dream', 'Zip Gun Boogie', 'New York City', 'Hot Love' and 'Get It On'.

Midway through the performance Bolan uncharacteristically threw in one new song, then titled 'You Damaged The Soul Of My Suit'. Even more extraordinary was the song itself – an admission perhaps that something had pierced the protective armour of Marc Bolan, perhaps? He shies away, typically, from any further elaboration during the course of the song, leaving another interesting thought hanging as a loose end. If anything had damaged the soul of Marc's suit, it was the absence of a genuine subculture during the mid seventies. Having always defined himself against the grain of the mainstream, Bolan inevitably got caught up in the confused direction of that decade; he had no obvious place. The youth cults which provided him with the springboards to activity had been dissipated and, to cap it all, he had been weakened by self abuse.

When the transformative zeal of the sixties had given way to the individual hedonism of the early seventies, Bolan was perfectly poised to clean up. His paper-thin adherence to the ideals of the alternative society took a back seat as collective defeatism took solace in spectacle. Glam had provided a moment's pleasure; but Bolan's moment had passed. The teenybop era was in decline; pop culture had already begun to look back on itself, celebrating the glory days of rock 'n' roll, garage rock and psychedelia. Iggy and the Stooges and the Velvet Underground were being eulogised in lavish retrospectives long before punk arrived. Disco music, which more or less dispensed with 'stars', filled the void and Bolan had been consumed by it. In the mid-seventies, Marc Bolan found himself in the unusual position of struggling against the grain.

# CHAPTER ELEVEN

'Listen, I was the originator of Punk Rock. We had a big
sign on the Strip that read, "The Cosmic Punk Comes", and
no one got it.'
Marc Bolan, *Record Mirror & Disc* magazine, June 1976

'We'd go up and tell him what we wanted to see him do,
which was play more guitar solos, and do an album of
really raw stuff. He'd say, "That's interesting, guys, I'll have
a word with my manager." He was doing a really wild
version of "Debora" on the tour, but I think the management
were against releasing it.'
Captain Sensible

In contrast to Bolan's fortunes in the States, David Bowie finally
made the big breakthrough with *Young Americans* in the spring
of 1975. He had always threatened to be Britain's only real export
from the glam era, discounting, of course, Elton John and Rod
Stewart, who were always perceived as apart from the genre.
Marc had presumed that he could conquer by virtue of his
advance publicity and well-practised larger-than-life character.
But American rock fans didn't like hearing how he was bigger
than the Beatles back home, and when they went to find out for
themselves, they were disappointed by a series of unexceptional
stage shows. Bowie had been more astute. He recognised that
Americans were more used to dealing with rock stars dressed in
lumberjack shirts and faded blue jeans, and sought to balance
the decadence of his image with a mixture of professionalism
and artistic credibility.

Bolan imagined that longer guitar solos and the injection
of some black music influences would be enough to belie the
impression that T. Rex were a lightweight export from the image-
obsessed British Isles. Bowie was far more flexible, dropping his
backing group, the Spiders From Mars, when he switched musical direction, and recruiting experts to assist him, be they ace

session musicians like Herbie Flowers and Tony Newman, or choreographer Toni Basil who helped him devise a spectacular stage show. 'Marc's problem was that he always wanted to be the sole creator,' recalls Tony Visconti. The tables had turned; and the tensions between the Bolan and Bowie camps continued to charge their friendship with a competitive rivalry.

David Bowie had recently landed a part in *The Man Who Fell To Earth*. Not to be outdone, Bolan began to envisage his own *Billy Super Duper* project in cinematic terms, while between them the pair made tentative steps towards a film soundtrack collaboration unrelated to either. Neither was committed enough about a joint venture to take this any further than discussion stages.

Neither did Marc take too kindly to receiving advice when Bowie offered it. 'They tried something out,' says Visconti, 'but I heard that all they did was argue. Marc just couldn't get real with David. Bowie thought he was getting somewhere for a while, and Marc seemed to be taking it well, but in the end he just left saying, "Go fuck yourself." He wouldn't listen. Gloria was powerless and all his musicians ended up as sycophants. He always wanted mediocrity around him so that he looked good.'

It was less a bid for renewed artistic credibility than a decision to turn his back on America which prompted Bolan to raise his profile in Britain during 1975, though his mind was further concentrated by two other pressing matters. The EMI contract was due for renegotiation by the end of the year and his increased visibility, preferably coupled with a hit single or two, would give him added muscle at the negotiating table. Also compelling him to return to a more settled lifestyle was the news of his imminent fatherhood.

Although heavily pregnant, Gloria Jones joined Marc in London's Scorpio Studios at the end of August, where T. Rex recorded a Christmas 45, added final mixing touches to the forthcoming 'Dreamy Lady' single, and ad-libbed a heavily phased vocal piece, 'Reelin' An A Rockin' An A Boppin' An A Bolan'. Several fans were invited into the session, which carried on until the early hours of the morning, and after the work had been completed Marc arranged for them all to be driven home. He wasn't only recording in London again: he had rented a three-storey house at 25 Holmead Road, just off the Fulham end of the King's Road.

Bolan wasn't always so keen when fans started to congregate around his house, especially in the months after the birth of the baby. His publicist Keith Altham remembers that, 'He went through a period of being quite Howard Hughes-like, to the extent that he even imagined that fans were bothering him. One day, my partner knocked at his door and there was no answer. As he walked back down the path, Marc peered out from an upstairs window and whispered, "Are they still there?" The road was absolutely deserted. "There are about twenty of them; they're hiding under the bridge. Get down by the gate, and when I open the door, make a run for it." It was a real performance of paranoia.' Bolan's committed core of followers were devoted enough to justify what appeared to be delusions of fanmania but, despite the brave attempts to explain away his fall from grace to cynically inclined journalists, T. Rex were now generally regarded as a hangover from a previous pop age.

When Bolan was invited by television producer Mike Mansfield to appear on a new Saturday afternoon teenage pop show called *Supersonic*, he agreed, seizing on the opportunity to win over the next generation of teenyboppers. Mansfield still believed in the power of the stars of old, and invited names like Gary Glitter, the Sweet and David Essex on to his elaborately designed and suitably over-the-top stage sets. What Bolan didn't realise was that children's television was to provide him with his chief outlet for the rest of his career, more often than not performing watered-down versions of his former musical glories.

While recording his first *Supersonic* appearance, Marc received a call that Gloria was in labour and he rushed to be beside her in a private room at a hospital in St John's Wood. He was delighted that the child, a boy named Rolan Seymour Feld Bolan, was born on 26 September, making the family a trio of Librans, which, he liked to believe, was the sign of strength, determination and success. The source of the name was so obvious that even Marc admitted to keeping up with the David Joneses: 'Bowie called his child Zowie Bowie so I thought I'd call mine Rolan Bolan,' he said. Drawing from his own experience, he strongly believed in the importance of the mother figure in a parent–child relationship, and, though the birth inevitably prompted him to reassess his lifestyle (a process that occurred gradually over the next few months), it didn't stop him accepting any offer that raised his public profile. Marc needed all the exposure he could get.

A unique opportunity came after an appearance on Thames Television, when he upstaged *Today* interviewer Allan Hargreaves by firing his own questions at the other studio guest, Telly Savalas (star of *Kojak*). Producer Mike Housego was sufficiently impressed to offer Marc a thirteen-week stint as a guest interviewer on the early-evening show, a six-minute slot that also gave him the opportunity to plug his latest songs. 'It's fun doing interviews because they can't bull me; I'm the biggest bullshitter of all time,' he said in October as the series got under way. Unfortunately, the commission didn't last its full course, although Bolan entertained guests such as Marvel Comics boss Stan Lee, Keith Moon, John Mayall, Angie Bowie and Roy Wood before the idea ran out of steam.

As winter approached, Bolan was in better spirits than he had been for many months. He seriously considered finding a more permanent base for his family, and made plans for a saturation tour of Britain in the new year, to accompany the release of the album that had been in the can for the best part of 1975. The recent *Today* appearances sent his imagination into overdrive, and before long, he was telling interviewers that he had been offered a late-night chat show and was making plans to interview twentieth-century legends like Greta Garbo, Ingmar Bergman, Orson Welles and Salvador Dali. It is a pity he didn't always display such impeccable taste when it came to the realities of his career.

Bolan's positivism extended to a rare critique of his own work in interviews around this time. He admitted that T. Rex had turned into a money-making machine, and that some of his recent records had been 'below par'. He had even begun to rethink the very parameters of rock 'n' roll within which he had worked for the past two decades. What had now become a 'huge art medium, an audio-visual art form' was tailor-made for some of Bolan's ideas but, disappointingly, his hyperbole wasn't matched by the resolve to put these into practice.

Bolan put opportunism before a measured response to the decline that had set into his career, as his autumn 1975 single made clear. Billed as 'T. Rex Disco Party', the lead track was 'Dreamy Lady', a glorious variant on the C/Am/F/G sequence that Marc had first used to good effect back in 1969 on 'Catblack (The

Wizard's Hat)'. The song utilised the disco ballad format and, unlike some of his earlier, more forced excursions into contemporary black music, it sounded naturally suited to his style. 'Dreamy Lady' was an exercise in what Bowie liked to call 'plastic soul' but, as with his own recent funk collaboration with John Lennon on 'Fame', British audiences didn't readily accept the musical turnaround.

Marc promoted the song on *Supersonic* by rising from the floor on a star-shaped platform, a throwback to the January 1974 tour, but the appearance was notable for delivering one of his most startling image transformations yet. It is always easy to draw links between events with the benefit of hindsight, and Bolan's claim to have been the Godfather of Punk has gained considerable credence over the years. Transvestism, or at least a flamboyant blurring of sexual identities, hadn't faded when its two main protagonists, Bolan and Bowie, switched their attentions towards America. *The Rocky Horror Show* and *Cabaret* provided the new focal points for the chic appeal of decadence. Bolan brought this transgression of conventional mores on to children's television, looking every inch the precursor of Siouxsie Sioux who, a year later, would become the first female punk 'star'. Dressed in a tight blue zip-up jumpsuit, with a black feather choker around his neck, Bolan's streaked hair had been crimped into sharp, dagger-like strands, while his face provided the punchball for all manner of cosmetic appliances, including over-rouged cheeks and panda-like eyes. Back in 1975, it was too far over-the-top to be considered a threat, but what may have been a ploy to divert attention away from his excess pounds provided the punks with a lasting image.

In his guest round-up of the week's single releases in *Sounds* magazine Gary Holton of the Heavy Metal Kids wrote that he had all the old Tyrannosaurus Rex albums and that 'Dreamy Lady' sounded like a return to them, an example of how critical faculties seemed to desert the music industry during the mid-seventies. Musicians, critics and audiences alike were all left clutching at straws. As nostalgia and pastiche replaced the rhetoric of youth rebellion, it really seemed as though the heart and soul had been ripped out of rock 'n' roll. Whereas Bolan had once shown reluctance to alter his winning style, he now sought to capture the mood of the month, dip it in the pot named T. Rex, and hope the audiences would return to him on a piecemeal basis. But 'Bolan's Jive In '75', the slogan which accompanied the single, was a lonely one; the 'T. Rex Disco Party' stalled at Number Thirty.

The records may not have been selling like they once did, but now that he was back in England, it was difficult to keep Marc Bolan out of the public eye for long. Keith Altham says, 'People would do an interview with Marc even when things weren't going well, because they knew they could get good copy from him. The media really liked people like Marc, and in many ways he made my job easier for me. I'd phone him up and say there's a page going in the *Mirror* this week, and he'd say things like, "What shall I be this week? Bisexual? Trisexual? Shall we say I take a gold bed with me on the road?" He loved a bit of outrage.

'The only other person who has a grasp of the media that comes anywhere near Bolan's is Mick Jagger. But Jagger is pre-meditated; Marc was instinctive, and I think people warmed to him because of that.'

Towards the end of the year, Marc was explaining away the film with David Niven and Capucine, stating that it had been cancelled due to lack of funds, but he spoke enthusiastically of his new projects. There were no less than four albums on the horizon, two of his own, and one apiece, which he had been producing from Gloria and Richard Jones. The ambitious rock extravaganza he had been toying with since 1970 still nagged at the back of his mind, coming to the fore whenever he was asked about his future plans. Referring to *Billy Super Duper*, he described it as 'a very intricate science-fiction story, full of more imagery than you've heard on any album ever. It's a combination of *The Children Of Rarn* album, which in fact I never recorded, and *2001* and *A Clockwork Orange* all sort of squashed together. It's got some amazing characters, places, worlds, planets, galaxies . . . everything's stuck in there. It'll take you days to get through it.

'There's a huge booklet enclosed with the album. It's an immense work. It's not a concept album as such, just a story set to music with lots of images. I think it will be important, an important album.'[1] So important, in fact, that Marc never found time to think it through to completion, despite telling reporters that he was off to Los Angeles for Christmas to finish work on it.

Nevertheless, the intergalactic imagery of *2001*, the urban street gangs of *A Clockwork Orange* and the mystical fantasy of *The Children Of Rarn* continued to provide Bolan with his raw material. Had he been able to draw his sources together and deliver his *chef d'oeuvre* at this stage in his career, it may well have backfired on him. Again, his instincts were correct. It was the singles market, and the younger audiences who inhabited it, which needed the biggest shake-up and, with a mixture of design and default, that is the level on which Bolan continued to operate. *Billy Super Duper*, the futuristic street punk, remained on the back burner, but his spectre nevertheless haunted Marc's subsequent work.

Caught between Bolan's commitment to simple, if elaborately dressed street songs and his perception of rock's capacity to become a huge audio-visual art form came 'Christmas Bop', the seasonal single recorded at the end of August. It was cloth-eared and ham-fisted, quite unlike the Spector-influenced song penned by Marc's friend Roy Wood a couple of years earlier. Whereas Wizzard's 'I Wish It Could Be Christmas Everyday' radiated a warm, celebratory glow, The 'T. Rexmas' Marc promised conjured up a Christmas spent alone huddled round a one-bar electric fire. It very nearly appeared, but Marc spared his blushes by calling a halt to its production. It couldn't even go out to fans as had the 1972 Christmas fan club freebie (a Beatle-esque collage of lunacy which contained an early version of 'Christmas Bop'): by the end of 1975, the fan club had ceased to exist.

After spending Christmas in the States showing off Rolan to his maternal relatives, Marc and Gloria returned to Britain to maintain and perhaps raise the profile established during the previous autumn. Publicist Keith Altham had little difficulty in placing Marc in magazines and newspapers, and news of the forthcoming series of T. Rex concerts was still deemed important enough to be front-page news in some of the rock weeklies. 'The idea of Marc Bolan is still as a big superstar, whether people like it or not,' he told one interviewer, in between trawling the more familiar ground of projects with Bowie, a forthcoming poetry book and how good his latest record was. The events of the past few months, including the birth of his son and the lifeline thrown by television producers, were also beginning to have an impact. Marc told *Super Star* magazine that 1976 was going to see a clean-living Bolan: 'I'll be getting my kicks from playing to the kids again for the first time in three years. I suppose you could say I've rediscovered my original dream all over again.'

Marc's original dream had been fame. He had shown great determination in achieving that goal, transforming intense self-love as a teenager into slavish devotion by half the world's teenage population. The hard work had been done. Whtever he did next could never detract from the fact that, in his mind, Marc Bolan already *was* a pop-music legend. The difference between Marc Bolan pre- and post-stardom was that, earlier in his career, he was willing to force the hand of chance, always seeking to nudge destiny a little closer. By the mid-seventies, he was generally content to let it take its course. If he was offered children's television spots, he'd do them; if someone gave him a million pounds to turn *Billy Super Duper* into a full-length feature film, he would have done that. In the meantime, he made slight adjustments to his music, appeased the record company by undertaking infrequent tours, and pleased himself by running rings around a steady stream of interviewers. Being allowed to live out the role of the star seemed to inoculate Bolan from the harsh realities of a world that had moved on from T. Rextasy. 'Marc was never a has-been in his own eyes,' exclaims Jeff Dexter, who began to see a lot more of his old friend again after Bolan's return to London. 'He didn't hear other people. His world just wasn't that real.'

Being thrust onto a stage to entertain paying customers who chanted your name incessantly as they awaited your appearance was Marc's kind of reality. Seeking adoration was the drug that tempted him back into the mainstream pop world. But whoever planned the schedule for the *Futuristic Dragon* tour had misjudged by combining essential appearances at major British venues with several dates in smaller provincial towns. To cover their costs, the smaller venues were forced into charging above-the-odds prices for tickets, with the result that T. Rex played to a number of half-full houses during the four-week tour, which took up most of February and the first week of March.

The plan was to extend the theme of the album into the concert halls with an elaborate stage set, something that Bowie would have seen through to perfection. For Marc, the inspiration was more important than the execution, and the grand idea was quickly whittled down to a simple dragon backdrop and his own scarlet *Futuristic Dragon* suit, trimmed with leopard-skin patterned velvet. A thick blond streak had been dyed into the front of his hair, crowning one of the least appealing images of his entire career. Sometimes Marc appeared drunk on the tour. At one concert, in Folkestone, he opened up to his audience, citing that being a superstar 'only gave me problems', as he reminisced about the days of being a 'flower child' while introducing 'Debora', which formed part of the acoustic set. (This almost became a request spot. Joyously received sing-along versions of songs like 'Ride A White Swan', 'Life's A Gas', 'Conesuela' and 'One Inch Rock' provided an intimacy missing between Bolan and his audiences since 1972.) It was all a far cry from the slick performances of his contemporaries, and a welcome lapse of 'professional' values that would be exceeded by a new breed of younger groups later in the year.

Marc Bolan still occasionally made the front pages of the pop press. He could even inspire members of the audience to jump on stage and mob him, which was what happened in Sunderland, when one fan pulled him off his stool, forcing him to take a few minutes off-stage to recover. But he couldn't come up with a hit record. Both *Futuristic Dragon* and 'London Boys', the single that followed it midway through the schedule, flopped badly – quite a feat while on an extensive nationwide tour with his face all over the music press and beyond. When pressed to explain the less-than-flattering crowds at some of the gigs, Bolan explained, 'I did this tour without any publicity just to get the feel of things again. Now I want to do more live shows. I was the first artist to play Wembley and I did it twice with 20,000 there each time. I feel like doing it again and I know that they'd sell all the tickets in a day.'[2] If Bolan believed that, then his sense of reality had parted company with the last vestiges of conventional wisdom.

Bowie's old friend George Underwood, who designed the first Tyrannosaurus Rex album sleeve, had been commissioned to paint Bolan astride a *Futuristic Dragon* for the new LP sleeve. It was unflattering to Bolan, begging cynical observers to quip that Marc was now the cartoon character he had always threatened to become. Because the recordings were several months old, Bolan was strangely reluctant to give it the hard sell, preferring to state how much time he had spent working on it.

The sleeve wasn't the only link with Bolan's past: several of the songs were reminiscent of former T. Rex glories, in what was something of a retreat from the diversions taken on *Bolan's Zip Gun*. Clearly, Bolan had tapped into the muse which guided him through the early seventies. The concept of the album title was never developed much beyond the grand 'Futuristic Dragon (Introduction)', which heralded the Dragon as a ''lectronic saviour' who, like most Bolanic icons, brought old wisdom into a contemporary or futuristic world. The overall sound was more unified, though, marked by the return of strings, a horn section and some exquisite backing vocals (courtesy of Gloria and Tyrone Scott, who had also joined T. Rex on the recent tour).

Two songs, 'Dawn Storm' and 'Chrome Sitar', were probably Bolan's most effective album tracks since the days of 'Cosmic Dancer' and 'Spaceball Ricochet': angrier, musically more dense, but no less indicative that he had not lost the ability to write emotionally charged music. 'Jupiter Liar' returned to the old-style Bolan boogie, albeit in slightly more pedestrian fashion, while 'All Alone' and 'Casual Agent' featured good vocal performances prompted by some of Marc's most playful lyrics in a long time. Nevertheless, *Futuristic Dragon* failed dramatically in its attempt to massage his career back to life.

'London Boys', the single recorded long after the album was completed, had been chosen in place of the more soul-influenced 'Sanctified' as the follow-up to 'Dreamy Lady', but it only added to the dismal picture, failing to secure a Top Thirty placing. Characterised by a trite chorus – 'Oh yeah we're the London Boys' – it nevertheless revealed Bolan overtly retracing his steps, evoking his mod days by name-checking Petticoat Lane and the London-to-Brighton scooter run. The underlying philosophy of those times, 'Changing life patterns to get to the top', is clearly stated, as is what Bolan found when he finally got there – uncertainty. The single formed part of one of Marc's latest projects, *The London Opera*, which had been prompted by his appearances as a television interviewer. A second track, written for and débuted on the *Today* programme, was 'Funky London Childhood', a John Lee Hooker-like boogie, the only new song featured on the tour. Both songs were featured when T. Rex recorded a studio session for London's Capital Radio, broadcast in March, alongside 'New York City' and the old Marty Wilde hit 'Teenager In Love'.

Marc had not remained in London for any length of time since 1972, and his return was marked by a nostalgic retread of his youth (which found an outlet in *The London Opera*), a tendency towards reworking the songs of that era ('Rip It Up', 'Ain't That A Shame', 'Teenager In Love' and 'Stand By Me' had all been covered during the winter months), and jam sessions with old friends like ex-Move and Wizzard main man Roy Wood. 'I haven't played for so long with someone I appreciate,' he told Wood during a home session where they ran through old rock 'n' roll favourites like 'Twist And Shout' and Buddy Holly's 'Oh Boy', and discussed plagiarism ('I nicked that off a Howlin' Wolf song,' Marc said of 'Jeepster', before protesting that 'I never stole anything in my whole life'). A Bolan/Wood collaboration was being hinted at by Marc in the press, but it wasn't really on the cards. Marc never collaborated with anyone: his friends were also his competitors.

Going back to his youthful interest in rock 'n' roll led Marc to American rockabilly of the fifties, and he even spoke of spear-heading a rock 'n' roll revival show. 'I'd avoid the overdone things like "Blue Suede Shoes" and "Johnny B Goode",' he said, inviting the interviewer to 'Imagine "Teenager In Love" with Cat Stevens, David Bowie and myself doing the three-part har-monies. I'd have Gloria and Tina Turner in there too.'[3] It was idle fantasy, but Bolan's back-to-basics attitude was real enough and he asked Jeff Dexter to find him the cheapest studio in London in an attempt to recapture the mood. Coincidence, per-haps, but Decibel Studios in his old stamping ground of Stamford Hill seemed to fit the bill, and Bolan recorded a new song there called 'I Love To Boogie'.

For years, Marc, like most pop and rock musicians, had based his riffs on the blues and his chord sequences on tin-pan alley traditions. As Tony Visconti remembers, 'Marc never stole; he was always *influenced by*!' The line was always a thin one, as George Harrison discovered to his cost when the publishers of the Chiffons' 'He's So Fine' successfully sued him for plagiarism on 'My Sweet Lord'. Marc was so pleased with his new rockabilly-style song that the intention to release 'Bolan's Zip Gun' (actually a vocal version of 'Theme For A Dragon' from *Futuristic Dragon*) as a single was quickly scuppered. Instead, 'I Love To Boogie' appeared on 45 at the start of June.

' "I Love To Boogie" was written in ten minutes in the studio after putting together these nine rockabilly LPs in my head,' Marc bragged to a *Record Mirror & Disc* reporter. ' "Hot Love" I did

the same. The middle eight's from "Heartbreak Hotel".'
Bigmouth had struck again, but he'd opened it too soon. On the
same day, news broke in *New Musical Express* that a group of
aggrieved rockabilly aficionados were planning to hold a 'burn-
in' of copies of the latest T. Rex record at a pub in the Old Kent
Road, East London. Bolan had apparently ripped off an obscure
rockabilly recording from 1956 by Webb Pierce called 'Teenage
Boogie'. A spokesman for the Teds, disc jockey Geoff Barker,
told the paper, 'The records are so alike it can't be coincidence.
He's kept the basic melody and simply changed the chorus
lyrics . . . even the guitar solo is a rip-off.'[4]

Bolan soon began to backtrack, claiming that he was simply
trying to rework Carl Perkins's 'Honey Don't', but behind the
scenes some heated correspondence was exchanged between the
publishers of the song and Bolan's London office. An attempt
was made to place an injunction on the single but, according to
Jeff Dexter, Tony Howard enlisted the services of a musicologist
to dissect both songs, and the findings were sent to the publishers
of 'Teenage Boogie'. The parameters of the debate were sufficiently widened to cast doubt on Marc's alleged plagiarism, and
it was pointed out that 'Teenage Boogie' itself was based on a
riff that had been around long before the song was written. The
matter went no further. Bolan, meanwhile, mischievously played
around with the two songs at home, blasting Webb Pierce's
version on his stereo, before launching into his own composition
on his acoustic. He probably wore a big smile on his face
too.

In spite of his regular ventures into the recording studio,
Marc felt he had nothing suitable for a B side. Songs like 'Soul
Of My Suit' and 'Funky London Childhood' deserved better,
while the recently recorded cover versions wouldn't swell the
depleting Bolan coffers. For the second time in a row ('Solid
Baby' from *Bolan's Zip Gun* had backed 'London Boys'), he dipped
into his own archive and dug out an old song, 'Baby Boomerang'.

Blissfully oblivious to the controversy surrounding the
single, one Bolan fan enthusiastically dashed off a letter to *Record
Mirror & Disc*, stating that, ' "I Love To Boogie" sounds so fresh
compared with all the current chart sounds, which proves Bolan
is a true original.' Bryan Ferry, the Shangri-Las, the Beatles and
the Beach Boys were all riding high with songs made popular
during the sixties, so perhaps she had a point, but Marc's return

to a minimalist rock 'n' roll sound had already been preceded by a new breed of gritty R&B groups on the pub circuit, and was currently being taken to new extremes by a little-known quartet of young London boys calling themselves the Sex Pistols.

The punk underworld had yet to touch the life of Marc Bolan, though he had belatedly discovered Lou Reed in the summer. The success of 'I Love To Boogie' had been encouraging and, oblivious to happenings in venues like the 100 Club and the Nashville, he confidently ploughed himself into completing a project which had been discussed, started, shelved and discussed again since the end of 1973: Gloria Jones's solo album, co-produced by Bolan. There had been a minor interruption at the end of June when his wife sued for divorce, citing Gloria Jones as the third party; but while Marc was unhappy at the prospect of a financial settlement, the hearing, planned for 5 October, was seen as little more than a formality. On that day, the deputy judge Donald Ellison said, 'I am satisfied that the husband committed adultery with the co-respondent, and that the wife finds it intolerable to live with him.' A decree nisi was granted, which was to become absolute a year later.

The birth of Rolan hadn't deprived Gloria of the opportunity to return to her musical career, and she made several appearances with funk act Gonzalez during the summer, most notably supporting Bob Marley at Ninian Park, Cardiff, on 19 June, and at the Wigan Casino (where, due to the popularity of her songs like 'Tainted Love', she held something approaching legendary status). Gonzalez helped out on her album, and there were contributions from Ray Parker and the Sisters Love vocal group, percussionist Ollie Brown and Billy Preston (who both accompanied the Rolling Stones that summer – Jones and Bolan were among the backstage liggers at one of the Earls Court performances).

The hands of Bolan ostensibly rested on the controls, though he also wrote several of the songs and played guitar on many tracks. 'High', 'Sailors Of The Highway' and 'Drive Me Crazy (Disco Lady)' (originally titled 'Ghetto Baby') had been salvaged from the aborted Pat Hall album; 'Get It On' (parts one and two) was from the T. Rex back catalogue, while 'Cry Baby' was a reworking of 'Savage Beethoven', a 1975 out-take and 'Tell Me Now' had been specially written for the record. Both 'Get It On' and 'I Ain't Going Nowhere' had preceded the album during the year on singles, but neither made much impact. It was no surprise, then, when the *Vixen* album appeared at the end of the year and quietly disappeared with a minimum of fuss.

Gloria's career kept her away from Bolan and, at times, out of England completely, so Sid and Phyllis Feld adopted the role of active grandparents, looking after Rolan in their flat at 9 Inglis House, Whitnell Way in Putney. The flat came gratis, by virtue of Sid's position as caretaker of the council block, a post he had taken during the early seventies in spite of Marc's occasional offers to transform his parents' lives by directing a large sum of money their way. 'They never wanted to change their lifestyle,' says Marc's brother Harry. 'They were so proud of Marc when he really made it, but it never affected the way they lived. Dad put his whole heart into that job. He'd do the bins at six in the morning, get all his work done early, and from opening time to closing time he'd meet his friends in either the Angel or the Green Man pub.'

It was only when Marc gave his Rolls-Royce to his father as a birthday present that Sid and Phyllis tasted luxury though, more often than not, the vehicle was parked outside one of the local pubs. Meanwhile, Phyllis was persuaded to quit her clerical job at London Transport Stores in Fulham, which conveniently gave her more time to look after Rolan while Marc and Gloria were working. It wasn't the sort of upbringing Marc Feld had been used to, and there was a thread of traditionalism that ran through Bolan to suggest that he may have had doubts about the arrangement. But with both his and Gloria's career in transition, there was little alternative.

*The Wilderness Of The Mind* was the title of a second book of poetry Marc intended for publication in 1976, but nothing was forthcoming. Whether the book would have found Bolan exploring the workings of his psyche and reporting his findings in a comprehensible manner is, despite its title, extremely unlikely. His inability rigidly to pursue an idea far beyond its original conception was further evidence of his sensualist attitude towards experience. He would 'go with the flow', ascribing the many twists and turns of his personal life to abstractions like 'destiny' and 'the vibe'. He had been Mighty Joe Young, Elvis Presley, the Face, the hippie, the glam idol, the drunk, the creative nerve centre, the lonely star at the epicentre of a whirlwind. He had increasingly gorged on a shifting parade of characters, in a manner entirely befitting the twentieth-century condition of the multi-faceted personality. Human identity had come under such an assault, from psychologists who professed that you weren't what you thought you were, to political philosophers who decreed that history shapes men and not vice versa. The possibility of the empty vessel ready to be shaped by society at the heart of every human being, and the tension between that and the Romantic notion of there being something more, is suggested by *The Wilderness Of The Mind*. It was one of his most appropriately chosen titles.

In public terms, Marc had been called back from the wilderness, but had yet to find his station in society. With a head full of grandiose aspirations unwilling to take shape into a hard, saleable product, he once again settled for whatever came his way, which was more small-screen exposure. Ever the opportunist, Bolan accepted Mike Mansfield's idea of a *Rollin' Bolan* television special for *Supersonic*, filmed in Wimbledon. What had been missing ever since Marc made it with T. Rex was foresight. He could never envisage much beyond preserving the stardom he had once craved and achieved. His new-found purpose, prompted by the birth of Rolan and nurtured by a more settled life in London, was to recapture something of that original fame: getting beyond it had proved insurmountable. Without any obvious market, or indeed, musical direction, he chose to let fate take its course.

*Rollin' Bolan*, broadcast in late August 1976, marked the final appearance of T. Rex with Steve Currie and Davey Lutton, Currie, originally the least-satisfied band member, had stayed the course far longer than anyone had expected. Never the most animated of backing musicians, he looked jaded by the end of his tenure, and apart from some work with Chris Spedding in 1977, he followed Steve Peregrine Took, Bill Legend and Mickey Finn into relative obscurity. Sadly, like Took, he made one final appearance in the music press in May 1981, when his death was reported following a car crash in Portugal. After Currie had split with his wife, his girlfriend Peta Heskell moved into his Twickenham home in 1979, before the pair emigrated to Portugal a year later. Some time around midnight on 28 April 1981, Steve was returning to his home in the village of Val Da Parra when, only half a mile away, his car veered off the road and he was killed. No other vehicle was involved.

Alongside 'I Love To Boogie' and 'New York City', his two biggest hits in recent months, Marc also played the unreleased 'Funky London Childhood' and 'The Soul Of My Suit' at the Wimbledon Theatre, together with one new song, 'Laser Love'. Having evoked a nostalgia for his teenage days on his previous two singles (he even looked like a chubbier version of Bolan *circa* 1966 while promoting 'I Love To Boogie'), Marc continued to mix up musical styles and visual image when 'Laser Love' appeared on 45 in September. The press loved what Marc called his 'Bolan-tino' look, a heavily made-up hybrid of the Latin matinée idol and a china doll, although the healthy coverage wasn't matched by the record, which was perceived to be a pastiche of the Rolling Stones. The riff was the idiot brother of 'Brown Sugar', and the newly recruited second guitarist Miller Anderson's fine slide playing was very much in the style of ex-Stone Mick Taylor. Technically, the recruitment of Anderson (who had once played with progressive blues outfit Savoy Brown) had upped the ante considerably, as confirmed by the twin guitar work on the B side, 'Life's An Elevator' (which, with painful predictability, Marc described as going 'up and down').

By the time of his next television appearance, promoting the single on *Top Of The Pops* early in October, the reliable rhythm section of Tony Newman and Herbie Flowers had become part of what the newly made badges proclaimed, 'A New Age Of Bolan'. Another design stated 'T. Rex Unchained', an indication that the recent line-up changes had given way to a more versatile and positive T. Rex. Bolan was genuinely excited about his group again, after the initial disappointment of hearing that Currie had quit in the wake of Lutton's departure. Nevertheless, he chose to mime to the song alone when he appeared on Granada TV's *The Arrows* show. Also on the set was June Bolan's new beau, Paul Varley, drummer with the resident band.

Although the impression was now that he was more in control of his career, Marc was still content to respond rather than to initiate. He had always been something of a sponge, in the best sense of the word, absorbing styles and ideas and then shaping them to fit his own needs, but now his creative capacity had become rather saturated. Everything he digested oozed back out in a slightly soggy fashion, rather than being reconstituted into something that exceeded the sum of its parts. Even the idea of recruiting first-rate musicians had been suggested to him. 'It was my idea to get good session musicians,' says Jeff Dexter, 'and I convinced Marc that the band David Bowie had used was the right one. It was good for him, and everyone hoped it would make him work harder with that calibre of musician behind him. By that time Gloria was working with Gonzalez and doing her own thing, and it seemed right that he should be one of the boys and make it with a boys' band. Of course, he said the whole band was his idea, but that's the way he was.'

There was no doubting the technical abilities of the backing musicians: the team of Dino Dines, Miller Anderson, Herbie Flowers and Tony Newman was undoubtedly the most accomplished backing group Marc ever had. But with the captain, if not exactly out of control then at least out of his depth in terms of navigation, T. Rex was akin to a well-equipped vessel adrift in a placid, uninspiring sea. Several pirate ships, bearing representatives of the most bizarrely clad and, arguably, the most ideologically threatening of the white youth subcultures, began to roam the waters. Marc Bolan, however, while not oblivious to the noisy brigands, was still seduced by the brightly lit horizon in the other direction.

Among those continuing to beckon was television producer Mike Mansfield, whose unstinting belief in the dramatic power of the Big Star (faded or not) had done much to bring Bolan back into the public eye. But riding around like a charioteer on a decidedly shaky white swan for a timid, badly mimed rerun of 'Ride A White Swan' did little to instil public confidence in him. Marc Bolan looked ripe to join the many ageing rock 'n' rollers or out-of-favour sixties acts on the chicken-in-a-basket circuit.

When few were listening, any exposure was welcome, and Marc was happy to join the line-up for Mansfield's *Supersonic* Christmas special, organised in conjunction with the *Daily Mirror* Pop Club and filmed at the Theatre Royal, Drury Lane, in London, on 19 December. The main focus of the show was Gary Glitter, making the first of his many comebacks, while the rest of the bill was suitably lightweight for what was – in the presence of Princess Margaret and her children – a Royal occasion. Joanna Lumley and Russell Harty presided over the event, which also included recent hit-makers like the Glitter Band (now a separate entity from their 'Leader') and Linda Lewis, and the up-and-coming John Miles and Tina Charles. Marc, with his new-look T. Rex, performed 'I Love To Boogie', 'The Soul Of My Suit' and

'New York City', before reappearing sandwiched between Twiggy and Marti Caine for the all-star sing-along of 'We Wish You A Merry Christmas'.

When punk groups started breaking through towards the end of 1976, Bolan's initial reaction was, like most among the established rock community, one of confusion bordering on hostility. 'This so-called punk rock thing. It's not selling. The kids don't want it,'[5] he miscalculated in September 1976. In the same breath, he happily threw himself into the ring, picking up on what he perceived to be the *Zeitgeist* of the new subculture. Name-dropping early sixties US girl group the Angels and film director Federico Fellini, pop falsetto Frankie Valli and Hollywood iconoclast Orson Welles as 'punks', Bolan at least understood the new movement's need to reject conventional icons. (In counting himself above and beyond 'old fart' status, his apparent conceit was partially correct. Bolan, like Rotten, Strummer, et al., had managed to get up the noses of the rock *cognoscenti* for several years, and the punks' overriding sense of style warfare and celebration of faded glamour created a space within which glittering oldies like Marc and Gary Glitter could enter.)

Marc Bolan sensed – and welcomed – the dynamism of punk rock but didn't believe in its new ambassadors. He rejoiced in the controversy it created but feared for his own privileged place as master of the grand pop statement. After citing 'My love is as strong as the raging sea' as the crucial line in 'Laser Love', he claimed, 'You can't get any punkier than that, can you?' Punk meant a lot of things to a lot of people, but Marc's reading of it, at this early stage, seemed incomprehensible. Nevertheless, it provided him with a new topic on which to pontificate in the rock press. While most of his contemporaries sneered scathingly at what appeared to be a noisy coup attempt by a cabal of shockingly clad musical heathens, Bolan's gradual warming to the 'new wave' was prompted by a mixture of positioning and opportunism. In the eyes of his critics, Marc had dressed up his lack of musical sophistication in a showy display of grand statements and even grander costumes. New spokesmen like Sex Pistols boss Malcolm McLaren and Mr Punk Rock himself, Johnny Rotten, ridiculed the complacency and simple pop/rock categories of the middle-class rock élite. At the heart of the punk maelstrom was a contradictory mix of dour workerism and intricate elegance, poverty chic and painful parody, righteous indignation and ironic distance. The attempt to tear up the old critical categories encouraged Marc to reposition himself within the new scheme of things. Age alone excluded most of Bolan's generation, but his long-professed street-wise attitude, his continued belief in rock's appeal to youth, and the fact that most of the new wave were the Children of *his* Revolution grown up, created the right conditions for a mutual appreciation society.

The shock of the new embraced the voice of the old in February 1977, when Bolan invited the Damned, who had beaten the Sex Pistols in getting the first UK punk single out, on his March tour of Britain. 'He saw me wearing a Bolan T-shirt in a music paper photo, and I think that did it,' says the Damned's Captain Sensible, who first saw T. Rex in concert at the Weeley Festival in 1971. 'He had a bit more perception at the time. He saw through the shit that the likes of the *News Of The World* and *The Sun* were saying, namely that punk rockers were just a bunch of boneheads.

'At the time, there were a lot of people stopping you in the street and punching you in the face because you dressed in punk gear. It was quite good for anyone to say anything nice about the groups at that time. When Bolan said we were all right, that something was happening around the punk thing, it was very controversial.' Captain Sensible also confirms that the new wave perceived Bolan in vastly different terms from the majority of the old guard. 'His music said it all,' states the bassist-turned-guitarist. 'He was out on a limb, destined to make weird records with weird lyrics, doing something that nobody else could understand. Bolan wasn't the seen-it-done-it-all merchant: he had fresh ideas.'

The first evidence of these 'fresh' ideas appeared in the form of the *Dandy In The Underworld* album, issued in February 1977. Preceding it was a cover of Phil Spector's old Teddy Bears' hit, 'To Know Him Is To Love Him', which was credited to Marc Bolan and Gloria Jones. Backed by a new version of 'City Port', a song originally taped for the Pat Hall album sessions, the single failed to register at all, despite a television appearance where, for once, Bolan was placed in the uncomfortable position of sharing the limelight with another performer.

Characterised by a hint of minimalism in its production, the

*Dandy* album, mostly recorded at AIR Studios in London, paid lip service to the musical credo of the Blank Generation. Yet despite Bolan's growing affinity with the new movement, his haste in getting the new-look T. Rex into the studio ensured that Marc drew from the spontaneous energy of the new wave, but he didn't share in its anger or the sense of alienation that marked it out from the highly charged rock of old. The mixed results of the album didn't quite warrant Bolan's claim that he was 'sounding marvellous again'. Most songs were preceded either by a maxim ('A fool's lament is the wise man's milkshake', instructed Bolan on 'I'm A Fool For You Girl') or a guide ('Jason B. Sad' was 'A distant boyfriend of Johnny B Goode'), but any conceptual unity, beyond the black-and-white sleeve symbolising a return to stark simplicity, was only cosmetic.

As always, the album title hinted at a concept woven around a central character – the 'Dandy' – but despite the inclusion of 'Funky London Childhood' (rewritten as 'Visions Of Domino'), and a faint recapturing of youth on the pedestrian R&B of 'Groove A Little' and urban strife on 'Teen Riot Structure', there was neither the unity of *The London Opera* nor any real answer to 'Anarchy In The UK' or the songs on the Buzzcocks' 'Spiral Scratch'. The title track, described by Marc as 'A Bolanic revision of Orpheus Descending', kicked off the record dramatically, though, with Bolan lurching back to the Greek mythology which had fired him during the days of Tyrannosaurus Rex. The best-known modern interpretation of the Orpheus legend was by Jean Cocteau in his 1950 film of the same name (*Orphée*), which plays on the idea of self misrepresentation, and where the analogy with Lacanian psychology is furthered when Orphée is told, 'Watch yourself all your life in a mirror and you will see death at work.'

Marc had begun to watch himself again, to the point where on 'Dandy', he could at last survey, and begin to come to terms with, the debris of his fractured career. 'Distraction he wanted, to destruction he fell', he sang over an impressive backing, before asking 'When will he come up for air?' and, more to the point, 'Will anybody ever care?' The final verse moved further away from the metaphysical discourse on death of the original Orpheus legend, towards a restatement of Marc's difficulty in altering the course of his life. Having evoked his own exile into mythology at eighteen, which reached a self-indulgent peak in those 'cocaine

nights' in the States, Bolan tried to envisage a future beyond the
seductive underworld that had first called him via his mirror back
in Stoke Newington. Aware that it was his entry into the sphere
where imagination and star-fantasies could blossom without con-
straint which provided him with his basic life impulse, he could
only see uncertainty after any metaphorical 'coming up for air'.
Smash his mirror world and Marc Bolan might go with it.

'Change is a monster,' he continued, 'changing is hard.' The
*Dandy In The Underworld* album marked the closing of the plastic
soul chapter of his career, and a reacquaintance with the tight
simple rhythms of his youth. Yet in terms of the unfolding teen
riot structure of 1977, Bolan let a mixture of opportunism and
nostalgia override what his head told him. He instinctively understood that the new musical movement sought to tear away the
mystique of stars by bridging the gap between audience and
performer. It created anti-stars, and in a final act of sacrilege,
spat on the whole mod credo of upward mobility, and trampled
the rotting vestiges of the Romantic artist philosophy to death.
The veil of creative genius, behind which artists hide, had been
demystified. Marc Bolan, the man who thought in terms of high
art while preferring to occupy low art spaces, was perplexed by
the aesthetic conflict prompted by punk, but could also read it
in terms of his own original aspirations. It seemed like *everyone*
could do it, but Johnny Rotten, Captain Sensible, even young
Dee Generate were all, in Marc's eyes, victims of a quirk of
nature. Like himself, they were destined to exceed their given
role in life, able to transcend the bounds of working-class resignation and inertia, fulfilling dreams fed to them in magazines
and on screen, which were then re-created in the bedroom, taken
out onto the street and into the sphere of public entertainment.

After several years spent nursing his own will to self-
destruct, Bolan had at last connected with a new youth culture,
white, British, essentially working class, which threatened to
destroy existing codes and structures, both in the music world
and beyond. In siding with the emerging if still subordinate punk
movement, Marc teased out new meanings for himself, which
were used to revive his flagging career. 'I have been sitting
around waiting for the pop climate to change,' he said in February
1977, 'for something like punk rock to come along. I consider
myself to be the elder statesman of punk. The Godfather of Punk,
if you like.'[6] For the first time in years, Bolan could scent real

success again, and a massive exertion of will sent him onto a new health regime, cutting out fatty foods, alcohol, and donning a tracksuit and trainers for daily exercises. Perrier and lemon replaced beer and brandy, and omelette or grilled fish with raw vegetables supplanted fry-ups. It was a commitment he maintained, with a few exceptions, for the rest of his life. The Damned's Captain Sensible remembers Bolan's daily routine, and the high-spirited mood of the T. Rex camp during the March 1977 tour. 'Marc was chirpy and happy to be out touring,' he says. 'There was no sense of him being in any way a has-been. He paid for us to go out with him, and we all travelled together in the same coach. While we were stuffing our faces with egg and chips in the service station, we'd see Marc jogging past our window every few minutes. He didn't smoke, drink or do drugs, though he was still a bit portly at that stage. I've still got the copy of the *Dandy* album he gave me, where he signed it, "To the Captain. Keep it clean. Marc." He was very together.'

By all accounts, Bolan enjoyed the nine-date tour and played well throughout its duration. It was probably the most accomplished set of T. Rex performances since he had enlarged the group from a duo into a four-piece. His confidence was reflected in the choice of material which, instead of shunning new songs in favour of the tried and tested – and by 1977 somewhat tiresome – hits, was divided equally between the old and the new. Only on 'Hang-Ups' and the predictable finale of 'Get It On' did Bolan veer towards playful indulgence and the rapport with Miller Anderson was particularly notable, producing some well-crafted guitar and vocal interplay on 'The Soul Of My Suit'. Unfortunately, Miller was disappointed by Marc's willingness to mime on the constant stream of children's television appearances and he left early in the summer, although his final performance with T. Rex was a rare live version of 'Dandy In The Underworld', performed on Granada's *Get It Together* at the end of June.

Bolan's courting of the young punk audience via a high-profile tour did not translate into an upward turn in record sales. The *Dandy* album spent a mere one week in the Top Thirty, while even a *Top Of The Pops* appearance couldn't help 'The Soul Of My Suit' into the singles chart. Punk rock, like Bolan, may have created a lot of noise in terms of publicity, but it, too, wasn't a particularly strong-selling phenomenon. The goodwill was extended further when Johnny Rotten, the Damned and Billy

Idol lined up alongside Lionel Bart, Donovan and Mike Mansfield at the *Dandy In The Underworld* launch party, held at the Roxy club in Covent Garden. The punk Mecca was an obvious choice of venue for Bolan to confirm his allegiance to the new wave, yet while the Damned's audience had appreciated Marc's excessive on-stage camp, Bolan was generally regarded as an amusing throwback to Liberace starlust, a parodic prince of showbiz panache. Marc, though, was only beginning to get the joke.

Before the British tour, he had taken T. Rex over to France for a few warm-up dates, which included an appearance at Le Nashville in Paris. While there, he reacquainted himself with the statues and paintings in the Louvre which had fired his imagination during the Riggs O'Hara expedition in 1965. After seeking out the statue of Hercules, he wrote in his tour diary that it was 'just the artistic inspiration to key the Bolan brain for boogie'. (Also in the Louvre is a Magritte painting of a tree titled *16th September*.)

Reading Gore Vidal's *Myron* and jamming with Steve Harley were just two other influences on Marc that spring, but the overriding impression he gave was of a man once again beginning to work to sustain and regenerate his career: it had taken punk to provide that impetus. As Bolan sought to join the Velvet Underground, Iggy Pop and Captain Beefheart as the acceptable face of the old wave, he had maintained his commitment to London by purchasing a spacious Victorian house in September 1976. Situated at 142 Upper Richmond Road, East Sheen, just a short drive away from his parents' flat in Putney (and close to where he made that disastrous live début in 1966 at the Pontiac Club), the property, with high ceilings and wooden floors, never really acquired any traditional sense of domesticity. Marc would often conduct his business lying prostrate on his large bed, surrounded by racks of stage clothes and unpacked boxes, as bemused workmen continued their renovations around him.

Marc spent much of 1977 between the twin axes of his southwest London home and his central London office at 69 New Bond Street. When he took over the building towards the end of 1973, he had originally sub-let offices to the likes of the Who, Pink Floyd, and concert tour manager Peter Rudge. As the fortunes of T. Rex and the Wizard group of companies changed, both Marc and 'manager' Tony Howard were forced to give up their elaborate suite of offices, and Pink Floyd and their manager Steve O'Rourke ended up sub-letting to Bolan.

This economic reality was partially hidden by Marc's continued high-media profile, which climaxed in a tetchy performance for the final *Supersonic* show at the end of March 1977. Spirits were high as cameramen and artists dressed for the occasion in a variety of outfits, and Marc – slimline in his green jacket and drainpipe trousers – seemed to be joining in the fun. After performing 'The Soul Of My Suit', his band were joined by regulars including Elkie Brooks, Alvin Stardust and Dave Edmunds' Rockpile for an all-star finale of 'Sweet Little Rock 'n' Roller'. Unfortunately, the boisterous Captain Sensible (in a nurse's uniform) and Damned drummer Rat Scabies (fresh from setting fire to his kit when the *Dandy* tour called in at the Rainbow in London) were unceremoniously booted out when they tried to join in, while Marc stormed off after a cameraman, eager to get a good shot of Alvin Stardust, had pushed him aside. He returned briefly, wearing a 'Marc Bolan Rules OK' badge, before calling it a day and hopping into a limo.

The demise of *Supersonic*, which had provided him with a lifeline to the teenage pop world, briefly cast Marc adrift, although Granada Television's *Get It Together* was still there for a live promotional appearance to tie in with the release of 'Dandy In The Underworld' as a single (with the reference to 'cocaine nights' edited out). By this time, 29 June 1977, Bolan was beginning to resemble the Marc of old, and when he wasn't hamming it up, the similarity to the Pink Floyd castaway Syd Barrett was uncanny. Once again, his hair sprouted a mop of cascading corkscrews and his body was slimmer than it had ever been – but the sense of regeneration was not borne out in record sales and, again, the single flopped.

Two lifelines were hurled in his direction early that summer. The first enabled him to capitalise on his hip elder-statesman image by contributing a monthly column for *Record Mirror* (ghost-written from Marc's notes by his publicist Keith Altham), where he pontificated on the current music scene, peppering his genuine enthusiasm for punk rock with the occasional lapse into self-mythology. Pictured only half mockingly with a crown and sceptre, ensuring that the star, if not the class, system should remain, Bolan kicked off with what was akin to a verbal recreation of the opening surge of electricity on '20th Century Boy'. 'I love the raw-edged energy and freshness new wave has brought to the British rock scene,' he wrote. 'The music of now is NOISE, be it beautiful, elaborate, complex, clean or bestial, primitive,

political or raw.' He then went on to discuss his relationship to
the new music, firstly by comparing its impact with the R&B
boom, Led Zeppelin and the birth of heavy metal, and glam rock,
which was 'me, Bowie, Alice Cooper and a couple of other people'.
Socially, and stylistically, Bolan still sought to maintain his sense
of Apartness. 'I'm a classless person,' he wrote, before ending
some comments regarding punk fashions with the recommendation to vary the styles a bit: 'I had imagination,'[7] he concluded.

That Bolan's imagination moved in mysterious ways was
confirmed in his second monthly message, in July, when he
unveiled his ideal supergroup: Leslie West (lead guitar), Steve
Jones (rhythm), Marc Bolan (vocals), Billy Preston (organ), Chick
Corea (synthesiser), Bob Dylan (harmonica), David Bowie (sax),
Iggy Pop and Lou Reed (backing vocals), with Sid Vicious and
Captain Sensible providing Stereophonic Spitting. It was as
ungodly as it was unlikely, but the only real stranger to the
list was Chick Corea, a techno-jazz rocker, who satisfied Marc's
continuing need to ally himself with musical experimentalists as
well as the new iconoclasts.

If Chick Corea seemed out of character, then Bolan's comments regarding non-musical concerns were encouragingly
astute. The world outside, or at least the negative aspects of it,
rarely intruded into Marc's mental framework, but after bemoan-
ing the media's role in almost willing the violence between Teds
and punks, he clearly saw music, perhaps for the first time in
his life, as a force for social and not just individual change.
'"Anarchy In The UK" and "God Save The Queen" are going on
all around us,' he wrote. 'Just pick up a newspaper and read
about Grunwick, Enoch Powell or the Jubilee celebrations. The
Pistols are a bloody good mirror. Anyone who thinks things are
not in a mess just does not look around them.'[8]

Bolan, whose life's work had been fuelled by a displacement
of the mundane/real into the symbolic world of subcultural
refusal and artistic freedom, recognised that punk rock operated
on a different level from his own, but he increasingly saw a role
in it for himself. After catching Siouxsie and the Banshees at the
Music Machine a few weeks earlier, he considered producing
them. The band, then in its formative stages, had inherited
Bolan's highly defined sense of drama, while the inclusion of
'20th Century Boy' in their set further aroused Marc's sense of
being a punk progenitor.

By the time of his third *Record Mirror* column in the first week of August, Marc Bolan had met Muriel Young and Mike Mansfield for lunch in Rags restaurant, where they discussed a new idea for a television pop show. Marc instantly took a liking to it, especially when Young, the producer, developed it into a six-episode series called *Marc*. He immediately accepted the proposal from Granada Television and, prompted by Jeff Dexter and manager Tony Howard, began scouting round for potential guest artists.

In his initial enthusiasm, names such as Presley, Sinatra, Vera Lynn, the Rolling Stones, Parliament, David Bowie and Iggy Pop were mentioned (in his column), but the reality of the children's 4.15 p.m. light entertainment slot was more suited to Stephanie De Sykes, Showaddywaddy, the Bay City Rollers, Mud, Rosetta Stone, and a regular dance troupe called Heart Throb. Marc fell into line, mixing contemporary versions of his hits with recent singles, throwing in some teenage favourites like the old Marty Wilde hit, 'Endless Sleep' and Chris Montez's 'Let's Dance' for good measure. What made *Marc* particularly notable was the regular outlet it provided for new wave acts such as Generation X, the Jam, Boomtown Rats, the Rods and Radio Stars, a group of old wavers dressed up as new, fronted by his ex-John's Children colleague Andy Ellison. 'I was jogging down the King's Road towards the studios where we were rehearsing,' remembers Andy, 'and I heard this Mini hooting at me. The window went down and it was Marc and Gloria. We talked about Radio Stars, and he told me about his television series starting soon, and said that I must come and do it. I never thought he'd get back to me, but not long afterwards, we were invited to do the show.'

Andy Ellison wasn't the only old acquaintance reunited with Marc for the series. David Bowie had a new single to promote, and agreed to fly in from Switzerland for the filming at the start of September. A year earlier, Bowie had said, 'I never had any competition, except Marc Bolan back in England . . . I fought like a *madman* to beat him. Knowing theoretically there was no race. But wanting passionately to do it.'[9] With Bowie's career still on the ascendant, both critically and commercially, and Marc confident that his own high profile was winning over both the straight teenage and the punk audiences, the pair decided to share the stage for a memorable climax to the last show in the series. Bowie pulled up at the Manchester studio in his limousine, with an entourage including Coco Schwab, his publicist Barbara de Witt and a bodyguard. The convivial backstage atmosphere was aided by the presence of long-standing friends like Jeff Dexter, B.P. Fallon and Keith Altham, while Marc's growing confidence with each successive show was threatening to explode. Altham had invited several journalists down to witness the historic occasion of Bowie and Bolan playing together in public for the first time, but Bowie's camp were not amused by the publicity.

The atmosphere was tense, but in fact, the tears came after the show. Having written 'Standing Next To You' in the dressing room hours earlier, Marc and Bowie were ready to unleash their impromptu duet, having performed their respective solo material (Bowie premièred 'Heroes', while Marc delivered a particularly strong revival of 'Debora') earlier in the day. Time was running out and the production crew were threatening to pull the stops at 7 p.m. With just seconds to go, Marc hopped on centre stage to take his place standing next to the world's second most famous ex-mod. He should have been elated, but the pressures of the day had taken a visible toll on him. There was a look of genuine sadness in his eyes as he gave an abrupt 'Thank you and good-bye' to the camera, in the thoroughly camp style he had been cultivating all year, before he bade a second farewell. 'From all of the boys in the band, David, everybody, all the cats, you know who they are. This is a new song.' Bowie counted the group in and the same ascending eight-note riff that the Beatles employed for 'Lady Madonna' got things under way. But despite several attempts to get it right earlier in the day, Bowie missed his vocal cue. Eventually, he found his way in, singing, 'What should I do . . . ', just as Bolan tripped into his microphone and off the stage. The camera zoomed in on Bowie's resigned grin before the technicians switched off the cameras. Marc Bolan had bowed out of his final television appearance, his final public performance in fact – an ungainly exit which left audiences frustrated that the duet was never completed, but which somehow crystallised the unfulfilled promise of Bolan's last few years.

The television show concentrated Marc's mind away from the failure of his latest single, 'Celebrate Summer', which, despite a blistering few seconds of noise guitar during the break, remained firmly in up-tempo pop, rather than the new wave category he claimed for it. Even before the announcement of his television series, Cube Records (inheritor of the Fly catalogue) had already decided to capitalise on Bolan's raised profile by compiling three songs from his 1970–71 heyday – 'Ride A White Swan', 'Jeepster' and 'Monolith' – with the previously unreleased 'Demon Queen' onto the *Bolan's Best+1* EP. That neither release made any impact suggests that Marc's comeback, as signified by his new-found health and his mates down at the Roxy club and the Vortex, was to return him to a cult status not dissimilar to that afforded him during the late sixties. The difference was that, in common with Andy Warhol, it was Marc Bolan's name, not necessarily his work, that was held in high esteem. Like Warhol's book of observations, *From A To B & Back Again*, Bolan's records now filled the remainder shops. Both icons retained titles in the new dynastic arrangement of 1977, but their use was strictly emblematic, as surnames steeped in the mystique of the individual's public quest to establish a strong sense of difference.

Punk rock maintained a troubled relationship with the star system, but in terms of his status within the movement, Marc Bolan functioned less as its Elvis Presley and more as its Cliff Richard. That is not to belittle his influence. It could be said that Marc, together with Bowie, Roxy Music and Alice Cooper, planted the seed for the movement, which only later was augmented with the sound of American excess from the Stooges, the Velvet Underground, the New York Dolls and the Ramones. Nevertheless, in 1977 Marc Bolan was too closely bound up with teenage dreams and pubescent idolatry to be taken seriously by those fans who had grown up and got guitars of their own. His new records weren't able to compete with the earthy primitivism of the Clash and the Adverts, though the punks' willingness to court the overblown (even a touch of nostalgia, maybe) made it a prudent moment to begin compiling a retrospective collection in time for the Christmas market. 1973's *Great Hits* had been deleted, and EMI wanted a replacement collection on their new budget-price NUT series. Colin Miles, who was handling the programme, had a meeting with Marc early in September at EMI's Manchester Square offices. 'He arrived brimming with confidence,' recalls the A&R man, 'a wonderful elf-like character playing the part of the camp glam rock star to the hilt. I worked on the assumption that artists aren't necessarily the best judges of their own work, and had drawn up a provisional track listing.

But there was a problem. He desperately wanted "Jitterbug Love" (the B side of "Children Of The Revolution") on it, whereas I had pencilled in "The Soul Of My Suit". When I told him I disagreed with his choice, he suddenly became very animated and took off on this Nureyev-like ballet routine, complete with sweeping arm gestures and spinning round on the floor. It was mind-blowing. There was Marc Bolan dancing round my office telling me I'm crazy because I don't like "Jitterbug Love". I quickly concluded that the song really ought to go on the record after all, and he calmed down.'

On Friday 9 September, Marc returned to EMI in his fake leopard-skin suit for a photo shoot for the forthcoming collection, provisionally titled *Solid Gold T. Rex*. Earlier that day, he had entertained a fan who had travelled down to see him. 'It was in my office in Victoria,' remembers Keith Altham, 'and before the fan arrived, Marc was going through his "Do I have to?" routine. But typically, when it came to it, instead of just spending half an hour, Marc stayed with him for a couple of hours, even taking him out in his car round London.'

The fan, Dave Rooney from Birmingham, arrived brandishing a 'Marc Bolan Is God' badge, which delighted Bolan, as did the news that an event was being held in Earls Court early in October to celebrate his thirtieth birthday. The badge, and the idea for the party, had been conceived by two London-based fans, Ros Davies and Colm Jackson. They had met Marc during the *Dandy* tour and, realising how accessible he was, started the *Hard On Love* Bolan magazine with a view to becoming the officially sanctioned British-based branch of the fan club. The 'Bolanites Unite' event was intended as the first step towards establishing ties with Wizard, and when Rooney mentioned it to him, Bolan immediately volunteered to turn up and play. 'I shall make a conscious effort to go through what I consider to be the Marc Bolan song book . . . my best songs.'[10] He even talked about calling up Mickey Finn and Steve Took to help him out.

Marc discussed many topics that afternoon, enthusing about his new version of 'Debora', describing the cratefuls of poetry he had amassed, and his hopes for a live album to be recorded on the next T. Rex tour. He also gave an insight into the fractured state of the modern mind, the kind of mind that had seen Mark Feld become Marc Bolan, that repository of ideological contradictions, of conflicting drives and desires. 'People don't understand you can be five people at the same time,' he said, knowing that he had subsumed many facets of his own character in his quest to become Marc Bolan the Star. That persona had undoubtedly taken over and clouded the subtleties in his thinking during the previous few years, depriving him of the imaginative gift he once wielded, a gift which was now poised to return and lift him out of his current malaise.

Everyone else was geared up for a revival of Bolan's fortunes. Marc had been extremely prolific during the previous months, and not just in terms of his public profile. He had also been recording hours of home demos alone, with Gloria Jones, Steve Harley, even some with David Bowie. Bolan and Bowie, together with Gloria, worked on a compelling – and vicious-sounding – collaboration titled 'Madman', which signalled a real stylistic shift towards a more anguished contemporary electric sound. Or perhaps the future of the prolific songwriter who had been long practised in the art of working with simple chords, really lay in talent-spotting and record production for the new wave? He may have possessed the will to proceed, but in September 1977, as his thirtieth birthday approached, Marc Bolan had yet to settle on the way.

# CHAPTER TWELVE

'I got a phone call from the Press Association. "Have you got a picture of Marc and Gloria together?" Fuck off!'
Keith Altham

'It seemed ironic that he was in a Mini and not a Mercedes. That would have saved his life.'
Pete Sanders

'I still feel really sad when I see him on television. He was a real giant, up there with Tim Buckley. What a tragedy his death was.'
Danny Thompson

'It would have been nice to have met up again as a couple of fifty-year-olds.'
John Peel

On 18 September 1976, *Record Mirror* reported that Marc signed the Morton's restaurant club book twice to please the hat-check girl. It was a popular eating haunt for celebrities, particularly among Jewish entertainers. A year later, in the early hours of 16 September 1977, Marc Bolan was back there again.

It had been a long day. Filming for the television series had finished, Gloria was back in Britain after a short visit to the States, and her brother was staying with them at the Richmond house. Richard Jones had only been in the country a matter of days, but he had already hatched some tentative plans with Marc to break into the new video market. Before arriving at the restaurant in Berkeley Square, Marc Bolan had filled his day as he often did, meeting old friends, doing a spot of recording and talent-scouting on the club scene. The only out-of-character event that day was an appointment with his dentist. Marc had got the rest of his body into shape, now he wanted some minor cosmetic work on his teeth. He was fast-approaching thirty, and was determined to grow old beautifully. Having sorted out the final arrangements for a bridge, the conversation with his dentist turned to less painful matters, and bottles of wine were opened.

Some time during the evening, Marc also put in an appearance at the Speakeasy, where Jeff Dexter was checking out a new punk band fronted by Andy Allan, son of Elkan Allan, producer of *Ready, Steady, Go!* 'Marc got arseholed at the Speak before they went on to Morton's,' Dexter recalls.

Shortly after midnight Marc, with Gloria and Richard, arrived at Morton's. An old friend, Eric Hall, was also there, but he left around one o'clock. The Bolan camp ate in the upstairs restaurant to the gentle sounds of a blonde singer-pianist named Victoria before adjourning to the bar downstairs, where a quartet of saxophone, trumpet, bass and piano provided some light music. As the high spirits began to flag, Marc persuaded Gloria to take over at the piano. By this time, less than a dozen guests remained, lending a mood of intimacy as she serenaded her lover with several romantic songs.

Marc kept an account with a car-hire firm, which he used on formal occasions, or when the situation otherwise demanded it. When the party left Morton's after several hours' drinking, at around 4.00 a.m. on Friday 16 September, the roads were peaceful. They decided to make their own way back to Bolan's Upper Richmond Road West residence.

Gloria drove Marc in her purple Mini 1275 GT. (That Tuesday, the car had been taken to a garage in Sheen, where the wheels were balanced and a tyre had been replaced. Unbeknown to its occupants, the pressure in the offside tyre was only 16 pounds, 10 pounds less than it should have been, and two nuts on the offside front wheel were not even finger tight.) Richard and Vicki, the young singer at the club, followed close behind.

Just before 5.00 a.m., the convoy had crossed Putney Bridge and was on the final lap home. Richard Jones remembers seeing the tail lights of the Mini vanish over the hump-back bridge along Queens Ride, a treacherous B road that skirts the southernmost part of Barnes Common. The tree-lined road was still engulfed in darkness, but as he approached the bridge Richard Jones could see rising steam. After jumping out of the car, his worst fears were immediately confirmed. The front of the Mini had almost completely caved in, crushed on impact as it careered off the road on the bend immediately beyond the bridge. It had smashed into a tree and the passenger's side had taken the brunt of the collision.

Richard Jones looked inside, and saw his sister, barely conscious and wedged between the steering-wheel and her seat. The engine of the car had trapped her foot under the clutch, but she was still breathing. Marc, whose fear of machines had always prevented him from learning to drive, remained in the passenger seat, but the impact on the left side of the car had been so great that the seat had turned over 180 degrees and was in the back half of the vehicle. There was no doubt in Richard's mind that Marc Bolan, motionless in his orange Lycra glittered trousers and fluorescent green and white top, was already dead.

On Tuesday 20 September, Gloria Jones, still suffering from facial injuries and unable to speak because her jaw had been wired up, received a visit from Marc's manager Tony Howard. For four days, she had been inundated with well-wishers and flowers, but the news that Marc was dead had been kept from her until she herself was off the danger list. Tony Howard had arrived to tell her the painful truth.

That same day, an extraordinarily large gathering of people flooded through the gates of Golders Green crematorium – Marc's family, representatives from his record company, friends and associates from the music industry and beyond, and a huge gathering of fans.

The sombre atmosphere was inflected with an overriding sense of unreality. No one there expected to mourn the death of someone so young, and yet many had come to pay their respects to someone they hadn't even met. But, in a way, they had known him. The public Marc Bolan had been every bit as real as the private Mark Feld. There was no great divide: he invented fictions and hopped from character to character but that, too, was part of the real Mark Feld. The reality of the fans' collective imagination is also an essential part of the Marc Bolan story. Located in it are the same drives, the same transcending of barriers, that prompted Mark Feld to embark upon the kind of life he chose for himself.

When Rabbi Henry Goldstein spoke of the two Marc Bolans, 'the real one – a good-natured boy who loved his parents – and the image projected on stage', it was no more than anyone expected. But behind the platitudes lay a multi-faceted network of feelings that Marc had a desperate need to talk about but rarely believed he could understand. His favourite pair of black velvet trousers, with the red and green diamond pattern down the sides of each leg, and a silk top with the letters MARC emblazoned on the front, had been singled out to clothe his body for the cremation, but, in accordance with the Jewish faith (which states that the body leaves the physical world in the same naked state in which it entered), these were probably never used. The ex-Stamford Hill mod would have appreciated that.

# APPENDIX ONE

# MARC BOLAN & T. REX:
# A Recorded History

This is a selective guide through the minefield of Marc Bolan's recorded work, concentrating on records issued during his lifetime and important posthumous releases. I have not name-checked every release. Those wishing to purchase each and every reissue, compilation and remix, should check out the back issues pages of *Record Collector* magazine, where the ins-and-outs of Bolan's catalogue have been copiously documented.

## THE SOLO YEARS

Until recently, the Mark Feld/Toby Tyler recording of Dion DiMucci's 'The Road I'm On (Gloria)' was only thought to have survived on a scratched one-sided EMIDISC acetate. This passed down the line from June Bolan to Paul Sinclair, eventually ending up in the hands of enthusiast Marc Arscott, who released the disc as a limited edition one-sided single, 'The Road I'm On (Gloria)' (March 1990; Archive Jive TOBY 1).

In 1991, a second EMIDISC acetate emerged, coupling that same version of 'The Road I'm On (Gloria)' with a cover of Bob Dylan's 'Blowin' In The Wind'. This subsequently sold for £4200 in auction, and the purchasers intend to recoup their investment by releasing it officially.

More recently, though, a reel-to-reel master-tape of the entire session has turned up at a London auction house. This contains two different mixes of both tracks, three unmixed takes of 'The Road I'm On (Gloria)' and six of 'Blowin' In The Wind' – a priceless piece of Bolan recording history that will hopefully find its way on to the specialist collectors' market before too long.

There are two singles from Marc Bolan's short spell with Decca Records, 'The Wizard'/'Beyond The Risin' Sun' (November 1965; F 12288) and 'The Third Degree'/'San Francisco Poet' (June 1966; F 12413), although he is known to have recorded several other titles for the company which have since been lost. These include 'That's The Bag I'm In', 'Rings Of Fortune', 'A Soldier Song', 'Highways', and 'Reality'. At least one former associate holds tapes from this era, but they are, for the foreseeable future, 'inaccessible'.

Marc's liaison with Simon Napier-Bell yielded some fascinating solo recordings, though only 'Hippy Gumbo'/'Misfit' (December 1966; Parlophone R 5539) appeared at the time. Potential follow-up singles, in the shape of 'Jasper C. Debussy' and 'The Lilac Hand Of Menthol Dan', were recorded and eventually released years later: 'Jasper C. Debussy'/'Hippy Gumbo'/'The Perfumed Garden Of Gulliver Smith' (August 1974; picture sleeve; Track 2094 013) and 'Return Of The Electric Warrior' EP: 'Sing Me A Song'/'Endless Sleep'/'The Lilac Hand Of Menthol Dan' (March 1981; picture sleeve; Rarn MBFS 001).

*The Beginning Of Doves* album (June 1974; Track 2410 201) contains several Bolan demos from 1966 and 1967, and remains an essential landmark in the development of a recognisable musical and lyric style. Napier-Bell, finding himself at a loose end, 'jazzed up' these demos (throwing in the previously unheard 'I'm Weird' and 'Horrible Breath (You Scare Me To Death)' for good measure on *You Scare Me To Death* (October 1981; with booklet; Cherry Red ERED 20).

## JOHN'S CHILDREN

Very little John's Children material featuring Bolan emerged at the time, but a lot has crept out in recent years. The original recordings are: 'Desdemona'/'Remember Thomas A'Beckett' (April 1967; limited number with picture sleeve; Track 604 003); 'Midsummer Night's Scene'/ 'Sara Crazy Child' (June 1967; release cancelled, though a handful of copies were distributed at the John's Children Club; 604 005); 'Come And Play With Me In The Garden'/'Sara Crazy Child' (August 1967; limited number with picture sleeve; 604 005; Spanish and German editions of this single feature an extended version of the B side with additional Bolan vocals); 'Go Go Girl'/'Jagged Time Lapse' (October 1967; A side is a version of Bolan's 'Mustang Ford' and features Marc on guitar; 604 010).

The best entry into the wayward world of John's Children is *A Midsummer Night's Scene* (1987; inner sleeve; Bam Caruso KIRI 095), which include the original three Bolan recordings with the group, plus several of the band's other singles.

The same label released a 12" edition of 'Midsummer Night's Scene' backed with three recordings which had been preserved on acetate. These include band versions of Marc Bolan's 'Jasper C. Debussy' (retitled 'Casbah Candy') and 'Hippy Gumbo'.

More recently, two John's Children mini-albums, titled *Playing With*

*Themselves vols 1 & 2* (Zinc Alloy Records MLP 9001/2; 1990/91) have appeared in Germany, featuring several performances with Bolan still in the group. The most tantalising recording of Marc Bolan actually fronting John's Children is the version of 'Hippy Gumbo' that appeared on the *Midsummer Night's Scene* CD, followed by the brief segment of 'Sally Was An Angel' on *The Beginning Of Doves* album. The complete version still exists, where Bolan can be heard sharing the verses with Andy Ellison.

A couple of oddities remain: the version of 'Desdemona' recorded specially for radio air-play (with the offending lyric altered to 'why do you have to lie' and with a keyboard overdub) turned up on *Marc: The Words And Music Of Marc Bolan, 1947–1977* (April 1978; 2-LPs, gatefold sleeves; Cube HIFLY 1). Meanwhile, Andy Ellison's 'You Can't Do That' solo single (SNB SNB–3308; May 1968) featured Marc's 'Cornflake Zoo' on the B side, with an audible Bolan vocal line and guitar part.

Several other Bolan-era John's Children recordings remain in private collections. These include: 'Mustang Ford' (as 'Go Go Girl' but with an extra guitar overdub and Bolan's original lyrics; 'The Perfumed Garden Of Gulliver Smith'; 'Midsummer Night's Scene' (a different take, three instrumental try-outs and an alternate mix); 'Daddy Rolling Stone' (two versions); 'Leave Me Alone' and two instrumental versions of 'Jasper C. Debussy'.

## TYRANNOSAURUS REX

The essential recordings can be found on the following Regal Zonophone releases: **Singles** – 'Debora'/'Child Star' (April 1968; limited number with picture sleeve; RZ 3008; No. 34); 'One Inch Rock'/'Salamanda Palaganda' (August 1968; limited number with picture sleeve; RZ 3011; No. 28); 'Pewter Suitor'/'Warlord Of The Royal Crocodiles' (January 1969; RZ 3016); 'King Of The Rumbling Spires'/'Do You Remember' (July 1969; limited number with picture sleeve; RZ 3022; No. 44); 'By The Light Of A Magical Moon'/'Find A Little Wood' (January 1970; RZ 3025)

**Albums** – *My People Were Fair And Had Sky In Their Hair But Now They're Content To Wear Stars On Their Brows* (July 1968; with lyric sheet; mono/stereo [S]LRZ 1003; No. 15); *Prophets, Seers And Sages The Angel Of The Ages* (October 1968; with lyric sheet; mono/stereo [S]LRZ 1005); *Unicorn* (May 1969; mono/stereo [S]LRZ 1007; No. 12); *A Beard Of Stars* (March 1970; with lyric sheet; mono/stereo [S]LRZ 1013; No. 13). Once again, refer to *The Beginning Of Doves*, which includes the duo's earliest sessions, taped for Simon Napier-Bell. Another title from this period, 'Sleepy Maurice', survived on acetate for almost twenty-five years before appearing on a limited edition single released in November 1991 (picture sleeve plus insert; Tyrannosaurus Rex Records TYR 001).

An acetate of 'Chateau In Virginia Waters' appears to have survived from the Joe Boyd session taped late in 1967, but this has yet to find its way onto the market.

We can expect the release of Tony Visconti's original two-track stereo audition tape in the near future. This includes all the songs that later appeared on the debut Tyrannosaurus Rex album, plus unique recordings of 'Hippy Gumbo', 'Lunacy's Back' and 'Puckish Pan'.

*Across The Airwaves* (February 1982; Cube/Dakota ICS 1004) is a collection of recordings made for BBC radio, and includes eleven Tyrannosaurus Rex recordings. Six of these are with Steve Took, including two from the duo's first session appearance late in 1967; and all five from the first electric session with Mickey Finn from November 1969.

Fly cashed in on Bolan's new-found popularity in 1971 with *The Best of T. Rex* (March 1971; Fly TON 2; No. 6) which features two unreleased Tyrannosaurus Rex performances, 'Once Upon The Seas Of Abyssinia' and 'Blessed Wild Apple Girl' both out-takes from *A Beard Of Stars*. These were originally taped with Steve Took, but his part was wiped and replaced by Bolan and Visconti doing a good imitation of him.

Other rare Tyrannosaurus Rex material has slipped out on several singles, including yet another out-take from 1969, 'Demon Queen', on the flip of the 'Bolan's Best+1' 7" (August 1977; Cube ANT 1); and two first album out-takes in 'Rock Me' (alias 'Puckish Pan') and 'Lunacy's Back' on the 'Mellow Love' 12" (January 1982; Marc On Wax SBOLAN 13).

## T. REX

**Singles** – Initially, Bolan offered value-for-money three-track singles, including material that wasn't available on LP, but after a while, he decided that the albums needed single tracks to boost sales. Towards the end of his career, he reverted back to the exclusivity of single material, although posthumous repackages have since meant that almost all of these recordings have been transferred on to album (if not CD).

'Ride A White Swan'/'Is It Love'/'Summertime Blues' (October 1970; picture sleeve; Fly BUG 1; No. 2); 'Hot Love'/'Woodland Rock'/'King Of The Mountain Cometh' (February 1971; BUG 6; No. 1); 'Get It On'/ 'There Was A Time'/'Raw Ramp' (July 1971; picture sleeve; 7/71; No. 1); 'Jeepster'/'Life's A Gas' (November 1971; BUG 16; No. 2); 'Telegram Sam'/'Cadillac'/'Baby Strange' (January 1972; T. Rex Wax Co. T. REX

101; No. 1); 'Metal Guru'/'Thunderwing'/'Lady' (May 1972; MARC 1; No. 1); 'Children Of The Revolution'/'Jitterbug Love'/'Sunken Rags' (September 1972; MARC 2; No. 2); 'Solid Gold Easy Action'/'Born To Boogie' (December 1972; MARC 3; No. 2); 'T. Rex Christmas Record' (December 1972; flexi-disc free to Fan Club members); '20th Century Boy'/'Free Angel' (March 1973; MARC 4; No. 3); 'The Groover'/'Midnight' (June 1973; MARC 5; No. 4); 'Truck On (Tyke)'/'Sitting Here' (November 1973; MARC 6; No. 12); 'Teenage Dream'/'Satisfaction Pony' (as Marc Bolan or Marc Bolan & T. Rex; January 1974; MARC 7; No. 13); 'Light Of Love'/'Explosive Mouth' (July 1974; MARC 8; No. 22); 'Zip Gun Boogie'/'Space Boss' (November 1974; MARC 9; No. 41); 'New York City'/'Chrome Sitar' (July 1975; MARC 10; No. 15); 'Dreamy Lady'/ 'Do You Wanna Dance'/'Dock Of The Bay' (September 1975; MARC 11; No. 15); 'London Boys'/'Solid Baby' (February 1976; MARC 13; No. 40); 'I Love To Boogie'/'Baby Boomerang' (June 1976; MARC 14; No. 13); 'Laser Love'/'Life's An Elevator' (September 1976; MARC 15; No. 41); 'To Know Him Is To Love Him'/'City Port' (as Marc Bolan & Gloria Jones; January 1977; EMI 2572); 'The Soul Of My Suit'/'All Alone' (March 1977; MARC 16; No. 42); 'Dandy In The Underworld'/'Groove A Little'/ 'Tame My Tiger' (May 1977; picture sleeve; MARC 17); 'Celebrate Summer'/'Ride My Wheels' (August 1977; picture sleeve; MARC 18).

**Albums** – There have been endless reissues of the original T. Rex albums, sometimes with variable sound quality, often in different sleeves. Stick to the originals, which came with unique packaging and on better quality vinyl. If you insist on fresh copies, then you're best advised to seek out the superior Japanese pressings, which are also better packaged than their UK counterparts. At the time of writing, there has been no comprehensive reissue series reinstating the remastered Bolan catalogue successfully on to CD in Britain, though the potential to undertake such a project is well within the bounds of possibility.

T. Rex (December 1970; semi-gatefold sleeve; Fly HIFLY 2; No. 13); *Electric Warrior* (September 1971; with illustrated inner sleeve and black-and-white poster; HIFLY 6; No. 1); *The Slider* (July 1972; with inner lyric sleeve; T. Rex Wax Co. BLN 5001; No. 4); *Tanx* (March 1973; illustrated inner sleeve and black-and-white poster; BLN 5002; No. 4); *Great Hits* (September 1973; with colour poster; BLN 5003; No. 32); *Zinc Alloy And The Hidden Riders Of Tomorrow Or A Creamed Cage In August* (February 1974; inner lyric sleeve and gatefold cover; BLNA 7751; No. 12); *Bolan's Zip Gun* (as Marc Bolan & T. Rex; February 1975; inner sleeve and die-cut cover; BLNA 7752); *Futuristic Dragon* (January 1976; inner lyric sleeve; BLN 5004; No. 50); *Dandy In The Underworld* (February 1977; inner sleeve and die-cut cover; BLN 5005; No. 26).

**Miscellaneous Releases** – 'Oh Baby'/'Universal Love' (credited to Dib Cochran & The Earwigs; August 1970; Bell 1121); 'Blackjack'/'Squint Eyed Mangle' (credited to Big Carrot; August 1973; EMI EMI 2047); 'Sunken Rags' (acoustic version) appears on the *Glastonbury Fayre* album (July 1972; 3-LPs, fold-out sleeve, with booklet and inserts; Revelation REV 1/2/3).

## RELEASES FEATURING BOLAN AS A GUEST/SESSION ARTIST

This area has always been shrouded in myth and rumour, the seeds of which were usually implanted by Marc himself. As Tony Visconti has confirmed, the much touted Bolan/Bowie collaborations amounted to almost nothing, at least during the years up to 1974. Only 'The Prettiest Star'/'Conversation Piece' (March 1970; Mercury MF 1135) can be confirmed as a genuine collaboration.

Marc sang a brief line on Marsha Hunt's version of 'My World Is Empty Without You' which appeared alongside three Bolan originals (none of which featured him) on her *Woman Child* album (November 1971; Track 2410 101).

As Bolan increasingly partied on the superstar circuit, he invariably ended up at several big-name recording sessions. One of these was for Alice Cooper, where it's now virtually certain that he contributed guitar to the 'Hello Hurray' single (February 1973; Warner Brothers K 16248, No. 6) and to 'Slick Black Limousine', an out-take from Cooper's *Billion Dollar Babies* album, which ended up on a free flexi-disc (February 1973; Lyntone LYN 2585) given away with *New Musical Express* magazine.

The friendship with Ringo Starr resulted in very little genuine collaborative work, excepting the *Born To Boogie* film. Starr recorded the T. Rex-like 'Back Off Boogaloo', while Bolan played guitar on just one song, 'Have You Seen My Baby', which appeared on the *Ringo* album (November 1973; gatefold sleeve and lyric booklet, Apple PCTC 252; No. 7). One further superstar collaboration, with Ike and Tina Turner, came in the midst of his American adventures. Marc played guitar on the second side of the 'Sexy Ida (parts one and two)' single (June 1974; United Artists UP 35726).

Eight tracks were completed for the aborted Pat Hall solo album during the winter of 1973–1974, with Bolan playing guitar and trying his hand at producing. Some of the backing tracks were salvaged and utilised for Gloria Jones' Bolan-produced *Vixen* album (December 1976; EMI EMC 3159), for which he contributes guitar parts throughout. He also overdubbed an additional lead line on the single version of 'Go Now'/'Drive Me Crazy (Disco Lady)' (February 1977; EMI EMI 2570).

Marc made two notable guest appearances as guitarist during the final months of his life: on 'If I Just Can Get Through Tonight' from

Alfalfa's self-titled LP (April 1977; EMI EMC 3213); and on *Amerika The Brave* which later turned up on Steve Harley's *Hobo With A Grin* album (July 1978; EMI EMC 3254).

## IMPORTANT POSTHUMOUS T. REX RELEASES

Dozens of unreleased T. Rex recordings have appeared since 1977, scattered over a bewildering variety of releases. The chief outlet for these has been Marc On Wax, the record company wing of the Marc Bolan Fan Club, whose efforts really got underway in 1982 when they managed to licence the 1972–1977 recordings owned by Wizard Artists Ltd.

Starting from a decidedly amateur base, Marc On Wax has to be congratulated for making available so many previously unissued recordings, though its approach has been criticised in some quarters, by those who insist that the material should be presented more methodically and with greater regard to quality control and standards of professionalism.

Most controversial was the decision to 'remix' T. Rex recordings in an attempt to make them sound contemporary. Interestingly, when Levi's commissioned a T. Rex song for their summer 1991 advertising campaign, they opted for a pristine December 1972 recording of '20th Century Boy'. I have not included these remixes as part of this discography.

**Live Recordings** – In the absence of a *Born To Boogie* soundtrack album, there was no record of T. Rex in concert (apart from on bootleg, of course) until the aptly titled *T. Rex In Concert* (August 1981; gatefold sleeve; Marc On Wax ABOLAN 1) which, despite the involvement of Tony Visconti, remains a poor-quality document of scrappy performances from 1971. (It's likely that the performances are taken from the August 1971 Weeley Festival and a date on the autumn tour later that year.) *T. Rextasy* (May 1983; LP + 12"; gatefold sleeve; early copies with a free poster; Marc On Wax ABOLAN 5) was a considerable improvement, although it includes some wild mixing and an overdubbed bass part.

1991 finally saw the release of the *Born To Boogie* soundtrack (2 LPs, with 16-page photo-booklet; gatefold sleeve; Marc On Wax MARC LP 514), featuring the live material from the film, suitably doctored at the time by Marc and Visconti. Also included is the Tea Party sequence and several of the humorous sketches.

**Studio Recordings** – The first major posthumous release was the previously mentioned *Marc: The Words And Music Of Marc Bolan, 1947–1977* set. Compiled by Tony Visconti, it covered the best of the 1967–71 era, and included 'The Children Of Rarn Suite', complete with sympathetic overdubs by the producer. The suite later reappeared in the form of a 10' (June 1982; with 12-page booklet; Marc On Wax ABOLAN 2), with the bonus of the original unadorned demo tape on the other side of the disc.

Another early T. Rex rarity to appear was 'One Inch Rock' (an acoustic demo version, probably an out-take from the 1970 *T. Rex* album), together with the similarly-dated instrumental title track on the 'Deep Summer' 12" (July 1982; Rarn MBFS RAP 2). Two full studio albums of Bolan out-takes appeared during the early eighties, featuring material that spanned the 1972–1977 period. *Dance In The Midnight* (October 1983; double gatefold sleeve; Marc MARCL 501) and *Billy Super Duper* (August 1984; inner sleeve; Marc ABOLAN 4) offered welcome glimpses into the archive, but their thrown-together nature and the posthumous overdubs on some of the tracks didn't win too many accolades from collectors. Incidentally, the *Billy Super Duper* album was not the same as Bolan's unrealised 1975 project. Far more successful has been the recent *Rarities* series, which, at the time of writing, has delivered three volumes of untampered-with archive material. *Rarities Volume 1* (1991; Marc On Wax SPS 3) offers many acoustic demos recorded during 1972, featuring working versions of songs that later appeared on *The Slider* and *Tanx*, alongside several titles that never got beyond the work-in-progress stage. *Rarities Volume 2* (1991; Marc On Wax SPS 4) contains raw T. Rex studio demos for much of the *Zinc Alloy* album, while *Rarities Volume 3: The Savage Beethoven Album* (1992; Marc On Wax SPS 5) boasts a mixture of out-takes spanning the years 1971–1976. The *Rarities* series is by far the most important venture into the T. Rex archive yet, the main drawback being the lack of recording details to accompany the releases (see 'A Secret History Of T. Rex' below). *The Marc Shows* (1989; gatefold sleeve; Marc On Wax MARCL 513) contains a selection of old hits and rock 'n' roll covers recorded for the summer 1977 Granada Television *Marc* shows. This project was slightly marred by the fact that original master tapes couldn't be located, and so the material had to be taken directly from the film soundtrack. Intriguingly, masters had been located several years earlier for the two complete tracks ('Sing Me A Song' and 'Endless Sleep') which appeared on 'The Return Of The Electric Warrior' EP.

Some previously unissued material has also been scattered across several single releases. One of the most essential of these is the 'Christmas Bop' EP (December 1982; 12"; picture sleeve; Marc On Wax SBOLAN 12EP), which includes the unissued 1975 title track, all of the material from the 1972 Christmas flexi-disc, plus acoustic versions of 'King Of The Rumbling Spires' and the previously unheard 'Savage Beethoven'.

Another mid-seventies acoustic recording of a Tyrannosaurus Rex song, 'Magical Moon', accompanied the standard 7" of 'Think Zinc' (June 1983; picture sleeve; Marc On Wax SBOLAN 14); while the 12" edition (SBOLAN 14EP) was backed by two rock 'n' roll covers, 'Rip It Up' and 'Teenager In Love'.

The original studio version of 'Funky London Childhood' appeared on the flip of the 12" edition of 'Sunken Rags' (July 1985; picture sleeve; Marc On Wax 12 TANX 2); a full version of 'Down Home Lady' backed the 'Sunken Rags' 7" (picture sleeve; TANX 2), while acoustic demo versions of 'Cadillac' and 'Truck On (Tyke)' appeared on the flips of two 'Get It On' 12" remixes (yellow vinyl 'Dusk Mix' and blue vinyl 'Dawn Mix' respectively) in 1987.

When Marc on Wax reissued the T. Rex Wax Co. albums in October 1983 in new sleeve designs, the version of 'Teenage Dream' on the *Zinc Alloy* album (MARCL 505) inadvertently appeared without its early fade. Other anomalies include a different take of 'New York City' on the *Till Dawn* album (irrespective of the remix and Bill Legend's re-recorded drum part), while the title track is slightly longer than the original version.

**Radio Recordings** – *Till Dawn* (November 1985; 2-LPs, gatefold sleeve; Marc On Wax MARCL 509) includes one disc featuring acoustic versions of material from *Electric Warrior* and *The Slider* recorded for American radio in 1972. Indispensable is the aforementioned *Across The Airwaves* collection of recordings made exclusively for BBC radio. Alongside the Tyrannosaurus Rex material are ten songs taped during 1970 and 1971 as T. Rex. Most notable is the appearance of the previously unheard 'Sailors Of The Highway', which was subsequently recorded by Pat Hall, and later Gloria Jones. The complete 7 November 1970 broadcast appeared as part of 'The Peel Sessions' series of 12" EPs (July 1987; Strange Fruit SFP 031).

The Tyrannosaurus Rex Appreciation Society issued *Honey Don't* (March 1990; with plastic outer sleeve; TS 14971) which, despite including three excerpts of poetry recorded for *Top Gear* in 1968 and 1969, featured material exclusively from the T. Rex era. The sound quality on the featured US radio sessions, two of which were recorded during the spring 1971 T. Rex tour (work-in-progress for *Electric Warrior*, plus a version of Carl Perkins' 'Honey Don't' and a jam called 'I Love The Way') leaves a lot to be desired. The third session, dating from 12 September 1972 and recorded for WBCN Radio in Boston, includes unique versions of 'The Slider' and 'Left Hand Luke And The Beggar Boys'. A Fan Club flexi-disc (December 1981; Cube/Dakota) coupled a brief Christmas jingle recorded for the Bob Harris Radio 1 show with 'Sailors Of The Highway'.

**Interview Discs** – The two best known interview discs have appeared on 7". The first (BINT 1) came with early copies of *Marc: The Words And Music . . .* , which included excerpts from a 1973 conversation with Stevie Dixon, backed by tributes from Steve Harley, Jennifer Sharp and John Peel taped in 1977. The free flexi 7" (Lyntone LYN 10086) accompanying the first 20,000 copies of the 'You Scare Me To Death' single, contained an interview with Marc conducted by *Melody Maker*'s Chris Welch.

The earliest recorded interview to appear on disc are three excerpts of an amiable chat with John Peel, which originally appeared on a Blue Thumb promotional single pressed for the 1969 US tour. These snippets are currently available on the B side of the 'Sleepy Maurice' 45.

America seems to have provided the bulk of the interview material available on disc. In 1971, Marc spoke to radio DJ Michael Cuscuna, and the best bits were pressed up for a Warner Brothers promotional album (PRO 511) as *The Electric Warrior Interview*; while a year later, the religious broadcasting service What's It All About? manufactured a promo-only pressing of a 7" interview single.

Since Bolan's death, *Where's The Champagne* (March 1982; picture sleeve; Rhino RNDF 252) and *Marc Bolan – The Interview* (June 1982; What Records W12 2401), dating from 1971 and 1969 respectively, have appeared. Also look out for the excellent Australian *20th Century Boy* triple album (1981; fold-out sleeve with inserts; EMI MARC 1) which, as well as providing the only comprehensive overview of Marc's career from 1965–1977, also includes several interview snippets at the end of each side. A poor quality interview picture disc, recorded in the US in 1972, has appeared on the Baktabak label.

**Miscellaneous Posthumous Releases** – Two other albums are worth a mention. Firstly, the budget-price *Solid Gold T. Rex* (June 1979; EMI NUT 5), chiefly because it was the compilation Marc was working on at the time of his death; and *The Unobtainable T. Rex* (September 1980; EMI NUT 28), which gathers up just about all the single material that had yet to find its way on to album (excepting 'Laser Love'). This is by far the most convenient introduction to the rewarding world of the T. Rex B side.

## A SECRET HISTORY OF T. REX 1970–1977

Lack of definitive documentation has left collectors confused about the origin of many of the recordings which have turned up on bootleg and 'official' releases since 1977 (and some which have yet to enter general circulation at all). Drawing on a combination of documentary evidence, the opinions of several experts, and a dose of old-fashioned aural judgement, I have attempted to map out the more likely origins for much of this material.

This is best achieved by grouping songs chronologically. In some cases, these recordings may be genuine out-takes; in others, many of the songs are little more than cast-offs, jams, or simply sketches for future reference. The information is intended as a rough guide, rather than the definitive statement on the matter. Please note that many alternate takes of well-known material also exist, but I've generally excluded these unless they are markedly different (e.g., an acoustic version of an electric song).

**1970:** 'Alligator Man' (demo), 'Dark Lipped Woman' (demo, possibly '71), 'Meadows Of The Sea' (demo), 'The Motivator' (demo).

**1971:** 'Bolan's Blues', 'Cosmic Dancer' (electric version), 'Honey Don't', 'Life's A Gas' (demo), 'My Baby's New Porsche' (demo), 'Spaceball Ricochet' (acoustic), 'The Children Of Rarn', 'The Slider' (demo), 'Thunderwing' (acoustic).

**1972:** 'Auto Machine' (acoustic), 'Birmingham' (demo), 'Broken Hearted Blues' (demo), 'Buick Mackane & The Babe Shadow', 'Canyons', 'Children Of The World' (acoustic), 'City Port (Fast Punk)', 'Did You Ever' (acoustic), 'Electric Lips (Sting Me Baby)' (acoustic), 'Ellie May' (demo), 'Fast Blues (Easy Action)', 'Ghetto Baby' (acoustic), 'Is It True' (acoustic), 'Jet Tambourine', 'Just Like Me' (acoustic), 'Left Hand Luke' (demo), 'Mad Donna' (acoustic), 'Mister Motion' (acoustic), 'Over The Flats' (demo), 'Rabbit Fighter' (demo), 'Rainy Monday' (demo), 'Rollin' Stone' (acoustic), 'Sailors Of The Highway' (acoustic), 'Shake It Wind One', 'Shame On You' (acoustic), 'Slider Blues' (acoustic), 'Space Ball Boot' (demo), 'Street Back' (electric), 'Sugar Baby (Rabbit Fighter)', 'Unicorn Horn, Work With Me Baby' (demo), 'Would I Be The One' (acoustic), 'Zinc Rider' (demo).

**1973:** 'All Of My Love', 'Candy Store' (demo), 'Dance In The Midnight', 'Delanie (Everyday)' (demo), 'Down Home Lady' (demo), 'Freeway' (demo), 'High Wire' (demo), 'Hope You Enjoy The Show', 'I'm Comin' To Rock 'n' Roll' (demo), 'I Wanna Go' (demo), 'Look Around' (demo), 'Metropolis' (acoustic), 'Misfortune Gatehouse' (demo), 'Mister Motion' (demo), 'Organ Thing' (instrumental), 'Plateau Skull', 'Rush', 'Sailors Of The Highway' (slow demo), 'Saturation Syncopation' (demo), 'Saturday Night', 'Shadow Babe' (demo), 'Shake It' (demo), 'Shut Down' (demo), 'Sky Church Music', 'This Is My Life' (demo), untitled jams with Danny Thompson on double bass, 'You Ought To Know' (demo), 'You're So Fine' (demo).

**1974:** 'Do I Love Thee', '11.15' (jam), 'Every Lady', 'Pale Horse Riding', 'Sparrow', 'The Children Of Rarn', 'Video Drama'.

**1974–1975:** 'Bolan's Zip Gun (Theme For A Dragon)', 'I Never Told Me', 'Sanctified', 'Saturday Night'.

**1975:** 'Ain't Nothing Like A Sad Man', 'Ain't That A Shame', 'Angel When I'm Mad', 'Big Black Cat', 'Billy Super Duper' (full 8-minute version), 'Bombs Out Of London', 'Bust My Ball', 'Brain Police', 'Depth Charge', 'Dynamo', 'Everyday' (possibly 1976), 'Get Down', 'I Believe', 'I Have Seen', 'King Of The Rumbling Spires' (acoustic), 'Lock Into Your Love', 'Magical Moon' (acoustic), 'Metropolis Incarnate', 'Teenage Angel', 'Over You Babe', 'Petticoat Lane', 'Reelin' An A Rockin' An A Boppin' An A Bolan', 'Sad Girl', 'Savage Beethoven', 'Stand By Me', 'Teenage Boychild', 'There Goes My Baby', '20th Century Boy' (re-recording), 'Walking Through That Door', 'You Damaged The Soul Of My Suit', jam with Roy Wood (includes 'Oh Boy', 'Fire Brigade', 'Jeepster', and 'Tonight's The Night For Love'; possibly 1976).

**1976:** 'Love Charm', 'Love For Me', 'Rip It Up', 'Teenager In Love', 'Write Me A Song (Supertuff)'.

**1977:** 'Foxy Boy', 'Hot George', 'Love Drunk', 'Madman', 'Mellow Love', 'Messin' With The Mystic', 'Purple Prince Of Pleasure', 'Shy Boy', 'Sing Me A Song', 'Sitting Next To You (Standing Next To You)', 'Skunk City', 'Smash Bash Crash (21st Century Stance)', 'Stay Hungry', '20th Century Baby', 'Young Boy Of Love'.

# APPENDIX TWO
# SOURCES

*Note*: All other substantial quotes, unless otherwise identified in the text, are drawn from personal interviews with the author. Full publishing details of all books mentioned in the Sources are to be found in the Bibliography (pp. 286–289).

## CHAPTER THREE

1 'Ain't No Square With My Corkscrew Hair' February 1976 interview by Spencer Leigh, *Stars In My Eyes*.
2 'Marc Bolan: Superstar Of The Seventies', *The Weekly News*, 3 June 1972.

## CHAPTER FOUR

1 *Beat Instrumental*, February 1971.
2 'Faces Without Shadows' by Peter Barnsley, *Town*, September 1962.
3 Quoted in *The Marc Bolan Story*, George Tremlett.
4 *Sunday Mirror*, 14 May 1972.
5 *Record Mirror*, 8 January 1972.
6 Sleeve note on *Bob Dylan* LP, CBS (S)BGP 62022, June 1962.
7 Quoted in *Electric Warrior: The Marc Bolan Story*, Paul Sinclair.
8 Albert Goldman, 1974, quoted in Dick Hebdige's *Subculture: The Meaning Of Style*.
9 *Evening Standard*, October 1965.
10 Derek Johnson, *New Musical Express*, 26 November 1965.
11 *Sunday Mirror*, 14 May 1972.
12 *She*, 1971.
13 Private collection.
14 *David Bowie: The Pitt Report*, Kenneth Pitt.
15 *New Musical Express*, 10 August 1968.

## CHAPTER FIVE

1 *John's Children*, Dave Thompson.
2 'John's Children, First Of The Anti Lust Groups', by Keith Altham, *New Musical Express*, 13 May 1967.
3 Quoted in *John's Children*, Dave Thompson.
4 Interview with Dave Rooney, 9 September 1977.

## CHAPTER SIX

1 *Days In The Life: Voices From The English Underground 1961–1971* edited by Jonathon Green.

## CHAPTER SEVEN

1 *David Bowie: The Pitt Report*, Kenneth Pitt.
2 'Blind Date', *Melody Maker*, 25 January 1969.
3 Interview with John Peel, 1969 Blue Thumb radio promo 45.
4 Quoted in *Electric Warrior*, Paul Sinclair.
5 'Took Talks About T. Rex', *New Musical Express*, 15 April 1972.
6 'But The Bopping Imp Keeps Bopping' by Chris Welch, *Melody Maker*, 11 October 1969.
7 *Sound + Vision* box set sleeve note, Rykodisc Records RCD 90120/21/22, 1989.
8 *The Record Producers*, John Tobler & Stuart Grundy.
9 *David Bowie: The Pitt Report*, Kenneth Pitt.
10 *New Musical Express*, 15 November 1969.
11 Interview with Penny Valentine, *Disc & Music Echo*, 11 October 1969.
12 *David Bowie: Moonage Daydream*, Dave Thompson.
13 *Real Life*, Marsha Hunt.
14 *Sound + Vision* box set sleeve note, Rykodisc Records.
15 'Tyrannosaurus Rex Are In Good Elf' by Chris Welch, *Melody Maker*, 14 March 1970.
16 *Stars In My Eyes*, Spencer Leigh.
17 Late 1971 interview with Michael Wade, *Vox Pop: Profiles Of The Pop Process*.
18 *Record Collector*, 1987.

## CHAPTER EIGHT

1 *ZigZag* No. 21, 7 July 1971.
2 *Disc & Music Echo*, November 1970.
3 *Rebel Rock: The Politics Of Popular Music*, John Street.
4 'Marc Sells Out . . . To The Cosmos', *Disc & Music Echo*, 8 May 1971.

5 *Days In The Life*, Jonathon Green.
6 Beautiful Dreamer: A Tribute To Steve Took, *Rockerilla*, May/June 1991, Nigel Cross.
7 Quoted in *Electric Warrior: The Marc Bolan Story*, Paul Sinclair.
8 *Jackie*, 1972.

## CHAPTER NINE

1 *Stars In My Eyes*, Spencer Leigh.
2 Charles Shaar Murray, *Cream*, May 1972.
3 Interview with Caroline Boucher, *Disc*, 9 December 1972.
4 *New Musical Express*, 23 September 1972.
5 Interview with Andrew Jackson, 1987, *King Of The Mountain Cometh: A Tribute To Marc Bolan*, 1991.
6 *Children Of The Revolution: Gum Into Glam 1967–1976*, Dave Thompson.
7 Charles Shaar Murray interview with David Bowie, *New Musical Express Greatest Hits*, 1974.

## CHAPTER TEN

1 *Stars In My Eyes*, Spencer Leigh.
2 Interview with Mark Wesley, Radio Luxembourg's 208/*New Musical Express*, 10 June 1972.
3 *New Musical Express*, June 1974.
4 *Jackie*, 1972.
5 *Stars In My Eyes*, Spencer Leigh.

## CHAPTER ELEVEN

1 'Marc Of The Dragon', *Sounds*, 22 November 1975.
2 *Stars In My Eyes*, Spencer Leigh.
3 *Stars In My Eyes*, Spencer Leigh.
4 *New Musical Express*, 26 June 1976.
5 *Record Mirror & Disc*, 18 September 1976.
6 *The Sun*, 18 February 1977.
7 *Record Mirror*, 4 June 1977.
8 *Record Mirror*, 2 July 1977.
9 *New Musical Express*, 3 June 1976.
10 Interview with Dave Rooney, London, 9 September 1977.

# APPENDIX THREE
# BIBLIOGRAPHY

I am gratefully indebted to the writers and publishers of all the material I've consulted during the course of writing this book.

The following biographies provided the basic source material:

Bolan, Marc, *The Warlock of Love*, Lupus Music, 1969

Bramley, John & Shan, *Marc Bolan: The Illustrated Discography*, Omnibus Press, 1983

Dicks, Ted (ed.), *Marc Bolan . . . A Tribute*, Omnibus Press/Essex Music, 1978

Sinclair, Paul, *Electric Warrior: The Marc Bolan Story*, Omnibus Press, 1982

Thompson, Dave, *John's Children*, Babylon Books, 1988

Tremlett, George, *The Marc Bolan Story*, Futura, 1975

Welch, Chris & Napier-Bell, Simon, *Marc Bolan: Born To Boogie*, Eel Pie, 1982

Williams, Dave, *Marc Bolan: The Motivator*, Silver Surfer, 1985

Those wishing to keep up with events surrounding the Bolan legacy (which takes as many dramatic twists and turns as he ever did) are invited to enter the domain of the fanzine. The central focus remains The Marc Bolan Fan Club, which produces a regular glossy A5 publication, *Rarn*. Life isn't that simple, though, and while *Rarn* offers good photographs, and details of future Marc On Wax releases, for many, the real debate resides outside the mainstream. This usually concerns disagreements over the official, posthumous presentation of Bolan's life and work. Years of internecine conflicts climaxed in 1991 with the formation of the Marc Bolan Liberation Front. The MBLF produces its own regular newsletter, *The Corkscrew*. Also in there somewhere are several other regular DIY publications, including *Nameless Wildness*,

*Cosmic Dancer, Gypsy Explorer* and *Rumblings,* the mouthpiece of the Tyrannosaurus Rex Appreciation Society.

Other sources consulted during the course of my research are as follows:

Barnes, Richard, *Mods!*, Eel Pie, 1979

Bennett, Mercer, Woolacott (eds), *Popular Culture and Social Relations*, Open University, 1986

Campbell, Colin, *The Romantic Ethic and the Spirit of Modern Consumerism*, Basil Blackwell, 1987

Chambers, Iain, *Popular Culture: The Metropolitan Experience*, Methuen, 1986

Chambers, Iain, *Urban Rhythms: Pop Music and Popular Culture*, Macmillan, 1985

Cohen, Stanley, *Folk Devils and Moral Panics*, MacGibbon & Kee, 1972

Cutler, Chris, *File Under Popular: Theoretical and Critical Writings*, November Books, 1985

Dyer, Richard, *Stars*, BFI, 1979

Frith, Simon (ed), *Facing The Music*, Mandarin, 1990

Frith, Simon, *Music For Pleasure*, Polity, 1988

Frith, Simon & Goodwin, Andrew (eds), *On Record: Rock, Pop and the Written Word*, Routledge, 1990

Frith, Simon & Horne, Howard, *Art Into Pop*, Methuen, 1987

Gibran, Jean & Kahlil, *Kahlil Gibran: His Life and World*, New York Graphic Society, 1974

Gibran, Kahlil, *The Prophet*, William Heinemann, 1976

Gillett, Charlie, *The Sound of the City*, Souvenir Press, 1983

Green, Jonathon, *Days in the Life: Voices From the English Underground 1961–1971*, William Heinemann, 1989

Harvey, David, *The Condition of Postmodernity*, Blackwell, 1989

Hebdige, Dick, *Subculture: The Meaning of Style*, Methuen, 1979

Hewison, Robert, *Too Much: Art and Society in the Sixties – 1960–75*, Methuen, 1986

Hoggart, Richard, *The Uses of Literacy*, Chatto & Windus, 1957

Hunt, Marsha, *Real Life*, Chatto & Windus, 1986

Lacan, Jacques, *The Four Fundamental Concepts of Psychoanalysis*, Hogarth Press, 1977

Laing, RD, *The Divided Self*, Pelican, 1965

Leigh, Spencer, *Stars In My Eyes*, Raven Books, 1980

Mabey, Richard, *The Pop Process*, Hutchinson Educational, 1969

Manlove, CN, *Modern Fantasy*, Cambridge University Press, 1975

McAuley, Ian, *Guide to Ethnic London*, Michael Haag, 1987

McRobbie, Angela (ed.), *Zoot Suits and Second-Hand Dresses: An Anthology of Fashion and Music*, Macmillan, 1989

Melly, George, *Revolt Into Style: The Pop Arts In Britain*, Penguin, 1970

Napier-Bell, Simon, *You Don't Have To Say You Love Me*, New English Library, 1982

Neville, Richard, *Playpower*, Jonathan Cape, 1970

Pitt, Kenneth, *David Bowie: The Pitt Report*, Design, 1983

Platt, John, *London's Rock Routes*, Fourth Estate, 1985

Rogan, Johnny, *Starmakers and Svengalis*, Queen Anne Press, 1988

Savage, Jon, *England's Dreaming*, Faber & Faber, 1991

Schaffner, Nicholas, *Saucerful of Secrets: The Pink Floyd Odyssey*, Sidgwick & Jackson, 1991

Shaw, Arnold, *The Rock Revolution*, Collier-Macmillan, 1969

Street, John, *Rebel Rock: The Politics of Popular Music*, Blackwell, 1986

Swinfen, Ann, *In Defence of Fantasy*, Routledge & Kegan Paul, 1984

Thompson, Dave, *Children of the Revolution! – Gum Into Glam 1967–76*, self-published

Thompson, Dave, *David Bowie: Moonage Daydream*, Plexus, 1987

Tobler, John & Grundy, Stuart, *The Record Producers*, BBC Books, 1982

Tolkien, JRR, *The Lord of the Rings*, Allen & Unwin, 1968

Wade, Michael, *Voxpop: Profiles Of The Pop Process*, Harrap, 1972

Wicke, Peter, *Rock Music: Culture, Aesthetics, Sociology*, Cambridge Press, 1990


Several essays also proved useful:

Cross, Nigel, 'Beautiful Dreamer – A Tribute to Steve Took', in *Rockerilla*, May–June 1991

Fowler, Peter, 'Skins Rule', in *Rock File*, Gillett, Charlie (ed.), New English Library, 1972

Hebdige, Dick, 'Towards A Cartography Of Taste 1935–1962', in *Popular Culture: Past And Present*, Waites, Bennett, Martin, (eds), Croom Helm, 1982

Marwick, Arthur, 'A Social History Of Britain 1945–83', in *Introduction To Contemporary Cultural Studies*, David Punter (ed.), Longman, 1986

Murray, Charles Shaar, 'Hello. I'm Marc Bolan. I'm A Superstar. You'd Better Believe It', in *Shots From the Hip*, Penguin, 1991


Also of great help were the pages of the popular music press, including:
*Beat Instrumental, Cream, Disc & Music Echo, International Times, Look-In,*

*Melody Maker, New Musical Express, Record Collector, Record Mirror & Disc, Record Mirror, Rolling Stone, Sounds, Superstar* and *ZigZag*.


Lastly, I consulted a number of non-music magazines and newspapers: *Jackie, She,* the *Sunday Mirror, Town, The Observer,* the *Sun,* the *Weekly News,* and *New Left Review*.

# INDEX